D1414718

LIFTING THE VEIL

JOHN SIMPSON is foreign affairs editor of BBC News. Since joining the BBC in 1966, he has been a foreign correspondent, political editor and news presenter. He has written six other books on current affairs. He was awarded the CBE in 1991. He is based in London.

TIRA SHUBART is a writer and television producer. She has worked for the American Networks, the BBC, and now writes for several publications and makes documentary films for Frontline News Television.

Lifting the Veil

Life in Revolutionary Iran

John Simpson and Tira Shubart

CORONET BOOKS
Hodder and Stoughton

Copyright © 1995 John Simpson and Tira Shubart

The right of John Simpson and Tira Shubart to be identified
as the Authors of the Work has been asserted by them
in accordance with the Copyright, Designs and
Patents Act 1988.

First published in Great Britain in 1995 by Hodder and Stoughton
First published in paperback in 1995 by Hodder and Stoughton
A division of Hodder Headline PLC

A Coronet paperback

10 9 8 7 6 5 4 3 2 1

A CIP catalogue record for this title is available from
the British Library

ISBN 0 340 65725 1

Printed and bound in Great Britain by
Cox & Wyman Ltd, Reading, Berkshire

Hodder and Stoughton
A division of Hodder Headline PLC
338 Euston Road
London NW1 3BH

To the memory of Narcy Firouz,
generous host, good friend and witty companion
whose views on Iran and Persian character
have influenced this book from start to finish.

Contents

List of Illustrations

Ayatollah Khomeini's tomb at Behesht-e-Zahra in south Tehran.

Mahmoudi, our driver and companion. (*Mike Goldwater/Network.*)

Street scene in Tehran with portrait of President Rafsanjani. (*Mike Goldwater/Network.*)

Street in scene in Tehran with portrait of Ayatollah Khamene'i. (*Mike Goldwater/Network.*)

Keepers of the revolution: a Pasdar and Gendarme. (*Mike Goldwater/Network.*)

Family on a motorcycle. (*Mike Goldwater/Network.*)

Pasargardae: Cyrus's tomb and the disintegrating remains of the Shah's saluting base of 1971.

Friday Prayers. (*Mike Goldwater/Network.*)

The theocracy: mullahs in Qom. (*Mike Goldwater/Network.*)

Worshippers at a shrine. (*Mike Goldwater/Network.*)

Islamic Justice: the mullah presides over family court in Rey.

Den of Spies: the walled compound of the former US embassy.

Islamic Justice: the mullah presides over family court in Rey.

Den of Spies: the walled compound of the former US embassy. (*Mike Goldwater/Network.*)

Skiing in the Albourz Mountains.

Introduction

We were driving southwards out of Tehran towards the old city of Rey, once the capital of Persia. At the head of our convoy was a Mercedes with the splendid figure of a black-robed mullah sitting in the back seat. One by one in the heat haze the cars turned into the yard of the Sadi Tile and Ceramic Factory. The mullah had been invited to lead the midday prayers here, and we were going to film him as he did it.

For a few minutes nothing happened. The mullah sat in his Mercedes while someone went to tell the management he had arrived. At last a little deputation came out and welcomed him with the requisite degree of ceremony. He indicated us with a sweeping gesture and the deputation shook hands with the males in our team. When they came to Tira Shubart they gave her an embarrassed little half-bow; since she was a woman it would be unIslamic to touch her. There was nothing intentionally rude about their greeting; on the contrary, they were positively ingratiating. It was just that they weren't used to having distinguished guests who happened to be female.

The awkward moment passed, and they led us into a grimy office building, up the stairs and into a room with a long table. The six of us sat on one side, the twelve people from the factory sat on the other. In the middle of the table were samples of the tiles the factory produced; boring, run-of-the-mill stuff which owed nothing to Iran's artistic heritage. A dish of apples, grapes and cucumbers had been set out for us, and an elderly man hobbled in with a brass tray bearing glasses of tea. At this point someone realised that one member of our group was a descendant of the Qajar dynasty, which was overthrown by Reza Shah in the 1920s; and that put an end to all discussion of British television or the manufacture of tiles.

The managers, who had all been factory workers before the overthrow of the Shah in 1979, questioned him with exaggerated respect about his genealogy and royal connections. It was like watching Bolsheviks brought face to face with a Romanov; except that most Iranians instinctively feel that the Qajars were the true royal family and that Reza Shah, who had started out as a mere soldier, and his son Mohammed who was overthrown in 1979, were upstarts. The managers, you knew, would go home that night and tell their wives proudly who they had met. As for the mullah we had come to film, he began by looking affronted by all this attention paid to someone else, but ended up rather pleased: after all, his significance was even greater as a result. The rest of us were treated like royalty ourselves.

It was time for prayers. The mullah led us outside and into the prayer room which was a huge room in the factory. Several hundred people were there, no doubt because the management wanted a big turnout for us. Men and women were separated, as Islam requires, but merely by lengths of canvas hung from a rope across the room. The mullah launched into a series of politically correct chants: 'Death to America, Death to Britain, Death to Israel, Death to Salman Rushdie, Death to Saddam Hussein,' and then (rather like a disc jockey making a special dedication for our benefit) 'Death to the BBC.' Everyone echoed the slogans obediently, but it was all perfectly friendly; there was no question of putting these threats into practice. After all, we were their guests and they felt flattered that we should be there. Whatever regime may be in power and whatever orthodoxy may be current, most Persians remain hospitable, generous, easy-going, and quick-witted.

The mullah began his sermon. All through the chanting and the initial prayers he had been holding a copy of a book in English. We recognised it at once, of course: it was *Behind Iranian Lines*, the book about everyday life in Iran which I had written in 1987, with research and several chapters by Tira Shubart. It was during the writing of it that Tira and I had first made the mullah's acquaintance. The back cover showed me sitting beside him, with a large picture of Ayatollah Khomeini on the wall behind. The mullah took the text of his sermon from the book. After he had read out a passage he said it wasn't altogether accurate, and misunderstood many things about Iran and the Islamic Revolution; but it was an attempt to be fair. They should never, he told the congregation, simply assume that everyone from the West was an enemy. There was a pause, and people nodded in agreement. Soon afterwards they were chanting the death threats again.

To be publicly praised by a pro-government mullah in Iran might seem like getting a favourable review in *Pravda* for a book on Stalin's Russia. We have no intention, however, of being the Sidney and Beatrice Webb of Iran; indeed, as a result of our activities both of us have been barred from returning to Iran, and after the publication of this book the ban will no doubt be reinforced. Yet as the mullah realised, we have tried to be fair, and to give a picture of what life is really like there: not the lurid, tabloid-newspaper version, but a rounded and objective account which acknowledges the positive as well as negative sides. As a result, it probably won't please anyone in Iran: the government cannot bear criticism of any kind, and the exile groups find it hard to accept that anything the Islamic Republic does can possibly be less than evil and criminal. That is too bad: our aim is to describe the realities of everyday existence there, not to make propaganda.

This book grew out of the one the mullah brandished in the factory. Two-thirds of it are entirely new. Iran has changed significantly since 1988, when the original was published: the war with Iraq came to an end, the *fatwa* was declared against Salman Rushdie, Ayatollah Khomeini died, Ali Akbar Hashemi-Rafsanjani became President, there was further Iranian involvement in terrorism abroad, corruption reached new heights and so did dissatisfaction with the regime. Above all, the hopes that Rafsanjani's less dogmatic approach might bring greater liberalisation and an end to Iran's international isolation have mostly come to nothing.

Over the years we have visited Iran both together and separately, and our experiences have therefore been different. We have shared the writing of this book equally; most of the chapters are in the first person singular, and we have tried to make it clear in the first few paragraphs of each whether it is Tira or John who is speaking. We hope that this will not confuse or irritate the reader too much. At the head of each chapter we have put a quotation from *A Mirror For Princes (Qabus Nama)*, the masterwork by Kai Ka'us Ibn Iskandar, Prince of Gurgan. This delightful and wise ruler wrote his book in the year 475 after the *Hijra* (AD 1082) 'to warn his favourite son and destined successor against the pitfalls on life's journey and to direct him in the path likely to lead to the greatest benefits'. The quotations are from the 1951 translation by Professor Reuben Levy.

When *Behind Iranian Lines* was written we had only been in Iran for eighteen weeks between us. Now we have spent a total of nine months there, in sixteen separate visits; few if any British, and no American, journalists have had as much time as this in the Islamic Republic. Together or separately we have travelled through large parts of the country, from the shores of the Persian Gulf in the south to the Caspian Sea in the north, and from the Kurdish and Arabic-speaking areas to the Turkoman territory of the north-east, in cars, planes, helicopters, boats, by horseback and on foot. The great majority of these journeys were made alone or with friends; the regime in Iran is very different from, say, Saddam Hussein's Iraq, Asad's Syria or the old Soviet Union, where spies and 'minders' surround you and you can see only what the authorities want you to see. The problem, for a foreign journalist, is to get a visa to enter Iran in the first place. Once you are there, it is easy to travel without official supervision.

We have been helped by a great many people who told us their stories and sometimes took risks on our behalf. It would not be doing them any favours to name them, but they will know who they are: especially those friends who lent us horses and taught me to ride; who designed a pair of cufflinks and explained to a Persian goldsmith the use of studs on a dress

shirt; who helped us with our Persian; who crushed a group of interfering
Revolutionary Guards by saying that if they didn't know what we were
doing there, they weren't important enough to have been told; who
benefited from the *sabzee*-tying ceremony; who drove into no-man's-land;
whose nickname was 'Bertie'; who slaughtered their best fat-tailed sheep
for us; who planted Buno Avenue; who does everything in sevens; who,
when in London, likes to eat at a particular Szechuan restaurant in the
King's Road; who gave us an Islamically correct clock; who follows the
Great Game from Tehran; who work for the BBC Persian Service; who is
a fellow member of the Chelsea Arts Club; who works at the bank; whom
we first met at Jules Bar; as well as the guru of The Mall and so many
other friends in Tehran, Isfahan, London, Oxford, Paris, Washington,
Brussels and (not least) somewhere in the Australian outback.

South Kensington, September 1994

1

Khomeini's Legacy

John Simpson

*The onerous part of the pilgrimage is the journey, which it would not be
an act of wisdom to enjoin on them that could not equip themselves for it,
for to undertake the journey without proper equipment would be to invite
destruction.*

A Mirror For Princes

As you drive south out of Tehran, the saffron- and rust-coloured mountains
of the Albourz range fade and the greenness, fed by mountain streams,
turns to brown aridity. The altitude drops, the temperature rises, the
buildings and the fields become an indeterminate dusty yellow-grey. It
takes a long time to fight through the squalid, poverty-stricken suburbs
of south Tehran and the chaotic traffic jams which build up in its streets;
but then, once you have reached the drab, endangered countryside beyond,
a new highway emerges from the tangle of roads which lead southwards
in the direction of the open plains.

A few miles farther, and the highway runs past a little colony of
undertakers' shops which display newly carved gravestones in their
forecourts. Some of the stones already have the full details of the
deceased carved on them and are ready for laying down. Others carry
only the phrase 'In the name of God, the compassionate, the merciful'
and are still waiting for a customer. Others again are entirely blank.
This is the area around Behesht-e-Zahra cemetery, where the mortuary
industry thrives. In the crumbling houses on its edges live the women
whose job it is to lay out the bodies and to weep at the graveside, adding
numbers and dignity to the mourning families.

Overlooking the cemetery is a mosque with a huge gold-coloured
dome. The dome is said to be covered in gold leaf, but it already
looks tarnished and there are those who say the money which was
donated for the purpose went astray. The dome lacks the shapeliness
of the classical Persian mosque; it has a squat, ungainly look, as if it

were designed by committee. Perhaps its roundness has something to
do with the speed with which it was constructed – faster than any
other building project in post-revolutionary Iran. The signs in Farsi
and English read: 'To Imam's Khomeini's Holy Tomb'; the assumption
was that it would become a place of pilgrimage to match the seven holy
sites of Shi'ia Islam. It hasn't. Khomeini's tomb has none of the bustle
of the shrine of Fatima in Qom or Imam Reza's shrine in Mashhad. The
vast parking lot is rarely even half full.

It is Friday. Midday prayers, the most important of the week, are
about to be celebrated. Inside, the mosque seems as large as a football
field, divided up by pillars and lit by huge, elaborate chandeliers. Its
vastness mocks the small number of people who have gathered there:
perhaps five hundred in all, scattered in little knots around a building
capable of holding tens of thousands. By no means all are there to pray.
Dozens of families, who have merely come for a day out, are picnicking
on the blankets they have brought with them for the purpose, leaning
against the cool marble walls. Those who are there to worship sit on
magnificent Persian carpets in front of the mullah who is leading Friday
Prayers. There are only about a hundred and fifty of them, men and
boys. A smaller number of women sit together, farther off, their black
chadors contrasting starkly with the handwoven silk carpets. Nearby,
children are playing on the polished marble floor, sliding in stockinged
feet as though on an ice rink, chasing each other or dragging each other
along, their shrieks louder than the prayer leader's chants. Nobody minds
the children; there is so much space here that they are able to give the
prayer session a wide berth.

In the centre of the shrine are the ultra-devout: two dozen or so men
and women who hold on to the bars of the cage surrounding Ayatollah
Khomeini's sarcophagus, too deep in their own world to be distracted
by the children or anything else. They bow their heads against the
bars in prayer, or gaze at the tomb as if mesmerised, or sit quietly
weeping. Others push their heads against the bars or reach their hands
through them. The object of their devotion is a marble slab covered by
a rich cloth, green for Islam. Beneath this slab lie the mortal remains
of Ayatollah Khomeini, buried with his face pointing towards Mecca.
Revolutionary Guards, their arms folded, stand and talk quietly among
themselves, watching to see that the mourners do not get out of hand,
and that there are no terrorist attacks or demonstrations. The sound
of the prayer leader's sermon mingles with the quiet chatter of the
picnickers and the occasional shriek of a running child, echoing up into
the coolness of the dome high above.

The contrast with the day on which the shrine was opened could
scarcely be greater. On 4 June 1990, the first anniversary of Khomeini's
death, there was an atmosphere of wild hysteria in the vast crowd that
thronged the place. For days beforehand the mourners had worked up

their religious fervour in classic Shi'ia fashion: processions of men and boys had whipped themselves endlessly and bloodily with flails as they marched around the mosque. Thousands of families had camped in the grounds outside in the broiling heat. Inside the mosque vast crowds swirled around the sarcophagus, chanting and beating their chests. That day the centre of Tehran was deserted. Those who had no interest in what was going on stayed indoors or had already left for the countryside, unwilling to draw attention to their disenchantment with the regime.

At Behesht-e-Zahra a fleet of helicopters flew back and forth, carrying VIPs and foreign journalists: there was no possibility now of getting to the shrine by road. This was to be more than a ceremony of mourning; it was a demonstration of the Islamic Republic's international influence. There were pilgrims from the entire world of Shi'ia Islam: from Lebanon, the Gulf, Afghanistan, the states of what had formerly been Soviet Central Asia, and from the wider diaspora. The official estimate for the attendance at the ceremony, eight million, was an absurd exaggeration, but there were certainly a quarter of a million mourners in the mosque itself and more forced their way in all the time.

In June the temperature at Behesht-e-Zahra regularly approaches 100 degrees Fahrenheit. Inside the mosque it must have been at least 120. The reek of sweat mingled with the sickly scent of the rose-water which was sprayed over the near-hysterical mourners in order to cool them down. The atmosphere lacked the insane edge of Khomeini's funeral, the year before, when his coffin had been tipped over by mourners crazed with grief and the frail white body had slipped out of its shroud and bobbed over the heads of the crowd. Still, inside the mosque, the masses rippled and swayed forward, steam rising from their bodies in the unbearable heat as they swept towards Khomeini's sarcophagus like an unstoppable tide. The Revolutionary Guards had to cling to the bars around it, interposing their bodies to stop the worshippers from damaging the tomb in their frenzy and self-abandon. To those of us on the fragile platforms which had been erected for the television cameras, it was an unnerving sight. A sudden surge of new arrivals through a side door foundered on the fifty or so wheelchairs of supposedly privileged war veterans. The wheelchairs were overturned in the crush, their metal snapped and bent, and the terrified, vulnerable occupants were pitched out and crushed underfoot in the crowd. Dozens of people suffered heart attacks that day, and the bodies of those who had fainted from the heat were passed to safety over the heads of the crowds like driftwood on the waves; though sometimes they would sink below the surface and disappear for minutes on end, until finally they were hauled up again and passed along towards the doors.

A little more than three years later it is hard to associate all this with the cool murmurings in a largely empty shrine. Outside, by the reflecting pool, there are more picnickers: quiet, relaxed family groups, mullahs sitting importantly upright while their wives and children hand them food to save them from the unseemly effort of reaching for it, groups of women chatting and laughing, men dozing in the shade of the scrubby bushes which were trampled underfoot by the devout crowds of 1990. Alongside the stalls selling food there is one where you can buy souvenirs: T-shirts, key-rings and posters bearing the stern likeness of Khomeini, as well as his books and pamphlets in half a dozen languages, indifferently printed. The food stalls are open for business but the one selling souvenirs is unattended and locked. You have to examine the goods through the glass, a little like looking at Khomeini's sarcophagus.

The people sitting outside have not come to visit the mosque. A picknicker explains that the forecourt also serves as a rest stop for bus passengers. He waves towards one end of the car park, where a dozen long-distance buses are waiting. 'The buses come up from the south,' he says. 'They stop here before the last part of the journey into Tehran. The drivers have their tea over at that tea-house, and we are having our meal here where the children can play. I wish there were more trees here,' he adds. For him and most of his fellow passengers this is just a convenient stopping-place. Less than four years after the death of the man who headed the revolution and founded the Islamic Republic, the religious significance of the place is distinctly secondary. The government which Khomeini left behind him may still be in place, but its power and authority have faded, like the memory of the scenes of wild mourning. Now everyone is waiting to see what will happen next in Iran. Khomeini's final act before he died was to construct a political dead end for his people.

The wild enthusiasm which brought about the revolution was precisely that: an enthusiasm. It faded quickly, as enthusiasms do. People soon became disenchanted with the notion that they were expected to become better morally, especially when it was abundantly clear that many members of the clergy and of the government of the Islamic Republic were themselves corrupt. The experience of government under Iran's clerical rulers proved to be a depressing one. By the late 1980s the rivalries and feuds within the government were becoming profoundly damaging, and during the first half of the 1990s President Rafsanjani was seriously weakened by the opposition of his political enemies. Ministers battled against ministers, ministries against ministries. Any political initiative was liable to be aborted by an *ad hoc* alliance of other figures within the government. Iran was stuck in a political and economic gridlock, from which there seemed to be no escape.

On 6 October 1978, the plane bringing Ayatollah Ruhollah Khomeini to the final stage of his exile landed at Orly Airport on the outskirts of Paris. In the airport terminal his flowing robes and black turban drew a good deal of attention, but he kept his eyes on the ground the whole time, determined not to allow anything that was evil in this Western environment to impinge on his consciousness. He climbed into the little car owned by one of his exiled supporters, Abol-Hassan Bani-Sadr, who was later to become President of Iran. As Bani-Sadr drove him down the motorway and into the narrow streets of the featureless suburb of Cachan, where his flat was, Khomeini resolutely refused to look out of the window. Their route did not take them to the centre of Paris, and Khomeini never visited, let alone saw, the city whose environs provided the springboard for his return.

When he came to France, Khomeini had been in exile for fourteen years. He had first been imprisoned for the leading part he took in the violent demonstrations of 1962–3 against the Shah's attempts to redistribute land to the peasants, allow greater freedom to women, and permit non-Muslims to take up posts in local government. The following year, after a period of house arrest, he was forced to leave Iran. He settled first in Turkey, and then in Iraq, in the Shi'ite holy city of Najaf. After 1975, when the Shah staged a diplomatic *rapprochement* with Iraq over the Shatt-al-Arab waterway dispute and cynically cut off support for the Iraqi Kurds, the flow of Iranian pilgrims wanting to see the holy places of Najaf and visit Khomeini greatly increased; and when the pilgrims returned home they often took with them tapes of Khomeini's sermons. But as long as Khomeini stayed in Iraq he did not represent a revolutionary threat to the imperial power in Tehran.

Some autocrats who are overthrown are the passive victims of events; not so the Shah. He was the engineer of his own downfall, and his greatest diplomatic triumphs made the revolution against him possible. His success in persuading the Arab members of the Organisation of Petroleum Exporting Countries (OPEC) to raise the price of oil to unprecedented heights in 1973 brought a flood of sudden wealth pouring into Iran, causing corruption and social dislocation on such a scale that the political system he had built up was unable to cope with it. Finally, he presented the incipient revolution with its leader when, in the aftermath of his diplomatic triumph with Iraq, he decided to do something about Khomeini. In the summer of 1978, in obedience to the instructions issued by the Ayatollah in Najaf, crowds of his supporters boiled on to the streets of Iran chanting, *'Dorud bar Khomeini'* – 'Long live Khomeini!' In reply, the Shah asked President Saddam Hussein of Iraq to expel Khomeini; and Saddam Hussein, anxious to keep on good terms with Iran, agreed. By making the request, the Shah expedited the revolution against himself, and Saddam Hussein, by agreeing, created a chain of events which led to his ill-judged invasion of Iran two years later and ultimately to the disaster of the Gulf War of 1991. It is not necessary to share Ayatollah Khomeini's views of his destiny to see that everything his enemies did, for whatever motive, seemed to further the interests of the revolution.

The Iraqi government gave Khomeini forty-eight hours to leave Najaf, and he hurriedly alerted his followers abroad and made his preparations. The message reached a medical laboratory in Texas, where one of his strongest supporters, Ibrahim Yazdi, was carrying out research into the treatment of cancer. Yazdi, a subtle-minded and ambitious man who was by now a naturalised American citizen, left immediately for Najaf. He arrived there before the forty-eight hours were up: if the revolution were about to begin, he wanted to claim his place in it. His first suggestion was that Khomeini should go to Kuwait, where the Shi'ia faith is strong; the Kuwaitis, however, refused to accept so difficult a visitor, and the refugees went to Baghdad to search for another place of refuge. In Paris meanwhile another Iranian exile, Sadeq Qotbzadeh, managed to persuade the Quai d'Orsay, the French Foreign Ministry, to give Khomeini a tourist visa. The even more difficult task of persuading him to accept it was entrusted to Abol-Hassan Bani-Sadr. Khomeini had profound doubts about the wisdom of going to live in a Western country which was so manifestly full of impurity; but Bani-Sadr eventually persuaded him that he had no real alternative.

He looked after Khomeini in his flat in Cachan for a few days, while the conversion work on a house in the village of Neauphle-le-Château in the countryside outside Paris was completed. Years afterwards, there was still a mild sense of scandal in Neauphle about the nature of the work that was required to make the house habitable for Khomeini. The workmen were, for instance, instructed to dismantle the modern lavatory and replace it with the type that had two porcelain steps on either side of a hole in the ground; the same firm had removed precisely that kind of lavatory from a dozen houses in the area over the previous decade. Planning permission for these and other changes, which would normally have taken weeks, was arranged in a day. Four new telephones and two telex lines were installed with extraordinary speed: the Quai d'Orsay has remarkable influence when it chooses to exert it. Khomeini had always refused to use a telephone, but at the age of seventy-eight he learned the advantages of instant communication. From then on he was in regular contact, through his lieutenants, with those inside Iran who were preparing for the revolution.

If going to live at Neauphle made it easier for him to communicate with his followers in Iran, it also brought Khomeini to the attention of the world at large. During the summer a French television team had penetrated to Najaf to try to interview him, only to find that forty Iraqi soldiers were deployed around his house to stop them. At Neauphle there were no barriers of any kind. During his first ten days there he complied with his undertaking to the French government not to make political statements in public. Still, the French media did not give up their efforts, and on 17 October he talked for the first time directly to a Western audience.

The second French television channel, Antenne-2, recorded a rather stilted interview with Khomeini that day. In it he said he was prepared to urge his followers towards armed insurrection against the Shah, who was, he said, kept in power by the United States; the central themes of the next few months were present from the beginnings of his time in the West. During the 195 days from this television debut to the moment of his return to Iran, he was interviewed 132 times: a remarkable degree of activity for a man in his eighth decade. Much has been made by Iranian royalists of the effect of these interviews in creating a revolutionary climate within Iran; but their real result was to bring the confrontation between the Shah and the Ayatollah to the attention of the outside world. In Iran itself it was the regular telephone calls from Neauphle and the smuggled cassettes of sermons which were of critical importance.

As the BBC's diplomatic correspondent, I had been visiting Iran to report on the increasing disturbances there since they had broken out the previous August. Now I went to Neauphle to interview Khomeini myself. The camera crew and I drove out of the centre of Paris early on a fine cold December morning, with the shadows lying long and sharp across the road, and reached the village at about eight-thirty. We stopped at the Café des Trois Communes in the centre of the village for a coffee and a croissant. The windows were steamed up – eight-thirty is a busy time in French cafés – and the bar was full of regulars. The atmosphere was heavy with tobacco smoke and the noise of the conversation as we clattered in, carrying our gear: camera, recorder, lights. The chatter died away and the heavy red faces of the French countryside turned to inspect us as we scraped our chairs on the wooden floor and filled the sudden silence with a discussion of what we were going to order.

'Iranians,' said one of the regulars dismissively, and turned his back on us. The others followed suit. To them we were simply extensions of the Ayatollah's entourage, foreigners whose generic name was 'Iranian', and who did nothing but take up tables in French cafés which could be put to better use by Frenchmen.

It was not difficult to find the Ayatollah's headquarters in the Route de Chevreuse: the police had established a road block outside it. On the other side of the road from the headquarters was the smaller house where the Ayatollah and his immediate entourage lived. We parked a little way away, outside a house with wooden shutters whose crossbars were painted white and stood out like large Zs. The lace curtains twitched slightly: either a Neauphlienne had still not been sated by the arrival of strangers, or the French equivalent of the Special Branch and the FBI, the Renseignements Généraux, had found themselves a warm billet. From an unmarked Simca parked across the road, we were being watched speculatively by two men in civilian clothes.

'You have an appointment?' The question was directed at me through the Simca's window. A gun lay on the back seat. I did not have an appointment; but I used, unknowingly, a technique which had been employed for centuries by Shi'ites: *khod'eh*, or the telling of a deceptive half-truth if it is necessary to protect the faith. Protecting the BBC's investment in sending me here, I replied that a Mr Yazdi wanted to see me. I had obtained the name from the previous evening's *Le Monde*, and it would have been truer to say that I wanted to see him. The policeman made a delicate gesture with his gloved hand, which I took to mean that he was letting me past even though he did not really believe me. By this stage the Renseignements Généraux, like the French government itself, had come to a kind of understanding with the Iranian exiles; I noticed, as I passed the car, that a small heater was keeping the occupants warm, and that an electrical flex which powered it ran from the car and snaked up the slope into Khomeini's headquarters.

Inside the gate I talked my way past a fierce-looking but pleasant young man in an open-necked shirt, dark suit and scrubby beard, and went up the steps of the house to the front door. There was an air of undirected bustle. More young men, built along much the same lines as the one by the gate, were speaking into telephones and cutting articles out of newspapers or talking and laughing. Little attention was paid to me, as I stood there adjusting to the warmth and the thick atmosphere. No one, I noticed, was wearing shoes; and assuming this was some religious custom I did not understand, I took my own shoes off. I found out later it was merely to protect the carpets from the mud of Neauphle. An old man with one eye came past with a metal tray and two or three cups of unclaimed tea on it, and he courteously offered me one. Someone noticed me then, and I invoked the name of Yazdi.

When he entered the room, Ibrahim Yazdi, the American cancer researcher who was to become his country's foreign minister, turned out to be a pleasant-featured man in his early forties with a neatly clipped beard and horn-rimmed glasses. His English was perfect, with a slight American accent.

'You wish to interview the Imam,' he said.

The title surprised me; until then I had heard it applied only to the great figures of the Shi'ite faith, eleven hundred years earlier. I assented, and he outlined the rules. All questions were to be submitted in advance, and put to the Ayatollah by him, and no supplementary questions were to be asked. I disliked this procedure, but there was no alternative.

'What are your questions?'

I tore a page from my notebook and wrote the questions out one by one, as they occurred to me. I still have the piece of paper:

1   Is it your intention to lead a revolution against the Shah, or do you simply wish to force him to change his policies?

2 What kind of government do you wish to see in Iran, and what form would an Islamic Republic take?

3 What would be the attitude of an Islamic Republic to the United States and the Soviet Union? Or to Britain, which has played an important part in your country's history?

4 Would there be a place for foreign companies in an Islamic Republic?

It all seemed extremely speculative. The Shah was still strong, and the prospect that a revolution in Iran could be organised from a village in the French countryside was inherently unlikely. The judgement was not mine alone; it was being made by the government of every major country in the world. Yazdi looked at my questions, and said we could have our interview that afternoon. In the meantime, we were free to film the Ayatollah at his prayers.

During my visits to Iran in the previous summer I had seen his face a thousand times, printed on posters, stencilled on walls, embroidered on banners. It was still a shock to encounter the Ayatollah in the flesh. As he walked slowly out of his house and across the road, the posters and stencils and banners came to life. Those heavy black eyebrows, that hawk-like nose, the white beard, the still-grey moustache constituted some of the most readily identifiable features in the world. His black turban, which indicated descent from the Prophet, accentuated the high forehead with its powerful lines which made his face look angry, even in repose. He wore a neat grey tunic under black robes, and walked slowly past us, taking no notice of the camera. His eyes were as ever on the ground, to avoid the sight of impurity. He looked the very personification of revenge.

A group of about thirty men and twenty women waited in the garden outside the blue-and-white prayer-tent. They fell back to let him pass and then followed him in, the men first. The women formed a solid mass of black at the rear of the tent. Khomeini was at the front, with a small knot of mullahs in white turbans around him. His quiet, toneless voice was almost lost in the heat and press of the tent, but it was his movements that everyone followed: he was the first to kneel and the first to rise, and latecomers at the very back stood on tiptoe from time to time to catch a glimpse of the back of his head. As always, Khomeini's mastery over himself was complete. He showed no emotion of any kind, then or later. Seventy years of rigid self-control had eradicated everything: anger, hatred, pleasure, happiness, relief. Already, even before he returned to Iran, he was indistinguishable from the icon.

At three o'clock that afternoon we presented ourselves at the Ayatollah's house and began making arrangements for the interview. The room where it was to take place was small, almost square, and

had only one window. The walls were covered with an incongruous
pattern of pink roses and some blue flower unknown to botany. We
took off our shoes, not knowing whether the room might be holy or the
presence of the Ayatollah might make it so. Within a few minutes we
had the room as well-lighted as a studio set, and all that was required
was the arrival of the principal performer. But it was another fifteen
minutes before the door opened. I was aware of the rustling of subfusc
robes and the manifestation of a powerful presence. Outside, he had been
impressive but isolated, a figure in a landscape. In this small, brilliant,
overheated room he was overpowering.

I tried to shake hands with him, uncertain of the protocol involved
in greeting somebody whose followers called him 'Imam'. He ignored
my outstretched hand, but in such a way that I might think he was
busying himself with his robes; it was not an ungracious gesture
on his part, merely one that thrust aside as meaningless anything
but the essentials of the relationship between us. My role, as far
as he was concerned, was that of an emissary from a country of
which he did not approve, speaking to him for reasons which did
not interest him; he would probably have preferred to spend the time
in religious contemplation. But a clear pattern had established itself:
people came to Ayatollah Khomeini thinking to use him for their own
ends, and instead found themselves serving the ends that he himself
served.

Any interview between a journalist and a politician represents a
balance of interest: the journalist wants strong, enlightening material,
the politician wants to present his views to a wider audience. Khomeini
might not have been a politician in the usual sense, and he did not need
to speak to Western journalists in order to ensure that people in Iran
heard his views. But he gave interviews at this time for two reasons:
firstly, because his advisers, more worldly than he, had faith in the
power of foreign newspapers, radio and television and persuaded him
to speak to them; and secondly, because it was a way of demonstrating
to the governments he regarded as Iran's enemies – Britain, the United
States and the Soviet Union – that he could not be deflected from his
declared purpose. Each interview he gave was intended to weaken the
support which each of those governments gave the Shah.

And so the balance of interest between Khomeini and the journalists
who interviewed him differed from the usual one. They came to him
because he was exotic yet accessible, a curiosity as well as a figure
of menace: he spoke to them to further his revolutionary ends. Who, in
Lenin's phrase, used whom? Khomeini's ability to play down the fiercer,
more reactionary elements in his political programme was impressive.
His advisers, once again, had briefed him well; he always left his
interviewers with the impression that human rights and the equality
of women, in something like the Western sense, would be assured.

No doubt they – we – wanted to be reassured; but there seems to have been a distinct element of disinformation involved.

Now Khomeini settled himself down cross-legged on a large square of foam rubber, which rested on a rough blanket on the floor. His back was against the wall with its red and blue flowers. The powerful lighting deepened the furrow between his eyebrows as he stared at the brown Baluchi carpet in front of him. He looked at me only twice during the entire interview: once at the end of his first question, and once at the end of his last one. On each occasion it was to mark an important point with some force. Yazdi translated my questions, and Khomeini answered them in a voice that was quiet and level. His words were chosen with care:

> The Shah has ruled Iran as though it were his private estate, his property, to do with as he chooses. He has created a dictatorship, and has neglected his duties. The forces of Islam will bring this situation to an end. The monarchy will be eradicated . . .
>
> The Islamic Republic will be based on the will of the people, as expressed by universal suffrage. They will decide on the precise form it takes. Every political party which works for the good of the country will be free. But there are aspects of life under the present corrupt form of government in Iran which will have to be changed: we cannot allow our youth to be corrupted and our Islamic culture to be destroyed, and drugs such as alcoholic beverages will be prohibited . . .
>
> We are hostile to governments which have put pressure on Iran, which have forced the Shah on Iran, and which have made Iran suffer at their hands. But we are not hostile to the citizens of those countries. We intend to reject a relationship which makes us dependent on other countries. As for the Soviet Union, we are not afraid of it or of its influence. But we have bitter memories of the British, because they ensured that Reza Shah [the Shah's father] came to power, and for half a century we have been under the domination of this man and his son.
>
> There will be a place for foreigners and their companies if they go about their daily business. But there are many foreigners who work against the interests of our people and help the Shah and his regime. They will not be allowed to remain in our country.

At last the audience was over. Yazdi folded up the piece of paper with my questions on it and handed it back to me. The Ayatollah, after his dark, penetrating glance at me, raised his arms slightly. The two men who had sat behind him throughout helped him with reverence to his feet. In its way, it was a significant interview, delivered in the fashion of an oracle: everything in it came true, but not in the way one would have thought at the time; especially the passage about universal suffrage and the freedom of political parties.

Ibrahim Yazdi followed his leader out, and they were met by Sadeq Qotbzadeh. Abol-Hassan Bani-Sadr came from an inner room to join them. All three represented the more liberal westernised tendencies within the incipient revolution. Within a few years the first would become foreign minister, and then be disgraced and forced to remain on the outer fringes of Iranian politics; the second would also be foreign minister, and would later be executed for treason; the third would be elected President, and afterwards forced into exile. They would have done better to remember the child-devouring habit of revolutions, just as the Carter administration in Washington would have done better to take notice of the force with which Ayatollah Khomeini said, 'The monarchy will be eradicated,' and the powerful look he gave as he said it. So, if the contents of the interview were reported to him, would the Shah himself.

I next went to Neauphle-le-Château in January 1979, eight days after the Shah had fled Iran. The brief Kerensky-like government of Dr Shahpour Bakhtiar was trying to hold the country together. Neauphle itself was in a state of permanent demonstration now. The students who wandered endlessly up and down the street between Khomeini's headquarters and his house had no clear idea what they expected to happen when they went back to Iran. Most defined the future solely in terms of the past: they wanted a society which was different from the one they had known in Iran, a society where, they said, every fourth person was an informer for SAVAK, the Shah's fearsome secret police, and you had to stay quiet if you wanted to avoid trouble.

'We want to say what we think without getting locked up,' one student said.

Others pushed their way into the group surrounding us to describe their experiences: being spied on, threatened, losing their government grants, fearing reprisals against their families at home if they criticised the Shah abroad. The women were fewer in number than the men, but no less vociferous. All of them wore some form of *hejab*, Islamic dress, even if it were only a headscarf; all believed that women in general would be freer under the new dispensation. Probably not many of them would have shown an interest in religion a year or so earlier, but they had been attracted by the political philosophy of Dr Ali Shariati, who introduced the concept of the 'oppressed masses', a concept which had a significant influence on Ayatollah Khomeini. Shariati had demonstrated that Shi'ia Islam could be an intellectual force in its own right, as effective as liberal democracy or Marxism. To people who were experiencing the sudden shock of life at a Western university for the first time, Shariati's theories provided a sense of purpose and of moral strength.

The news from Iran was conflicting. Yazdi and Qotbzadeh twice announced that the Ayatollah was about to return, and both times the journey had to be postponed for lack of assurances about his safety. In the streets of Tehran there were daily clashes between the demonstrators and the military. The government of the country had come almost to a halt. Day by day, Bakhtiar's power declined. His last real sanction was to postpone Khomeini's return. But it could not be done indefinitely; and on 31 January he announced that the Ayatollah's plane would be permitted to land at Tehran airport.

The crowds at Neauphle went wild with joy, and the competition began for seats on the flight. My office did not want me to go, preferring that I should stay and 'anchor' the news from Iran in the studio in London every night; but I had decided privately that I would catch the plane no matter what happened, a broadcasting stowaway if necessary. It was going to be one of the turning points of modern times, and I did not want to stay at home and read about it in the newspapers.

Air France had agreed to fly Ayatollah Khomeini back to Iran in a Boeing 747 with a volunteer crew. It would only be taking half the usual number of passengers, in case the plane were refused permission to land and had to fly back to Paris. No more than two hundred seats would be available, a third of them for Khomeini's party. The plane was to leave from Charles de Gaulle Airport at one o'clock the following morning, and the tickets were to be issued at seven that evening outside the headquarters building in Neauphle. Although it was a little before midday, a ragged queue for tickets began to form immediately.

I decided to join it. I knew I was on the provisional list for seats, but experience suggested that those who presented themselves and refused to go away invariably did better than those who trusted in the promises of officials. I sent my colleagues off to the Café des Trois Communes, and took my place in the queue of hopefuls. It was several degrees below freezing and my brand-new Loden coat, bought in the Rue du Faubourg St-Honoré, did not altogether keep out the chill. I waited for seven hours, unable to move in case the people in the crowd behind me edged me out of my place. Conversation with the Iranian enthusiasts around me ran out quickly. Sometimes the queue would move a few paces; sometimes there was a scuffle as a latecomer tried to force his way in. There was nothing to do, nothing to read, nothing to eat, and nothing much to think about.

The waiting ended in a sudden blaze of action and shouting, for which our seven hours in the cold had not prepared us. Names were called, and those who were not there to answer did not get tickets. It had been dark for some hours, and people had to use cigarette lighters to read the list of favoured names and count out the money: five hundred dollars each, or the equivalent in French francs. There was anger and despair. Several hundred-dollar bills and a couple of tickets blew out of someone's hand, and vanished in the mud and darkness. People kept arriving late and shouting out their demands and pleas. As for me, I took the two tickets we had been allocated, paid, and headed off. The waiting and the cold had sapped everything except the desire to get warm and eat something. I left the late arrivals to their Hieronymus Bosch experience in the dark, scrabbling on the ground, fighting and bewailing their losses. The Café de Trois Communes was exerting an attraction I could no longer resist.

At Charles de Gaulle Airport that night our suitcases were weighed and checked in, and a mysterious blue tag with the figure 2 was stuck across each of them. One of the baggage handlers called out, 'This way to the death-flight.' We laughed, to show that we were not scared; though I, for one, certainly was. My throat was dry, and I was prey to sentimental thoughts about home. The reports from Tehran indicated that the armed forces were deeply divided. Some officers and men seemed determined to support their current master, Dr Bakhtiar. Many of the ordinary soldiers wanted to follow Khomeini and the cause of religion. The rest still kept their loyalty to the Shah. Who knew which tendency we would land among?

I looked around me, and detected the same anxiety among many of my fellow passengers. There was only one good thing about it, I thought; the office had assigned me a cameraman who was one of the few people I would actually want to be with in a tricky situation: a short, spry, nautical-looking figure in his fifties called Bill Handford, with the sharp blue eyes of a sailor and a bristly beard which would later be much admired by the ayatollahs and mullahs we were to meet. Throughout our experience of the coming weeks, he never once complained. Bill Handford had filmed in Vietnam, the Nigerian civil war, in Northern Ireland at its worst; maybe a plane trip to Iran with an ayatollah was nothing very serious, after that.

There was, fortunately, no shortage of space on the plane. Khomeini and his supporters and advisers took over the first-class section, which left us with two or three seats each. The discreet curtain dividing first-class passengers from the lower orders was kept firmly drawn. A regular undertone of prayer filtered through it, and those Iranians who had not been able to get seats in first-class stood or knelt in the aisles. I struck up a conversation with a British acquaintance of mine, who was based in Paris. He was not happy to be on the plane. 'I'm their Paris correspondent,' he kept saying. 'The only reason I'm here is because this whole thing is starting from Paris. What do I know about Iran? Nothing. So why did they send me? Because I'm their Paris correspondent.' The litany continued, and I moved away.

A little later in the flight I fell into conversation with a returning Iranian student. 'I am hoping with great sincerity,' he said, 'that this plane will be shot down.' Another student interrupted. 'That wouldn't be right at all. I want to sacrifice my life too, but I want us to land and take part in the revolution. That would be a far better sacrifice.' With such difficult moral choices under discussion, I envied Bill Handford's ability to fall asleep immediately.

An amusing, phlegmatic Air France steward brought us dinner. There was no alcohol on the drinks trolley, by the strict instructions of the Ayatollah. For me, practical anxieties were beginning to take over: we would need to do some filming on board. I applied at the dividing curtain, and was told that my request would be considered. I settled down for an uneasy sleep, nervous about what the morning might bring.

Three hours later it was light outside the aircraft, and coffee and croissants put a little life back inside me. There was a stir at the front end of the plane, and Sadeq Qotbzadeh emerged from behind the curtain, like Chorus in a Shakespeare play. He climbed on the foremost row of seats in our section, his back to the place where the film would have been projected if the Ayatollah had permitted such a thing on his flight.

'I have a serious announcement to make,' he said in French, looking down at a piece of paper he was holding. Everyone went quiet.

'We have just received a warning over the aircraft radio that the Iranian air force has orders to shoot us down directly we enter Iranian airspace.'

Someone – it may have been the correspondent based in Paris – asked nervously if we would be turning round. 'Certainly not,' said Sadeq Qotbzadeh.

'What's he saying?' I heard Bill's voice ask me, quietly.

'You don't want to know,' I said, but I told him anyway.

'Hmmm,' he said sceptically, giving me a sidelong look. He had heard warnings like this before.

Qotbzadeh, meanwhile, had climbed down and was walking along the aisle with the practised skill of a public relations man, seeking out the television cameramen and the photographers.

'You can film the Imam now. But be brief.'

I picked up the sound-recordist's gear and hurried forward with Bill.

'No journalists, just cameramen,' Qotbzadeh said, trying to hold me back.

I reminded him that we had been allocated only two tickets, and had been forced to leave our sound-recordist in Paris, to follow on later. Qotbzadeh smiled and let me pass.

The Ayatollah was sitting at the front of the first-class compartment, on the left-hand side, looking out of the window: there were no impurities at this height. The whirring of the camera – we were still using film then, rather than video – caught his attention, and he turned to face us, calm and passionless. I asked him a question about returning to Iran. His son Ahmad, sitting next to him, translated it into Farsi. The Ayatollah lowered his head without answering, and looked out of the window again. A few minutes later, a better-phrased question from a French correspondent elicited the most famous remark of the trip.

'We are now over Iranian territory. What are your emotions after so many years of exile?'

'*Hichi*,' was the answer: 'Nothing.'

Question and answer exemplified a mutual incomprehension. To Westerners, and to westernised Iranians, it sounded as though he cared nothing for the country he was about to plunge into revolution. We expected some sign of emotion, but emotion was not in Khomeini's line. He had spent his entire life ridding himself of false, personal, human feelings. It is permissible for a Muslim to express his love for Allah through the love of a person or place, but not to love them strictly speaking for their own sake. Ayatollah Khomeini did not.

The Prophet Mohammed returned from his *Hegira*, the flight to Mecca, in order to carry out the first Islamic Revolution; Khomeini, too, was returning from a *Hegira*. Such moments were not to be debased. The news of his reply to the French correspondent's question was passed incredulously from one journalist to another at the back of the aircraft, and as we took note of it each of us remembered that we were now flying over Iran, and that Sadeq Qotbzadeh had warned us we might now be shot down.

Nobody shot us down, though, and we continued our flight to Tehran, seeing at last the snowy peaks of the Albourz Mountains below us. Many of the Iranian exiles in our part of the plane gave away to an unIslamic outburst of rejoicing, though some glanced nervously at the curtain to check that they were not being overheard and disapproved of. A thin yellowish sunshine cut through the cloud cover as we descended. Tehran lay spread out below us, as peaceable and featureless as any city looks from the air. People were crowding together in their hundreds of thousands, their millions even, waiting for us to land; but from this height they were invisible.

The pilot's voice came over the loudspeaker: 'We have not received permission to land. Until we receive this permission we shall be obliged to circle over the city. You may experience some discomfort.'

We experienced discomfort in fairly large quantities. A passenger aircraft like a Boeing 747 is stable and pleasant enough when it flies in a straight line, but when it circles at low altitude for half an hour or more it can induce airsickness and earache in the most seasoned traveller. Bill Handford caught my glance and winked; but the gloomy British journalist of my acquaintance was in an ecstasy of unhappiness. 'I am the Paris correspondent,' he intoned. 'What am I doing here?'

And then, at last, it was over. The revolutionary welcoming committee on the ground had completed its negotiations with the air force men who were running Mehrabad Airport, and the Boeing's agony of circling was at an end. We set a straight course for the runway, and the wheels touched the ground of the country the Ayatollah felt nothing about returning to. The exile was back, his *Hegira* over; the final phase of the revolution was about to begin.

2

Revolution

John Simpson

Once you engage in battle it is inexcusable to display any sloth or hesitation: you must breakfast on the enemy before he dines on you. When you have arrived in the midst of the fray, be remiss in nothing but take no precautions for your own life; he that is destined to sleep in the grave will never again sleep at home.

A Mirror For Princes

A revolution is the most disturbing and enthralling event imaginable. Wars usually generate more confusion and boredom than unalloyed fear, and from your small patch of hillside or bundu you have no idea what is going on anywhere else. The information you receive has usually been distorted long before you hear it, and it is almost invariably censored when you try to report it. In a revolution, by contrast, you can see what is happening for yourself, and there is neither time for it to become distorted nor sufficient organisation on the part of whatever authorities are left to censor what you want to say. The action takes place before your eyes; there is no question who has won or lost.

You need have no personal sympathy whatever with the motives of the revolutionaries to find yourself swept up in the violent excitement of it all. The crowd carries you along like a river in flood, and the hundreds of people who swarm around you, shouting and waving their makeshift weapons in the air, are your devoted friends, ready to sacrifice their lives to protect you and very happy indeed for you to witness and record their heroics. A revolutionary crowd is awesome. There is nothing so cruel, nothing so courageous, nothing so stupid, nothing so noble, nothing so good at improvising solutions to the most impossible problems. Intelligent, prudent people find themselves abandoning their individuality and becoming part of a wild, unstoppable mob; and if you are with them you too become caught by the general animal magnetism.

The Iranian Revolution, like the French and Russian revolutions, succeeded because of the dynamics of the crowd. There were of course organising minds behind it, but the crowds were the vehicle they used, and without the angry power of the people on the streets the old political order would have remained unchanged. The revolution against the Shah took most of a year to accomplish, and it was done by a process of savage attrition. The constant demonstrations in the streets sapped his confidence in himself, and the fear his subjects had of him. There is something self-legitimising about very large gatherings of people: they regard themselves, and others regard them, as embodying the will of the nation as a whole. In the case of Iran, the process which began slowly and in fear among small groups of people ended up as the genuine expression of the great majority of the country.

As early as September 1978 it seemed plain to those of us who were on the streets every day, watching the mood of the crowds, that the Shah's position was in danger, yet there was an understandable reluctance among foreign governments to believe it; most of them had too much to lose to want to face up to the prospect. I suggested in a BBC broadcast in the first week of September that the Shah might be forced to give up his powers and become a constitutional monarch. There were streams of complaints about this rather timid forecast, including a private one from the Foreign Office. A young American of seventeen, who spent a great deal of time with Iranians of his own age, saw the signs more clearly:

> During that winter, when there was martial law, there was one form of defiance that many people took. They would climb on to their roofs at sunset and call out 'Allahu Akbar! Allahu Akbar!' You could hear it across the city and up the mountainside: 'Allahu Akbar ... Allahu Akbar ...' It reverberated through the winter air. It was then I realised that a change was coming.

On 31 December 1977 President Jimmy Carter and his wife spent their New Year's Eve in Tehran as guests of the Shah. As midnight struck, Carter raised his glass in a toast to the coming year and to the Shah's rule. Iran was, he said, 'an island of stability in one of the more troubled areas of the world'. It seemed true enough at the time. The large majority of the population accepted the Shah's rule without question, and although there was opposition from the left and from some elements among the clergy it was mostly too frightened to express itself publicly within Iran. The events of the year which President Carter had toasted with such apparent confidence were a process of sudden erosion of this fear, and of the Shah's nerve. Yet as so often happened with him, he created his own problems through overconfidence.

Three or four days after his triumphant celebration of the new year with the president of the United States, someone (it has never been finally established whether it was the Shah himself, or the SAVAK, or the cabinet) instructed the information minister, Darioush Homayoun, to send an article attacking both the left-wing and the religious opposition to the newspaper *Ettelaat*. Signed with the pseudonym 'Ahmad Rashidi-Motlaq' and entitled 'Iran and the Black and Red Reactionaries', the article was published on 7 January 1978. It included a scurrilous personal attack on Ayatollah Khomeini, hinting that he was homosexual and accusing him of being a British agent: he was, it said, 'an irreligious adventurer who was linked to the centres of colonialism ... and the more superficial and reactionary colonialists'. He had been recruited by the British in India in his youth, according to the article, and they were paying him through an Arab intermediary to conduct a campaign against the Shah.

There was an immediate outburst of anger in the holy city of Qom, where Khomeini had many allies and close supporters in the theological colleges. The city shut down completely, and two days after the article appeared a crowd of several thousand students marched through the streets in protest. They were confronted by a large contingent of armed police, who opened fire on them. More than fifty students were killed, and the pattern which was to bring the Shah down a year later began: forty days after their deaths, there were mourning processions in various parts of the country. These were declared illegal, and the police opened fire. Someone else was killed, and there was cause for another mourning procession: which in turn would be fired against. At the time it was known in the slang of the Tehran streets as 'doing the forty-forty'.

By August, after months of this, the Shah was in considerable trouble; though it was not yet obvious that it would be terminal. On the 19th, a few days before I arrived in Iran for the first time, a fire broke out at the Rex Cinema in Abadan during the showing of a controversial film called *The Deer*. The film, which was made by an Iranian director, contained some implicit criticisms of contemporary life in Iran, and was regarded as being hostile to the Shah; it had received a certificate from the censors only after a number of cuts had been made. Four hundred and ten people, including many women and children, died in the fire; all the exits had been barred. The government claimed that it had been the work of religious fanatics, but Khomeini insisted it was the SAVAK, and most people seemed to agree. The fire was certainly started deliberately, and by this time the government was so nervous that it established a board of inquiry and invited several foreign journalists in Tehran to put questions to the men who had produced the inquiry's report. I was one of the journalists, and was told that it was most important that I should ask hard-hitting questions, so that the viewers would accept that the report was genuine. It did nothing to dispel the view that the Shah's secret service was responsible.

It was during this visit that I first saw the revolutionary crowds in action in the streets; and although I was not there for the 'Bloody Friday' massacre of 8 September 1978 at Jaleh Square, when more than fifteen hundred people were killed, I returned in time for the next big round of demonstrations and shootings. On 5 November the biggest crowd since the start of the troubles began to gather in central Tehran. My colleagues this time were the famous BBC cameraman Bernard Hesketh and his sound-recordist John Jockell, who were later to win many prizes for their coverage of the Falklands War. Bernard was the oldest man on either side to be involved in the war, yet he 'yomped' across the islands and into Port Stanley with Royal Marines and Guardsmen half his age. By midday, when nothing very much had happened, I left them to carry on filming while I went back to our hotel three miles away to telephone a report. We arranged to meet at two o'clock.

'I'll find you round here somewhere,' I said. It seemed a sensible enough arrangement at the time.

But the telephone call took three hours to come through, and when I was finally able to leave the hotel the sky was black with the smoke from a dozen big fires. The taxi-driver we had hired for the day was old and cowardly, with a face like a lugubrious sheep. He refused to drive me back to the town centre, on the grounds that I would be killed and the car burned. There was no doubt which he thought was the more serious. I cajoled and raged and offered him money: a bonus of £100 plus a written indemnification against any damage or loss. He refused. As a last effort to get him to change his mind, I said I would have to walk if he wouldn't take me.

Having committed myself, I felt I had at least to set out; and having set out, it was just as difficult to go back as it was to keep on. I was nervous that Bernard and John would think I had abandoned them, and that overrode even my fear of walking through the streets. This fear was not altogether misplaced. There were fires and barricades at every intersection along the way, and a million or more people were on the streets. Anyone from Britain or the United States could expect rough treatment, though we were usually safe enough when we were working: the camera was the only passport we needed. Without it, I felt very alone. I walked with an artificial air of purpose through the noise and smoke in my conspicuous Austin Reed sports jacket, the stench of burning tyres and burning buildings in my nostrils and the sound of thousands of chanting voices in my ears. People screamed in my face and threw things at me, but although I must have passed through ten or eleven barricades no one stopped me. On the two occasions when it looked as though somebody might, I glared at them like the Victorian engraving of Sir Charles Napier outstaring the tiger in the Indian jungle. It seemed to work.

It was a very long three miles, all the same, and it soon became obvious that with so many people running through the streets our rendezvous could never have been possible. I was nearly three hours late by now, and had to shoulder my way through the crowds. That made it slightly safer, since no one could see me coming and react to my presence; with the natural courtesy of the Persian they made way for me, and by the time they had properly worked out who I might be, I was gone. But I was hopelessly lost; the landmarks had been blotted out by the sheer density of people. I had only one concern: to avoid being swept away by the crowd, and to keep to my own purpose. In the noise and the weight of numbers this was becoming difficult. By now I was very tired.

And then I caught sight of them. It was so unlikely that I shouted out loud; not that it mattered, in that degree of noise. To have come all this way in the largest crowd I had ever seen, and to have stumbled on the only two people in it whom I wanted to meet, seemed quite extraordinary; but there, ten yards from me, a little above the heads of the crowd, was the outline of our camera. I fought my way over to them.

When I reached them, though, I found that Bernard and John had problems of their own. The crowd was angry about something which had been broadcast by the BBC Persian Service the previous night, and although Bernard had pulled the BBC stickers off his camera most people knew perfectly well who we worked for. I make it a rule never to pretend I do not work for the BBC; as long as the monthly cheque keeps coming in, it seems the only decent thing to do, and in this case there was no point in denying it. Bernard explained the situation hurriedly to me, brushing aside my efforts to tell him how difficult it had been to find him. I now realised we had two things to worry about: firstly our safety, since the crowd had become extremely hostile, and secondly the safety of the pictures which Bernard had already filmed, and which sounded remarkable. A few minutes before my arrival, it seemed, Bernard and John had filmed a group of soldiers surrounded by the crowd which had been entirely friendly. At first the soldiers had fired on the demonstrators, but then some of them had broken down in tears and gone over to the crowd, handing them their guns and tearing the insignia off their uniforms. The demonstrators had carried the soldiers away shoulder-high.

At that point a man, beside himself with emotion, had made his way to the fringe of the group of demonstrators who were surrounding Bernard and John, and had begun screaming that his brother had been shot dead by the army the previous day, and that the BBC had failed to report it.

'That proves it, my friends,' he was shouting as I looked round and saw him. 'They're in the pay of the Shah.'

The mood of the people who heard him turned instantly from helpfulness and friendship to savage hatred. There was no time to try to soothe them down, or explain things away. The noise, the emotions, the tension, even the smoke that lay heavily in the air, all made quietness and rationality impossible. They pressed in even closer, and a small man who had pinned a picture of Khomeini on to a broom-handle started beating me in the face with it. Others, including a student who had spent a term at Norwich Polytechnic and had been acting as a translator until a minute or two before, started pulling us about and wrenching at our clothes. I could feel the material of my conspicuous jacket ripping, and I realised with a stark horror that they were going to tear us to pieces. I had seen it happen to other people; now it was going to happen to us.

When I had watched it happen during a demonstration earlier, it had seemed to me that the victim had yielded quite soon to the overwhelming mood of the crowd, giving himself up to it rather than fighting to stay alive. Even being a victim of the crowd was, I felt, a part of the sense of joining the common purpose. I was determined not to yield to this animal magnetism. Violent, contorted faces pressed into mine, screaming insults. My face was covered with spittle. A dozen powerful hands gripped me. And all the time the little man with the picture of Khomeini on the broom-handle carried on beating me about the face.

If it hadn't been for that, I should probably have succumbed. It is impossible to fight off so many people at such close quarters; not even Sir Charles Napier could have done it. But you can grab hold of a broom-handle. I did so at first out of pain and instinctive rage, and I lunged back at him with it, missing him. But when I had it in my hand, and had wrestled my arm free, I waved the stick with its picture of Khomeini in the air, and did the first entirely intelligent thing I had done all day. I shouted, *'Dorud bar Khomeini!'* – 'Long live Khomeini!'

That so simple a device should have worked is an indication of the ease with which the collective emotions of a crowd can be turned. All three of us were released, our equipment was picked up and handed to us, and we had some difficulties persuading them not to carry us shoulder-high ourselves, like the soldiers Bernard and John had filmed earlier. We were very shaken and very relieved, and the knowledge that I had contravened all the BBC's rules of balance and objectivity bothered me not one little bit. I have the picture of Khomeini in front of me as I write, complete with the holes from the drawing-pins which fixed it to the broom-handle, a few small rust-coloured stains from my blood, and the creases where I had folded it up and put it in my pocket, a gift from the little man who had been hitting me with it a few moments before. I regard it with some affection; I think it may have saved me from the nastiest death of my imagining.

The crowds which gathered in Tehran three months later, on 1 February 1979, to welcome Ayatollah Khomeini back from exile were quite possibly the largest group of human beings ever assembled together in one place on one day for a single objective. And in contrast to the angry mood of 5 November and all the other bitter days of confrontation with the army and the SAVAK, the mood was one of joy. The Shah had gone into exile, on the pretext that he was paying a state visit to Egypt. The prime minister he had appointed, Dr Shahpour Bakhtiar, was nominally in charge of the government, but he was clearly a brief interim figure who would soon be swept away by the sheer weight of support for Khomeini. It was only a question of time.

Meanwhile in the country as a whole there was a state of near-ecstasy. Central to the Shi'i faith is the belief in the Missing Imam, Mohammed al-Mehdi, who disappeared in AD 880 and is expected to come again bringing righteousness and judgement to the earth. When Khomeini, whose followers called him 'Imam', returned to sweep away the old, failed political system of Iran and establish it with an Islamic Republic, the clear blue skies and bright sunlight of that day seemed to them to take on the transcendent quality of a Second Coming. Some days before, a Tehran magazine had published a poem entitled 'The Day the Imam Returns' by Taha Hejazi, which showed how people's expectations had risen to chiliastic heights:

> The day the Imam returns
> No one will tell lies any more
> No one will lock the doors of his house;
> People will become brothers
> Sharing the bread of their joys together
> In justice and sincerity.
> There will no longer be any queues:
> Queues for bread and meat,
> Queues for kerosene and petroleum,
> Queues for cinemas and buses,
> Queues for tax payments,
> Queues for snake poison
> Shall all disappear,
> And the dawn of awakening
> And the spring of freedom
> Shall smile upon us.
> The Imam must return
> So that Right can sit on its throne,
> So that evil, treachery and hatred
> Are eliminated from the face of time.
> When the Imam returns,
> Iran – this broken, wounded mother –
> Will forever be liberated.

An old system had died, a new one was being born; people invested the moment with every quality they wanted to see applied to their daily lives. Those who had flocked to the poor, ugly slums of Iran's cities from the quiet villages, those who had been shocked by the sudden social changes of five years of immense oil wealth, those who had witnessed the corruption of a Third World country with First World wealth – for all of them, the revolution seemed to promise a return to decency and sanity. And for the urban middle class, who had benefited from the wealth but had often been disturbed by the effects of it, there seemed to be the chance to start again on a better, cleaner basis. If there might be a darker side to the revolution, no one wanted to think about it. For the moment, everyone's wishes, political, social and personal, seemed on the point of coming true.

All through the night, in this highly-charged spirit of expectation, volunteers had been at work on the roads which the Ayatollah would take from the airport, washing and cleaning them to make sure they would be worthy of him. Later, there were to be reports that among the chants that arose from the enormous crowds as Khomeini's car passed by were some that made the reference to a Second Coming explicit: 'The doors of paradise have opened again!' 'Now is the hour of martyrdom!'

When the Air France Boeing landed at Mehrabad, and Bill Handford and I had filmed the Ayatollah's triumphal appearance at the top of the aircraft steps, our immediate part in the day's proceedings was over. We made contact with the correspondent and crew who were to take over from us, and were at last able to collect our belongings and relax; we had been working for twenty-six hours.

Khomeini's party swept ahead of us into the special terminal building for passengers making the *Hajj*, or pilgrimage to Mecca. Our luggage lay unclaimed and isolated on the carousel. There seemed little point in hurrying anywhere: the roads were all blocked off for the Ayatollah's arrival, and there was no transport of any kind to be found. Bill and I sat side by side on a wooden bench, talking or dozing and luxuriating in the fact that for a few hours at least there was nothing for us to do. On the other side of a pair of glass doors Khomeini was speaking to a gathering of several hundred mullahs who had come from all over Iran to welcome him. His quiet voice did not penetrate the doors, but the fierce applause with which his words were received did. The heat and emotion of the moment must have been intense.

And then suddenly the glass doors opened and Khomeini appeared, almost carried by two mullahs. His arms were over their shoulders, his head hung down on his chest. A group of mullahs followed, and we could hear the cries and murmurs of dismay from the others who had been listening to him. Bill and I took a moment or two to react. The group around Khomeini took no notice of us, and we pushed our way with the camera into a waiting room where they had laid the Ayatollah down on a couch and a doctor was already bending over him. Nobody stopped us filming.

For a moment or two there was utter silence. Khomeini lay on the couch, his eyes shut, while everyone stood and watched him, frozen. Then the eyes opened.

'*Ab,*' he said faintly. 'Water.'

Someone put a glass of water tenderly to his lips, and he drank from it. Then, very slowly, he sat up and thanked them for the care they had shown him. The heat, the tiredness, and perhaps in spite of himself the emotion of the return had caused him to faint. It was an uncharacteristic moment of weakness, and one which he must have determined would not be repeated again on this transcendent day; and we, by chance, were the only ones outside the circle of the faithful to have witnessed it. But there had been a moment when Bill and I had both thought we had got one of the best scoops of the century.

As the Ayatollah was driven away from the airport, no one who watched his blue Mercedes pass can have had any idea of the problem that had briefly arisen. For them, all that was visible was the icon: Khomeini sitting straight-backed, waving only occasionally, and with the fierce, purposeful, unforgiving expression which was reproduced in every one of the thousands of pictures of him lining his route. Khomeini knew his Persians well: they are a people who respect firmness and strength. Groups of his closest supporters had been going the rounds for several days making sure that only pictures which showed him as the stern avenger were on display. Any which showed him smiling or even looking mild were taken down.

By now the crowds had been waiting for more than eight hours. As they caught sight of the Mercedes, complete with its escort of motorcycle outriders, a roar went up and was relayed all along his route: a travelling chain of noise which stretched for half a mile or so at any given moment. Like the portraits of the Ayatollah, most people were not smiling. Their emotions went much deeper than that. Their expressions were serious and triumphant, and they chanted the words of prearranged slogans and waved their fists in time to the chanting with a ferocious confidence. Between two and three million people saw the Mercedes pass. They lined the route twenty deep, they climbed into the boughs of even the most feeble trees, they clung precariously to the steel skeletons of unfinished buildings along the way. Every inch of every wall and post seemed to be covered with pictures of him, and a new banner was on display: a clenched fist in black surrounded by faces representing political prisoners, and over it the words '*Allahu Akbar*' – 'God is great'. It was the first flag of the Islamic Republic.

Khomeini had decided to stay aloof from the opposition politicians who had remained in Iran during his fifteen-year exile. He was not going to ally himself with anyone else. Instead of accepting their invitation to a meeting at Tehran University, he headed straight for Behesht-e-Zahra cemetery, eighteen miles away in south Tehran, to pay his respects to those who had given their lives for his cause during the year of clashes with the police. But it was clear that the crowds were so immense along the road that his Mercedes could not make it in safety. The army, which had scarcely made an appearance of any kind, had offered its services to Khomeini's supporters, and the man who had never made a telephone call until four months earlier completed the last three miles of his journey in a helicopter.

At Behesht-e-Zahra itself the pressure of the crowds was indescribable. The sheer weight of bodies broke up and displaced the gravestones which were set in concrete in the ground. There was serious doubt whether the helicopter could put down without injuring or killing people; and then one of the marshals had the idea of taking off his belt and swinging it round his head, which both cleared the area round him and imitated the action of a helicopter's rotors. Soon all the marshals were doing the same thing over the full extent of the area which had been selected for the helicopter to land.

Behesht-e-Zahra is vast, and Khomeini had time to visit only one part of it: section 17, chosen because the seventeenth day of the Persian month of Shahrivar (8 September in the Western calendar) was Black Friday, the day in 1978 when the Shah's troops had killed hundreds of demonstrators in Jaleh Square and elsewhere in Tehran. As the returning Imam sat on a chair in section 17, surrounded by people who had each lost a member of their family in the campaign against the Shah, his quiet words were relayed by loudspeaker to the thousands who had crowded into the cemetery to hear him:

'I have suffered many difficulties and have witnessed a great deal of pain, and I do not know how to thank these noble people who have sacrificed everything for their revolution.'

He appealed to the army's generals to join the cause of the people, and warned the government of Dr Bakhtiar that he would stop their mouths and appoint a new government with the support of the people.

'We will cut off the hands of foreign agents,' he went on, to a roar of approval. A mistranslation of this, giving 'correspondents' instead of 'agents', was nervously passed from one journalist to another that day, until the mistake was rectified.

In his office in the centre of Tehran, meanwhile, Dr Bakhtiar himself, a forlorn but gallant figure, sat almost alone, a few guards outside his door but almost no civil servants left in the building to do his bidding; they had mostly gone to witness the Ayatollah's drive through the city.

'I am going to do my best to have good relations with him,' he told a resourceful Western journalist who had stopped by to ask how he was planning to deal with Khomeini.

Bakhtiar was an impressive man with a long and honourable record of opposition to the Shah, but his moment had passed. Although he still occupied the post of prime minister, power had long since ebbed from him – had never, indeed, belonged to him. Yet it had not entirely passed to Khomeini. The army, the sixth most powerful in the world in terms of numbers and equipment, was still in being; and although it had been badly depleted by desertions those who had remained loyal still looked like a force which could do a great deal of damage if it chose. President Carter had sent General Robert E. Huyser as his personal representative to show support for the Bakhtiar government, but Huyser had been warning the military not to consider carrying out a coup. As events showed, it would probably have been impossible anyway, but this was not the impression of many people at the time. Bloodshed on a large scale seemed increasingly likely.

At seven-thirty on the morning of Saturday 3 February, two days after the Ayatollah's return, our taxi (driven by a man named Mahmoudi, who will feature later in this personal history) nosed its way into a narrow street not far from the Majlis, or parliament. The shops in it were closed and shuttered. The external appearance of the houses was deceptively small and mean; behind the mud-coloured walls they were often grand and sometimes magnificent, with fountains playing in the walled gardens. The street was full of people, all heading in the same direction, and we had to slow down to their speed.

'Just close now, Mr John,' said Mahmoudi, and showed us where he would wait for us. The alley down which we had to go was too narrow for his car, and was blocked by a group of heavily-armed men, some of them Shi'ites from Lebanon and Iraq. We were still some way from our objective, but the chanting we could hear indicated the direction we should take. Occasionally the hurrying crowd would pick up the chant as they pushed each other along: '*Allahu Akbar, Khomeini rahbar!*' – 'God is great, Khomeini is our leader!'

There were three of us now: Bill Handford's sound-recordist, David Johnson, had joined us. Dave was a sailor, like Bill, but his physical opposite in every way. Where Bill was small and wiry, David was enormous, and he had such a savage scar down the side of his face that people always seemed to think twice about interfering with us. The two of them were known to their colleagues as Bill and Bulkhead.

Here in particular Dave's size and strength were great assets. The end of the alleyway was entirely packed with chanting, excited people, and the dozens of armed guards who were supposed to be keeping the approaches clear had long since given up, powerless against the sheer weight of numbers. For at the end of the alley was the Alawi Girls' school, which had been selected as the Ayatollah's headquarters; and the Ayatollah himself was to give his first audience there this morning. Slowly, a few inches at a time, we squeezed along the edge of the crowd, pushing our way along beside the wall. Dave was first, and we moved in his wake; but for someone who suffers, as I do, from claustrophobia and the dislike of crowds it was a very trying experience. As the masses of people swayed and shifted, we would find ourselves jammed hard against the wall, in constant danger of having the breath knocked out of us or even (I felt) getting our ribs stove in. There were times when I was afraid I might give way to my phobias and start yelling in panic, though in that narrow space and with all the noise of the chanting few people would have noticed.

At last, however, Dave's strength and our joint determination got us to a narrow gate and we were pulled in by the guards as though they were rescuing drowning men from the water. We found ourselves in the yard of the school. Before the turbulence of the immediate pre-revolution period this school had had three hundred pupils. Now we were shown into the assembly hall. On the walls were texts enjoining the girls to be quiet and good, together with maps of various parts of the world. A large group of journalists, gathered together from places all over those maps, were waiting for Khomeini's first news conference on Iranian soil.

It took a long time. Yazdi and Qotbzadeh, both looking nervous, translated Khomeini's answers into English and French respectively. Most of what he said was intended to weaken Dr Bakhtiar's grip on power. He also repeated his appeal to the generals:

> Certain talks have taken place and, should it become necessary, more will take place. We shall call on them to act in their own interest as well as those of the people, for the army is one with the people; it is the people's brother. The army must not use its machine-guns against the people. We do not want our soldiers to be under the thumb of foreigners. They should be independent. They are our sons, and we love them as such.

A Frenchwoman with a harsh voice asked if the Ayatollah's followers had weapons. In the pause while he formulated his answer in his mind the noise of the chanting outside filled the room: '*Allahu Akbar, Khomeini rahbar!*'

'When the moment comes,' he said slowly, 'we will get arms from the proper places. We will work together in the streets.'

And so it was to prove.

*   *   *

During the week that followed, Bill Handford, Dave Johnson and I were out of Tehran, finding out what was happening elsewhere in the country. It was a difficult decision to take, since no one knew when the moment of revolution might come, but it turned out to be the right decision. In Isfahan we found that the revolution had already started, and the Islamic Republic had established itself without bloodshed. In Tehran, however, the deadlock continued. Khomeini had named his government, as he had promised; the rival government of Shahpour Bakhtiar continued to crumble; and the strength of the armed forces was further and further eroded as more detachments of soldiers and airmen marched to the Alawi Girls' School to pledge their loyalty to the Ayatollah.

When Mahmoudi drove us back to Tehran on the evening of Friday 9 February we found the city in a state of wild confusion and excitement. Road blocks had been set up, cars were burning, and the revolutionaries had guns for the first time. During the day crowds had attacked the air base at Doshan Tapeh, outside Tehran, and most of the NCOs had gone over to them. After a fierce battle the base had been captured and large quantities of arms and ammunition seized. They were carried off to Tehran University, the nerve centre of the revolution. Khomeini's supporters already held the streets, and as we drove to the InterContinental Hotel we saw hundreds of people building barricades to protect themselves against the counterattack which everyone knew would come soon. The Imperial Guard had mostly remained loyal to the Bakhtiar government.

Saturday 10 February began badly. Joe Alex Morris, a correspondent for the *Los Angeles Times* who was a general favourite at the InterContinental, was out early in the streets. He had taken refuge in an upstairs room, close to a gun battle. He was just raising his head to look out of the window when he was hit in the forehead by a stray bullet. He died instantly.

The barricades were everywhere now. They were usually wretchedly inadequate affairs, made up of everything that came to hand: balks of timber, gates, rocks, cars which had been abandoned by their owners. The Chieftain tanks of the Imperial Guard would, I felt, ride over such things without noticing them. As we drove round the streets, filming and being stopped constantly by vigilantes, I tried to explain to the makers of the barricades how flimsy their constructions were. They just laughed. There was a wildness in the air, a feeling that nothing mattered. A millennial event was about to happen which would cancel out the past and usher in a new age. Drivers passing the barricades would offer their precious cars to make them stronger; shopkeepers would open their stores and hand out their stock of food to the revolutionaries, without being asked.

As the morning wore on, the tension grew. Flatbed trucks drove past at speed, carrying groups of young men and women who held on grimly or waved pieces of white cloth. The smoke from dozens of fires built

up over the city, as it had done on 5 November; but this time the
revolutionaries were setting fire to the barricades to give themselves
the illusion of greater safety. For once the alley leading to the
Alawi Girls' School was almost deserted. We found six or seven
youths guarding the entrance. They wore blue uniforms and their
faces were blackened as a form of camouflage. They had been on
duty there all night, they said; everyone else was off fighting.

But fighting where? It was proving frustratingly difficult to find where
the battles were going on. We could hear gunfire in the distance, and
we saw dozens of trucks and ambulances driving at speed through the
streets. Twice we hurried to a place where we had been told there was
fighting, only to find that it had ended half an hour before. All that
was visible was a pile of cartridge cases from a light machine gun
and traces of blood on the roadway. My greatest fear was that the
revolution had started in earnest and that we would not find anything
to film.

An ambulance went past us, its rear doors open to show a bare
stretcher inside drenched with blood. Whoever had been wounded had
already been taken to hospital, and the ambulance was looking for more
cases to bring in. I could hear automatic fire not far off, and a helicopter
gunship appeared a couple of miles away, hovering over a revolutionary
strongpoint somewhere in south Tehran and pouring fire into it before
banking steeply and moving off. A truck passed us, the body of a man
lying on a bloodstained sheet on the back of it, surrounded by red
tulips: the symbol of martyrdom. The signs of violent conflict were
all round us, but we were unable to track it down. Each decision we
took seemed to be the wrong one.

The curfew was extended. Anyone found in the streets between
four-thirty in the afternoon and five the following morning would,
a government announcement said, be shot on sight. There was panic
then, and Mahmoudi had to pull into the side of the road to avoid
the wild driving of people who had done enough sightseeing and were
desperate to get home. At the barricades some of the revolutionaries
had brought out portable television sets – somehow, a very Persian
thing to do – and a pro-Khomeini group had set up a television station
of their own. We found one group of people sitting on the ground beside
a white Paykan car, watching a small yellow television on which a
flickering black-and-white Khomeini was enjoining people not to obey
the curfew but to stay on the streets.

We looked carefully at our map, and listened to Mahmoudi's advice:
when the tanks came, they would take the route that led past the
InterContinental. It seemed the best place to be, as well as the most
convenient, and we settled down with the revolutionaries waiting in the
road outside. Three fires were kept burning all night long, partly to keep
the 150 diehards there warm, and partly to attract the attention of the

Imperial Guard; the revolutionaries took pride in offering themselves as a target. An hour or so later, just after midnight on what was to prove the culminating day of the revolution, Sunday 11 February, I grew bored with making light conversation with the would-be martyrs and sat on the pavement to jot down some notes by the fitful light of a burning tyre. Neither the grammar nor the descriptive power adds up to much, but they give a sense of the atmosphere as the long night drew on:

Barricades scarcely strong: 1 large old US car (Buick) dragged up, tipped on side. Other barricades even smaller and mostly composed of rubbish from nearby tip. Unlikely give us much protection. Smoke and sparks go up from fires in streets all round. Smoke hangs over dark street, stench of burning rubber. Each tyre lasts good hour, and no shortage. Biggest crowd round car with bullhorn inside: symbol of leadership. Owner tempted to use it from time to time to chant '*Allahu Akbar*' etc, but as night goes on, instinct fades. Ambulance sirens go, but nothing passes us. Some cars and m/cycles still on streets even now. Gunfire? Rare. Waiting. When will tanks come?

They came, as they always do, at dawn: twenty-six Chieftains by my count, some with rubber treads and some with metal ones which ground their way into the tarmac and left marks which were still visible when I went back seven years later. The noise of clanking, grating metal could be heard half a mile away, and the remnants of the 150 defendants who had lasted out the night fled precipitately, leaving behind them the Molotov cocktails they had spent much of the night filling. The lead tank, finding only an upturned Buick and some skips filled with rubble in its path, scarcely checked its speed at all. It struck the Buick's roof with a grinding sound and flipped it aside as though it were made of tinfoil. The Buick crumpled up and lay in the middle of the road, twitching every now and then as another Chieftain struck it in passing.

Now there was no shortage of good pictures. As Mahmoudi drove us through the streets, a look of intense concentration on his face and his round, greying, bullet head thrust forward, it seemed clear that we were going to see a fight to the finish today. Most of the barricades which were left had been reinforced properly with sandbags, and the men behind them had automatic weapons. Everywhere, people were being taught how to load and fire them. There was a constant rattle and crack of gunfire, though it was hard to tell what was for practice and what was aimed at the enemy. The revolution had its own cavalry now, too: motorcycles with armed and helmeted passengers on them, driving fast to the places where the fighting was beginning.

The men who drove them were known as the Motorcyclists of Allah. From them, at last, we found out where the main battle was going on: at the Eshratabad Barracks.

On our way, I saw a sight which we could not pass without stopping to film. Mahmoudi was driving fast down the main Shah Reza Avenue. Ahead of us was one of Tehran's ugly overpasses, which carried the road over the intersection with Hafez Avenue. There was smoke everywhere, and the sound of explosions, but I could see a crowd of two or three hundred outside a police station close to the overpass. It was here, during my first trip to Iran the previous August, that two of my colleagues and I had been held after we had been arrested by a senior officer of the SAVAK. We had had an unpleasant time in this place, threatened with shooting and kept for hours without food, water, or the chance to relieve ourselves, even though one of my colleagues was ill with a stomach complaint. The British Embassy, which I had managed at some risk to telephone, had done nothing to get us out; in my experience British embassies rarely do.

Now the place was under siege, and as we ran along the overpass to get a better camera angle the crowd broke in through the main entrance and ran through the offices, looting and smashing and attacking the detectives and SAVAK men who were unfortunate enough to be inside. We could see the crowd clearly through the windows, as they tipped out the contents of the drawers and showered the street below with the filing cards of suspects. I caught up a handful as mementos; one of them carried nothing more than the name and address of a suspect and the words 'Attended a Communist meeting'.

Unpleasant things were going on inside the police station now and, as we filmed, uniforms, some of them wet with blood, were thrown out of the windows and landed ludicrously on the branches of a tree outside, like washing hung out to dry. I urged Bill to finish filming; I had no desire to see anything else here. As we made our way on foot along the overpass a helicopter gunship came swooping low over the nearby buildings, attracting occasional riflefire from the ground. We were dangerously vulnerable: there was no cover of any kind, and we were the only people on the overpass. If you are under a helicopter, it seems to have omniscience and perfect vision. I felt naked and trapped. I was nervous enough to move away from the other two, across the road, in order to present a less compact target. It was an impulse I felt ashamed of, especially when the helicopter veered away, the faces of its crew clearly visible, and headed off for more promising targets.

Mahmoudi dropped us at the end of a long street which led to the Eshratabad Barracks. He would probably have driven us further; gunfire did not seem to scare him particularly. But people on the street corner were lying on the ground and making urgent signs to us to get out of the line of fire, and it seemed safer for him to park while we went forward on foot.

'Waiting here, Mr John,' said Mahmoudi, and I knew he would. We set off down the street towards the fighting.

It was the most difficult thing we had to do the whole day. A great many stray bullets were coming down the street in our direction. Some splattered against the walls or sang off the brickwork, leaving sudden white marks on the dull grey brick. They were mostly about two feet above our heads, though some cracked nastily in the air closer than that. Absurdly, the words of an Irish folk song floated into my mind:

> *The pulse of an Irishman ever beats quicker*
> *When war is the story or love is the theme.*

As the holder of an Irish passport, which I use in preference to my British one in difficult or unpleasant places, I found this was true enough: my pulse was indeed beating extremely quickly. The couplet which follows was unfortunately less true as I found myself humming it under my breath:

> *And place him where bullets fly thicker and thicker,*
> *You'll find him all cowardice scorning.*

The other two earned my admiration: Bill, striding forward in his tweed jacket as though he was on his way to make a documentary about country sports, and Dave, whose size made him a greater target than any of us, keeping up with Bill and carrying the heavy recorder which was linked to Bill's camera by a thick umbilical cable. Despite his fierce appearance I knew that Dave was anything but fierce; he disliked this kind of thing intensely, and usually managed to avoid it. That only made my admiration for him all the greater. For someone not normally particularly brave to behave so well under those circumstances was impressive, and he managed to stay hooked up to Bill's camera during the entire time.

We stopped a couple of times to decide what we should do, but by now the excitement of the event had taken over. We wanted to know what was going on at the end of the road even though the bullets were starting to fly thicker and thicker. When we got there the layout of the battle became clear immediately: it was a T-junction, and the insurgents were along the right-hand bar of the T. They were keeping up a heavy fire against the barracks, which were close to the point where the left-hand bar joined the main stem of the T. The soldiers inside were returning the fire with interest, and it was their wilder shots which had been coming down the stem of the T towards us.

We arrived in time to see the end of the battle. The attackers were still being pinned down and had taken some heavy losses. A number of injured men were being carried off past us, under fire. But soon after Bill stationed himself out in the open, filming, with Dave and I standing rather more nervously beside him, the fire of the defenders began to grow weaker and more intermittent. The revolutionaries, seeing this, charged across the open space and broke through the main gate. Soon it was all over. The soldiers were surrendering in twos and threes, and the attackers were driving trucks into the perimeter wall of the barracks in order to create new ways in. Soon hundreds of men were streaming out, laden with rifles, handguns and ammunition.

'This'll win us an award,' Dave said when we'd finally finished filming and were thinking about going back to find Mahmoudi. I was too new to television to know what really constituted good pictures, but Bill wasn't satisfied.

'You couldn't see it all clearly enough,' he grumbled.

He was, I felt, being too rigorous, but it didn't matter anyway; the pictures which he and one of his colleagues had shot on the day of the Ayatollah's return later won the BBC the most prestigious international news prize of the year at the Monte Carlo festival.

Vae victis. That evening a line of men with scarves tied over their eyes was led into the complex of houses and storehouses around the Alawi Girls' School. They were wearing civilian clothes, but they were all senior military men. They had been captured in the course of a day which had seen their authority, the forces they commanded, and the government they served all smashed beyond hope of recovery. They entered the room like blind men, their arms resting on the shoulders of their guards. A group of us, all foreign journalists, had been allowed in too. The scale of the victory was still sinking in. The storerooms behind the school yard were filled with more weapons and stocks of ammunition, all of it captured, than I had ever seen in my life.

We had been invited here so that we could question some of the prisoners. The most important of them was General Mehdi Rahimi, the martial law commander for Tehran. When we were seated around a large table he and his deputy, General Mohammed Ali Noruzi, were brought in and their blindfolds removed. In the intense heat of the room, with the occasional noise of gunfire outside as the delighted revolutionaries let off their weapons in celebration of their victory, both of them seemed completely bemused. It still seemed unlikely that civilians who, the previous night, didn't know how to build a decent barricade or fire a gun, could possibly have defeated men like these two, who had possessed the power of life and death over a capital city until that day.

Rahimi was a heavy-featured man with silver hair and sharp, intelligent eyes. He was dressed in a bush shirt and trousers, and there was a cut on his right cheek. He bore his sudden change of fortune with remarkable composure, and behaved with quiet dignity.

> My name is Mehdi Rahimi. I am the military governor of Tehran. I was arrested this morning as I was walking in the street to my office. Someone captured me and brought me here.

His quiet Farsi was translated into English by the ubiquitous Ibrahim Yazdi. We were invited to put our questions. Some people, particularly the Americans among us, shouted them out, concerned only with trying to get precise answers to questions that had been unclear all day. It seemed to some of us, though, that there was more here than a matter of simple information. We were looking at a man who would be dead very shortly. Even if his orders had brought death to hundreds of people over the previous few days, he deserved the decency of being able to talk about himself and his situation. I interrupted the flow of questions about how many men he commanded and when he had last seen Bakhtiar with one of my own: how had the revolutionaries behaved towards him?

> In the beginning we were treated very harshly. We were insulted, and people threw stones at us. But I have to say that we also received words of comfort, and orders were given that we should not be hurt.

His deputy, General Noruzi, was smaller and gentler-looking, and less uncompromising. Rahimi had plainly decided, however, that he would not dishonour himself in his own eyes. He spoke of the orders he had given during the previous few days.

'All nations need fatherly punishment from time to time, even if it has to be taken to the point of killing people ... There was disorder, and it was necessary to send in forces to restore order.'

'Whom do you recognise as your overall commander now?'

'My commander-in-chief is His Imperial Majesty, the Shah.'

'Do you believe your life is in danger from the decision of the court which, we understand, will try you?'

General Rahimi smiled slightly, looked up, and lifted his hands a little, as though all these questions were an irrelevance.

'I came into this world once, and once I will leave it.'

By the next morning, Monday 12 February, the last pockets of resistance were dealt with. A total of 654 people, the new government announced, had died in the fighting; 2,804 had been injured. The man whom, after General Rahimi, the revolutionaries most wanted to capture managed to give them the slip: Dr Shahpour Bakhtiar, having seen his brief power evaporate around him, was smuggled away to the territory of his tribal kinsmen, the Bakhtiaris, and later surfaced in Paris; one day the Iranian regime would send its men to murder him there.

It says a great deal for the traditional forms of politics in Iran, which were every bit as civilised as those of Western Europe, that the man who gave orders that Bakhtiar should be protected and helped to escape was Dr Mehdi Bazargan, whom Ayatollah Khomeini had named as prime minister in the new, revolutionary government. Both Bazargan and Bakhtiar were politicians of an older, pre-revolutionary stamp, and they had known each other well in the days when they had found themselves isolated by the Shah's one-man rule. Now that Bakhtiar's life was in danger, his successor took the very considerable personal risk of saving him. Word of this soon got out, and the fiercer, unforgiving spirits in the new regime found his action in helping Bakhtiar escape both incomprehensible and treacherous. Bazargan was not to last long as prime minister.

That morning Bill Handford, David Johnson and I drove out early to the Niavaran Palace, the Shah's residence in the foothills of the Albourz. We watched as the last remnants of the Imperial Guard, the Shah's 'Immortals', drawn from the best recruits in the army and commanded by officers from the best families in Iran, piled up their uniforms on the back of a flatbed truck and stood around, chilly and embarrassed, in their underwear. All of them had sworn a personal oath to defend the Shah with the last blood in their bodies, yet no single drop of blood had been shed in the capture of the palace. The fact was, the Immortals (whose grand nickname derived from that of a brigade, ten thousand strong, in Achaemenian times; whenever a man was lost, another would step forward to take his place, ensuring that the regiment never died) had long received such pleasant postings in Tehran and elsewhere that their social and ceremonial functions had undermined their military abilities.

Not everyone had given up so easily, though. On Wednesday 14 February, after being held for three days and subjected to a number of futile interrogations, Generals Noruzi and Rahimi and two others were found guilty of 'causing corruption on earth' and 'fighting against Allah': crimes that had not existed until that day. They were taken up to the roof of the Alawi school and shot. General Rahimi faced his firing squad with the shout *'Javid Shah!'* – 'Long live the Shah'.

By comparison with some of the others, Rahimi and Noruzi were lucky; at this stage of the revolution their captors were still anxious to show that they were not like the SAVAK, who tortured their prisoners. With the capture of General Nassiri, the SAVAK's commanding officer, however, this changed. Nassiri was hanged until he was almost dead, then cut down and beaten savagely. Both his legs were broken, and his face was badly mutilated. Then he was paraded on television. When questions were put to him, he could answer only with sign language.

Nevertheless when a soldier referred to 'that Shah', Nassiri summoned up his last reserves of strength to rebuke him and tell him to call the Shah by his proper title, His Imperial Majesty. Nassiri was a cruel man, and he had directed the SAVAK during one of its worst and most repressive phases; but he was no coward. Some of these men may have reflected that if the Shah had kept his nerve as they had kept theirs, the revolution might not have happened.

3

Breaking Through

Tira Shubart

Except when on a journey, do not ride an ambling horse, because while riding an ambling horse a man holds himself in a bad posture. In the town, therefore, and in your own precincts, ride a spirited and high-stepping horse, so that because of the horse's mettle you are prevented from being careless of your own person.

A Mirror For Princes

Seven years passed after the revolution before John was able to return to Iran. The Islamic Republic had developed an intense dislike of the BBC, and anyway preferred to create its new–old society out of the sight of Western journalists. John had communicated his interest in Iran to me, but as a woman as well as a journalist I was likely to find it even more difficult to go there. Nevertheless, after a great deal of effort, we were both finally given visas.

By this time, travelling to Iran had become a little easier than in the early days of the revolution. Iran Air, with its Islamic dress code and ferocious service, was no longer the only way to go. Now several far more comfortable Western carriers flew the route, and senior Iranian officials often travelled first-class with them, in preference to their own national airline. There were plenty of foreign businessmen and diplomats on the flights, but rarely any journalists.

As for Iranians, it had become much easier for them to obtain passports, and far more of them were travelling abroad. Many who had gone to live in the West after the revolution had made their peace with the new regime, and preferred to overlook the inevitable restrictions in order to have the pleasure of living at home again. Only men under thirty-five had to be careful about returning, since while the Iran–Iraq war was still on they could be forced to join the army.

The salesman in the London office of Iran Air handed me my ticket and a tourist map of Tehran with a melancholy smile. 'It has all sorts of useful telephone numbers on the back,' he murmured. 'Like the central morgue.'

Iran Air's customer relations policy was not reassuring.

It was August, and John and I were going to take a holiday in Iran. We had received the first tourist visas which the Islamic Republic had ever issued to British citizens, and they were for an unprecedentedly long period: a month. Up to then journalists had been invited in only for short, unsatisfactory, highly supervised trips to cover the war at moments when Iran had recovered some territory or made a strategic foray into Iraq. Women journalists were not allowed on these trips at all.

The only other Westerners who could go to Iran were those with something to sell; especially weapons. The Islamic Republic was not interested in dollars, marks or pounds if they came from the pockets of tourists. Tourism meant an invasion, no matter how slight, of Western culture, which threatened to dilute the revolutionary fervour. Some Westerners, travelling in convoy on overland trips across Asia, were given transit visas of seven days to enable them to drive across Iran from the Turkish border to Pakistan or vice versa; but they were not allowed to visit Tehran. Altogether, including visitors, the foreign wives of Iranians and a very small number of people who had been permitted to stay on after the revolution, there were only around three hundred Western Europeans in the country at any given time. There were also about two hundred Americans. They were all the wives or widows of Persians, and all had dual Iranian and American nationality.

It took five months to persuade the Iranian Embassy to accept my visa application, and when an official telephoned and asked me to come to the Embassy and fill out a visa form, I felt my tenacity had been rewarded. Later I realised that it had probably taken so long because of Iran's haphazard bureaucracy: notes not taken, letters unfiled and telexes transmitted weeks late to Tehran.

I felt pretty good, all the same, and thought I should dress up properly for my trip to the Embassy, to show them I knew how to behave. I turned for advice to the back of the tourist map:

'HOW TO DRESS: According to Islamic rules, travellers are kindly requested to wear decent clothing and ladies should observe the Islamic outfit – large scarf and loose long dress with trousers or long thick socks – during their trip to Iran.'

I wasn't going to Iran yet, but I was going to Iranian territory. I arrived at the Iranian Embassy decent, Islamically correct, and very hot. But it seemed a small price to pay to enter into a society that had once again become as mysterious and remote to outsiders as it had seemed to the travellers of Elizabeth I's times.

I had learned already that the Embassy of the Islamic Republic of Iran had refined bureaucratic obstruction to an art form. After I had stumbled into the consulate wearing my thick socks, my large scarf and my long loose dress, hot even in the mild English summer, I found that the visa form expected me to list every country I had ever visited, the purpose of my visit to it, and when it had taken place. I also had to provide an almost genealogical degree of information on my family, and enough detail about the money I was taking to satisfy a tax inspector. When I eventually finished filling out the form and took it to the fierce-looking woman presiding at a large desk, she looked dismissively at what I had done and pointed to the part where it said that three identical applications were required: photocopies were not acceptable. It took me another half-hour. Then I handed everything in, including the three photographs which showed me peering out from an oversized black headscarf, and £15 for the visa fee and finally walked out of Iranian territory into the weak London sunshine. Out of prudence and good manners, I waited until I had cleared the field of vision of the security camera above the embassy entrance; then I unknotted my scarf and took off the long loose black raincoat I had worn over my shirt and trousers. I could feel the fresh air again. That, I was to find, was a rare pleasure in Iran.

At Heathrow Airport a couple of Sundays later, in August 1986, I joined the queue to check in for Iran Air flight 710 to Tehran. Iran began here. Around me, Iranians jostled for position with their overloaded baggage trolleys. Under conditions of stress the charming side of the Persian tends to come to the fore; anyone who needs help, especially an obvious foreigner, can expect any number of small acts of kindness and useful pieces of advice.

The flight was supposed to take off in less than an hour, but the check-in procedure had not even started. The mountains of luggage indicated that we were in for a long wait. In addition to an average of three suitcases per person there were uncountable numbers of boxes bound with string and masking tape, containing every conceivable electrical and electronic device. The distinctive green and gold of Harrods shopping bags was everywhere.

Persians have the ability to turn most events into social occasions, and in the check-in queue we were soon telling the people around us why we were travelling to Iran, and listening to their reasons for visiting England. With some it was obvious: several of them were young men who had been wounded in the war with Iraq and had been in London for medical treatment. They were bearded, their shirts were buttoned at the neck but they were not wearing ties. They were gaunt and sallow, and they looked to me as though they had been in every television report about revolutionary Iran that I had ever seen.

There were plenty of older men in carefully pressed suits, slightly out of fashion, who were very definitely wearing ties; some of these men were returning for the first time since the revolution. There were several elderly women, some of them wearing *chadors*, who had been visiting their sons and daughters who were studying, or maybe exiled, in Britain. The women were usually accompanied by young men who pushed their luggage trolleys to the counter, helped them with the formalities, escorted them to passport control and then said goodbye. I felt they exuded a kind of relief at the idea that they weren't catching the plane as well. There were various younger women too, trying to control their children's games of hide-and-seek among the luggage trolleys.

Several people asked me politely if I was sure I was in the right queue. They found it hard to believe that a woman who didn't look like the wife of an Iranian should be making the journey. One or two of the women said in their self-deprecating Persian way that I must be very brave to want to go to Tehran, but a smartly-dressed Iranian woman of about my age left her own queue and came over to reassure me.

'I know there are a lot of problems, and there will be all sorts of things you won't like, but I promise you, you will have a good time.'

She smiled and wandered back to her place in the other queue. I was to find that everything she said was true.

We boarded our Iran Air flight twenty minutes after it had been scheduled to leave. Two stewardesses greeted us gloomily at the door, the pallor of their unmade-up faces accentuated by the black hoods they wore over their heads and shoulders. They looked, I thought, like medieval nuns from a particularly strict convent. Next to them stood a bearded, tieless man in plain clothes: security. He glared at each of us in turn, and some of the women passengers reached for the scarves that were draped on their shoulders and hurriedly tied them over their heads as if a chilly breeze had suddenly begun to blow. Other women, in the expensive clothes that were obviously their usual dress in London, brazened it out a bit longer; the time for *hejab* would come soon enough.

Below us was the English Channel; we had left British airspace. I was never so aware of leaving familiar things behind. Usually I had visited countries which I knew, or which at least were places that I had clear expectations about; Iran was *terra incognita*. A few minutes later there was an announcement:

'Ladies and gentlemen, in honour of the Islamic Revolution in Iran, ladies should now respect the Islamic dress and headscarf.'

The ways of the West had finally to be abandoned; the Islamic Republic of Iran started here. I looked around and saw that I was one of the last to make the necessary adjustments. Some had wrapped themselves in *chadors*: the figure-encompassing cloak of thin black cotton which covers the head and body down to the ankles, and has to be held together at the neck with one hand or if necessary with the teeth. Other women wore the less traditional *roupush*, a baggy, loose raincoat-like covering. Their headscarves were mostly black, dark brown or grey:

dull, gloomy things which deadened their faces immediately. Some women (usually the better-dressed ones) were prepared to take a mild risk or two. One wore a black headscarf with white flowers on a bright blue background, another had a scarf which was mostly dark blue but had some pink design on it. I buttoned up my *roupush* and tied my headscarf, pulling it further down on my head so that no hair would show, then glanced at the woman opposite me. She gave me a reassuring smile and rolled her eyes upwards in humorous resignation.

By now people were wandering up and down the aisles, the women kissing their friends, the men shaking hands with each other and exchanging notes about their trip to Europe. A middle-aged man with a shock of prematurely (but only just) white hair stretched out his arm as though he didn't realise his new gold-and-diamond Rolex was showing. An attractive older woman, after glancing up the aisle to make sure none of the Iran Air staff were watching, pulled a pearl necklace from underneath her dress to show off to her friend. In the open spaces by the galleys and the emergency exits, half a dozen men were praying. Two were disabled ex-soldiers; one was in a wheelchair and the other, who had lost a leg, sat on the floor, his crutches beside him. A young bearded mullah, wearing a black turban that denoted he was a *sayyeed* – a descendant of the Prophet – led the prayers. I could hear the Arabic words faintly: '*Allahu Akbar … Bismillahir rahmania rahim … Alhamdulillahi rabbil-alamin…*' After the prayers the mullah turned sharply, imperiously away, leaving the others to help up the man on crutches.

The front of the aeroplane was curtained off from those of us with economy seats. That didn't stop the children from darting behind the curtains and continuing their games in the first-class area, though they were usually ushered out quickly. A number of the older men occasionally peered behind the curtain to see who was there. The woman in the aisle seat across from mine leaned over to me.

'We call it mullah class,' she said. 'The government keeps those seats for them.'

It was my first clear sighting of the revolution's new and privileged élite.

The flight took well over five hours, but at last the pilot announced in Persian and in English that we should prepare for landing. Below us the lights of Tehran were clearly visible, even though the city had already been bombed a number of times. We made a perfect touchdown at 4.05 a.m. My reassuring neighbour leaned over again.

'These pilots are trained to a high standard,' she informed me. It was the first pro-Iranian thing she had said. Then she added, 'They were all trained in London before the revolution.'

We disembarked under the baleful gaze of the bearded security man. Two elderly buses had pulled up beside us. A number of passengers raced to the first one and jumped on. Walking slowly and awkwardly in my unaccustomed clothes, I could only manage to get on to the second bus. Directly we reached the terminal building I began to realise how important it was to get there fast. I was right at the back of a long, slow-moving queue of about a hundred people, having been overtaken by everyone except the most seriously crippled ex-soldiers and the oldest of the women in *chadors* with their impossible amounts of hand-luggage. I looked at my watch: 4.45 a.m.

By now the women who had been talkative and friendly on the plane were noticeably quieter. I looked up and caught my first glimpse of a group of Revolutionary Guards. They were standing on the staircase above the arrivals hall looking down at us searchingly, a handful of unshaven and bleary-eyed men and a couple of women in *hejab*. It was hard to see what they were looking for: an individual suspect, perhaps, or any sign that someone was breaking the Islamic dress rules. Either way, they exuded an air of disapproval: by the mere fact of having travelled to the West, the Iranians from my flight had made themselves suspect. Only those who were wearing *chadors* seemed at ease; all the other women had tucked their hair firmly under their headscarves. A marked silence descended on us as we shuffled forward every three or four minutes, our passports in our hands. When I finally reached the head of the queue and handed my passport to the Revolutionary Guard in the little glass box, he had to look at me and my passport photo several times; a headscarf alters your whole appearance.

IN THE NAME OF GOD, FOR THE ATTENTION OF DEAR IN-COMING PASSENGERS, WELCOME TO OUR COUNTRY IRAN. That was cheery enough, I thought as I reached the next control point. Someone handed me a form in Persian, then stamped it with relish and determination. I stopped at the next desk, behind my fellow passengers, but a woman placed her hand on my arm and told me the desk was for Iranians only. I had time, therefore, to read the rest of the welcoming sign; only now it wasn't so welcoming.

DEAR PASSENGERS, IN CASE YOU HAVE FOREIGN EXCHANGE (F.E.) PLEASE GET F.E. DECLARATION FORMS, AS YOU WILL NOT BE PERMITTED TO TAKE OUT ANY F.E. WITHOUT THIS FORM YOU ARE REQUESTED TO TAKE GOOD CARE OF IT. OTHERWISE YOU WILL FACE DIFFICULTIES FOR WHICH THE CUSTOMS OFFICIALS ARE NOT HELD RESPONSIBLE.

All official notices at airports contain a certain hint of menace: the threat of 'difficulties' is, after all, the main sanction any bureaucracy can wield. But here in Iran you knew they meant it.

At the next desk a couple of women were thumbing with the speed of bank clerks through the wads of pounds and dollars and francs which everyone was thrusting towards them. One man was singled out for no apparent reason and searched with brutal thoroughness. Perhaps he looked like a smuggler who was concealing valuable hard currency; perhaps the security guards simply pulled someone out at random from time to time to remind us all of the 'difficulties' that we might encounter if we ignored the advice on the posters. The man didn't complain; if he had, something worse might have happened to him. Much better to regard all this as a form of physical airport tax, levied on the passengers in part-payment for whatever pleasure they had gained from visiting Europe. When my turn came, the woman behind the desk let me off lightly: she flicked through the money I handed her and wrote down the amount I had declared without properly checking it.

By now it was still only five-thirty. I thought we had made our way through the system with remarkable speed; the stories about waiting for three or four hours seemed to have been greatly exaggerated. I rode the escalator up to the baggage hall, and found myself in a scene of utter desolation. Luggage in huge quantities had been piled up around the slowly moving carousels, and three great queues, each of a hundred or so people, were waiting for the customs search which was being carried out in minute detail. There were only three customs officials on duty. The London flight had apparently arrived within a few minutes of one from Turkey, which had been just as crowded as ours. There was a remarkable silence in the great hall, but it was the silence of resignation. And yet I soon realised that very quietly, in groups of twos and threes, people were being sociable again. Here in the customs hall there was no point in pushing to get ahead in the queue. Since there were only three people to search our luggage, they would do it more quickly if they were left in relative calm rather than being besieged. The collective Persian will was at work.

At last I spotted our luggage on the ancient carousel. The few luggage trolleys had vanished, so I lugged the cases along the floor and joined the queue. It seemed to take about fifteen minutes for each passenger to be searched; that represented too many hours for me to want to work out. But the friendliness of our fellow passengers was an important compensation. Particularly that of the women: with the eyes of the Revolutionary Guards on them, the men were more reluctant to speak unless their wives had started the conversation. I embarrassed three or four men without meaning to, by introducing myself and holding out my hand, Western-fashion. It is deeply unIslamic for a man to touch a woman in public. In each case, though, good manners outweighed their discomfort, and they shook my hand. It was only later that I realised the full extent of their courtesy.

I started to enjoy this business of sitting on my luggage and talking to the people round me. I also realised now that there were other Westerners in the queue. An Englishwoman in her early thirties, whom I had earlier mistaken for an Iranian because she had spoken to her children in Persian, told me in a strong Manchester accent that she and her Iranian husband had lived in north Tehran since before the revolution. Her Persian was fluent, and when her husband lost his job she had gone out to work and made enough money to keep them both. They had, she said, decided to leave Iran the previous year, because of the Iraqi bombing; but now the pull of the place was too strong, and they were back. She had prepared herself carefully, though. She opened one of her suitcases to show me. It was entirely filled with Tampax and toiletries.

Another Englishwoman, hearing us talking, came over. She had never liked living in Iran, and the sight of so many people waiting to have their bags searched was almost too much for her.

'I'd forgotten how bad it is here,' she said, the lines of her face deepening as she spoke. 'Once I've got through all this, and seen everybody, I'm getting out for good.'

'What about your husband?' I asked.

She skipped a beat and raised her eyebrows. 'That's his problem,' she said.

She had met him at university. Their backgrounds were entirely different; her family had little money and he was extremely wealthy. At first Iran had seemed romantic and exotic to her, but things had changed in the country, and presumably in her marriage as well. Only the most adaptable Westerners, like the woman with the case full of Tampax, would be likely to make a success of living in Iran now.

A third Englishwoman, tall, pretty and vague, wandered across to us. She had lost one of her suitcases, but was philosophical about it. Her calmness seemed more remarkable when I discovered that this was her first trip to Iran; she had married an Iranian doctor a few weeks earlier in Britain. He was, she said, waiting for her in the arrivals hall. The only worries she seemed to have were about her pets, two dogs and a cat, which had arrived on a Lufthansa flight the previous day. She hoped that they had been properly looked after. I admired her very English concern; as long as the animals were all right, the lost luggage and the long queues didn't matter.

(A few years later, when I had travelled a great deal more in Iran, I told a Persian friend of mine in Tehran about meeting the three Englishwomen at the airport: especially the one with the two dogs and the cat. She laughed.

'That sounds very much like Liz, the woman who married my cousin,' she said, and picked up the telephone to speak to her. It was.

The next day we drove to a lovely house high in the foothills of north Tehran. Liz greeted me in the same friendly, vaguely distracted manner that I remembered from the airport. She had made the transition to life in Iran happily and was living in this pleasant place with two small children, her husband and, of course, her pets. By now only one dog was still alive and the cat was geriatric, but she had acquired a variety of other animals including a goat which had been brought to the house to be slaughtered for one of the Islamic feast-days; characteristically, she had turned it into a member of the household and would sometimes put it on a lead and take it for walks.)

Two hours after I had first settled down to talk to Liz and the others in the customs hall, I reached the head of the queue and lifted my bags on to the trestle-table where a female customs official was waiting to search them. The light of enthusiasm shone in her eyes, a hard and vindictive enthusiasm which drove her to open everything regardless of whether it was worth inspecting. Each book I had brought with me was examined with care, to see if it might contain some passage offensive to the faith or critical of the Islamic Republic, every article of clothing was pulled out and held up, every item of toiletry was opened and sniffed. The salami I had brought as a gift, two and a half feet long of pungent Italian sausage, provoked a good deal of suspicion: it was unopenable, powerful-smelling, and of no obvious political or religious use. Baffled, the searcher put it on one side for later examination.

My music tapes caused a more specific problem. Ever since Ayatollah Khomeini's speeches were smuggled into the Shah's Iran in cassette form, tapes had been a source of suspicion to customs officials. I offered her my Sony Walkman headphones so she could listen to The Grateful Dead. Instead, she swept the entire pile of cassettes aside with distaste. It took her twenty minutes to check everything, but at the end I was free. Nothing bad had been found, and all I had to do was repack my belongings and move on to the sixth and last checkpoint.

That was a mere formality: another passport inspection, very cursory, and a glance at the piece of paper the customs woman had given me. It was seven forty-five. We pushed our way out into the noisy arrivals hall, and came face to face with a vast crowd of relatives and friends. The noise, the fatigue, and the sense of having had my possessions rifled combined to make me sick of the entire experience. I fought my way through the main doors and let my cases slip to the ground. The air was warm and fresh, like the waters of a summer lake, and the topmost peaks on the mountains above were touched with the first rays of the sun. A warm, dry savour hit me: the smell of dust and animals and open plains. Opposite, in the growing light, a couple of strident signs had been erected to uplift the spirits of returning Iranians and raise the political consciousness of new arrivals. WE ARE WITH THE INNOCENTS OF THE WORLD, said one. The other read, VICTORY IS OURS. At that moment, I shared both sentiments.

4

Gridlock

Tira Shubart

If you wish to buy a house, buy one in a street where prosperous people reside and not on the outskirts. Do not buy one which lies under the city wall, or one which is cheap because it is in a state of dilapidation. Also look to your neighbour. There are four things which are great misfortunes: a bad neighbour, a large family, a quarrelsome wife and poverty.

A Mirror For Princes

At the front of *Tehran Today*, a street guide to the city based on the London A–Z, there is a helpful map labelled 'Tehran Urban and Suburban Railway Underground'. It shows an extensive Metro system with two lines; one goes from the northern suburbs through the centre to the poorer southern suburbs, ending at Ayatollah Khomeini's shrine; the other crosses from east to west, and reaches out to the rapidly growing suburb of Karaj more than ten miles away. Forty Metro stations are marked out within the area of Greater Tehran. In much smaller letters at the bottom of the map, the phrase '(under construction)' appears.

Each year that passed was supposed to see the Metro's completion. The endless delays gave it something of a mystical significance: rather as the French and British soldiers of the First World War believed that peace would come only when the leaning statue of the Virgin in the bomb-damaged town of Albert fell, many Tehranis came to believe that when the Metro was completed the regime would collapse. That provided an explanation of the long delays in finishing the work; but then every Iranian seems to have an implicit belief in the existence of secret explanations which confound everyday common-sense ones. The Metro system was planned by the Shah as part of his grand design for Iran to overtake France economically and militarily by 1993. Rejecting the Shah, Iran had instead found itself governed by those who wanted to live according to the ordinances of the seventh century. And so for years the various sites lay abandoned, open to the weather. It was only in October

1986, with little ceremony, that the work on the Metro began in earnest.

The purpose of the enterprise was to provide Iran's sluggish economy with an injection of public money, and relieve the traffic congestion in Tehran, but there was considerable opposition to it within the governmental structure itself. In the summer of 1987 the most powerful man after Ayatollah Khomeini, Ali Akbar Hashemi Rafsanjani, came to inspect the work and to give it his backing. Speaking without notes, Rafsanjani, a witty, quick-thinking man, said he knew there had been a good deal of criticism of the idea that so much money should be spent on the Metro at a time when every *rial* was needed for the war with Iraq. 'But,' he said, looking round at the serious-minded officials with him and grinning suddenly, 'just think how useful it will be as an air-raid shelter.'

Providing shelter from Iraqi Scud missiles during the so-called 'War of the Cities' was for years the only practical use the Metro served. Yet it was badly needed. In a city which is just as sprawling and just as dependent on its highway system as Los Angeles, cars and taxis were the only effective way of getting around. There was a dilapidated bus network, which during the 1980s was forced by sheer pressure of numbers to give up its Islamic segregation of male and female passengers; women, of course, were expected to sit at the back. After that, people could sit or stand wherever there was room. But the service was too irregular and expensive (in ten years the fares went up five-fold) to be either popular or effective.

It was July 1990, and I was back in Iran for my fourth visit. A television crew and I were working for an American news organisation. Waiting for me in the crowd of relatives and friends who pressed around the exit from the customs hall was a stocky, smiling figure with iron-grey hair: Mahmoudi, the driver that John and I had hired in 1986 when we had been here as tourists. We had found him at the Laleh Hotel, and as we sat side by side on the uneven back seat of his beaten-up white Paykan John said to me that he looked remarkably like the driver who had worked with him during the revolution.

'Did you ever,' John asked cautiously, 'work for the foreign television companies at the time of the *Enghelab*?'

'Yes, sir. Working for ABC, CBC, BBC. Name of Mahmoudi, sir.'

John dug me in the ribs in triumph.

'Name of John, Mahmoudi. You drove us to the Alawi Girls' School, and to the Eshratabad Barracks on the day of the fighting. Remember me?'

'Yes, Mr John.'

He said it quietly and without surprise, as though he had made the connection long before and had just been waiting politely for John to catch up. 'Now working for you again, Mr John.'

He put out his hand at a particularly dangerous point as we drove off, and shook hands in a dignified, ceremonious manner. It was a great moment.

Mahmoudi drove us everywhere during our month-long visit as tourists, and would be our driver on each of our trips together and separately from now on, sharing our travels and getting us out of trouble. Once, outside the main entrance to the Grand Bazaar in Tehran, I managed to anger a man who was collecting money for the war effort against Iraq. How I did it, I had no idea; but soon an angry group had gathered round John and me, shouting and getting bigger and more hostile all the time. It was the kind of moment when most drivers drift off and sit in their cars until everything is over. Mahmoudi, however, moved in quietly and calmly, not pushing anyone or shouting, just explaining things rationally and pleasantly to the man who was screaming the loudest. Gradually the man stopped shouting, and the crowd thinned out. We went back in silence to the white Paykan with Mahmoudi, and as we climbed in John started to thank him. Mahmoudi would not let him finish.

'No problem, Mr John,' he said.

Over the years he had made a studied effort to improve his English, just as I had tried to keep pace with him in Farsi. But communication had never been a problem: Mahmoudi had a way of guessing what we meant even when he could not understand the words. He was almost painfully generous, in the manner of so many Iranians. And if he said he would pick us up at four in the morning he would invariably be there at three-thirty, polishing his almost unpolishable Paykan with a piece of rag, as carefully as if it were a Mercedes.

He had spotted me some way back, as I came out into the arrivals hall in a little group of arriving passengers. He pushed forward, hands outstretched to take my cases. If we had been anywhere else in the world I would have thrown my arms around him, but here I had to be content with smiling at him. We walked through the chaos of the airport out into the cool air. There was the first hint of dawn in the sky, but the stars and a crescent moon were still bright. Taxi-drivers called out to us, offering their services, but we took no notice. Even from a distance I could recognise Mahmoudi's white car. It never seemed to look any worse, or any better: it was just another pre-revolutionary Paykan, and the only surprising thing was that he managed to keep it so roadworthy.

I looked out at the city as eagerly as I always did when I arrived back, forgetting my tiredness in the enthusiasm of the moment. It was a little before five o'clock, and there was very little traffic on the road. Within a few minutes we had reached the elegant monument which the Shah had erected to himself and his dynasty: the Shahyad, a soaring arch of white marble in a square which had been renamed 'Azadi': 'freedom'. Enormous rallies had been held here in the days of the revolution, with a million or so well-marshalled people surrounding the monument, while the more adventurous spirits in the crowd competed to see how high they could climb up its apparently sheer sides and stencil portraits of Khomeini on the stone. Now the stencils had long disappeared, and even the exhibition of photographs of the revolution which had replaced the old audio-visual display about the achievements of the Pahlavi dynasty were no longer on show: so few people came to see the exhibition that the city authorities had eventually closed it down.

By now the shops were starting to open, lit by the yellow glare of hurricane lamps or the blue of neon. Inside, the shopkeepers were laying out their stocks of vegetables, or piling up bolts of cloth, or heaving bloody half-carcasses of meat on to slabs while their assistants stood by, yawning. The sun was below the skyline still, and the light in the streets was dull and grey. The lamps shone on to the pavement in front of the shops, throwing its unevenness into relief. Tehran demands careful walking: the paving stones rear up every now and then, as though some powerful hidden force were starting to exert itself.

There is indeed a powerful pressure within the city: the enormous upward thrust of population. Areas which had been open land at the time of the revolution were now covered with concrete buildings. In 1978 Tehran had a population of six million and seemed overcrowded even then. By the early 1990s, although the precise figure was impossible even for census officials to determine, it was thought to be close to twelve million. In the country as a whole the population was approaching sixty million: it had nearly doubled in the fifteen years since the revolution began. Ayatollah Khomeini's regime had encouraged the growth in population during the eight years of the Iran–Iraq war, when losses were high and manpower was the only strategic advantage Iran had to match Iraq's superior supplies of weaponry.

At that stage the government used various forms of encouragement to persuade people to have larger families: extra ration coupons, subsidies for children's clothing, help with housing. When the war ended it became clear how serious a strain the growth in population was putting on the system, yet there was still a reluctance to introduce anything as Western-sounding as a birth-control campaign. In 1989 a system of free contraception and sterilisation in hospitals was introduced, but it was distinctly half-hearted. When occasional programmes dealt with the subject on television there were always loud complaints by conservatives. Now, I could see from Mahmoudi's car, there was a handful of posters advocating family planning along the main airport highway, which grew more crowded every year.

The growth in the population of Iran's cities could not be entirely blamed on the revolution, though. The process had begun in the first decade of the century, but the greatest increase came after the raising of the oil price in 1973. An unprecedented flood of wealth, job opportunities and corruption flowed into the larger cities of Iran, and had given rise to serious social dislocation. After that, the revolution brought millions more into the cities, searching for work and social benefit payments. Many were refugees who had lost their homes in western and south-western Iran when the Iraqis invaded in 1980. And although the three million refugees who had fled to Iran from Afghanistan since the Soviet invasion in 1979 were not supposed to settle in the cities, large numbers of them had ended up in Tehran as well.

Since few planning controls were enforced for the first ten years after the revolution, the working-class population of Tehran spread out into the plain, colonising areas which had previously been scrub and near-desert; the middle class had pushed their way up into the cool, wooded foothills of the Albourz Mountains, and the rich had sought refuge even further up the slopes, taking over the small villages which had once been a day's ride from the city. Alongside the streets in these cool suburbs were the clear, burbling channels or *jubs* which carried the streams from the Albourz down into the heart of the city, cooling it and providing the poor with their water. But by the time the *jubs* reached the overcrowded, insanitary slums of south Tehran the flow was sluggish and the colour muddy.

Many of the men who had come to Tehran in search of work and as a way out of their villages had given up trying to find housing; they simply camped out on the construction sites where their rudimentary skills had found them work. At first light, as Mahmoudi and I drove past, yawning men were emerging from their makeshift huts and gathering round the newly-lit cooking fires. In places, entire shanty-towns had sprung up on patches of wasteground.

We penetrated deeper into the city. There was no mistaking the signs of decay here. Among the parades of shops that were just opening for the day, plenty had closed down for good, looking like gaps in an uncared-for row of teeth. Plastic signs advertising bakeries or electrical goods shops or tailors were cracked and broken, and the walls were covered with graffiti and the tattered remnants of posters. Tehran had never been fortunate in its architecture, and the few grand nineteenth-century buildings and mosques that had survived the ruthless modernisation of the Pahlavis had long since been swallowed up behind charmless concrete and brick buildings. Nothing remained of the city walls, nor of the twelve tiled gates of Tehran, spectacularly rebuilt in the last century. They had all been destroyed as old-fashioned, and unrepresentative of the modernising spirit of the imperial dynasty.

The drab grey stucco façades of the buildings we passed were cracked and stained by the weather, and crisscrossed with cables strung across them to carry power to the shops and to the apartments above. The metal fixtures rusted, the dirt from the atmosphere lay thick on every surface, and not even the first sunshine of the day could make them look attractive. Sometimes a thin tree, planted by the roadside, would lean in towards the buildings, and in the branches would hang a birdcage; but the little yellow finch inside would be motionless, its feathers ruffled up, silent in spite of the morning sun.

Further down the street was a high wall covered with badly cracked plaster. A slogan had been recently sprayed across the wall: '*Marg bar bad...*' and then a word I couldn't read. Mahmoudi looked at it and laughed: it said 'Death to bad *hejab*'. I hoped at first it might be an indignant protest against Islamic dress for women; then I realised that it meant the exact opposite: Death to those who did not wear their Islamic clothing properly. It explains something about the lack of political moderation in Iran that the only way to express condemnation of others is to condemn them to death; the relatively mild formula of the West, 'Down with...', simply does not exist.

More than at any other time I could remember, there were signs of activity by political dissidents. A number of slogans had been painted on the walls, then scrubbed or whitewashed out by the local *Komiteh*, one of whose tasks was to look out for opposition graffiti and deal with it quickly. The ayatollahs are preachers: the word is important to them, and they knew the force that anti-Shah slogans had had before the revolution, when the SAVAK also had to keep the walls of the city ideologically clean. During the two or three years after the revolution, the political confusion of the time was reflected in the graffiti everywhere. Opposition groups like the Mojaheddin-e-Khalq, the Fedayeen, the Communist Tudeh Party, and even some remaining royalist elements fought out their political battles with the revolutionary government, in part, with spray-cans of paint and powerful slogans. But after the defeat of the opposition the old offending messages were obliterated. One, however, survived for almost a decade after the revolution: the nihilistic, or maybe ironic, message, 'Long live conflict!' Maybe the authorities thought it referred to the war against Iraq.

Nowadays the *Komitehs* selected the slogans which were to be painted on the walls from an official list, much as slogans for special occasions were worked out in the old Soviet Union; and they were often painted up by professional signwriters. They rarely touched great heights of creativity: 'Neither east nor west, but Islam!', 'Freedom is obtained by sacrifice', or more threateningly, 'I recommend women to forget their behaviour under the last regime and accept the Islamic code.' 'Death to America' and 'Death to England' are favourite stand-bys.

Sadly, I noticed that some of the most imaginative slogans and wall paintings had disappeared, presumably because they were out of date. The bright, funny caricatures on the walls of the military barracks near the airport had been painted over, for instance. During the Iran–Iraq war a splendid sequence of huge political cartoons had been on prominent display, showing Saddam Hussein as a puppet worked by Uncle Sam. And, to provide the balance that the government felt was necessary in the mid-1980s, a greedy Russian bear with a hammer and sickle attempting to claw the world in half.

After Ayatollah Khomeini's death, though, some of the more strident graffiti and cartoons quietly disappeared: particularly those which might offend Western countries with whom the Iranian government wanted better relations. The huge political drawings on the wall of the British Embassy compound on Ferdowsi Avenue were removed after Britain and Iran re-established diplomatic relations. The wall had been built in convenient sections, ten feet by fifteen, and an official cartoonist had turned each section into a painting in primary colours. Mrs Thatcher, portrayed as a feral, toothy blonde, was running away from 'Irlanda N' pursued by a volley of bottles and rotten fruit. Her arms and legs were shown as unIslamically bare and she trailed an inevitable handbag. A nervous Uncle Sam, his arms in the air, was being marched across the desert with a monster fountain pen like a gun barrel pointed at his back: meaning, presumably, that the propaganda of the Islamic Republic could rid Iran of American influence.

Further on, Saddam Hussein lurked nervously behind the paunchy figure of the Saudi king, who held out a battered dustbin-lid shield with a dollar sign on it. They were the kind of cartoons a newspaper might print in a far more moderate country than Iran, and there was none of the gore and obsessive concern with physical wounds which many official posters displayed during the war with Iraq.

By now we could see, above the surrounding buildings, the distinctive T-shape of the old InterContinental Hotel, whose name had been changed after the revolution to 'Laleh', or tulip: the flower of martyrdom. This was where John and most of the other foreign correspondents had stayed during the revolution, and it had been the press centre during the American hostage crisis of 1979–81 as well. It had a considerable hold on the affections of everyone who had stayed there at the time. The InterContinental was shot up, invaded, raided, searched for illicit alcohol; and the staff remained unfailingly courteous and helpful in spite of everything. I was once bequeathed a bottle of gin by an American correspondent, a friend of mine, who had hidden it in the air-conditioning duct of Room 617 during a raid by Revolutionary Guards. I never managed to undo the cover of the duct, so maybe it's still there.

Now I too had become used to the hotel, thinking of it as the Laleh even though John and most of the others always called it 'The InterCon' in memory of the earlier days. Now I scarcely noticed its increasingly shabby interior. I was planning to stay with friends rather than in the hotel, but I could not resist asking Mahmoudi to stop there briefly so that I could have a cup of tea and greet the hotel staff. I pushed open the glass door into the lobby where so much television equipment had been piled up in the past. Foreign camera crews could still fill the lobby during the occasional events that would simultaneously attract international interest and be considered a suitable showcase by the Islamic Republic; in practice that meant elections, earthquakes and funerals. It was dark and almost empty now: one of the power cuts which affected most parts of Tehran several times a week had just started.

The men at the reception desk remembered me at once (when John came here in 1986, after an absence of seven years, they recognised him as he walked across the lobby to register) and called out their greetings. I chatted with them about journalistic colleagues and the appalling level of the Iranian *rial*, then went round to the telephone room where the operators, who appeared to work around the clock, performed daily miracles with their antiquated switchboard. They took great pride in their work; often we would arrive back at the hotel at the end of the day to be told that a call to London would be coming through soon; normally it took up to three hours. The operators had guessed we would be back around this time and knew we always wanted to talk to our foreign desk when we returned. In later years a new German-designed telephone system eliminated the need for this admirable sixth sense.

I sat down in the lobby in the same old armchair, under the same enormous old colour photographs of a birch wood in autumn, and ordered tea and a moist slab of what Persians call 'English cake'. Apart from three German businessmen and their Iranian contact, I was the only person there. The upholstery was a little more frayed and the stains on the carpets had multiplied. Above, on the wall, was the familiar raffia-work sign that said, 'Down with USA'. There was another familiar fixture too: the free-standing noticeboard which had been there since before the revolution and read: 'Wedding arrangement is a fine art, especially when done by Hotel InterContinental Tehran.' A throne had been lost, tens of thousands had died in prison and hundreds of thousands on the battlefield, but the sign advertising wedding arrangements had scarcely shifted by more than a foot.

Outside, the streets were filling up with cars and people: men in open-necked shirts, long-sleeved for Islamic decency, carrying briefcases for their day at the office; women office workers, pale and unemotional in their hoods (known as *maghne'ehs*); mullahs, in the crisp grey robes that gave them the appearance of contented pigeons, walking past with the rolling gait that so many Persian men adopt: a side-to-side motion, rather than the angular, up-and-down lope of the European; older women, their faces masked by their *chadors*, whose black material made them look thinner and more bent. Now that the traffic was building up, filling the entire street with fumes and the sound of car horns, some scooters and motorbikes were taking to the sidewalks, weaving slowly in and out among the crowds of people.

'Traffic is more bad now,' Mahmoudi announced with cheerful resignation when I returned to the car. He meant that the roads were noticeably more jammed since my previous visit. For those working in the private sector, running a car was still reasonably cheap. The most popular cars in Tehran were small Renaults, which like the British-designed Paykans of the 1970s were built from imported kits in an Iranian factory. They cost less than $8,000 in 1993, although to order one in white, inexplicably the most popular colour in a dirty city, was $700 extra. Japanese cars, three to four times more expensive and quite prestigious, had become increasingly common, particularly the four-wheel-drive Patrol. Insurance cost as little as $50 and a tankful of petrol only $5, yet parking and traffic fines were very expensive: an illegal U-turn carried a fine of $30. As for the street system, it had become even more chaotic: there were diversions everywhere, caused by street resurfacing or by ambitious construction projects to build more overpasses and bypasses. None of them seemed to have any effect on the painfully slow flow of cars. Tehran, like the Iranian system of government, was increasingly sclerotic; everyone forecast its imminent death, and yet it managed somehow to keep going.

Mahmoudi turned off the crowded road on to a side-street. This was a new short cut. There were few cars and we sped along, appreciating the breeze that our speed generated. After a minute or two we found ourselves in the middle of three lanes of cars, held up by an ineffectual policeman some way down the road. Between him and us a superannuated set of traffic lights changed intermittently, but no one took any notice of them. An urbane Persian friend of ours had once murmured, as he forced his way across an intersection, 'Traffic lights are like all the other rules here: we regard them as being purely advisory.' Life in Tehran is largely about getting away with things. The Islamic Republic, in trying to make people pure, had not turned them into good drivers. Cars insinuated themselves in and out of the lines to gain a little advantage. Beside us, a battered blue bus lumbered slowly forward, exhaust belching out smoke the colour of its paintwork, brakes shrieking at every touch on the pedal. In between the cars, in the tiny spaces that not even the Tehran drivers could use to their advantage, motorbikes wobbled in and out. One middle-aged man on a Honda carried a large, *chador*-wrapped woman as a passenger, sitting sidesaddle. She gripped the seat frame tightly with one hand and held the *chador* over her mouth and nose to keep out the exhaust fumes. If she used both hands to grip the motorbike, her *chador* would only cover her mouth and the fume intake would increase. What she could not do, for the sake of Islamic decency, was to sit astride the motorbike or grip her husband around the waist.

On the opposite side of the road was a checkpoint for cars heading into the heart of the city. At the beginning of the revolution, in a popular, common-sense move, the authorities had decided to ban all private cars from the centre of Tehran for five days a week during working hours: Saturday to Wednesday from 7.30 a.m. to 1.30 p.m. It worked for a few years. Every road into the centre was blocked off during those hours, and the only vehicles the police would allow through were those which carried an official sticker. These regulations were still observed, but tens of thousands of other drivers had managed to acquire the official sticker, which now cost $200.

In the middle of the gridlock that spread across all four arms of an intersection, there had been an accident: two cars had collided, leaving a small heap of orange and white plastic shards in the road. Iranian law, which in this case owes nothing to the revolution, insists that no car can be moved after an accident until the police arrive, on pain of a heavy fine. A white four-wheel-drive Nissan Patrol from the local *Komiteh* had drawn up alongside. Four tough, self-reliant men in olive-green fatigues and beards were inside, and the two at the back cradled machine-pistols. They were all equipped with walkie-talkies; there was a good deal of expensive equipment riding in this patrol.

The *Komiteh* man sitting behind the driver said something into his walkie-talkie and got out, throwing his gun carelessly on to the seat: he wouldn't be needing it to clear the traffic. The appearance of the *Komiteh* was usually not welcome. At best it meant interference and a lecture, sometimes a fine to be paid, official or otherwise, and at worst being bundled into their vehicles and driven off to be questioned and perhaps charged. But now it meant that the traffic would start moving again. The *Komiteh* man threaded his way between the cars, stopping occasionally to direct individual drivers. Then he dealt with the two cars which had collided. The dispute between the drivers had stopped the moment the *Komiteh* arrived: these were not the kind of people you argued with. The horns had stopped blaring everywhere too, and within three minutes the entire traffic jam started to clear. It was an impressive performance, and the *Komiteh* man knew it. A few minutes later, he walked slowly back to the Nissan which started up with a roar and made a sharp U-turn, its tyres squealing as it drove off at speed.

Here in the centre there were fewer signs of economic decay. Each parade of shops seemed to contain at least one florist's and one place, neatly kept, where you could buy cakes and boxes of expensively presented nuts: Iranian social life revolves around exchanges of expensive little gifts. The signs displayed by the shops were smaller and neater than in the past, since for a time shopkeepers paid tax according to the size of their advertisements. Altogether, although times still appeared to be hard, it seemed to me that life for the better-off in Tehran was picking up a little. I did not, however, expect anyone to confirm this to me: social life also revolves around a certain obligatory pessimism about the way things are going.

I was getting tired, and it was a considerable relief when Mahmoudi manoeuvred on to the slip road for the Bozorg Rah-e-Modarres motorway. Our destination was north Tehran where it would be cooler and calmer. As the motorway swung to the right, I caught sight of the Albourz

Mountains. The sun had burned through the morning mist and the air was clear enough up here to see the perfect snow-capped peak of Damavand mountain 18,000 feet above us, reddish in the morning sun. The mountain's base was swallowed in mist and it seemed to float above us: a good omen, I felt.

5

The Insecure Throne

John Simpson

If you should have an enemy, be neither afraid nor anxious. Yet never remain uninformed of your enemies' doings whether they are secret or open; never feel secure against his mischievous activity against you, and be constantly planning how to outwit and injure him. Make continual inquiry about the state of his affairs and the opinions he expresses, keeping both ear and mind alert for them; thus you may keep the door of calamity and misfortune closed for yourself.

A Mirror For Princes

Niavaran is a small, unremarkable suburb clinging to the lower slopes of the Albourz Mountains. A few shops, a tea-house or two, expensive (and many not so expensive) houses straggle up the hillside. A few decades ago it was a pleasant hill village, but now the roads to it are bigger and busier and each year more houses are built there by the well-to-do who wish to escape the heat and pollution of the city. Nowadays Niavaran is part of the municipality of Tehran, which has spread northwards to encompass it: though the city centre lies ten miles away and a thousand feet below to the south.

The shops in the centre of Niavaran are unremarkable too: a bakery which produces the various types of bread that are the staple of Persian life, a flower shop, and several shops selling pastries and nuts. Until January 1979 each of these shops carried large photographs of the Shah, the Empress, and usually their eldest son for good measure, since this, if anywhere, was the Shah's home village. He had chosen the pleasant, dry, sparse air of the Albourz for his summer palace, and he and the Empress came to like it so much that they lived there during the other seasons as well, spending more time at Niavaran than at any of their other residences.

The display of imperial photographs by the villagers was not simply intended to be ingratiating. The people who lived here, unaffected by the expansion of Tehran until the palace was built, were bedrock royalists, men and women of peasant origin who had always revered their Shah regardless of the dynasty and its political weakness or strength. Hardy, traditional mountain villages like this provided the best recruits for the Shah's army. But although he appeared nightly on the television screens of Iran, they rarely saw him in person. There had been so many attempts on his life over the years that he showed himself to his people as little as possible, and the villagers at Niavaran were lucky to get more than two or three glimpses of him a year.

When he visited the Golestan Palace in the old centre of Tehran for some ceremonial occasion, or went to the airport to fly further afield, he would go by helicopter. It was partly symbolic: the monarch flying serenely above the turmoil below. It was also prudent, and his security advisers and his own instincts, together with the appalling traffic of Tehran, dictated that he should avoid going anywhere by road if he could. The mass of his subjects were no more hostile to him than Tsar Nicholas II's had been in the years before the Russian Revolution: on the contrary, like the last Tsar, the Shah was mostly regarded with respect, even adoration. Yet there had been a continuing threat to him from extremists throughout his reign.

In February 1949, when he was twenty-nine and had ruled for nearly eight years, a man posing as a photographer fired five shots at the Shah from a range of six feet. One shot struck him in the face and another in the shoulder, but he was not badly hurt. The Shah later wrote of the incident:

> The man threw down his gun and tried to escape, and in their fury at this assassination attempt, some of my young officers unfortunately killed him. He must have been a curious character. We discovered that he had been friendly with various arch-conservative religious fanatics, yet in his flat we found literature of the Tudeh or Communist party. His mistress was the daughter of a gardener at the British Embassy in Tehran.

The remarkable cocktail of motives suggested there – Marxism, Islamic fundamentalism and the faint yet intriguing link with Britain – provided the Shah with suspicions which, during the immense upheavals which resulted in the revolution thirty years later, formed themselves into a certainty in his mind. His bloodstained uniform was placed on reverent display at the Iranian Officers' Club in Tehran, and remained there until, in February 1979, the Officers' Club was sacked and the uniform torn into shreds by people who shared some of the opinions of the would-be assassin of February 1949.

After that the Shah rarely moved among ordinary people again. This was not, however, the impression given by the officially controlled news media. On the main freeway out of Tehran to the west, miles from any centre of population, a curious dilapidated shed-like structure still stands by the roadside, its corrugated-iron roof rusting, its seats broken or plundered. This is the stand from which, year after year, the Shah would review his armed forces. His personal helicopter would land nearby, and he would be driven fifty yards or so through cheering crowds of soldiers dressed in civilian clothes. He would then take his seat in the reviewing stand while the hugely expensive military equipment on which he lavished the resources of the state was paraded along the roadway in front of him. Then, when the review was over, he would drive back the fifty yards to his helicopter. That night's television pictures, carefully shot and edited, would give the impression that the Shah was going freely among his people. For most of his reign he could have done so; but he and his advisers preferred to play it safe.

The sight of the Shah's helicopter flying over Tehran, closely accompanied by another in order to confuse any attempt at mid-air assassination, was therefore a paradigm of his rule: distant, abstracted, separated from his subjects by superior technology. Yet he always wanted the appearance of closeness. The way he was portrayed was a matter of obsessive interest to him. In the year before the revolution the Shah would regularly hunt through the articles about himself and the Iranian crisis in the British and American press, firing off orders to his ambassadors in Washington and London to protest in the strongest terms about any critical references with no regard for their significance, nor for the quality of the newspapers which printed them.

The Shah's ambassador in London, Parviz Radji, found it just as hard as his master to distinguish the substantial from the ephemeral. The diary which Radji later published showed a natural concern with what was being said about Iran, but it was as though both he and the Shah felt that all would be well in Iran if only things could be presented more favourably. This is a classic symptom of the court mentality, and Radji, as a protégé of the Shah's fiercely devoted twin sister, Princess Ashraf, was a consummate courtier. The less subservient friends of the Shah in Britain and the United States noticed with some anxiety from the mid-seventies onwards how difficult it was to penetrate the screen of nervous, flattering courtiers around him and his more realistic Empress. Any warning about the danger this screen represented would be silently deflected by officials whose jobs depended on their ability to avoid upsetting the Shah. Radji's diary for 27 September 1976 contains an account of his conversation with the forthright Sir Denis Hamilton, an executive of Times Newspapers, the company which then owned the London *Times* and *Sunday Times*. Sir Denis was a supporter of the Shah, Radji noted.

But he thinks the Shah can no longer be spoken to. Every time a reference is made to some of the more contentious issues of his rule, there is a display of clout [sic] from the Court, threatening a unilateral break in economic and commercial links. 'I've seen,' he goes on, 'how ministers treat him – all that bowing and hand-kissing . . .'

I sent a cable to Tehran, retaining most of Denis Hamilton's observations but omitting the reference to the Shah's treatment of his ministers.

Princess Margaret was forthright too. Arriving at the Embassy during an anti-Shah demonstration in 1976, she told Radji that she was quite used to that sort of thing, having experienced many pro-IRA demonstrations in the United States. She added, 'But, of course, you have torture, which we don't.' Radji claimed to be amazed at how misinformed the Princess was about his country, even though the Shah had himself defended the use of torture in interviews with *Le Monde* and CBS. The SAVAK, he said, used the same methods as any other secret service. 'Who,' he asked with that mixture of cynicism and naïveté which marked so many officials under the Shah, and so many of their successors under the Islamic Republic, 'doesn't have a secret police?'

In 1975 the Secretary General of Amnesty International wrote: 'No country in the world has a worse record of human rights than Iran.' Not long after Princess Margaret's remark to Parviz Radji, the Shah claimed that there were three thousand political prisoners in Iran; various human rights organisations put the number at between 25,000 and 100,000. Amnesty International estimated that there had been more than three hundred executions for political offences between 1972 and 1976. No independent investigation was allowed into the growing reports of torture in the Shah's prisons. In a speech after the revolution, Ayatollah Khomeini claimed that 100,000 political prisoners had been executed during the Shah's reign; the true figure is still disputed. The intensity of the repression was, however, as fitful as most of the Shah's policies. Like his ambassadors and political advisers, the generals whom the Shah appointed to command the SAVAK during the 1970s were more concerned to please him than to tell him the truth. As a result, the sudden swings of imperial policy, from toughness to liberalisation and from concession to martial law, were ordered on the basis of intelligence which was, until the very end, filtered and pasteurised to render it acceptable to him.

During his last year in power the Shah's obvious unfamiliarity with the mood of most Iranians became a growing embarrassment to his ministers and supporters. He was also under increasing pressure from President Jimmy Carter's administration in Washington to improve Iran's human rights record. In May 1978 he had made a poor impression during a news conference with several Iranian newspaper and television correspondents. At times his answers to their ingratiating questions were haughty and dismissive; when someone asked him about the continued existence of Rastakhiz, the only legal party in Iran, which he had founded himself in 1975, the Shah replied, 'Has multi-party democracy proved to be such a bed of roses in the West?' That created further anger abroad; yet few Western observers noticed that during the same news conference he seemed deeply indecisive in his approach to the growing unrest in Iran. Over the previous few days there had been several demonstrations in the Tehran bazaar, and the army had had to fire live rounds into the air to disperse one crowd. The Shah himself had cancelled an official visit to Bulgaria on the pretext that he was suffering from a cold. None of the foreign correspondents attending his news conference dared to ask him about the disturbances; in the Shah's Iran, journalists were courtiers too. Nor did the Shah mention them. He merely seemed vacillating and insecure.

Television interviews with the Shah had always been common enough in the West, as part of his projection of himself as the builder of a Great Civilisation. He had given so few interviews to his tame press and television at home that they were watched with great care for the light they shed on his current mood and concerns. His apparent lack of self-confidence now made a deep impression in a country which had come to expect strong, ruthless leadership from him. He had controlled any political opposition with such intensity ever since the disturbances of 1963 and 1964 that any sign of its weakening was certain to have a serious effect. Throughout the summer of 1978, convinced that the Shah's grip had started to relax, people took greater and greater risks in opposing him.

In July hostile graffiti began appearing on the walls of Tehran, and the SAVAK was not always fast enough in painting them out. By the end of August the demonstrations were bigger and better organised than they had ever been. Each time people found they could make their protest without being shot down or arrested, they were emboldened to come out on to the streets again. Under American pressure and the Shah's own weakening resolve, Iran had become a textbook example of the dangers that befall a repressive government which finds itself obliged to liberalise. During one large demonstration at the beginning of September, a few days before the Jaleh Square massacre, a middle-aged man wearing a suit and tie broke away from the main body of marchers and ran over to us as we were filming. He was waving a 100-*rial* note, and as he stood in front of our camera he exaggeratedly inscribed a large cross over the face of the Shah on the front of the banknote. A well-known writer on Iran, who was standing with me at the time, said, 'If a man like that doesn't care about being recognised, it means he isn't afraid of the SAVAK any longer. And if he isn't afraid of the SAVAK, then the Shah's had it.'

Such momentary insights changed people's perceptions of the Shah's chances of survival as much as the daily parade of trouble on the streets of Iran. The British ambassador, Sir Anthony Parsons, a witty, unstuffy and clear-sighted man who was remarkably helpful to me even though the BBC was one of his bigger problems in dealing with the Shah, went to see him when he returned from leave in mid-September.

I was horrified by the change in his appearance and manner. He looked shrunken: his face was yellow and he moved slowly. He seemed exhausted and drained of spirit. But he was ready to discuss the internal crisis without reserve or inhibition and gave me the unprecedented impression that he would welcome my personal view. He even asked at one point if we could influence the moderate mullahs into a more tractable frame of mind. I replied that, because of his suspicions of us, I and my immediate predecessors had avoided all contact with the religious classes. He must know that, and it was no use his expecting us now to do something which, if we had done it before, would have wrecked our efforts to build a good working relationship with him. The Shah smiled and accepted my point.

Just as his interviews on their domestic television had convinced many Iranians, with their swift political instincts, that the Shah was in serious trouble, so the interviews he gave to the Western media presented people in the outside world with clear indications that he was starting to lose his grip. In October, speaking to a correspondent from *Le Figaro*, he described the situation as 'discouraging' more than twenty times during the hour they were together. A few days before, he had been interviewed for American television (he rejected all requests from me, apparently on the grounds that the BBC was working against him) and seemed to find it hard to concentrate on the questions. He rarely lifted his eyes from the magnificent carpet. The pauses between the questions and the Shah's answers grew longer and longer, and the answers themselves more and more vague. It was deeply embarrassing to watch. The fact that the Shah was fighting a courageous battle against cancer, and was receiving a debilitating and painful course of treatment for it, was a carefully guarded secret; no doubt that accounted in part for the inadequacy of his public performances. According to someone who was close to him during those months, the Shah was also suffering a good deal of pain in his feet, possibly from gout, which troubled him physically more than the cancer. In the circumstances, his advisers should have told him not to give any more of these disastrous interviews. No one of course did.

The Shah's mood was not always so negative: but even journalists who interviewed him at more confident moments found him strangely unaware of the true nature of the problems he faced. Time and again he would refer to Communist, or British, instigation of the rioting. An Iranian sociologist, Ehsan Naraghi, was consulted by the Shah on a number of occasions during the last few months of his reign. In his book *From Palace to Prison* Naraghi presents himself in a highly favourable light, far-sighted and liberal in everything he advises the Shah to do (one of the reasons why one trusts Sir Anthony Parsons's account is that he is so frank about the few misjudgements he himself made). Nevertheless Naraghi no doubt quotes the Shah accurately on the subject of Britain:

> The calls for the Shah to reign and not to govern [the Shah tells him] were merely the slogan of all those abroad who wished to see him turned into a puppet. The British, for example, had no wish to see real power established in our country . . . The Americans are a different breed. But they allowed themselves to be swayed by the British who fear our prosperity and our power. It would suit London to see a weak king, manipulated by their agents.

Until the moment of his departure from Iran, and indeed until the moment of his death, the Shah never understood the nature of the revolution against him. Nor did he understand the mood of the people who brought it about. He knew almost nothing of what was going on in the streets of his cities. But then he never saw the city streets with his own eyes: he flew over them in his helicopter, and relied on his secret policemen and his courtiers to tell him what was happening. He knew that his father had created a similar system, and that it had led to his isolation and downfall, but he believed that he himself was so aware of the dangers that such a thing could never happen to him. This wasn't true; and it brought about his destruction.

There was a depressing lack of mutual loyalty between the Shah and his courtiers. When the demand began to grow for an end to corruption, the Shah scarcely paused before offering up loyal and sometimes honest servants to appease the mob and buy himself a little more time. His prime minister for thirteen years, Amir Abbas Hoveyda, was a decent and honourable man who had tried in 1977 to curb the corruption emanating from the imperial family itself. He himself lived quietly and simply, but he had incurred the anger of the generals who ran the martial-law government of the Shah's last months and was among those arrested for corruption in November 1978. The Shah did nothing to protect him, and seemed embarrassed when people mentioned Hoveyda's name in his presence. Hoveyda refused to escape before his arrest ('I have a lot of detective stories to read and must stay where I am to finish them!' he said when Sir Anthony Parsons warned him that he was likely to be picked up soon). He was still in prison when the Shah left the country, and was shot soon after the establishment of the Islamic Republic.

Yet if the Shah showed little loyalty to his servants, his servants often showed little real loyalty to him in return. The ministers, ambassadors and generals who toadied to him were usually much more concerned with their own careers than with the future of the imperial throne. They too bear a good deal of responsibility for his, and their, downfall.

Nowadays Davoud lives in exile in Paris. He longs one day to return to Iran, but only on his own terms. He does not believe this will be possible under the Islamic Republic. He comes from an aristocratic family, and grew up wanting to be a soldier and serve his country like his father and grandfather before him. He looks after himself as carefully now as he did when he was in Iran, maintaining the sort of self-discipline that he learned in the army. He was sent to study at a military academy abroad and joined the Immortals when he returned, like many other young men of good family. He commanded the soldiers who guarded the Niavaran Palace.

The Immortals comprised a number of regiments, including heavy artillery, anti-aircraft units, an armoured detachment and various types of special forces. For Davoud it was a great honour to be asked to join the Immortals; it also meant that he would be posted in Tehran near his family and friends, and receive extra allowances.

We had a pretty cushy life. We lived in a little village with houses and flats. It was in Aqdasiyeh which was west of Niavaran. It was a beautiful area, right up on the mountainside. Officers and NCOs could rent houses and towards the late 1970s officers could buy houses at a very good mortgage rate. Despite all that, I left the Immortals less than a year after I joined because I realised that, as soldiers, they were rubbish. Only spit and polish, nothing else.

Davoud was adventurous, and took the opportunity to work with a British SAS team which was giving anti-terrorist training to the Iranian army. The Iranian special forces unit which was set up as a result was a good one. When it competed against similar groups from the other armies of the CENTO (Central Treaty Organisation) alliance, the Iranian team usually came first, particularly in things like shooting and desert manoeuvres. Davoud first became involved in anti-terrorist activities in the late summer of 1978.

There was to be an opposition meeting where Bakhtiar and others were speaking. It was at a place called the Karvansarasangi on the road to Karaj, a private orchard which was owned by a supporter of Bakhtiar's. We first reported to our base and were ordered to wear civilian clothes. Then we were armed with lengths of cable and sticks.

When we got to Karvansangeh we surrounded the orchard where the meeting was being held. There were quite a few SAVAK whom we knew because the Special Forces were cooperating with them. Our anti-terrorist group was a combination of army, police and SAVAK. So together we surrounded the people; there were probably 600 of them. We pushed them out of that orchard, herded them out really, and created a corridor that they had to run through. As they did we beat them. Then we smashed up their cars. We wanted to give them a taste of direct action in order to give them a shock, Bakhtiar and all those idiots. I promise, if we had been able to continue like that, the revolution wouldn't have happened. The people would have lost their nerve.

After that, Davoud's unit started going to the mosques in south Tehran, dressed in plain clothes. The mullahs in these mosques were starting to give political sermons, questioning the vast differences in wealth between the people in north Tehran and the poor in the south.

As soon as the mullahs would start to talk about such matters, political matters, we'd make a *salovat*. When somebody shouts *salovat*, everyone around must complete it by reciting a long chant in Arabic which starts 'We pray to Mohammed and all his lineage . . .' It goes on for a few minutes. But we would deliberately do this at the wrong moment, when the mullah was becoming very political. It was a useful way of interrupting and confusing the situation, but still being correct in their terms. We wanted to create an uproar. Because, you see, even then in the autumn, you could sense that they had no real organisation. You must remember that these were ordinary working people, the ones we saw in the mosque and elsewhere. They were not brave. They were taking tiny, tiny steps against the Shah. But each time they took a tiny step and weren't stopped, they took another and another. Martial law hadn't yet been declared either, so the authorities wouldn't let us close down the two or three mosques where the trouble was starting. Then the two mosques became twenty and twenty became two hundred and there was no way of stopping it. The steps became bigger and bigger.

When martial law was declared, Davoud's unit was instructed to mark out the strategic points on the streets which led to the various ministries, so that they could confront the crowds. The first big demonstration was at Ghaitariya, near the Soviet Embassy, which attracted more than 30,000 people. By that stage, according to Davoud, it would have been necessary to shoot or arrest four or five thousand people, and the decision was taken to allow the demonstration to go ahead.

Many times I was ready with my men to do anything to stop the demonstrators. I never shot anybody because I never had orders to do so. I would have, without any problem. My job was to protect the monarchy. The day we became officers we swore an oath of loyalty to the monarchy and I never forgot that.

Morale got worse and worse every day, especially in the Imperial Guard. After all, some of the first soldiers to turn on their officers were in the Immortals. It was in the mess-hall at the Lavizan garrison in north Tehran, right after Ashura [December 1978]. The officers were eating lunch and several soldiers came in and started shooting. There were many killed, fifteen I think, and many wounded. Some of the officers who were armed shot back and killed them, but one was just wounded. When they grabbed this soldier they screamed at him and asked him why he'd done it. The soldier told them, 'We went to our mullah and asked him what can we do, what can we give to the revolution?' He said 'Just kill your officers.'

Davoud retains a kind of loyalty to the Shah even now, though he blames him for getting rid of his best advisers and for listening to the Empress Farah, who advised him not to shoot down the demonstrators.

He was an intelligent man, he was very kind-hearted and he loved Iran, he loved Persians. But we are not Europeans. You cannot judge us or treat us the same way, we are different people with a different history. It is necessary to be rough. And the Shah's word should have been the ultimate law but he didn't have the guts to back it up. In the end he blinked. He should have let the army do its job. Before, in 1963 when there was trouble, Assadollah Alam, the Minister of Court, took charge and the army knocked everyone flying. Several hundred people were killed, but the trouble was stopped.

When the Shah fled the country, Davoud's sense of loyalty obliged him to stay even though plenty of other well-to-do officers were starting to leave themselves.

A number of officers banded together and we continued to fight, but there was no back-up. Several high-ranking officers, even generals, tried to do deals with Khomeini's people. Of course they were all killed. In the end we disappeared. I got out about three months after the revolution. I won't tell you the details, but

I left Iran through Kurdistan and into Turkey. I don't believe in the monarchy any more. When you think about it, it makes no sense. You can have one strong leader like Reza Shah but who comes after? His son wasn't capable and that's why I am here and not in my own country.

The first time I went to the Niavaran Palace, in August 1978, I was turned away merely for stopping our car at the gates to see if we could film. A sergeant of the Immortals marched over and ordered us to leave. The second time I went to the palace was on the morning after the revolution, 12 February 1979, when the Immortals were standing shivering in their underwear looking very mortal indeed. Their gaudy uniforms were piled up on the back of a truck, ready to be taken off for burning. The third time was with Tira in 1986, when the palace had just been opened as a tourist attraction.

It felt like visiting the Winter Palace in Leningrad in, say, 1925. On the gates of black, unornamented steel there were banners with slogans about the invincibility of the Islamic Republic and how it had smashed the corruption of the past. In the guardhouse, where the sergeants had once been posted, two watchmen in civilian clothes sat talking and laughing. They were in their mid-thirties, and seemed pleasant enough. One was tossing a handgun back and forth in his hands, but it had a brass cloakroom tag pinned to the trigger guard. That somehow reduced it to the everyday level of umbrellas and briefcases. I made a joking reference to the gun, and the man holding it explained that a senior member of the Revolutionary Guards was paying the palace a visit.

'The former palace,' I said, in mock reproof. I had used this feeble joke, which tested my Farsi to its limits, a couple of times before with street names from the Shah's time which had been rebaptised in suitably revolutionary fashion but whose new names no one could ever remember. The joke seemed to appeal to people. Now both the watchmen rocked with laughter, and the handgun slipped between the knees of its guardian, the barrel pointing perilously inwards. I considered making another joke, but doubted if my Farsi was up to it.

We left our bags and were handed another brass tag in their place. A small, elderly, unshaven man with an extremely dirty shirt gave me the most perfunctory of searches: a pat on the chest and on each of the pockets of my trousers. Since it was still lunchtime, the gun-minding watchman explained, there were no women searchers, so Tira could go in unchecked. Who, I asked, were they protecting the palace against anyway? The watchman smiled and brandished the revolver, making the tag jingle against the butt, to indicate that they were ready for anything and anyone, even if he couldn't precisely say which direction

the threat might come from. I stopped asking difficult questions and
bought two three-hundred-*rial* tickets instead.

. The grounds were kept remarkably well; it was hard to imagine that
when the Shah and the Empress were here, the standard of care could
have been higher. The grass, coarser than the English variety, was
manicured in parallel stripes. Geraniums grew in the star-shaped beds,
where the earth was newly turned and free of weeds. In the shade of
the tall maple tree which must have been planted when the original
palace was built, sprinklers trailed clouds of water which glittered
in the early-afternoon sunshine.

Seeing all this again, I found the memories remarkably fresh in my
mind. Even the neatness of the grounds was familiar, because the
imperial gardeners, in the absence of any instructions to the contrary,
had gone on working after the Shah had left. On Monday 12 February the
iron gates had opened and the camera crew and I had been swept in on
a flood-tide of demonstrators who were singing and chanting rather than
shouting slogans, and unarmed except for the occasional piece of wood.
We swept past the shivering, trouserless Immortals, unable for the time
being to stop and film them because of the pressure of the crowd. One of
them sat on the ground, hitting his head and looking up at the imperial
crest on the wall above him with an expression of utter despair.

It was less like the storming of the Winter Palace than a scene from
the French Revolution: the peasants and artisans breaking into the
grounds of the count's château. The crowd boiled along the pathways
and lawns, past the old house built by Reza Shah and towards the new
one his son had built in 1957. The mood was one of militant curiosity;
they wanted to see how he and the Empress had lived, not to burn the
place down to the ground. We raced along with them, Bill Handford
filming as he ran. Then a line of volunteers with armbands stopped us
at the point where the pathway opened out into an open area in front
of the main entrance to the palace.

One of the volunteers shouted out something to the crowd, and
everyone halted in a mood of disappointment; the looting fever was
undoubtedly on them, and if they had broken in, the contents, and
perhaps the building itself, would have been destroyed. But everybody
was obedient, and I realised then that the great majority of them were
probably not revolutionaries at all, but men and women from Niavaran
village: simple people who had always been royalists in their hearts.
They stood where they had been stopped, trying to peer in through the
windows twenty yards away, but there was little to be seen: a desk
with a few trinkets on it, some expensive curtains, a painting gleaming
faintly in the quiet darkness inside.

The volunteers took a step forward, and the crowd moved instinctively,
obediently, back. No one wanted trouble. Then they turned and walked
away, herded by the volunteers, their sticks and pieces of wood trailing,

casting occasional regretful looks back at the palace they wanted to be able to say they had seen. None of them paid any attention to the Immortals, who had been given blankets to put round themselves by now. We were not allowed to film through the windows of the palace, but the volunteers had no objection to our filming the grounds and the wretched Immortals. We got our pictures of them and of the quiet, wondering crowd, and left. With the fall of the imperial palace, the revolution was over.

Seven years later, Tira and I walked around the place where all this had happened, noticing the kind of things I had not had time to notice then: the nineteenth-century French street lamps, for example, painted a civic dark green and shipped in specially from Paris. On a line of shaded benches, which might or might not have been there before, a seated queue of quiet, polite citizens had formed, and moved up a couple of spaces to make room for us. We might all be waiting to apply for something: residents' parking permits in an expensive part of London, perhaps. The women were wrapped anonymously in *chadors*, but they looked as if they had money. There were two men, who also seemed to be middle class. They tried not to stare at us while we waited for a guide to come over and take our tickets. We were the first tour of the afternoon.

Despite its setting, the palace was scarcely handsome. It suffered from the faults that buildings of the mid-fifties usually do suffer from: a lumpish shape, too much concrete, and rooms which are never quite the size they should be. Even in 1957, when the Shah built it, it must have looked as though he thought he was buying style, when he was simply spending a great deal of money. The Niavaran Palace had its virtues, all the same. It was only two storeys high, and parts of it were attractively tiled in yellow and blue. It was not built to overawe the visitor, but to remind him that he was entering a family home; and for that reason perhaps the decision to open it to the public did not have quite the effect that its advocates in the Majlis had intended. It certainly did not appal the visitor with its extravagance, nor did it symbolise the immense corruption of Iran in the Shah's later years; instead, it shrank the imperial family to normal, understandable terms.

We walked in single file to the front door, over which a particularly disapproving portrait of Khomeini now hung, and took off our shoes in the porch in order to protect the carpets inside. This was where the huge dogs, beloved by the Shah and the Empress, used to come bounding out when visitors arrived, jumping up and leaving paw-marks on everyone's clothes. Inside, it was cool and surprisingly gloomy. We shuffled round while the guide told us, as guides will, the measurements of each room, the provenance of every major piece of furniture, the size of each of the great carpets which covered every floor. These were the only objects of serious artistic value in the house; the rest were mostly things which the Shah and Empress had received as presents from the rich and famous

like themselves. There was a dreadful gold-plated bowl from Richard
Nixon, with the presidential head, like the profile on a Roman coin,
superimposed on that of the Shah. No question which head was in the
place of honour: Nixon's was the one.

Soon the guide had ceased to bother about the six Iranians who were
on the tour with us, and gave his commentary in English.

'When they are wanting coolness or sun, they press this button
like I do, and see what follows.'

What followed was that a large panel in the roof opened slowly and
silently over the central atrium of the house, allowing the sun's rays to
cut downwards into the gloom and pick out the pattern on the largest
and most remarkable of the carpets. The guide pressed the button to
close the roof again. He couldn't resist playing with it once or twice
more, to show off its responsiveness. We resumed our exploration. The
house was neither grand, nor intimate, nor even very practical. Its
rooms, like those of Versailles, were all interlinked so that you had
to pass through each one to reach another.

The furniture seemed to have been chosen at random, with nothing
matching anything else; there was green, red, gold and white upholstery,
often in the same room, and everything from Second Empire to 1950s in
terms of style. It had nothing to do with the imperial family's taste: some
of the imperial furniture vanished from Niavaran before the new regime
imposed proper control, and replacements had been brought in from the
forty-five other Pahlavi family residences in Tehran without regard to
style.

The Shah's bedroom was austere: a narrow single bed in an alcove,
with a portrait of his father glowering on the wall. The Empress,
by contrast, slept in a vast gilded four-poster. Society portraits of
her and her children hung on the walls. The guide, with a touch
of salaciousness in his voice, allowed us a glimpse of the Empress's
clothes: glitzy robes of pink and blue and green, crammed together
in her surprisingly small dressing room, and (like Imelda Marcos) a
hundred or so pairs of shoes. By now, though, I found my reactions
had changed. It wasn't the imperial family which was lacking in taste,
it was we who gawped at their private belongings and passed judgement
on them. The Shah's regime may have been cruel towards its opponents
and corrupt in many of its dealings; but the Shah himself had paid the
price for it all, while many of the men and women who had a more
immediate responsibility for the repression and the corruption went to
live on the proceeds in the pleasanter cities of western Europe and
the United States. I felt suddenly that I couldn't take any more, and
we hurried out into the sunlight.

The Niavaran Palace had hinted at a private vulnerability in the Shah
which underlay the bombast of the Great Civilisation. It is there, too, in
his memoirs:

In my early years as King, and especially during the Mossadegh period, I went through acute anxieties; and it is perhaps no wonder that my hair is prematurely white. Without the ability to relax I would surely have disintegrated physically, emotionally and even mentally.

One of the few mistakes my father made was to rely upon a narrowing circle of advisers. Fearing Reza Shah, they flattered him rather than telling him the truth; and I am sorry to say they were by no means always incorruptible. My system is entirely different . . .

In 1971 the Shah was at the height of his powers. His rule was unchallenged, Ayatollah Khomeini was in exile in Iraq, the immense corruption that took root after he led the OPEC countries in tripling the price of oil still lay ahead. So did the diagnosis by two leading French specialists in 1974 that he had cancer. According to his calculations, 1971 marked the 2500th anniversary of the founding of the Persian Empire. It was also the thirtieth anniversary of the Shah's reign. The Shah wanted a pageant and chose to hold it in the ruins of Persepolis, built by the great emperor Darius. The occasion was celebrated in a fashion which may never again be equalled for ceremony, colour and sheer excess of every kind.

The tent city at Persepolis covered 160 acres, and 43,000 yards of flame-proof cloth in beige and royal blue was used to make the tents, which were grouped around a central plaza in which fountains played day and night. Each tent had a sitting room, two bathrooms, two bedrooms and a kitchen. The followers whom each of the main guests had brought with them were relegated to orange-and-white tents a little farther away. Maxim's of Paris provided the food, and the best French wines were brought in. Monarchs and presidents or their representatives from sixty-nine countries attended, among them President Podgorny of the Soviet Union, Vice-President Spiro Agnew of the United States, the Emperor Haile Selassie of Ethiopia (who brought a retinue of seventy-two and a chihuahua dog with a diamond collar), King Constantine of Greece, and Imelda Marcos of the Philippines (who brought only seventy-two pairs of shoes). Within a few years all of these people were disgraced or removed from office with the exception of King Constantine, who had been overthrown already. Wearing theatrical false beards and dressed in the uniforms of every Persian epoch since that of Cyrus, 6,200 soldiers marched past the assembled guests. Horse and camel cavalry, litters, chariots and tanks paraded past. Only one period was entirely left out: the Arab conquests which brought Islam to Persia.

About an hour's drive from the tent city at Persepolis, in the flat plain at Pasargadae, lies the tomb of Cyrus, the first great Persian king. It is a rectangular stone monument, a single chamber with a gabled stone roof, its simplicity mocking the grandeur and excess of later epochs. Scarcely anything here has changed since the day Alexander the Great came to pay his respects and was touched by Cyrus's modest request: 'Grudge me not this little earth that covereth my body.'

This was the site the Shah had chosen for the opening of the 2500th anniversary celebrations. Since the tomb stands alone, with only the rust-coloured earth of Fars around it, a special concrete platform was constructed for the Shah and the Empress. They arrived by helicopter from Persepolis to a carefully-staged reception in front of all the emperors, presidents and princes. Field guns fired an immense salute. Then in his high-pitched voice the Shah read an invocation which began 'O Cyrus, Great King, King of Kings' and ended 'O Cyrus, rest in peace, for we are awake.'

Nowadays, like the Great Civilisation itself, everything the Shah created for the celebration at Pasargadae has crumbled away. Only the tomb of Cyrus remains in its grand simplicity. Visitors are rare, and when Tira and I went there it took the ancient guide several minutes to find the book of tickets, pale green and yellow ones printed in Farsi and English, plainly dating from pre-revolutionary times. The price was pre-revolutionary too: ten *rials*, so little that it was hard to find the right money.

The guide hobbled after us.

'Tomb of Cyrus,' he said unnecessarily, jabbing in the direction of the incomparable monument with his stick.

Then he pointed to a flat rectangle of concrete, laid out in front of the tomb. The concrete was cracked and fissured, and desert weeds, thistles and coarse grasses had burst their way through it, turning it into rubble. In a few more decades it would disappear completely. The old man struck a pose and faced Cyrus's tomb, which rose up almost unaffected by two and a half millennia.

'Cyrus there,' he said.

Then he tapped his stick on the remains of the concrete base where the salute was taken in 1971, dislodging several fragments of decaying stone.

'Shah,' he said. 'Shah was here.'

He winked. I knew exactly what he meant.

6

The New Masters

Tira Shubart

The loftiest branch of learning is that of religion, the principles of which lie everlastingly in the declaration of the unity of God. The practical applications of that declaration constitute the provisions of the religious law, and its profession brings blessings both in this world and the next.
A Mirror For Princes

Half a mile from the Shah's former palace at Niavaran lies the village of Jamaran. The name is not attractive; it means 'the abode of snakes'. For almost ten years, until the middle of 1989, the place where the road to the village forks off from the main Shahid Bahonar Avenue was blocked by a Revolutionary Guard checkpoint. No unauthorised person was allowed to approach the village. The reason was not snakes, but national security: Jamaran was where Ayatollah Khomeini lived and worked.

The village had been selected for various reasons: its size, the ease with which access to it could be controlled, and its distance from the turmoil of central Tehran. Most important of all, it was tucked into the mountainside, which gave it a considerable measure of protection from air attack during the war with Iraq. Farther along the Shahid Bahonar Avenue was an elderly battery of anti-aircraft guns which had often seen action; the Iraqi air force had made several determined but unsuccessful attempts to bomb Jamaran. There was, supposedly, an internal danger as well. Various plots were alleged to have been organised to capture or kill Khomeini. It is hard, even now, to be sure how many of these plots amounted to anything more than the paranoid imaginings of the security service, or else were invented as part of the bitter infighting which went on continually around the person of Khomeini. None of the 'plots' went further than the planning stage; but many people were executed for their supposed involvement in them, all the same. Among them was the Islamic Republic's first foreign minister, Sadeq Qotbzadeh, who had been Khomeini's spokesman at

Neauphle-le-Château, and master of ceremonies on board his flight from Paris.

By no means all of Jamaran was taken over by Khomeini's entourage. In the immediate area of the village there were more than a hundred large, well-appointed houses owned by those whom the new regime called the *taght-ut-tee* (literally, idol-worshippers): wealthy people of the kind who were associated with the old regime. The higher up the foothills you lived, the greater your wealth was likely to be. Many of the houses were surrounded by big fences, which protected their terraced swimming pools and tennis courts from the attention of the new Islamic neighbours who had moved in: Khomeini's clerical courtiers. These were popularly known as 'Mercedes-Benz mullahs': ambitious men who had built homes here in order to be near Khomeini, or had moved into property confiscated from leading supporters of the *ancien régime*.

It was surprising how many potential class enemies of the Islamic government had chosen to stay in their houses, even though every trip in and out of the neighbourhood meant a compulsory search of cars, drivers and passengers at the road block on the corner of Jamaran Road and Shahid Bahonar Avenue. Most did their best to continue with their old way of life under the new system. One man took pride in the fact that he had never allowed his supply of bootleg vodka to run dry at his house in Jamaran. He always wanted to be able to offer his guests any drink they asked for. After Khomeini's death, when the road block had been dismantled and the siege conditions lifted, I asked him how he had smuggled the liquor through the checkpoints.

'I'd better not say,' he replied. 'You never know when I might have to use the same hiding place again.'

One pleasant spring morning in 1992 – John had stayed in Britain to report on the general election – I decided to be a revolutionary tourist. Mahmoudi of course knew the quickest route to Jamaran: he had often driven foreign journalists to the audiences Khomeini gave there. But he had not been back since Khomeini's death, and he was surprised to find he could now drive past the place where the road block had been, and was able to park near the lane which led to the Ayatollah's house. He put a heavy chain through the steering wheel and locked it on to the brake pedal – the usual anti-theft device in Tehran – and we set off on foot.

The guards were slumped inside their post at the top of the lane and barely glanced at us. Since they couldn't be bothered to raise the barrier, we simply stepped over it. We passed a souvenir shop that sold portraits of Khomeini, and turned down a small side path. A group of giggling schoolgirls rushed past us; it was the end of morning classes. Ahead of us walked several men in the olive green uniforms which were nowadays worn by both the Revolutionary Guards and the *gendarmerie*.

At the end of the alley was a simple, unimpressive building, the brickwork of its façade crude and unfinished. It looked altogether out of place in expensive Jamaran, and its simplicity gave the impression of being cultivated for effect. There were two doors; men went in through the larger one and women through the smaller. We found it hard to rouse the security staff from their noonday torpor and get them to let us in. I was given a cursory body search, nothing more than a pat-down, and was asked to press the shutter of my camera to show it was genuine. Then the guards slumped down in their places again, glad to be rid of us.

Mahmoudi and I wandered into a rectangular hall like a school gymnasium: it was the place where Khomeini used to appear in public during his final years, and I had seen television pictures of it many times in Tehran. As always, it seemed a great deal smaller in real life. The balcony where he used to sit above the level of the crowd had been glassed in. The microphone he had used was still there. In case we thought the glass was some kind of protection from the worshippers, a sign explained in delightfully faulty English:

> In the name of God the most high. All dear pilgrims should notice. This place where Imam used to seat and deliver speach, had not been covered with glass. It is covered after Imam departure for protection as a sacred seat.

But the effort of conserving the Ayatollah's balcony seemed to have exhausted the people who now looked after the place: beneath it, the plaster was peeling off the wall and had covered the kilims on the floor below with a fine white dust. The mural on the wall opposite, which depicted a vast crowd of pilgrims looking towards the Ka'bah in Mecca, was also showing signs of decay.

Mahmoudi and I left the mosque and followed a path leading up to a small house with a tiny cemented courtyard. Unlike many of his followers, Khomeini remained uninterested in material wealth throughout his life; the house showed that. As with the unfinished brickwork of the entrance to the complex, its very simplicity seemed almost ostentatious. I peered in through the window of the main downstairs room: it was small, and furnished with an undistinguished carpet, a cheap sofa, and an ottoman. On a small side-table, which was covered with a plastic tablecloth, was a telephone. The shelves behind the couch were empty except for a half a dozen books and, absurdly, a rolled umbrella lying on top of them. On the floor in front of the sofa was a pair of sandals, positioned as if the Ayatollah might be about to slip his feet into them. A young guard with a recently shaven head was looking after the display, but he scarcely noticed us. He was praying intensely and dramatically, making much use of his prayer beads. I interrupted him to ask if photographs were permitted. He turned and told me with tears in his eyes that he had worked there while Khomeini was alive. Now, he said, he spent his days in prayer.

In life, Khomeini had been an icon. Now that he was dead, some
people worshipped their notion of him still. Like Lenin, he had left
behind him a system and an idea of the state; and, as with Lenin,
the people who ran the state after his death changed everything. The
West regards Khomeini's revolution as Islamic fundamentalism, pure and
simple; meaning a religious obscurantism which wilfully tries to put back
the clock and return to an older social system, where women are forced
to cover themselves, banking is regarded with suspicion, and the Koran
is the only guide required to govern the state and administer the law.

The system Khomeini left behind him involved all of these things.
But there was much more to it. His politics were not merely a rejection
of Western secular values, they represented a form of populism which
at times seemed almost socialist. The purpose of the revolution went
beyond establishing a society based on the values and ethics of the
Koran; it was intended to achieve a basic shift of wealth and power
away from the established middle class and towards the dispossessed.
The people who thronged his coffin at his funeral maddened with grief,
and who continued to mourn him long afterwards, were from that class.
And yet the slums of south Tehran were as bad after Khomeini's death
as they had been before the revolution, and the differential in wealth
between the slum-dwellers and the inhabitants of north Tehran was
much the same as it had been before the big upsurge in oil wealth in
1974. Even by the time of Khomeini's death in 1989 it was clear that
the revolution he led had been a profound failure in its own terms.

The revolution tried to create a society which was Leninist but not
Marxist–Leninist. That is to say, Iran still instinctively possessed a free
enterprise culture, but the government introduced the kind of controls
over people's movement, thought and behaviour similar to those in the
old Soviet Union. This was a failure too. Iran had always been an open
society, and even the people who were supposed to police the new system
often shared a more relaxed approach to life.

When John and I returned to London after our first trip to Iran
together in 1986 and reported on it for television, we received a good
deal of hate-mail, usually anonymous, from Iranian exiles. 'I don't know
what you were allowed to see, but...' they would say, or 'You were
only shown the places the regime wanted to take you to...' Yet this
was not true. Both of us had travelled widely in countries governed
by ideologically dogmatic regimes, from the Soviet bloc to Libya, Cuba
and China, and the freedom of movement we were given in Iran was
remarkable by contrast. There were various reasons for this. Firstly,
Iran had never been a totalitarian country, and the Leninist system of
spies and informers in every city block and every village had never
really taken root. Secondly, the lax habits of Iranian petty officialdom

meant that we never experienced real difficulty in going wherever we wanted and were rarely challenged or stopped. The mere fact that we were Westerners was usually enough to get us through any official checkpoint. At the start of a trip to central and southern Iran, which was to last more than a week, John discovered after we had spent an hour and a half driving through the worst of the Tehran traffic that he had left his passport behind. He decided to risk it, and carry on with the journey. We did not experience the slightest problem. On the two or three occasions when he was asked for his passport he simply produced his BBC identity card. It worked each time.

Finally, there was the unwillingness of the 'minders' from the Orwellian Ministry of Islamic Guidance to bestir themselves and help us. Many of them had second or even third jobs, and could not afford to come with us on our trips outside Tehran. Instead, they gave us permission to move around the country as we chose, although during the war with Iraq we had to sign an undertaking not to go to any of the front-line areas unaccompanied. On one occasion we insisted that someone from the Ministry should go with us: we wanted to go to the holy city of Qom and interview a senior cleric for BBC television. For the rest of the time we did not even tell the Ministry where we were going, nor did they ask. At no time during any of our visits were we followed, as far as we could tell. It is of course possible that Mahmoudi reported on us to the Ministry or to the security police, though knowing him this seemed unlikely. Anyway, we could easily have flown or gone by bus rather than drive, and nobody would have been the wiser.

By about 1984, the atmosphere in Iran was noticeably more relaxed than it had been. The revolution and its bloody aftermath were starting to recede in people's minds, and the fervour which had created it was fading fast. The regime's asceticism, which had originally seemed rather appealing to most Iranians, was fading too. By the mid-1980s it was apparent that the official corruption which had characterised the Shah's rule had returned. Revolutionary Guards were not immune to the offer of money, and if you were a businessman there was usually a government official or a mullah who would, for a consideration, put you in touch with the right people. The vanished class of courtiers was being replaced by a new élite. The atmosphere of intense religiosity had begun to change. It was much rarer to find people praying five times a day, as they did at the time of the revolution. Persians had rarely been very intense about religion in the past; now they were reverting to their old ways.

Immediately after the revolution some mullahs had condemned the use of telephones and watching television as worldly and dangerously westernised. Ten years later anyone who held those views ran the risk of being openly mocked. Practical considerations like the rapid growth in

population began to figure in public statements; the use of birth control
was advocated in Friday Prayer sermons. There were increasing signs
of common sense on potentially contentious issues such as the practice of
organ transplants. The religious conservatives had accepted the need for
income tax and sales tax: things some of them had once denounced as
unIslamic. And whereas some Muslim idealists had originally spoken
in almost Marxist terms of the withering away of government
and the establishment of 'pure Islam', by the end of the Islamic
Republic's first decade scarcely anyone questioned that the clergy were
administering an essentially secular state, even if some of them still
professed to regard it as the beginning of the reign of God on earth.

None of Iran's religious leaders had had any experience of the non-
Islamic world. Of the senior clerics who came to power in 1979 only
one, Ayatollah Mohammed Beheshti, had spent time abroad (mostly
in the German Democratic Republic) and had learned German and
some English. His more open ways and greater understanding of the
world outside Iran's borders might have made him a useful successor
to Khomeini, but he was assassinated in 1981. For the most part, since
the study of the Koran was assumed to contain everything necessary
for human life, no great attention was paid by those who ran the
government and the Islamic Republican Party to the detailed business
of administration.

The civil service was different. A large majority of the men and
women who had been in senior positions in the Shah's administration
had left the country after the revolution. Many of those who stayed
were imprisoned, and some were executed. The upper echelons of every
ministry in Tehran were almost entirely empty when the revolutionaries
formed their government. But men, and a smaller number of women, were
available to fill the places. The universities of Europe and the United
States were full of Iranian students in the last years of the Shah: many
of them had taken refuge there in order to escape prosecution at home.
It was people like these who flocked to Neauphle-le-Château to link up
with Khomeini's revolution, and who flew back to Iran to take part in
it, or to join in the business of reconstruction when the revolution was
over. They were young, energetic and well-educated; and they quickly
filled the upper ranks of the civil service.

A great many of them had been influenced by the writings of Dr
Ali Shariati, who had studied at the University of Paris from 1960 to
1965. After obtaining his doctorate there he returned to Iran. Already
there was a good deal of unease among the clergy about the Shah's
determination to westernise Iran, and when Shariati began lecturing on
politics and religion he quickly made an important reputation for himself.
Soon, cassettes of his lectures were being passed around among those of
the younger generation who had an education and a social conscience. He
appealed to many of them in a way that another teacher and philosopher,

Al-e Ahmad, older and more insular than Shariati, did not. Al-e Ahmad greatly influenced some groups of far-left-wing students and his writings had a pervasive effect on most aspects of opposition to the Shah; but it was Shariati who fuelled their resentment of Iran's dependence on, and cultural subservience to, the West.

He also articulated the alienation which so many better-off, young, Western-educated Iranians instinctively felt. He pointed up the contrast between what they had been taught abroad and what they knew to be happening at home. Young men and women who rejected all this as shabby and corrupt found that Shariati touched their innermost feelings. He died at the age of forty-four at Southampton, in England, having felt obliged to leave Iran. It was alleged that he had been poisoned by the SAVAK, but this was never established. His only real memorial is a long boulevard named after him in the north of Tehran, cutting through the wealthy suburbs of Qolhak and Shemiran, where people not known for their longing to return to their Islamic roots have homes. Under his influence the intellectual resistance to the Shah allied itself with the religious resistance; together, the two strands brought about the revolution. The generation which was attracted by Shariati provided the majority of government ministries in Iran with their senior civil servants: men whose loyalties to the clerics who ran the government were strong, but who came from a better-educated background than any cleric.

The revolution of 1978–9 was supported by a whole range of political parties and groups, most of which had been illegal under the Shah. The strange alliance of left-wing groups and religious fundamentalists, which had obsessed the Shah and bewildered outside observers, quickly broke up once the revolution was complete. The religious movement which had crystallised around the person of Ayatollah Khomeini was as ruthless as the Bolsheviks in stamping out its revolutionary allies. One of its victims was the Tudeh or Communist Party, largely controlled by Moscow, which had joined the alliance for purely tactical reasons. The Soviet Union was nervous about the prospect of a Muslim revolution in a neighbouring country as important as Iran, and instructed the Tudeh Party to break its links with the revolutionary government quickly. The Fedayeen, split into a minority and a majority faction, were well-disciplined and played an important part in the revolution itself, but soon fell out with each other and with their former allies. In 1981 the revolutionary government started arresting and executing large numbers of Fedayeen members, and effectively drove the group out of politics altogether.

The other main force in the revolution was the Mojaheddin-e-Khalq, a complex and interesting movement with a powerful flair for public relations. It was larger, more self-confident and more aggressive than the other groups on the far left, and was not prepared to be pushed aside. It had been founded in 1963 as an attempt to fuse Islamic fundamentalism with Marxism, influenced perhaps by the ideas of Ali Shariati. The combination was not always an easy one.

The US State Department believed that the Mojaheddin were as dangerous an enemy of the United States as the Islamic Republic itself, and in a report in the Congressional Record in 1992 it listed those whom the Mojaheddin had murdered: an American military adviser, Lieut. Col. Lewis Hawkins, in 1973; two US Air Force officers and a local employee of the American Embassy in 1975; and three American employees of Rockwell International in 1976. The State Department also maintained that the Mojaheddin had supported the takeover of the US Embassy in Tehran and the holding of the American hostages. By this stage the Mojaheddin had become by far the best organised of the Iranian opposition groups and had obtained a remarkable degree of international support. It now presented itself as a serious, democratic political party, and found the State Department report deeply embarrassing. It replied that at the time of the murders its top leadership had been in gaol, and that the murders of Americans had been the work of radical Marxist factions within the organisation, rather than of the group as a whole. It also claimed that it had not supported the takeover of the American Embassy; though, if so, it kept extremely quiet about it at the time, and certainly gave the impression that it approved of what was being done.

Abol-Hassan Bani-Sadr, who had played a key part in the revolution by encouraging Khomeini to go to Paris, was elected President of the Islamic Republic in 1980 with the support of the Mojaheddin and other radical groups. Khomeini, however, had begun to use a powerful term of abuse against the Mojaheddin, calling them *monafegin*, a word inherited from the time of the Prophet and meaning 'splitters' or 'hypocrites'. Soon Khomeini was openly siding with Bani-Sadr's political opponents. By the summer of 1981 it was clear that Khomeini was planning to depose Bani-Sadr as President, and in July he and the Mojaheddin leader, Massoud Rajavi, escaped to France together and set up their headquarters in a house in the village of Auvers-sur-Oise to the north of Paris. It looked like a conscious attempt to repeat the success of Neauphle-le-Château three years earlier.

During the four weeks before the two men left Iran, the Mojaheddin began an all-out campaign to overthrow Khomeini's regime. On 28 June sixty pounds of dynamite exploded at the headquarters of the ruling Islamic Republic Party in east Tehran during a secret meeting of the party's leadership. Among the dead were Bani-Sadr's main rival, Ayatollah Beheshti, who was the party's secretary-general, plus four cabinet ministers, six under-secretaries in charge of government ministries, twenty-seven members of the Majlis, and several other senior officials. Altogether, seventy-four people lost their lives in the explosion.

During the first week of August there were thirty attacks of different kinds, in which fifty people were assassinated and fifty more died in bomb explosions. It was beginning to look as if the Mojaheddin would destroy the entire structure of the regime. In the weeks that followed their bombs killed the new President, Mohammed-Ali Raja'i; the new prime minister, Mohammed-Javad Bahonar; the chief of the national police force; the heads of military intelligence, civilian intelligence, and counter-intelligence; the prosecutor-general; the leaders of Friday Prayers in Kermanshah, Kerman, Tabriz, Yazd, Shiraz, and a number of lesser towns and cities; the governor of Evin gaol; the leading theorist of the Islamic Republic Party; the governor-general of Gilan province; and a large number of judges, Majlis members, officers in the Revolutionary Guards and civil servants. Altogether more than two thousand senior figures are thought to have died in the Mojaheddin's campaign.

Their strategists believed the moment had come for a final push against the regime; and they began staging sudden armed marches through the streets of Tehran and other cities, which resulted in pitched battles with the Revolutionary Guards. The intention was to stretch Khomeini's forces beyond the point where they could cope; it was a tactic which had worked well during the revolution. But whereas the Shah's army had lacked experience in street-fighting, had been unsettled in its loyalties, and had conflicting orders about shooting to kill, the Revolutionary Guards had no such problems. On 27 September 1981 several hundred Mojaheddin fighters staged an all-out battle with the Guards close to Tehran University, and suffered heavy losses. It was the end of the Mojaheddin's hopes of toppling the government. From now on, there would be no question of permitting political opposition groups to operate openly in Iran, and an officially-encouraged paranoia created by the fear of assassination swept the country. Before the Mojaheddin's campaign, people had been executed in their hundreds. Now the regime's victims would be numbered in thousands.

The Mojaheddin settled into exile, operating through the National Council of Resistance (*Shawra-ye Melli-ye Moqavamat*). Over the years the Council has attracted large numbers of other groups and personalities – 109 of them at the time of writing – in an effort to give the appearance of a broad-based opposition. The claim to include the National Front, which had once been the main conventional political party opposing the Shah and was largely composed of liberal nationalists, but had broken up as a result of the pressures of the revolution. Significant figures like Shahpour Bakhtiar, who as prime minister had bridged the gap between the Shah's regime and the revolutionary government, appeared sympathetic to the National Council of Resistance (NCR).

Yet it was run in a fashion which made some NCR supporters feel distinctly uneasy. The Mojaheddin-e-Khalq remained at the heart of it, and Massoud Rajavi, the Mojaheddin leader, encouraged a cult of the personality which some of his opponents likened to the Moonies. Rajavi was in fact a quiet, impressive and rather unassuming man in person, but his followers were encouraged to think of him in hero-worshipping terms:

> You, Massoud, have saved me and given me a new life. It was you who illuminated history. It was you who bridged the gulf between us mortals and the Prophets. It was you who brought us closer to the Prophets and the Saints. It was you who saved Iran and the world from the false Islam cooked up by the corrupt, hypocritical and power-hungry clergy.

So runs a personal testimony from one of the organisation's newspapers, *Mojahed*, in 1985. Over the years that followed, the cult of personality grew. So did the similarity with the Moonies. The Mojaheddin's volunteers were required to live in communal households and hand over their financial assets to the movement. They also had to provide the supervisors with a full list of everything they had done during the day. The evening's prayer, which was compulsory, was followed by an equally compulsory chanted greeting to Rajavi. Self-criticism ceremonies were common.

Mojaheddin supporters needed the organisation's permission to marry, and there were sometimes mass weddings, Moonie-style. Marriage, indeed, seemed to play a remarkably important part in the Mojaheddin's system. Rajavi married the daughter of Abol-Hassan Bani-Sadr soon after they had fled to Paris, but by 1985 the Central Committee and Politburo of the Mojaheddin (for despite their efforts to woo American support there is a distinctly Marxist–Leninist tone to the organisation) were asking Rajavi to marry Maryam Azodlanu, the wife of one of his closest associates. The new Mrs Rajavi became co-leader of the organisation, equal with Rajavi himself; and the photographs of her, complete with headscarf, became as commonplace as his own. By 1994 Maryam Rajavi was the titular president of the organisation.

Its public relations system bombarded foreign opinion-makers with faxes, and its petitions against the cruelties of the Khomeini regime were signed by tens of thousands of people who might know little about the Mojaheddin but were certain that they disliked the reactionary policies of the Islamic Republic. Many leading figures in Britain, France and the United States lent their support to the movement's campaigns. Its publicity handouts were expensively produced, and it maintained a radio station and information centres in at least fourteen cities in Europe and North America. At airports and in the streets volunteers would stop passers-by, open elaborately compiled folders containing pictures of torture and execution in the Islamic Republic, and ask for their support.

The most generous supporter was President Saddam Hussein of Iraq. Sections of the Mojaheddin's organisation were based in Iraq, including its military wing, the National Liberation Army (NLA), which had its headquarters about sixty miles from the Iranian border. The organisation claimed that it had 40,000 troops, but 15,000 is probably a more accurate figure: one-third of them were women. Its weaponry was largely supplied by Iraq. In July 1988, during the last weeks of the Iran–Iraq war, NLA units were sent into Iran in an operation called 'Eternal Light', in support of a major Iraqi offensive. The NLA force, which had been told that ordinary Iranians would welcome it with open arms, briefly held the towns of Kerend and Eslamabad-e-Gharb. Soon, however, the Iranian army counterattacked and Saddam Hussein characteristically ordered the withdrawal of Iraqi air cover. The NLA's fate was sealed, and many of its troops were torn to pieces by local people. According to a report by the Congressional Research Service in Washington in November 1992, 'Saddam ... used the NLA as a bargaining chip in relations with Iran, unleashing the group when relations deteriorated and reining it in when relations improved.'

The Mojaheddin reportedly keeps an underground resistance movement within Iran, though whenever a bomb attack is carried out and civilians are killed the organisation's fax machines are quickly in use to deny any responsibility; the National Council of Resistance presents itself as a highly respectable body which does not wish to be associated with terrorism. It is hard to find any public sympathy within Iran for the Mojaheddin, however. Perhaps this is merely because the penalties for being a supporter are so great; but people often explain with a good deal of feeling that they could not support a group which helped Saddam Hussein against its own country, nor one which was so extreme during the revolution. Despite their impressive organisation and the large amounts of money they clearly have to spend, the Mojaheddin have not managed to persuade people in Iran that they would be a suitable replacement for the Islamic Republic.

After 1981 the Islamic Republic Party was the only political grouping which was permitted to organise or hold seats in the Majlis. Nevertheless it was a coalition, representing opinion from conservatism to radicalism and pragmatism, and in June 1987 it was abruptly wound up because the leadership was worried that the fierce political infighting at the heart of the IRP might begin to destabilise the Islamic Republic itself. For a time, no parties of any kind were permitted. But in the run-up to the parliamentary election of 1992, two political groupings were allowed to form and canvass votes in opposition to one another. Ludicrously, their names were almost identical: the Combatant Clergymen's Association, which was strongly radical and inclined to oppose the government, and the Society of Combatant Clergymen, which supported the government's efforts to open up the Iranian economy to the outside world.

What divided the factions in Iran was precisely the issue which divided the left and right in most Western countries: how much should the state involve itself in the economic and social life of the country? In Iran the radicals, who could usually rely on the support of Ayatollah Khomeini, regarded the state as the chief guarantor of their vision of the Islamic Republic. It had a duty to protect the moral standards which the revolution had established: which meant using the *Komitehs* and the Revolutionary Guards to police strict codes of dress and behaviour. Even more importantly, it meant that the state had to control the economy in ways that seemed almost Soviet, in order to cut out any unhealthy influence from the outside world and particularly the West. Iran, in the radicals' view, had to be a siege economy where there would be no borrowing abroad and no infiltration by foreign companies. Finally, they wanted an aggressive foreign policy in the Middle East and elsewhere, which would challenge Western interests and promote the spread of fundamentalist Islam.

The radicals were usually in the minority. Most of the deputies in the Majlis were supporters of the line which is known in the West as 'pragmatic'; that is, they accepted that the economy had suffered badly as a result of Iran's isolation from the outside world, and they blamed this isolation on the extremist foreign policies of the radicals: in particular, supporting terrorism in various parts of the world and the taking of Western hostages in Lebanon. As time went on, the fact that the divisions in Iranian politics had to be submerged instead of allowed out in the open began to cause very real problems for the government of the country. And by the 1990s it was starting to make Iran almost ungovernable.

Because it proved to be capable of a certain degree of adaptation the Islamic Revolution did not collapse when Khomeini died in 1989, as so many foreign commentators had confidently predicted. The revolution had dug itself in too well for that, and it had destroyed any serious alternative to itself. Nor was it dependent any longer on the personal charisma of a single leader.

Nevertheless Khomeini's death weakened the Islamic Republic in subtler ways. While he was alive he had always been able to quell the disagreements within the government and the clergy on any given issue by pronouncing his own opinion on it. After his death, there was no one to judge the disputes. The way was open for power struggles and for bitter disputes about policy. Khomeini had set out the qualities of purity and wisdom which someone holding the office of *velayet-e-faqih*, the Guardianship of the Faith, should possess, in Article 5 of the Constitution:

> The leadership of affairs and the guidance of the people is the responsibility of a just and pious law-giver who is aware of the spirit of the times, is courageous, and possesses drive and initiative. The majority of the people should know and accept him to be their Leader.

But no one really fitted this description, once Khomeini was dead, and the government could not agree on any single ayatollah to take his place. As a result, the Constitution had to be amended to allow the one person almost everyone could accept – the country's President, Hojat al-Eslam Ali Khamene'i, who was only a middle-ranking cleric – to be appointed. Ali Akbar Rafsanjani, the Speaker of the Majlis and commander-in-chief of the armed forces, who was closest to Ayatollah Khomeini and had become the most powerful political figure in the country as a result, insisted that on his deathbed the Ayatollah had named Khamene'i to succeed him as *faqih*.

Perhaps it was true. Khamene'i certainly had excellent revolutionary credentials: he was a student of Khomeini's, he had been imprisoned twice under the Shah, and had been seriously injured by a bomb at a Friday Prayer service in 1981. After his recovery he was appointed to the Supreme War Council. He had not, however, fulfilled the usual scholarly requirements which enabled him to be considered a senior religious figure. This was immediately rectified by a special meeting of the Assembly of Experts, which duly proclaimed him an ayatollah. It was a neat piece of theological manoeuvring, which solved the immediate problem of the appointment of the new *faqih*; but it gave plenty of scope to discontented clerics to question the validity of the whole operation.

Rafsanjani then took Khamene'i's place as President: which may have been the purpose behind the whole business. A round-faced, plump, smooth-chinned cleric born in 1934, Rafsanjani was another of Khomeini's pupils and was also jailed under the Shah. He took an active but not particularly prominent part in setting up the revolutionary *Komitehs* which established Khomeini's dominance in Iran in 1978 even before the Shah left. After the revolution he received another mark of status: he was injured in a Mojaheddin bomb attack. He was one of the founders of the Islamic Republican Party, and became deputy Minister of the Interior. But it was in the openness of debate in the Majlis that Rafsanjani emerged from the junior ranks of government and made himself the foremost power in Iran after Khomeini himself. In July 1980 his eloquence and his ability to chivvy the other members along were rewarded when he was elected Speaker. After that, with the proceedings of the Majlis being broadcast regularly on television and reprinted in the newspapers, Rafsanjani's rise was assured.

His alliance with the top leadership of the Revolutionary Guards made him the spokesman of the most effective military force in the country. This was essential when Iran's military position worsened in May 1988 in the war with Iraq, and he was appointed sole commander of all the armed forces. Seven weeks later, in July, Rafsanjani had persuaded Khomeini that the war was unwinnable. It was a decision which Khomeini reached reluctantly and with great bitterness, but it saved further unnecessary bloodshed and demonstrated the strength of Rafsanjani's political influence. His promotion to President, when Khamene'i took the post of *faqih*, appeared to set the seal on his power.

In the Majlis they were debating the economy. It was a heated affair, as Majlis debates often were. But the Speaker was there to ensure that the members observed the proper procedure, as in a Western parliament. On one of the benches at the back was a cleric in a white turban: a man with heavy-rimmed glasses and a knowing smirk on his face. He seemed interested in what was being said and followed the action carefully, but he rarely spoke nowadays, and the empty places around him seemed to indicate that his colleagues in the Majlis were not enthusiastic about being associated with him. Hojat-ol-Eslam Sadeq Khalkhali had once personified the farthest extremes of fervour. One of his milder proposals was to rename the Persian Gulf the Islamic Gulf. The Western media incorrectly promoted him to the rank of Ayatollah and nicknamed him the 'hanging judge' for his leading role in ordering the execution of hundreds of victims of the revolution. Khalkhali was yet another student of Ayatollah Khomeini, and served his apprenticeship as an organiser of many of the violent protests against the Shah in the early 1960s.

Khalkhali's loyalty to Khomeini during the years of exile in Iraq stood him in good stead when the Ayatollah returned. His ruthlessness was placed at the disposal of the revolution in the first days after the victory in the streets. At the start of the revolution, when General Rahimi and other military leaders were captured, there were considerable fears that a rescue attempt might be staged by the Americans or the Iranian army; Rahimi himself appeared to believe that such an attempt would be made. Khalkhali volunteered to conduct a rapid trial of the generals, after which they could be shot.

It was the start of a career during which Khalkhali sentenced several hundred people to death. Among them were Amir-Abbas Hoveyda, the Shah's former prime minister; a former senator aged 102 who had attacked Khomeini in a speech sixteen years earlier; an unknown number of wounded Kurdish prisoners, shot as they lay on their stretchers; and a sixteen-year-old boy whose pleas of innocence were dismissed on the grounds that if he were genuinely innocent he would go to Paradise anyway. During one six-week period in 1981 Khalkhali ordered the executions of two hundred alleged drug-users. Soon after he threatened the members of the imperial family with death, the Shah's nephew was murdered in Paris. In full view of the world's television cameras, he toyed with the charred remains of an American serviceman killed in President Carter's bungled attempt to rescue the American hostages in 1980. For most people who watched the pictures of the incident abroad, it fixed in their minds once and for all the notion that Iran had surrendered itself to medieval barbarity.

Some figures in the Iranian government believed that Khalkhali was a liability. But he kept his seat in the Majlis, and managed to be elected to the foreign affairs committee; when the peace negotiations opened with Iraq in September 1988, Khalkhali went to Geneva to act as the committee's observer. He was protected as long as Ayatollah Khomeini was alive because he was one of those with – as Khomeini put it – a 'commitment to Islam'. He and his fellow radicals continued to push for a state-dominated economy and an activist foreign policy.

Once Rafsanjani was in a position to determine the requirements for political advancement, after Khomeini's death, he built up the powers of the presidency with a series of constitutional amendments. As he consolidated his power, Rafsanjani began weeding out the radicals of whom Khalkhali was one. It was easy enough to get rid of cabinet ministers and administrative staff in the various ministries, but replacing the elected members of the Majlis was rather more difficult. First Rafsanjani enlisted his ideological allies in the Majlis to confront the radicals over their policies. Since the Majlis debates were broadcast on radio and television, it was a useful way of bringing the drive against them to public attention. During a debate at the end of 1991, Ghassem Sholeh Saadi, a deputy from Shiraz, asked the radicals what they could offer the country now that their previous policies had been so unsuccessful.

> Your political insight reached its peak when you called on the House to fight under the banner of Saddam Hussein when he invaded Kuwait. And then you wanted it to recognise the coup [of August 1991] in the Soviet Union. Might it not be better if you kept quiet for a while now?

Under the Islamic Republic, Iran became one of the few countries in the Middle East where people could change their government through the ballot box, highly restricted though the choices invariably were. There has long been a certain limited tradition of independence in the Majlis. The Shah tried to silence parliament when it became awkward; but instead of prohibiting elections to it, he controlled the candidates

who were eligible to stand. The Islamic Republic followed the same
pattern. Many parties were forbidden, and the counting of votes was
never carried out in the presence of independent observers. Nevertheless,
by comparison with most other Islamic countries, there was a democracy
of a kind.

Controlling access to the Majlis was therefore essential to Rafsanjani
and Khamene'i. They first turned to the Council of Guardians, the
committee responsible for making sure that all legislation passed by
the Majlis was compatible with the *Sharia*, or Islamic law. The Council
was packed with conservative clerics appointed by Ayatollah Khomeini,
who took the same view of the radicals as the President and the country's
new spiritual leader. They therefore devised a theological examination for
members of the powerful Assembly of Experts, which was effectively the
most senior religious body in Iran. Some members of the Assembly were
insulted at being subjected to this kind of scholastic scrutiny, and refused
to undergo the test. Others, Khalkhali among them, agreed to do so. It
was an error of judgement on his part. He failed the examination, as it
had been intended that he should, and was declared to be insufficiently
qualified to sit in judgement on the selection of a future spiritual leader.

Khalkhali's position was seriously weakened. He was next subjected
to a screening process devised by the Council of Guardians to check
the qualifications of those wanting to stand at the next Majlis election.
It was no great surprise when he was eliminated, together with a
number of other key radicals including Ayatollah Mehdi Karubi, the
Speaker of the Parliament. Khalkhali issued a statement blaming agents
of America for his political demise: 'We have become the target of
anger because of our courage, frankness and clear opposition to the
interests of the US in the region.'

By November 1991, one hundred radical Majlis deputies, suspecting
that they would be barred from standing in the April 1992 elections,
signed a statement openly challenging the position of Ayatollah Ali
Khamene'i and demanding that he should be replaced by Ayatollah
Hossein Ali Montazeri, the man whom Khomeini had originally named
as his successor and then dismissed three months before his death.
Afterwards Montazeri was banished to Qom. He had been a surprisingly
trenchant critic of the Islamic Republic's record. In a speech to the annual
conference of the Iranian Association of Muslim Students in October 1988
he had criticised the government for refusing to listen to the voices of
dissent, and for its abuses of human rights:

People have complained to me that their relatives, while serving
short prison sentences for political offences, have been executed
without any explanation. This is not how our Islamic justice should
operate.

A month later Montazeri attacked the use of arbitrary arrests and torture:

> All the present shortcomings – discrimination, social injustice, the low earnings of the deprived sectors of society, and soaring prices – are the natural consequences of the policies of your government. We are not going to solve anything by torturing, imprisoning and executing our opponents . . . The excessive internal policies of your government must end, and those responsible must be brought to justice.

His criticisms were directed against the radicals' way of doing things; and yet, three years later, when the radicals found their influence dwindling, they turned to Montazeri whom they then chose to view as a fellow victim of Rafsanjani's rise. By the autumn of 1991, the oppressive methods which Ayatollah Montazeri had condemned were used against a group of Majlis deputies who travelled to Qom for an 'unauthorised' meeting with Montazeri, their new figurehead. Two of the deputies were arrested and charged with 'conspiracy against Imam Khomeini's decrees'. Montazeri himself was allowed to continue teaching, but his offices were ransacked and some of his aides were arrested. Despite the fact that he was suffering from heart and kidney problems, Montazeri was not allowed to go to Tehran for medical treatment. The country's leadership, headed by Rafsanjani and Khamene'i, was determined that he should stay well away from the centre of political power.

The first parliamentary elections since Khomeini's death were scheduled for 10 April 1992. One-third of the list of three thousand candidates for the Majlis had been weeded out by the Council of Guardians. Electioneering took the form of a few poorly attended rallies in the street in front of the Majlis building: sometimes fewer than a dozen people would bother to stop and listen. Coverage of the election on television was heavily weighted in favour of Rafsanjani; not surprisingly, given that his brother ran the television service. There was little interest in the election among the voters. When a leading member of the pro-Rafsanjani Society of Combatant Clergymen gave a news conference, a German journalist asked him to explain what their platform was. The mullah looked surprised. 'That will become clear after the election,' he said.

The election was held, as always, on a Friday. Queues formed at many of the polling stations, and there were more women than I had expected: perhaps a third of all the voters. There were also plenty of young people. The voting age in Iran was fifteen, one of the lowest in the world, because the age of army service had been lowered to fifteen during the war with Iraq and the familiar argument had been put forward that those who were old enough to die for their country were old enough to vote for its government. The ballot papers had no names on them; the electors had to write in the names of the candidates they supported. Many people couldn't remember who was standing in their district, and there were long discussions about the way their names were spelled. It was scarcely a secret ballot in the Western sense, yet some degree of choice was being exercised.

Among the prominent names which everyone remembered was that of Ali Akbar Hosseini, a mullah who was also a television presenter and had not been involved in politics before. His programme *Ethics in the Family* was popular, especially among women; they responded by voting for him in large numbers. Hosseini's line on television had been moderately liberal: where there were family disagreements he advised everyone to talk things over, and he urged husbands to value their wives and to give them presents for their continual hard work. Among the other successful candidates were the president of Tehran University and several prominent doctors who were new to politics.

The real winner was President Rafsanjani. He had succeeded in creating a large and compliant majority for himself in the Majlis, and the people who had voted for him wanted him to have a free hand in government. The voting pattern showed plainly that people preferred reform to radicalism. That meant an end to economic hardship, and a greater opening to the West. Rafsanjani, the 'pragmatist', seemed to have the perfect qualifications to do the job. He had enjoyed the full backing of Ayatollah Khomeini, which meant that his ideological flank was secured; and yet he had the flexibility of mind to make the very considerable changes that would be necessary. Now, through ruthless manoeuvring, he had lined up the political pieces as well. Everything seemed to be in place, and the only problem would be if, despite everything, Rafsanjani failed to deliver. He would have no excuses then.

The problem he faced was two-fold. In the first place, the political process in Iran had genuine meaning: it was never simply a charade, as it was in the Soviet Union under Stalin or Brezhnev where the Party controlled everything and public opinion meant nothing. On the contrary, the fact that the debates in the Majlis were broadcast live on Iranian radio meant that Rafsanjani's opponents were able to appeal to public opinion very effectively, blaming him implicitly for so many of the things that were wrong with the country. And they also proved effective at using the procedures of the Majlis to frustrate him. His grand five-year plan for the economy was held up in the Majlis for an entire year by the political manoeuvrings of the radicals, who objected to the fact that it included a borrowing requirement of $27 billion from abroad. The plan was finally passed in 1990, but the delay had done considerable damage to Iran's economy in the meantime.

The second problem Rafsanjani faced was his failure to turn himself into a figure of real authority. There was no one to replace Ayatollah Khomeini. His death should in theory have made the government of the country easier, since it meant there was no longer an ex officio figure who could intervene in the political process at will. The radicals who had been able to get his backing on issues as varied as the *fatwa* against Salman Rushdie and the quality of programmes on Iranian television had lost their only trump card. From the day Khomeini died, their influence was weakened: his death removed the only referee in the often bitter political game. From now on there would be no one who could take the final decision between two factions or two ministers.

The political life of Persia has always been a matter of bitter infighting and plotting. For the most part Khomeini had used his influence to stamp out this kind of thing. Now the jostling for power became general. Every minister, every ministry, gradually joined the fight against every other minister and every other ministry. What one did, another would try to undo. This all-out bureaucratic warfare reached into every aspect of official life. In Iranian embassies abroad the staff, representing different government ministries in Tehran, would compete bitterly with each other for influence and contacts. Once when John was given a visa by the Foreign Ministry, the Ministry of Islamic Guidance sent an official to the airport to countermand it; and it was only because Islamic Guidance made a mistake about the time of the plane's arrival, and the Foreign Ministry official was more senior, that John managed to enter the country.

The competition stretched from this kind of level right to the very top of the political system. Rafsanjani and Khamene'i, having been close political allies at the time of Ayatollah Khomeini's death, gradually lapsed into rivalry as well. The country's economic problems gave a great deal of scope to Khamene'i to issue veiled criticisms of Rafsanjani; and clashes over the appointment of individual civil servants led to more bad feeling between them. Rafsanjani was never able to establish himself in a strong enough position to forestall the efforts of his rivals and enemies to manipulate his actions for their own political purposes. Instead of establishing himself as the most powerful figure in Iran, he became the leading symbol in most people's minds of the impossibility of achieving anything in the Hobbesian political war of every man against every man.

In June 1993, only fourteen months after the elections to the Majlis, Rafsanjani's first presidential term ended and he had to stand for re-election. Despite the pleasant early-summer weather there were no big queues outside the polling stations this time. Most people took the day off; they visited friends in the countryside, they walked in the Albourz foothills, they gave parties for their friends and relations. As I drove round the city, inspecting the polling stations, it was obvious that the turnout would not be high. Most people seemed to believe that Rafsanjani was incapable of honouring his promises, and they preferred to forget about the political process that day.

A little over half the electorate voted. Rafsanjani duly won a second four-year term (according to the Constitution it would have to be his last) but his reduced majority was seen as a weaker mandate, a protest vote about the economic conditions of the country and the lack of clear political direction. In the 1989 presidential election Rafsanjani had received 94.5 per cent of the vote; this time the figure was only 63.2 per cent, even though the three challengers who had been approved to run against him by the Council of Guardians (which Rafsanjani, of course, controlled) were all considered unelectable and were generally disliked. It is reasonable to assume, therefore, that most people who voted for them did so as a protest. In some provinces, especially those where there were large Kurdish populations, Rafsanjani's lacklustre opponents actually beat him.

A few days later those Tehran newspapers which supported Rafsanjani and his Combatant Clergymen party started a campaign to show that by the standards of other countries Rafsanjani had performed well. The *Tehran Times*, for instance, printed tables to indicate that his majority was greater than those of Clinton, Mitterrand or Reagan. It was scarcely very convincing, and the newspaper *'Salaam'*, which supported the radical faction, responded by showing that the turnout had in fact been distinctly lower than the official figure. Rafsanjani, who had once been regarded by the great majority of people as the one man who could bring Iran back to normality and a position of international respectability after the revolution, was now a lame duck.

On Tuesday 6 August, 1991, the house of Shahpour Bakhtiar in the Paris suburb of Suresnes was under guard by French paramilitary police, as it had been ever since the former prime minister had fled Iran in 1979. When one of Bakhtiar's aides, Fereydoun Boyer-Ahmadi, arrived at the house with two guests, the police guards admitted them after a cursory check. Boyer-Ahmadi was on a list of fifteen regular visitors to the house and Bakhtiar, who was now seventy-six, had spoken of him as a second son. Once inside, he introduced the two men as supporters from Tehran. In reality they were agents of the Ministry of Intelligence and Internal Security (*Vezarat-e Ettelaat Va Amniyat-e Kishvar*, or VAVAK, which had taken over most of the name and many of the employees of the old SAVAK). As soon as Soroush Katibeh, Bakhtiar's assistant, had left the room to make tea, the men leapt at Bakhtiar and stabbed him in the throat and body with a couple of kitchen knives which they found in the house. When he returned to the room Katibeh was also butchered. Boyer-Ahmadi, Bakhtiar's 'second son', a handsome, round-faced man, seems to have stood and watched the two murders.

He and the Iranian agents, Ali Vakili Rad and Mohammed Azadi, spent nearly an hour in the house before collecting their passports from the guards and leaving. They had apparently not been in contact with Tehran; it was two days before a British monitoring team in Cyprus picked up a message from VAVAK headquarters to an Iranian embassy in Europe asking for confirmation of Dr Bakhtiar's death and the bodies were discovered. Bakhtiar had been a particularly important target; if he had been captured at the time of the revolution he would probably have been executed then and there. Instead, he escaped to Paris and, as we have seen, joined forces with the Mojaheddin. Western intelligence sources believed that he had knowledge of clandestine forays into Iran by members of the opposition. On all three counts he was a marked man.

Meanwhile the first clues to the trail which led to the arrest of the murderers were discovered: bloodstained shirts and discarded Iranian passports in the Bois de Boulogne, a wallet, filled with Iranian, French and Swiss money, left by accident in a telephone box. From there, the French police traced telephone calls to a flat in Istanbul which was known to have been used by Iranian government agents. Eleven people, including five Iranians, were arrested in Turkey. The two suspects finally succeeded in crossing into Switzerland after a series of blunders; missing a train connection and being turned back on their first attempt by Swiss border guards who spotted the forged visas in their false Turkish passports. Azadi managed to slip out of Switzerland back to Tehran with the help of a contact but Vakili was picked up and extradited to France. Two more suspects in the case were arrested as well. As for Boyer-Ahmadi, he simply disappeared.

Under the direction of a magistrate who was an experienced investigator of terrorist crimes, Jean-Louis Bruguière, the French police launched a major murder investigation. Eighteen volumes of evidence were produced which showed links between the arrested suspects and the Iranian Foreign Ministry, the Telecommunications Ministry, the Ministry of Islamic Guidance and the Iranian television network IRIB. Most intriguing of all was a one-page document issued on the authority of Iran's foreign minister, Ali Akbar Velayati, dispatching one of the suspects, Zeinolabedine Sarhadi, to Switzerland. The French believed his mission there was to help smuggle Bakhtiar's killers out of the country.

There had always been speculation over the extent to which the Iranian government had been involved in the murder of opponents of the Islamic Republic. The chief question was whether President Rafsanjani, generally regarded as a moderate, knew of terrorist missions such as this and approved of them, or whether he was powerless to stop individuals or ministries from carrying out assassinations or bombings. According to the US State Department, the Iranian government committee which sanctions acts of terrorism and murder is the Supreme Defence Council (SDC), on which Rafsanjani has a seat. There is a great deal of doubt about this, however; the SDC is a large committee with a wide membership drawn from the armed forces which are traditionally more straitlaced than the intelligence organisations. It seems unlikely that such sensitive matters would be discussed quite so openly.

The case against Rafsanjani is not proven; but Velayati, his foreign minister, was always close to him, and if Velayati knew about the murder of Dr Bakhtiar then Rafsanjani is likely to have known about it too. And if he knew about the murder of Bakhtiar, it must be reasonable to assume that he knew about other terrorist attacks as well: the blowing-up of the Pan American jumbo jet over Lockerbie in December 1988, for instance, which – while the bomb was probably planted by two Libyan government employees – seems likely to have been carried out on the instructions of elements in the Iranian government in revenge for the shooting down of an Iran Air passenger jet by the USS *Vincennes* earlier in the year. Later, a small explosive device was planted under the car driven by the wife of the *Vincennes'* captain in a quiet suburban street in the United States. An eye for an eye is the governing principle of the Islamic Republic.

Since the revolution, more than sixty Iranian opponents of the regime had been murdered abroad. Members of the Mojaheddin-e-Khalq were particular targets and were assassinated in France, Switzerland, Italy, Pakistan and Turkey. According to the IRA, Iranian agents tried to persuade them to kill Mojaheddin figures in Britain in exchange for cash and weapons. Iranian Kurdish dissidents were also murdered in Europe and the Middle East. Non-Iranians were targeted as well: Turkish intellectuals, Saudis, and a Jordanian, all of whom had links of some kind with Iran. In the violent campaign against Salman Rushdie's book *The Satanic Verses*, the Japanese translator of the book, Hitoshi Igarashia, was murdered, the Italian translator was stabbed and beaten, and a Norwegian publisher was shot. Someone set fire to the hotel where the Turkish translator of Rushdie's book was staying, and distributors and bookshops selling *The Satanic Verses* were threatened. By no means all of these attacks will have been carried out on Tehran's orders, or even with Tehran's knowledge; but it seems reasonable to assume that some of them were; particularly those in Japan, Italy and Norway, where Iran maintains active embassies.

A defector from the VAVAK told an Italian magazine in the late 1980s that the organisation had an annual budget of £120 million ($180 million), and used the Bank Markazi Iran to channel funds to its operatives and informants in Europe, the Middle East and Africa. It was set up, improbably, by a boyhood friend of the Shah, General Hosayn Fardoost, who had been the head of the Imperial Inspectorate, one of the competing intelligence services which the Shah maintained. Despite their personal friendship General Fardoost became convinced during 1978 that the Shah's regime would not last much longer and he made secret contact with Ayatollah Khomeini during the last stages of his exile in Iraq. There were rumours later that he had passed information to the Russians, too, as an insurance in case a Marxist government came to power. No doubt he also kept lines open to the Americans and the British, as reinsurance.

Within days of Khomeini's triumphant return, Fardoost set up a successor organisation to the SAVAK, whose acronym was SAVAMA. At first a number of SAVAK employees were given jobs there, in exchange for handing over their files and their lists of contacts. Neither Fardoost nor SAVAMA were trusted, however; he was arrested and SAVAMA was stripped of most of its SAVAK graduates and metamorphosed into the VAVAK. Its job changed, from competing with and keeping an eye on the big foreign agencies – the CIA, MI6, the KGB and so on – to contacting and controlling terrorist groups and Islamic fundamentalist organisations abroad. In April 1987, for no very clear reason, the VAVAK decided to make an example of its founding father, the Shah's one-time friend General Fardoost. Iranian television broadcast an interview with him, in which he confessed to having been a British agent. At the end of the broadcast an announcer promised that Fardoost would soon give more details of his treachery. But he did not make another appearance. After a month, Tehran Radio announced that Fardoost, who was seventy-six, had died of a heart attack 'under intensive interrogation'.

The VAVAK maintains Iran's links with revolutionary and fundamentalist groups in Egypt, Morocco, Pakistan, Afghanistan and Turkey. In Sudan, the organisation became the main supplier and adviser to the fundamentalist regime of General Omar Al-Beshir, while, according to the US State Department, the Iranian Revolutionary Guards provided training for the Sudanese army. Iran's ambassador in Khartoum is thought to have been involved in the takeover of the American Embassy there. The VAVAK is also responsible for relations between Iran and the Lebanese Shi'ite organisation Hezbollah: for many years Iran's only important asset abroad.

It was not, however, an easy asset to manage. Hezbollah was filled with enthusiastic and pious Shi'ites, but they were independent-minded and did not take easily to being ordered about by Tehran. They kidnapped the various Western hostages on their own initiative, and when the VAVAK persuaded them to release the occasional one from time to time, it was never easy. A senior figure in the Iranian government once confided to John some of the problems they had in dealing with Hezbollah:

It isn't enough for us to tell them what they must do – release this hostage, or another one. We have to persuade them that we are not being weak, and that they will get some advantage out of it. These people are Shi'i, yes; but they are also Lebanese. They do not give up something in exchange for nothing.

It was relatively easy to persuade Hezbollah to give up two of its hostages in 1986, when Colonel Oliver North offered Iran missiles and other weaponry in exchange for them. But when the other Western countries refused to make such obvious concessions, Hezbollah became much more wary of handing over its most valuable acquisitions. In the end, Iran resorted to a complicated package of inducements (financial and in terms of materiel) and subtle pressures, many of them negotiated through Syria, to ensure that the American and British hostages were released.

American and Israeli officials have maintained that Iran was the guiding force behind other terrorist organisations in the Middle East: those in Egypt and Palestine, for instance. Yet there is little sign of outright Iranian involvement, particularly with the Palestinian group Hamas, which is careful of its reputation in the West and seems to avoid contact with Iran. As in Egypt, the fact that Iran is a Shi'ite country and most Middle Eastern groups are Sunni is a major obstacle to closer relations. All the same, there is a freemasonry among the various extremist organisations which regard Israel and the United States as their chief enemies, and as in the case of the Lockerbie bombing one group will often help another.

It is as well not to become too hysterical about Iran's terrorist links, however. As the murder of Dr Bakhtiar showed, the VAVAK is often clumsy and inefficient, and it is inclined to concentrate on easy, relatively safe targets: exiles who have no means of protecting themselves. Often the expertise of Hezbollah lies behind the bombings designed to make political points for Iran: the bombing of the World Trade Center in New York in 1993, for instance, or those in July 1994 at a Jewish community centre in Buenos Aires, which killed almost a hundred people, and at the Israeli Embassy in London. Iran had made itself a natural target for suspicion even though it had denied responsibility for the bombings: not only did the government in Tehran refuse to condemn them, but several Iranian newspapers described the explosions as legitimate targets in a just war. Yet it is almost certainly a mistake to assume that there is necessarily any overall control of terrorism by the Iranian government. In this, as in so much else, the infighting between the various ministries and agencies means that any number of groups are tempted to act on their own. It is one of the penalties of political weakness.

                              *   *   *

I was being driven too fast down the motorway in a comfortable German car, enjoying the spring day. My camera team and I had been trying to arrange an interview with a deputy minister and had run into a very Iranian combination of endless delay from some officials in the ministry and the seemingly sincere desire of others to help. In the car with me was one of the helpful-tendency officials, Hossain, a man who appeared to be refreshingly free from the anti-imperialist dogma I had been treated to earlier in the day. By chance, he had strolled through the office of the head of red tape when I was presenting my request. Now he and his driver were dropping me off at the Laleh Hotel on their way to an appointment somewhere else. No doubt he enjoyed the unusual experience of giving a lift in his ministry car to a Western woman.

Hossain was an intriguing character. He had travelled often in the United States and Europe and spoke good conversational English; and although he wasn't dressed in up-to-the-minute north Tehran style, his well-fitting cream shirt was clearly imported. His trousers were casual but well cut, and even his Islamically acceptable three-day stubble was carefully tended. He was fascinated by the Primaries for the 1992 American presidential election which were then in progress; in fact he was better informed about the campaign platforms of Clinton, Bush and Ross Perot than I was.

'Well,' he said when I told him so, 'I listen every night to reports of their campaigning on BBC World Service television. I get it on my satellite dish.'

He saw my surprise and asked teasingly, 'Would you like to know the latest football result in England? I can tell you that too.'

His parents had moved to Texas at the start of the revolution: an unusual background for a man who appeared to be in the fast stream of his ministry. I asked why he hadn't gone abroad like his parents. Hossain explained that his sense of justice and equality had been offended by the Shah's regime and he believed in the revolution. He had been in Jaleh Square on Black Friday, 8 September 1978, when hundreds of demonstrators had been gunned down. For Hossain and many others, Jaleh Square was an emotional turning point which had finally demonstrated the underlying brutality of the Shah's regime.

Inevitably, he was also out in the streets when Ayatollah Khomeini returned, and he had offered his services to the new revolutionary government. It was after the initial euphoria of the revolution that Hossain's family had decided to leave the country. When Saddam Hussein provided an unexpected source of unity for the new government by invading Iran in 1980, Hossain volunteered for the army.

'Even if I disagreed with some things that were going on,' he said, 'this was my country and we had been attacked. Of course I had to fight.'

He survived the war uninjured, although he lost many friends. When he returned from the front, he took up his old job in the Ministry once again, with the same quiet dedication that had taken him to the battlefield. His reward was rapid promotion.

Hossain still went to visit his family in America for a month every summer, and he appeared to like the country immensely. He told me about the places he had visited and films he had seen on his last trip, and I realised then where he had bought his clothes: The Gap, a mildly expensive chain shop with an outlet on every shopping mall in the United States. Over the next few days my colleagues and I saw a good deal of Hossain at the Ministry, and shared several midday meals with him at a local *chelo kebab* restaurant. One night we invited him to join us for dinner, but he refused on the grounds that his presence might make our Iranian friends uneasy. He grinned, and added that it might also inhibit us from drinking something stronger than fruit juice.

We went to Isfahan for a few days, and met him again on our return to Tehran. I told him how beautiful we had found it, and how many Iranian people seemed to be spending their honeymoons there.

'Maybe I should go and take some photographs to send to my girlfriend in New York,' he mused. 'Then she will remember that there are some things in Iran that are the best in the world. At the moment she doesn't want to come back because she doesn't want to wear *hejab*.'

Towards the end of our trip, we insisted that Hossain should join us for a meal at a friend's house. The friend, I said, certainly wouldn't be uneasy, and we were all happy to drink fruit juice for one night. He collected us at our hotel and we began the usual battle through the Tehran traffic. John and I sat in the back, chatting about our day, while Hossain and the driver talked to one another in the front. The radio was on loudly. We were laughing about something when we realised that Hossain and the driver had gone quiet: the radio was broadcasting the call to prayer. We stopped talking. Hossain opened the glove compartment and rummaged around until he found a cassette and put it into the player. A song that had once won the Eurovision Song Contest replaced the wail of the call to prayer. He and his driver resumed their conversation. So did we.

Directly we entered our friends' house we were on private property and I could take off my headscarf and my hot, uncomfortable *roupush*. Hossain smiled slightly when he saw how relieved I was to be getting out of my *hejab*. The dinner was pleasant, and everyone seemed relaxed. At the end, as we left, he shook John's hand as usual. As a good servant of the Islamic Revolution, he had never previously shaken mine. This time he raised his eyebrows and put out his hand.

'I think you won't mind,' he said as I took it.

Hossain was a loyal official who had fought for his country. But he was also a natural liberal, a man who believed that journalists should be allowed to work freely in Iran. The next time we were in Iran, one of our first calls was to his ministry. He wasn't there. I asked finally if he had changed jobs, but the answers always seemed evasive. Finally we heard that he had gone for his usual holiday to the United States some months earlier, and not returned. The Islamic Republic had finally become a little too restrictive for him.

7

The Second Sex

Tira Shubart

When you seek a wife do not demand her possessions also; and look well to her character, refusing to be enslaved by beauty of face – for prettiness, men take a mistress ... Someone asked Alexander why he did not marry Darius's daughter, who was very beautiful. He replied, 'It would be an ugly matter if we, who have become master of all men in the world, should have a woman as master over us.'

A Mirror For Princes

The sofas had been rearranged in a long S-shape to create a sort of catwalk down the middle of the big sitting room. We fidgeted expectantly, sipped our tea, and reached for the bowls of pistachios and dates on the table. There were eight of us altogether, and we had been invited to see the summer collection of one of Iran's few designers of *haute couture*. The designer was inventive and successful, and aged around forty. We will call her Nikki. In another part of the world her work would be in all the newspapers. Here in Iran she was showing her collection to us as though we were part of an underground resistance movement. If there had been any men here and the local *Komiteh* had heard about it, the consequences would have been serious.

Nikki showed her new collections twice a year. The previous summer her outfits had been loose and casual, in russets and golds and beiges. That winter she had concentrated on figure-hugging, sophisticated versions of the little black dress. It was Nikki who set the trends for the richest and most fashion-conscious set in Tehran. The women who wore Nikki's designs had no interest in the off-the-peg outfits from the expensive shops in north Tehran's Vanak Square, all shoulder pads and loud designs like a poor imitation of Ivana Trump. Nikki's outfits were simple and elegant, and didn't overwhelm a woman's personality. She was fastidious about the tailoring of every item that came out of her small workshop. The clothes were reasonably priced by Western standards, between $60 and $100. In Iranian *rials*, however, they were unthinkably expensive.

The show was, as usual, a success, and most of us made appointments to visit Nikki for fittings. One of the women was luckier and wouldn't have to wait for her new clothes; Dore, a perfect size eight, was always a model at these gatherings, and Nikki always gave her one outfit as a thank-you present. She usually bought three or four others as well. I selected two things, one casual and one formal. Back in London I received a lot of compliments on them. Nobody believed me when I said where they had come from.

Nikki was pleased with our appreciation of her collection. She was full of nervous energy but after a while she stopped pacing about the room and sat down. She balanced on the edge of the sofa, beautifully made-up and dressed in a handsome linen shirt and trousers of her own design, waving her hands expressively. The difficulty of finding materials that met her high standards was considerable.

'My dear, this year things are getting worse. I hunt and hunt for good fabrics and when I find something that I really love I buy up the whole stock, every roll of it. If I don't I always regret it. For example, that cloak Dore wore in the black patterned material: I can probably only make five or six of those because I wasn't quick enough when I saw the material. The worst thing is finding good buttons and belts, especially belts. Nobody in this country can make decent belts.'

Three of the women at Nikki's fashion show ran their own businesses, either in their homes or in private offices where they could wear what they wanted. Only on private property are women free to dress as they wish, and only the better-off middle-class women would normally wear 'indoor clothes' when they met men who were not close relatives. As for outdoor clothes, the choice is very limited. There is the *chador*, which you wrap around yourself and which covers you from head to foot. You hold it together under your chin with one hand, but if you are carrying shopping or pulling children along with you, or doing any kind of task, the only way you can keep it on is to grip it in your teeth: scarcely very hygienic. The *chador* is usually black, gloomy and forbidding, and is meant to be. It is also meant to reduce the distinguishing characteristics between one woman and another to almost nothing. The purpose of it is to protect men from the temptations offered by female beauty, though it can have the opposite effect. Persistent urban legends invest the *chador* with a mysterious, teasing quality. There is, for instance, a familiar Tehran story about a taxi-driver who drives a woman to her house and asks her for the fare. All she does in reply is to open her *chador*: she is wearing nothing under it. But for the most part the *chador* does what it is supposed to do: it brings a glum conformity to the streets of Iran.

The demands of office life have given rise to an almost equally dreary alternative, a long tunic worn with a separate, pull-over hood. This allows women civil servants to use both hands as they work: an office revolution

of a sort. The other form of *hejab*, which you only see in the cities, is
the *roupush*, a loose raincoat-like coat which buttons down the front
and hangs just below the knees. It has been adopted reluctantly by
middle-class women in the absence of anything more individualistic or
attractive. Private seamstresses make the *roupush* in all types of material
and most colours (though they usually avoid black), and embellish it with
grace notes like shoulder pads and large pockets.

You have to wear a headscarf with the *roupush*, and this gives scope for
further refinements. Silk designer scarves are popular. So are fringes and
beads. Often the materials and colours are coordinated with the *roupush*.
Women who dress like this tend to cover their hair as little as they can,
wearing their headscarves as far back on their heads as possible to show
the maximum amount of hair. Every lock of hair which escapes from its
Islamic confinement represents a small victory.

Challenging the system can of course be dangerous. Every neighbourhood has its *Komiteh*, whose members consider themselves guardians of
Islamic values. Morality squads patrol the streets, four to a car, watching
for women whose legs are bare beneath their *roupush*, or whose faces
have signs of make-up. Some of the squads are composed of women,
and they have a reputation for particular ferocity. Men usually deliver
a lecture on the pavement, but the female squads are inclined to order
you into their car and drive you to headquarters before fining you. The
fines can be anywhere between two and twenty dollars, and the wealthier
you look the more you are likely to have to pay. Serious infractions of
the rule can be punished by up to seventy lashes, but I have never
heard of any woman experiencing anything like the maximum penalty.
There are many cases where women have received half a dozen or
more lashes to the back of their legs or the palms of their hands for
'bad *hejab*'. And there are persistent stories about women being slashed
with razor blades or having acid thrown in their faces. Perhaps they are
true; but if so it does not happen often. The natural Persian tendencies
of timidity and self-dramatisation incline middle-class Iranian women
to repeat the stories; it makes them feel they are running greater risks
than they really are when they assert their individuality in face of the
state's demand for conformity.

Nevertheless every woman in Iran, whether timid or bold, undergoes
a far more serious scrutiny than any man. For middle-class women, the
balance between being yourself and avoiding trouble is a difficult one
to maintain. Dore, the model at the fashion show, told me that the key to
it was understanding when and where the rules subtly change:

'It's other people who make you uncomfortable, not just the *Komitehs*.
If you go down to the bazaar area, where the women are strict about
hejab, you don't push your sleeves up to your elbows like I do when I'm
in north Tehran. And people dress differently in different parts of the
country. In the north they're very liberal about their *hejab*, and you can

show your neck when you're up there. I've been hassled plenty of times, like any other woman – walking into a museum for example and being told to pull my scarf down over my hair. It's just part of everyday life. I've never been arrested by the *Komiteh*, but my mother has. She wasn't wearing socks one time and she made the mistake of answering back when they stopped her. You have to know where it's OK to do that.'

Dore sees it all with a certain sense of irony. She believes that the situation is abnormal, but she thinks it was just as abnormal in the 1970s, when her grandmother wore a *chador* and fashionable girls walked through Tehran in miniskirts as a challenge to conservative morals. For her the *roupush* symbolises the contradictions of forcing a particular code of behaviour upon people who don't believe in it.

'The *roupush* now has epaulettes and big buttons. I know it looks ugly, but I like it. The more ridiculous the better, I feel. For instance, the way the girls who are into pop culture wear fluorescent sneakers and Swatches under their *hejab*. And imagine wearing a *roupush* down to your ankles and a big hairstyle with a scarf thrown over it. I call that the *kakol*, which means a bird's crest. And it looks ridiculous. But it's a way of creating a different identity for yourself, because these people, the government, are trying to force something on you that just isn't possible, asking people to be religious when they aren't. You either believe in something or you don't. *Hejab* is really hard to believe in. You have to feel comfortable with your clothes. Our servant does not feel comfortable without *hejab*. She has to have her scarf on even if she is alone in the house ironing. She believes in it, she is used to it. I'm not, and my friends aren't. But we don't have a choice.'

In the eyes of its supporters, one of the most important tasks of the revolution of 1979 was to undo a process begun by Reza Shah forty-four years earlier in 1936: the forcible unveiling of women. In 1935 he ordered that teachers and schoolchildren should no longer wear *hejab*, and army officers – the chief supporters of his regime – were forbidden to appear in public with women who were veiled. On 8 January 1936 he went further: he attended a diploma ceremony at a training college for women teachers accompanied by his wife and two of his daughters, all of whom wore European dress. It was the first time any Persian woman had appeared unveiled on a public occasion. In the following years, Khomeini was to refer to Reza Shah's campaign for the emancipation of women as 'one of the darkest moments in the history of Islam', and said it gave women the choice of becoming prostitutes or staying at home. His own wife turned her back on the outside world for the sake of honour and religion. There was even a mullah in Shiraz who stayed in his house from 1936 until his death thirty years later, in case he might be forced to look at a woman who was improperly dressed.

Under Reza Shah's son, Mohammed Reza Shah, women were given the vote, and government programmes ensured that they were better educated and trained to take their part in the economic and political life of the country. The Shah's twin sister, Princess Ashraf, who was one of the royal group who appeared without a veil on that January day in 1936, was a powerful supporter of the emancipation of women. She used her considerable influence over her brother to encourage him to introduce a Family Protection Bill, which gave women the right, under certain circumstances, to sue for divorce, and obliged men who wanted to take a second wife to obtain the consent of the first one. Such measures undermined the whole basis of Islamic law, and threatened to turn Iran into a secular society along the lines of Turkey or Nasserite Egypt.

The Shah himself had married a young, well-educated and westernised woman, Farah Diba, in 1959. In his artless and revealing book *Mission for My Country*, published two years later, he wrote:

I think my matrimonial experiences and my general observation have taught me a little about women and their ways, and about how our wonderful Persian women can best realise themselves. My country has seen many startling social changes in the thirty-five years since my father assumed the throne, but seasoned observers declare that the most sweeping advances of all concern the emergence of our women. Now it seems to me the time is opportune for Iran's women to reappraise their needs and potentialities if they are most fully to enrich their own lives and those of their husbands, their children and their fellow-countrymen.

Impatience, hubris, and an absence of his father's ruthlessness are all apparent in that passage, and those qualities were to lead to the downfall of the Shah's hopes of turning Iran into a secular, westernised society in which women would play an equal part with men. Nevertheless, in the years before the revolution an unprecedented number of young women were educated at universities in Western Europe and the United States. They came back with very untraditional ideas about the way they should dress and behave in public, and the jobs they were qualified to do. But from 1978 onwards, a reaction set in among precisely these educated young women; and so while those who were slightly older were endeavouring to follow the Shah's line of emancipation, many of the more recent graduates were willingly putting on *hejab* and taking part in demonstrations.

The reasons for the change were complex, and had a good deal to do with the growing revulsion for the waste and corruption which the immense rise in oil prices of the 1970s had caused in Iran. The wholehearted adoption of Western values by the classes who had benefited from the oil wealth was keenly resented by more traditional Iranians. Opposition to the Shah took the form among many women of a return to the older Islamic certainties. Even though Reza Shah had founded Tehran University and ordered that women as well as men should be taught there, and his son had extended the education and advancement of women, this was no longer counted in the Pahlavis' favour by those women who had benefited most from the process. As the opposition to the Shah swelled and erupted on to the streets of Iran's cities, the *chador* which the Pahlavi dynasty had banned became the uniform of those who wanted to bring the monarchy to an end and replace it with an Islamic Republic which represented many different things to different protesters.

In March 1979, a month after he had returned to Iran, Ayatollah Khomeini preached a sermon advising women workers to clothe themselves in the *chador*. Immediately there was a protest demonstration by women in the centre of Tehran. Many of them, at some risk to themselves, had supported him publicly during his time in exile. Now they pointed out that the Koran did not impose a specific Islamic covering, but stated merely that women should 'cast down their eyes, and guard their private parts, and reveal not their adornment save such as is outward and let them cast their veils over their bosoms'. A year later, however, in 1980, *hejab* for government employees became compulsory and President Bani-Sadr announced that women should cover themselves because 'research proved female hair had a kind of radiance'. In April 1983 all women in Iran, whatever their religion or nationality, were obliged to conform to a ruling that only their face and hands could remain uncovered.

When Ali Akbar Rafsanjani became President in 1989, it looked for a while as though the rules on women's clothing might be quietly forgotten. The reports of a news conference which he gave for the Iranian press, soon after being elected, had an electrifying effect on middle-class people throughout Iran. Under the Islamic Republic, women journalists have tended to be particularly fundamentalist, and the custom was for them to sit separately from the men, wrapped in their *chadors*. For a moment after he walked into the room Rafsanjani said nothing, and merely looked at the press corps. Then he spoke.

'Can you tell me where in the Holy Koran it says that women are supposed to look ugly?'

If it seemed like the beginning of an entirely new approach, the hopes it raised were speedily disappointed. The behaviour, treatment and clothing of women was so central to the ethos of the Islamic Republic that the hardliners could never have considered any surrender on this issue. Nor did Rafsanjani have the power to force through the changes he would clearly have liked to introduce. Far from becoming easier and freer, the rules affecting women were if anything applied more strictly.

*   *   *

Mrs Barzin Maknoun, professor in charge of women's issues at the Institute of Cultural Research and Studies, was a forbidding figure as she sat on a sofa in a corner of a room on the seventh floor of an office block at Palestine Corner, Revolution Avenue. Her *chador* was wrapped tightly around her, and she wore heavy glasses with thick frames which depersonalised her face. You could have passed her in the street half an hour after meeting her and not recognised her among all the other earnest, frowning women in *chadors* and glasses.

Mrs Maknoun spoke the American-accented English which she perfected when she studied for her Ph.D. at the University of Illinois in the 1970s. She found it difficult to be personally friendly to me, and she made it clear that she expected me to misunderstand and distort her views. There were certainly some grounds for her hostility, at least in her own eyes; her husband, who had studied in the United States with her, was murdered outside their house in Tehran not long after the revolution by men she said were American agents. She offered no further details. In 1980, at the time of the American Embassy hostage crisis, she was involved in a lecture tour in the United States connected with her academic work. She insisted on wearing her *chador* throughout the tour, and received a great deal of hostility and personal abuse.

Despite her education, which was entirely Western, we had little common intellectual ground. Mrs Maknoun was a true believer. She maintained that the Koran was a perfect guide for all aspects of life, and the unspoken implication was that I too would benefit from following its teachings about women.

'The things that concern women in Iran are often misunderstood, purposely so, in the rest of the world. It is our task here to show what Islam says about these things, and about what the real Islamic woman should be. You have to study the Holy Koran, which shows that only Islam gives true rights to women – and more rights to women than to men. But women are not fit to have every kind of responsibility. A woman could not do what Imam Khomeini did, for instance.'

'You mean that women aren't the intellectual equals of men?'

'No, I don't mean that at all. What we believe is that men and women are actually equal, but that they're made differently. Men are stronger in some things and women are stronger in others. A woman can get as close to God as a man can, but in a different way. A man can use his intellect to get there, and a woman can use her high emotions. But they are both equal in the sight of God. You see, there are big differences physically between men and women, and these differences make it difficult for them to do the same things. A woman can be a mother and care for a child, because of her high emotions. A man cannot do that. His duties are to support his wife and his family, because he's made that way.'

'So you believe that the way women are regarded in the West is the cause of much of our social upheavals?'

'We think women should have different goals from men. The problems have come up because women in the West are trying to be the same as men. They're doing the same jobs as men, and that's why social problems arise. Women work outside the home, but they also have to take care of their children, because by nature she's the one who bears the child. The whole burden rests on women now, because they're trying to be equal with men. But Islam says no to all this. Islam says the best thing for a woman is to be a wife and mother. That doesn't stop a woman having a job or a profession – she can do that if her husband agrees, but her first job is to take care of her children. And it's the job of the man to take care of her.'

It was curious to hear these views from the lips of a successful professional woman in her forties, with a string of degrees. And it was difficult to debate an issue with someone who could take refuge behind the certainties of a revealed religion. She had all the answers, and they were infallible ones. Mrs Maknoun believed that the Islamic Republic and the laws concerning women were based squarely on the Koran and the teachings of Mohammed, so there could be nothing which needed changing. For her to entertain criticism of the structure of society in the Islamic Republic would mean calling into question the doctrinal theories on which it was based. Our discussion foundered. At the end of forty-five minutes I couldn't think of anything else to ask her. We tried not to be hostile as we parted; but you couldn't have called it a meeting of minds.

Persian women have always played an important part in their society. They have never been forcibly restricted to the home, as women in parts of the Arab world have been. They have traditionally played an equal part in family life, and often a dominant one. Traditionally, too, they have been well-educated, and that tradition continues under the rule of the ayatollahs, even though women can only be taught now by other women and cannot themselves teach male children older than seven. A woman who marries keeps her own money and her property, and can take it with her if the marriage ends in divorce. Women run offices, they own property, they control businesses, they drive cars. Women played an important part in the revolution, and have also entered into opposition against the regime; more than a thousand women have been executed for political crimes, real or imagined, since 1979. But the debate about women in the Islamic Republic has never stopped since the revolution; and it has taken both serious and ridiculous forms.

In 1979 there was a controversy about whether unmarried women should be allowed to ride in cars with men, but when it was pointed out that regulations could never be drawn up in such a way as to allow taxis, for instance, to take only women, the proposal collapsed. Two further attempts to set up a taxi service driven by women for women failed. There was also an attempt to stop women riding horses astride. This too was abandoned, though in theory there are only certain hours of the day during which women are allowed to ride at all.

The more substantial problems are concerned with employment and status. Many leading civil servants who run the country and were educated in the West do not object as much as the older clergy to the fact that women hold official positions. In the Foreign Ministry for example, where more than three-quarters of the civil servants have degrees from Western universities, an outsider will encounter women in middle- and high-ranking positions. Women have a similar prominence in the Ministry of Islamic Guidance, another ministry that deals with foreigners on a regular basis. In theory there is no bar to women working in most professions. Rafsanjani said in 1985 that there are only three areas of public life closed to women: the law, religion and the army. When he became President he continued to press for women to get more access to top jobs, and in July 1994 one of his deputies, Ayatollah Mohajerani, the vice-president for legal and parliamentary affairs, said in an interview on Iranian television that women were qualified to hold cabinet posts, and that the ban on women studying physics and engineering at university no longer applied. The presidential office even sponsored a bill to allow women to work in the armed services, though it did not specify in what capacity. Yet this change in emphasis has taken so long to work its way through the system that it scarcely seems to have any effect at all. Of the 270 members of the Majlis elected in April 1992, only three were women.

The Iranian clergy, the *ulema*, have traditionally looked to Arabic models rather than Persian ones in social matters. This is partly because Arabic is the language of Islam, and the writings in the Koran show a similarity to traditional Arab opinions on women. Consequently the *Sharia*, the religious laws which govern the Islamic Republic, bear little relation to Western ideas of equality between the sexes. Under the *Sharia* a woman's testimony in a court of law is worth only half that of a man's, and if a woman is murdered or accidentally killed the blood money that must be paid is only half that of a man's. The Islamic Republic made polygamy legal again, and men may have as many as four wives if they can show that they have the money to keep them. As with the Islamic punishment of criminals, there are many stories of men taking a number of wives, but it is very difficult to find proven cases. The custom of taking temporary wives, or *sigheh*, has been permitted once more. Although some consider it not much more than legalised prostitution, there are a number of conditions which protect the woman and any child that results.

From time to time the conservative clergy feel obliged to warn women about the moral dangers they face. *Jomhuri Islami*, the Tehran newspaper which is most associated with the Islamic hardliners, frequently runs articles on the subject. One carried a long warning to women not to smile at strange men, and to be careful not to stand near the windows in their houses, in case the neighbours saw them. 'Exposure without the Islamic cover could,' it said, 'invite dirty stares from strange men and arouse satanic lust.' If this happened, it might lead to 'loose behaviour' and 'corruption' of the women concerned.

One of *Jomhuri Islami*'s clerical supporters, Ayatollah Jannati, took more direct action to prevent moral corruption. During the 1994 Football World Cup, liberal elements in the government decided that women could be allowed to attend the opening match of the Asian Youth Games in Tehran. The teams consisted only of boys under the age of sixteen. But this was to be the first match where both men and women were spectators together since the revolution. A special gate and separate terrace was provided for the women to maintain a degree of sexual apartheid. But Ayatollah Jannati was outraged; he believed that women should not be allowed to see boys in football kit and possibly hear them utter swearwords in the heat of battle. There were also reports that teenage girls waited on the sidelines after the match in order to collect autographs from the teams. When women spectators arrived at the stadium two days later for the second game in the series, Ayatollah Jannati had mobilised his supporters; men with guns and truncheons stood at the women's gate, barring all women from the match. There would be no further opportunity for dishonour and temptation.

Islamic tradition places a woman under the protection of a man throughout her life; her father when she is young and her husband for the remainder. The nurturing mother is held up as the ideal image of a woman in the Islamic Republic, on television, in the cinema and in revolutionary poster art. When girls are growing up, they are urged to follow the example of Fatima, the Prophet's daughter: the perfect wife and mother. Nearly all the female virtues are defined according to a woman's relationship to men. But problems arise when women choose to move outside these connections. Recently the women's magazine *Zan-e Ruz*, or New Woman, has been addressing some of these issues.

Zan-e Ruz is the only women's magazine which is now permitted to be published. It is strictly and wholesomely Islamic, and it has a mission to show women how to lead a better life so that their husbands and children will benefit. It comes out monthly with a print run of 75,000, and is mainly distributed in Tehran. *Zan-e Ruz* is not a new magazine; it was established in the 1960s and was a little stodgy and worthy even then. In the 1970s it started to take on a mildly Islamic flavour: Ayatollah Morteza Motahari, the chief Islamic thinker on matters relating to women, was invited to submit articles about the position of women in Islam. This intelligent pre-vision ensured *Zan-e Ruz*'s survival after the revolution, when all the other women's magazines, mainly concerned with fashion, were closed down.

After the revolution Motahari's articles were published in book form under the title *The Rights of Women in Islam*. Motahari was a moderating force in the Revolutionary Council until his assassination by the Forqan terrorist group in May 1979. He was familiar with the writings of many Western philosophers and authors, and was notable for his sympathetic approach to the question of women's rights. Like Mrs Maknoun, his argument was that men and women possess equal, but not necessarily identical, rights:

> Man and woman are equal in their being human, but they are two kinds of human beings with two kinds of characteristics and two kinds of psychology ... Islam has not considered there to be identicalness or exact similarity of rights between men and women, but it has never believed in preference and discrimination in favour of men as opposed to women. Islam has also observed the principle of equality between men and women. Islam is not against the equality of men and women, but it does not agree with the identicalness of their rights.

The *Zan-e Ruz* offices are in the building of the Kayhan publishing company, which produces one of Iran's major daily newspapers as well as a number of specialised magazines. The offices have the air of bustling, slightly shambolic activity which large newsrooms always generate. The magazine is run by an editorial board of three women and a staff of four reporters, several of whom speak French or English and have studied for degrees in Europe. The editorial people occupy about a quarter of a vast open-plan office, divided off into small sections by glass partitions which do nothing to reduce the noise level. All the women wear tunics and hoods.

'Things are so much easier for us because we wear Islamic dress,' one of the editorial team told me, glancing at the occasional man who wanders past from one of the other magazines on the same floor. 'Nowadays when I talk with one of my male colleagues I feel that I can speak freely to him, without having to worry about any attraction. When we're covered like this it means we can talk to each other just as human beings, not as man and woman.'

Fatima, named after the favoured Islamic female role model, is in her mid-thirties, serious-faced, pale and with heavy glasses.

'Before the Imam returned, women were encouraged to regard themselves as just consumer items; the styles made men want to treat women as objects. Now women are well treated in Iran. We don't have the kind of rapes and attacks on women that you have in the West. I can walk in the streets of Tehran at night without fear, but Western women cannot go out in their cities at night-time. There is great respect for women in an Islamic society. And our dress is an important part of this.'

The issue of *hejab* is regularly mentioned in *Zan-e Ruz* in a favourable light, as if the writers feel they have to justify its existence as often as possible:

> It is right that women should stop paying attention to appearance and false adornment and that they should find their true place in the society and family by acquiring the Islamic identity.

Yet the women who determine the magazine's contents are increasingly aware of new social problems that have arisen for women in Iran; in some ways the humane influence of Ayatollah Motahari is still apparent. In 1993 the magazine started running a kind of agony column, with answers to readers' questions. They avoided the usual platitudes about the Islamic identity of women, and instead addressed the immediate problems of single women who did not have the protection of a traditional household: problems such as those of finding a place to live in Tehran, for instance.

Several people, from young students to unmarried career women and widows, told their problems to *Zan-e Ruz*. A woman who had recently started her first job wrote:

> In our society, women with no one to protect them have to deal with all sorts of problems. Our only sin is that we are single, but these landlords think that a single woman has no right to live. I can pay the rent, yet I can't see what it is the landlords think that stops them from renting a house to me.

A mother and daughter said they had had to search for weeks before they were accepted by a landlord 'in an area of Tehran which isn't safe'. The landlord wasn't safe either, as they found on their first night in their new flat.

'They trembled in fear until the morning,' the editor of *Zan-e Ruz* wrote, 'because a person had tried to enter their room with the use of extra keys and they had been unable to do anything.'

The editor's only suggestion was that government agencies should do more to help women who find themselves in such difficulties.

More serious problems were examined in an article entitled 'Escape from Hell', published by *Zan-e Ruz* in 1993. It was written by a young woman, Maryam, who had been pressured into an early marriage by her mother. Her story filled four pages in the magazine, and was noticeably free of any mention of religion. Maryam wrote that her mother was convinced that if she did not get married she would lose any chance of happiness; and she described the moment when, against her better judgement, she accepted an offer of marriage in order to stop an hysterical scene:

I tried to stay calm.

'Look, mother, there's no need for all this anxiety. Don't worry. I'll get married when the time is right.'

'The time is right now. Why don't you marry Behzad? Yes, Behzad, the Rahimis' son. They're rich ... They're kind, warm and polite ... Haven't they come to ask you to marry him two or three times already?'

'But Mother, this Mr Behzad you've chosen is only twenty, and anyway I really don't know him at all. The two or three times we saw him, he was so quiet and withdrawn, it seemed as though he didn't think it was worth talking to any of us.'

Even so, the marriage took place. Within a few weeks, the young bride realised that Behzad was a drug addict and used both opium and heroin. She described her life 'shut up with him in hell, a hell which he had been in since the age of seventeen. I tried to be patient, and help him cope with his problem, which was now my problem too ... But when I realised that nothing I could do was any use, I decided to tell my own family as well as his.'

That wasn't any help either; her husband's family, whom they lived with, accused her of lying. By this time Maryam was pregnant. She thought about an abortion, but decided against it. For five years, she put up with beatings and mental torture in order not to be separated from her daughter. Finally, in desperation, she told the police about her husband and they arrested him. Her parents-in-law were outraged. They maintained that she was unsuitable as a mother, and tried to obtain custody of their granddaughter. When she started divorce proceedings, even her own parents criticised her. 'Divorce is a bad omen,' her mother said. 'Divorce is dishonour, divorce is a sin!'

A year later she went to court and was granted a divorce, but she had to repay two-thirds of the gold coins which had been given to her as a wedding present by her father-in-law.

By the end, Maryam had shed her old life and started to regain her self-respect. Yet her parents soon started putting pressure on her to marry again. She said she only wanted to find a job so 'when I open my eyes in the morning, I realise that I have an aim in life. If there is some incentive, then I'll feel better and I'll finally have some chance of success.'

The *Zan-e Ruz* agony aunt replied to Maryam sympathetically:

My sister, you have put behind a very difficult time and now, thanks to God, you have the opportunity to begin a new life. Be optimistic about the future. In order to put the setback of your marriage behind you, you need some kind of incentive to make you happy and cheerful.

Then followed the practical advice: Maryam should allow the child to visit its father occasionally, as long as these meetings did not affect the child's behaviour for the worse. She should make sure that her husband paid her a proper monthly allowance, and should take the matter to court if he refused. And finally she should find herself a job. Underneath the article was an advertisement setting out Maryam's qualifications: it was her way of following the agony aunt's advice.

The frankness of all this is unusual for Iran, and it raises a number of issues which were never officially recognised at the beginning of the revolution: the existence of drug addiction, the discussion of abortion as an option (abortions are legal in certain circumstances in Iran), the pressure of in-laws, and the issue of custody of children who usually stay with their fathers after a divorce. There are thousands, perhaps tens or hundreds of thousands of Maryams in Iran, women who are not meekly satisfied with the part that they have been given in life, and who want something better for themselves. Merely to acknowledge this is to accept that the Islamic Republic is not necessarily able to provide the circumstances which every woman will find acceptable.

It can be one of the most impressive sights on earth. After the five-hour journey up over the winding roads of the Albourz Mountains and down through the humid sub-tropical forests called *jangali* or jungle (the word is the same in Persian and in Hindi, which is where the British picked it up) the road suddenly opens up. The Caspian Sea, more like an ocean than a lake, lies in front of you, stretching off to the horizon. All the way along the Iranian shore, little villages which were once fishing ports have been converted into resorts for holiday-makers from Tehran. But ever since the revolution business has been bad. A large number of the well-to-do people who used to come to the Caspian every summer left the country, and the villagers had to catch fish for a living once more.

Nevertheless the main resorts, Noshahr, Ramsar, Sari and so on, have managed to attract enough visitors to support the local community. *Chai-khanehs* – tea-houses – abound near the shoreline, and seaside shops sell buckets and spades and beach toys. Footballs hang in nets outside the shops, bumping against each other in the sea breeze. The casino at Ramsar, once a main attraction for wealthy Tehranis, is now a large restaurant, specialising in sturgeon kebab. Other casinos along the coast were shut down in 1979 and have stayed empty ever since. The houses of the rich, with their swimming pools and tennis courts, have often been confiscated by the local *Komitehs* or given to government ministries. Some are rented to foreign diplomats, glad to get away from the heat and noise of Tehran for the weekend. Others have been sold off cheaply to middle-class Iranians who would never have thought of owning a place on the Caspian before the revolution.

The beaches are often magnificent. But even from a distance there seems to be something curious about the swimmers. A large stain on the water surrounds them, as though someone had spilt ink there. When you get a little closer, you realise that the stain is the swimmers' *chadors* floating around them on the surface of the water. Two teenage girls are lying on air mattresses, their heads close together as they giggle conspiratorially, their *hejab* trailing off the edges into the water. After a bit they start to rock each other's mattresses back and forth in the water until one of them capsizes amidst laughter and shrieks. When the girl re-emerges, there is the briefest glimpse of a low-cut swimsuit. This beach is restricted to women and young children, and although the Islamic Republic dislikes beach holidays (in a broadcast of August 1979 Ayatollah Khomeini said, 'Islam does not approve of swimming in the sea') it is permissible if the sexes are strictly segregated and if the women wear Islamic dress, even in the water.

'I've told my husband that I hate these holidays,' Mahjan, a pretty, slim Iranian woman told me. 'It's all right for him and the children: they can dress normally. But imagine swimming in all this gear even with a bathing suit on underneath. When your *roupush* wraps around you in the water, it's like being caught by huge coils of seaweed. I don't think it's really safe, anyway. I always feel as though I'm sinking.'

Mahjan used to enjoy the Caspian Sea as a child, before the revolution. Since then, she has had several beach holidays but this will definitely be her last.

'This year I didn't even bother going into the water. My kids are old enough to be good swimmers, so I just sat in the shade, trying to stay cool, and kept an eye on them. When they were younger I would sit on the shore and make sandcastles with them, but now I get too hot. And if you are hot, the water seems so tempting. Well, it is refreshing for a minute or two, but then you have to face all that dreadful business of getting out, weighed down by your wet clothes and finding a place to change, or putting up with the clammy feeling if you don't.

'At the beginning of the revolution there was a lot more flexibility; I suppose the authorities were less organised. If we took a motorboat offshore, just out of sight, you could usually dive in, wearing something normal for swimming, and enjoy yourself. But then the *Komiteh* started their patrols in motorboats. You can see they love racing around at high speed and shouting orders whenever they have the chance. It's simply not worth the risk any more to have a swim without all the gear on. And the beaches are segregated, so I can't even sit with my husband or my brother. It's even more annoying when I see them wind-surfing or swimming out on the water. As for sunbathing – don't make me laugh, there's no such thing as an Islamic suntan! The only swimming I do now is at my cousin's house nearby. He has a large

pool in his garden – behind eight-foot walls. But when I get outside
those walls I really feel trapped.'

The greatest concession women are allowed to make to the fact of
being by the sea is that they can go barefoot on the sand. That, at any
rate, does not seem to be frowned upon by the *Komiteh*, who keep
watch on the beach. Further out, the *Komiteh* speedboat patrols make
slow passes along the shore to ensure that no one swims round from
the men's beaches to spy on the women or sails round on one of the
brightly coloured wind-surfers that cluster a few hundred yards offshore.
And yet something forbidden has happened here on the beach, all the
same: a boy and girl have written their names in the sand, with a heart
round them. No doubt the waves will wash it away before the *Komiteh*
see it. But the powers of the *Komiteh* can only stretch so far; not even
the Islamic Republic can pass laws that change the nature of people.

8

Islamic Justice

John Simpson

Inflict no punishment for a triviality, for fear that you yourself be made liable to penalties even when innocent; and let nothing rouse you to anger ... In my opinion, however, if a man commits a crime for which he must be punished, you should not inflict the full penalty but should pardon him, thus treading the path of clemency and mercy.

A Mirror For Princes

'We were having a small dinner party at a friend's home, only ten people. We had finished the meal and it was late in the evening, so we were sitting and having coffee and cake. Our host had been living in Paris and had just returned to Iran, so when the bell rang he opened the door without hesitation. There were seven *Komiteh* standing there demanding to know what was going on, so he shrugged his shoulders and said, "Come in and see for yourself." We couldn't believe he could be so stupid.'

Marjan lived in an expensive flat in the foothills of north Tehran. She supplemented her modest private income by decorating the houses of her wealthy friends. Her social life was elaborate and intense. She was always laughing, gossiping, and going to parties and dinners. Although she had not left Iran for more than a decade she dressed in clothes that would look smart in London or New York. She viewed the Islamic Revolution primarily as a fashion challenge. On this occasion, though, Islamic law was interfering with her life instead of merely with her dress sense.

'So there we were, men and women, friends together, with no headscarves or *roupushes* on. The *Komitehs* went crazy, searching the place for drinks, grass, and videos. They didn't find anything, but they arrested us anyway.

'First they took us to the *Komiteh* station and asked us for our names, then they left us sitting there because they didn't seem to know what to do with us. It was morning by the time they decided to take us to have our blood tested to see if we had been drinking. Actually we hadn't been drinking that night. We were annoyed, but we were still laughing a bit among ourselves because we knew they had not found anything bad in the house.

'At the hospital where we went for the blood tests, the ten of us were marched in by the *Komiteh*. We'd been taken there in separate cars for men and women, of course. The doctors must have known those guys because after one glance they rushed off looking busy. So we sat down and waited some more. Finally the *Komiteh* grabbed one of the doctors and demanded that he take blood samples and test us.

'The doctor just blew up and said, "Don't you think we have enough work here, serious work for people that are sick?"

'We had to be careful not to smile because he really lost his temper.

'So then they drove us to another hospital and found a doctor who came to look at us. He asked the *Komiteh* when they thought we had been drinking.

'"Last night," they said.

'"Well, that was almost twelve hours ago. They wouldn't have any trace in their blood now."

'This doctor looked like a sympathetic sort of man and obviously did not want to get involved.

'Back we went to the *Komiteh* station in the convoy of Nissan Patrols. We were never charged with anything specific, but we were in the system by then and they didn't want to let us go. Altogether we spent four days with the *Komiteh* at their gaol in the station and then we were transferred to prison at *Zendan Kasr* – the Castle Prison in Tehran. It actually wasn't so bad because my sister had been at the party and so we were kept together and could cheer each other up.

'They put us in a communal cell with about forty-five other women. There were bunk beds arranged in a U-shape on three levels and some people slept on the floor as well. The atmosphere was friendly, and everyone got together to help each other. And it was a very clean cell, because everyone was very neat, the way women usually are. We had had some money with us when we were arrested, which they let us keep, and so we were able to buy food from the outside: you are allowed to send out orders to the shop. And we hired one of the women prisoners, a young Kurdish girl, to cook our meals for us on the stove we shared in the cell. She washed our dishes and generally looked after things.

'We didn't want to touch the regular prison food because it contained powders which made you constipated. The shop had most foods and we were allowed pretty much anything except – in the women's gaol only – they wouldn't let us bring in cucumbers or aubergines or courgettes! Can you imagine what kind of minds think of something like that?

'I decided to be like a journalist in the gaol and interview everybody, so it would be an interesting experience while we were there. There were all sorts of women in the cell. There were more than a dozen prostitutes, mostly runaways. They were quite young girls – fourteen, fifteen and sixteen – usually very pretty. The *Komiteh* had picked them up for soliciting men. There were also four young teenagers who were in various stages of pregnancy, from six months on when it really starts to show. They had all ended up in gaol because their parents had registered a complaint against their boyfriends. So the *Komiteh*'s answer was to arrest the girls *and* the boys for unIslamic behaviour and lock them up if they wouldn't get married. Apparently most of them do get married in the end, because they're so frightened at being put in gaol. But there was one girl who insisted that she wouldn't get married. She had been there for a month before we arrived and was still there when we left. She was determined. She probably had her baby there.

'A mother and daughter were also in the cell together. They had been arrested for killing the woman's husband who had repeatedly raped the daughter. That was a very sad story and they cried a lot. We all felt very sorry for them and tried to comfort them. You could see there were some people who would be in gaol for a long time. They had no help from the outside and no money. And some were a bit simple-minded.

'We were finally released after five days in the prison because we arranged to give the authorities the deeds to our house for bail. It had taken a while for our relatives to organise all of that. Two months later we went to court and as there were no charges against us, they dismissed the case, returned the deeds and it ended there, no more problems. So I had my time in gaol. But we still have dinner parties, and the man who was our host that night has learned that when all his guests have arrived he shouldn't open the door to anyone else.'

Marjan's brush with revolutionary justice was fairly mild, but her arrest and detention had no basis in Islamic law as it was supposed to be interpreted in Iran. Even if people broke the law by drinking or watching illegal videos, the privacy of the home was supposed to be legally inviolable. The police or the *Komitehs* needed a search warrant showing a specific reason, such as searching for drugs, if they wanted to enter private houses. Yet many people were so intimidated by the *Komitehs* or the Revolutionary Guards that they opened the door to them and let them in anyway.

Shari was from a middle-class family, the kind that was regularly targeted for harassment by the *Komitehs*. Her experience had become increasingly common.

'I had just come out of the shower and was in my bedroom, wearing just my bathrobe. I was sitting in front of the mirror, brushing my hair, when suddenly the door was kicked open and a bearded *Pasdar*

[Revolutionary Guard] burst into the room. He looked around the room with what seemed like real hatred, and glared at me.

'"Get dressed decently and come downstairs," he shouted. I couldn't believe it. He had no right to come into my room without my husband; that is not correct behaviour in Islam. Well, I should have shouted back, but I was too frightened. I got dressed, put a headscarf over my wet hair and went downstairs. My husband was there, sitting very quietly, while the *Pasdars* searched the house. They said they had reports of drug-taking. Of course that was not true and after making quite a mess they left. Maybe they just wanted to look inside our house or get a bribe from us. My husband told me they didn't have a search warrant, but if you say no to these people, they will just make life more difficult later.'

In theory, Ayatollah Khomeini disapproved of such intrusions into people's homes. In a series of sermons which he gave when he was still in exile in Najaf, he stressed repeatedly that private property should be protected by law. When he returned to Iran in 1979 he made a point of telling the Revolutionary Guards that they must respect the homes of private citizens. This was duly enshrined in Article 47 of the Constitution. Khomeini maintained that this was an important difference between the Islamic Republic and the way in which Communist regimes treated their citizens. He pointed out, too, that the Shah had not been a great respecter of private property, and had often found reasons to confiscate the land, houses and even horses of people who incurred his displeasure.

Yet the Revolutionary Guards often ignored these pronouncements. The founders of the Islamic Republic may have wanted a clean break with the previous regime, but they were unable or unwilling to restrain their security forces from behaving in a way that was reminiscent of the worst excesses of the Pahlavi years. During the first two years of the revolution, bank accounts, land and houses were confiscated in large numbers by revolutionary tribunals. Many people who left the country were punished in this way. Any houses that were left unoccupied were liable to be confiscated. The usual policy was to confiscate first and sort out the rights and wrongs later.

In December 1981, after many abuses of this kind, Khomeini issued his eight-point declaration setting out the need to respect people's 'movable and immovable possessions'. For the rest of the 1980s the property of the middle class and wealthy individuals seemed a little more secure. There were fewer accusations of counter-revolutionary plots. But in the 1990s, as President Rafsanjani's power faded and the infighting between ministries and security agencies grew, low-level harassment and the confiscation of property became more common. It could sometimes take ten years for a case of wrongly confiscated property to be resolved, and getting back a house or land could turn into a full-time job. Sometimes it seemed that the propertied classes in Tehran talked of nothing else.

*   *   *

Ali had had a privileged upbringing. His parents sent him to boarding school in England and then to the prestigious Massachusetts Institute of Technology (MIT) in the United States, where he studied engineering. He returned to work in Iran after the revolution and welcomed the new regime because he believed it would bring an end to the inequalities which he, like many thoughtful people, had found distasteful. He offered his services to the new government as an engineer. Ali was a serious-looking man, prematurely bald; he usually wore tweed jackets, which he bought on his annual trips to London. He always spoke in measured tones, choosing his words carefully, and when he recounted his experiences with the law his tone was unemotional and factual.

'I worked for less than a year in the Ministry of Heavy Construction, and then I was sent abroad to complete my doctorate, at the Ministry's suggestion. The government paid for my studies and I was technically still a government employee. There was no question of not returning to Iran. I could have stayed in the States before, because I had a residency permit and could have gotten a green card with my professional background. I would have made more money there, but at the end of the day my family is here and it is my country. So there I was, studying happily in Massachusetts, when I had a letter from my brother telling me that my house had been confiscated. Because I wasn't living in it, the revolutionary tribunal thought I had left the country for good.

'Now that I'm back in Iran I often spend as much time trying to sort out my property as I do at my job. Being a government employee doesn't speed up the process, believe me. And my wife and I have to live in a rented apartment when we could be in a nice big house with a garden for our children. I'm quite certain that I will get my house back eventually, but it's a legal process that will take three years. I'd really have to draw you a flow chart to show you how it works.'

Ali took out a Mont Blanc fountain pen, and pushed aside the blueprints and computer printouts on his desk. He found a clean sheet of notepaper and carefully drew a chart with circles and rectangular boxes marked in English and Persian. Arrows and numbers pointed the way between the different positions.

'You start here at the *Dadgah Enghelab*, the Revolutionary Court. It's the first step, because they have to find your file. They're not judges, they're more like detectives. This is a three-stage process which can take weeks or months – usually months. After they find your file, they send you on to a second department. There are many different steps here, and I've had to return to that office nineteen times. The next step is the third court or department, where you may be sent back to second, as I was initially, but then after all the reasons for the confiscation have been found you go back to the first court – that's a judge attended by five or six mullahs – and then on to the *Ejarie Ahkam*, the Executive Court. There are essentially six stages of the hearing which are held there.

'After that point you may be sent back again to the *Dadgah* to search for further documents or evidence. Of course if the judges are changed for some reason, that may slow things down further. I am well into the home stretch now after two years. For me, it's a fairly straightforward process, because it's clear they shouldn't have taken my house away in the first place. We should get it back within a year. But nobody is going to refund the money we spent renting a place to live for three years. I can afford it, so it's not a big worry. But it shows you what kind of country we live in.'

Ali seemed more annoyed by the waste of energy and the inefficiency of the legal system than by the basic injustice of losing his house for several years. His engineering training had taught him to design systems which work. Justice, as practised in the Islamic Republic, did not necessarily match up to his standards.

> The human rights situation in the Islamic Republic of Iran is characterised by long-term political imprisonment after unfair trials, the widespread use of torture and the death penalty, and possible extrajudicial executions of opposition activists outside Iran.

So began the report on Iran by Amnesty International in November 1993. Since 1979, despite its repeated requests, Amnesty International had never been allowed to visit Iran to discuss the situation with the government, to observe political trials, or to visit prisons. Only one visit, to interview Shi'ia and Kurdish refugees from Iraq in the aftermath of the 1991 Gulf War, was permitted.

Although Article 168 of the Iranian Constitution promised that 'investigation of political and press offences shall be held in open sessions of the Courts of Justice in the presence of a jury', there were hundreds of documented cases where this had not happened. Secret trials appeared to be more common than open ones and charges brought against detainees were often not clearly stated or were subject to sudden change. Notification of arrest to the families of detainees could take weeks or even months and denial of legal representation for the accused was common. Former prisoners routinely relate that physical abuse and torture was used to obtain false confessions.

In the Islamic Republic there were 109 offences that are punishable by the death penalty. Some of these, such as prostitution and adultery, rarely resulted in execution. In 1983 the United Nations Special Rapporteur on Summary and Arbitrary Execution reported that 'between 4500

to 20,000' executions had taken place. Three years later Amnesty
International had recorded and verified the cases of more than 6,500
people who had been executed: only cases which could be fully
substantiated were included in this number. The worst year seems to
have been 1988, with at least 2500 political prisoners executed. Detailed
records and interviews with families showed that a total of 300 people,
both men and women, have been executed in each succeeding year. The
real number may well be considerably higher.

It could have been a magistrates' court in Britain, dispensing penalties
for traffic violations: there were the same formula judgements, the same
breathless speed of operation, the same resigned acceptance on the part
of the offenders. But in this court the judge, who was also a mullah,
was hearing minor criminal cases, and the punishment was whipping.

The accused shuffled into the dock and, if he was sensible, pleaded
guilty. The evidence was given in a fast monotone, the mullah paused
momentarily to reflect, and sentence was passed. Today, in the queue
of prisoners, there was a well-known lawyer who had been stopped by
the police on the way home and found to have a bottle of illicit Iranian
vodka in his car.

Being found in possession of alcohol was an offence, but not as bad
as being drunk. The only question in this case, therefore, was whether
the lawyer had taken anything from the bottle.

'No, I did not.'

The police and the *Komitehs* tended not to invent the evidence in these
cases, and the bottle was unopened. The arresting officer confirmed that
the accused man had not been drinking. The mullah looked down at the
piece of paper in front of him, and then up at the accused again.

'Twenty-five lashes.'

The accused in the previous case was also caught with a bottle
of vodka, but he could not deny that he had been drinking from
it. He had received eighty lashes – a penalty which might do him
permanent injury. Twenty-five was unpleasant, but bearable. The lawyer
had got off lightly, and he knew it.

He was taken down immediately to the basement of the court, and
into the whipping room. The guard was not rough with him: all this
is as much a routine as if he were writing out a cheque to pay his
fine. Inside, two men were waiting on either side of a low table. There
were straps for his wrists and ankles, and he had to lie down, still
wearing his shirt and trousers, while they were fastened. The waiting
was perhaps the worst part of it.

One of the men selected a whip, made of rigid leather. He took a step
forward, his right arm high above his head, his left hand holding the end
of the whip until the moment of the stroke. The whip whistled in the air

and came down hard across the lawyer's shoulders, just below his neck. The pain was intense, but he was determined not to scream or make a fuss. The tightness of the bonds helped him control his reactions.

'One,' intoned the assistant.

The next blow landed an inch or so below, on the upper shoulderblades. His clothing provided no real protection.

'Two.'

Each of the strokes was laid with care and skill, an inch or so lower than the previous one. The red and purple lines of bruising travelled parallel to one another down his back, over his buttocks, and down his legs to the ankles.

'Thirteen.'

Painful though the previous strokes had been, the remaining twelve were much worse: they covered the same area, back to the top of the shoulders. The lawyer found it helped to control the pain if he concentrated on every detail of it, examining it objectively as though it were happening to someone else: the sound of the whip in the air, the exact place it landed on his body, the precise physical reaction.

'Twenty-five.'

The straps were undone, and one of the men helped him off the table. His back felt as though it was on fire.

'Thank you,' he murmured, without thinking. The man said nothing; it was simply a job to him. The lawyer was free to leave, his penalty paid. The entire process, from walking into court to limping slowly, painfully away from it, had lasted less than half an hour.

It was curiously hard to find accurate statistics about the punishment of crime in Iran, and none were issued by the government. Each year an unknown number of executions, certainly in the thousands, took place for drugs offences and for other civil and political crimes. There was no doubt that punishment was more rather than less harsh, and often entirely arbitrary. It had been tempered, though, by the increasing corruption; criminals could often buy their way out of trouble. In some cases the punishments which were inflicted were clear violations of the Koran, and many of them would be regarded in the West, and by some people in Iran itself, as atrocities. Others were regarded there as entirely fitting: for instance, cutting off the hands of men convicted of theft.

In Shiraz in February 1986 four thieves, each of whom had received lesser penalties for previous convictions, had the four fingers of their right hands cut off. The following May another man found guilty of repeated theft suffered the same penalty in front of a big crowd in a park beside the main Tehran bus terminal. The commander of the Tehran judicial police, whose men were responsible for amputations and executions, said the sentences had been carried out there so that travellers would spread the word around the country. An electrically operated guillotine for cutting off hands was used at Qasr prison in Tehran in 1985, and in Mashhad the following year.

Iranian officials often find it difficult to understand why Westerners should be so horrified by an electric guillotine, which is manufactured in a Western country and is capable of amputating a hand cleanly in a tenth of a second. These are clear cultural differences between an Islamic society and a Western one: many Iranians, including those who disliked the ruthless justice in their own society, were genuinely puzzled at the unwillingness of Western countries to punish the abuse and murder of children more severely. In Iran, as in many other Middle Eastern countries, the molestation and murder of children was almost unknown and regarded, with horror and incomprehension, as one of the worst diseases of Western society. Rape and other crimes directed against women were also relatively rare in Iran.

Few Iranians, like few Americans, doubted that the death penalty was effective in some circumstances. The government of the Islamic Republic made a virtue of the fact that it put people to death 'mercifully': that is to say, they were shot or hanged. Iranian officials often took pleasure in pointing out that some of the methods of execution used for convicts in the United States – the gas chamber, lethal injections and the electric chair – were certainly not instantaneous, and that the condemned person suffered terribly. True enough, perhaps; though the same officials rarely liked to be reminded that hundreds, perhaps thousands, of 'political criminals' had been tortured to death in Iran. Often the bodies of those who had been arrested for political offences and had died in gaol were not returned to their families. The assumption was that the cause of death would be too obvious.

There were other forms of Islamic punishment which were equally abhorrent to Westerners. In 1986, for instance, Amnesty International was given details of eight cases of stoning to death for adultery. The Islamic Penal Code of Iran even specifies the size of the stones to be used:

In the punishment of stoning to death, the stones should not be too large, so that the person dies on being hit by one or two of them; nor should they be so small that they could not be defined as stones.

We could find no evidence, when we were in Iran, that stonings had taken place in any of the larger cities; but there were plenty of anecdotal accounts from country areas. In a village to the east of Tehran, for instance, an adulterer was buried up to his chest in the earth and his neighbours stood at the permitted distance and threw rocks of the prescribed size at him for half an hour or more. He remained conscious the whole time and called out to them, begging them by name to spare his life. Finally one man, taking a larger rock, ran over and smashed his skull with it. Another story tells of an adulterer who also took a long time to die and was eventually killed by a Revolutionary Guard who happened to be back in the village on leave. He shot him in the head. The soldier was charged with manslaughter, and sent to prison.

The documents which Amnesty International sent to the Iranian government, detailing its condemnation of political executions and torture as well as of Islamic punishments like stoning, received an almost puzzled response from one deputy during a debate in the Majlis in June 1987:

> Amnesty International's report describes execution, flogging and hand amputation as ... inhuman and cruel. If amputating the limbs of a person with gangrene is inhuman and cruel, then so is corporal punishment, execution, flogging, and the severing of hands. But the fact is, these punishments are not inhuman and cruel, they are of positive benefit to society and are carried out for the good of mankind.

Allamah Sheikh Mohammend Kashef Al-Ghita was an academic who specialised in the three branches of Shi'ia criminal law: *Hodud* or Penalty; *Qesaas* or Retaliation; and *Diyah* or Compensation. Like so many Iranian jurists, he was a man who had spent the greater part of his life in the study of Islamic jurisprudence. He had no doubts whatever about the system, nor about the truth and justice of what it propounded. And when he explained it to me, he certainly had no idea of the effect his words had on a liberal-minded, humanitarian Westerner:

> If an adult, sane man knowingly and deliberately has sexual intercourse with a woman who is forbidden to him, it is an obligation on the authorised judge to order him to be flogged with a hundred lashes; his head will be shaved and he will be forced to leave the city for a period of one year. But if he is in a position to satisfy his sexual urges in conformity with the law – that is, if he is married – he will be stoned to death as well. If the same applies to the woman, she too will be stoned to death; otherwise she will be given a hundred lashes.

Interestingly, though, Al-Ghita stressed that it was not at all easy to get a conviction in the courts for such 'crimes'. Adultery could only be proven if the accused person confessed four times, or if four just men, or three just men and two just women, had actually witnessed the act. The witnesses had to be unanimous. If there were fewer than the required number, those who gave evidence could theoretically be punished for slander, which carried its own unpleasant penalty of eighty lashes. In practice, if the only evidence against an offender was his own confession which he then disavowed, or if he repented of what he had done, he would not be stoned to death. The same rules applied to women. Anyone who was convicted three times for adultery would, however, be beheaded; and beheading was also the punishment for rape.

The cutting off of hands, or more precisely of fingers, was not the automatic penalty for theft. Indeed, according to Al-Ghita there should strictly be twenty-seven separate criteria of seriousness if a judge was to order a thief's hand to be severed. In practice, he accepted that there would usually be around six: if the criminal acted from greed rather than necessity, if he were an habitual criminal, if the victim was poor or sick, and so on. It seemed likely, though, that in the known cases of amputation a strict adherence to the criteria was less important than the desire to set an example to the community in general.

Murder, Sheikh Al-Ghita acknowledged, is the most serious crime. In practice, the penalty was usually a very long prison sentence accompanied by a large fine in compensation. But the principle of *Qesaas*, or retaliation, existed, and could be demanded by the family of the victim. *Qesaas* was rarer in cases of murder than of mutilation as a result of physical assault: literally, an eye for an eye and a tooth for a tooth. That became relatively common after the revolution. In 1986, for instance, a woman who had lost her left eye was permitted to gouge out the left eye of the woman who had attacked her, in a formal ceremony that was attended by both families. In the same year, a group of terrorists who were found guilty of planting bombs in Qom and other cities were sentenced to suffer 'retaliation' before they were executed. By Western standards these events are atrocities; but Iran had never claimed to be Western. The punishment of crime was a cruel and ugly business in many parts of the Third World, and the Middle East in particular. It would be a mistake to blame many of these things too closely on the Islamic Republic.

For a court of law, it was remarkably informal: just an upstairs room in a small modern building, with a desk, several chairs, a window that opened out on to a verandah, and a picture of Ayatollah Khomeini looking suitably severe. The divorce court in the town of Rey, just south of Tehran, was in session.

When we arrived, there were only seven people in the room: the judge, who was a mullah in his sixties with a long, ugly, intelligent face and humorous eyes set above an aquiline nose; his clerk, an ingratiating thirty-year-old, who scribbled notes on the case with a ballpoint pen on loose sheets of paper and pushed files or a copy of the Koran towards the mullah when he needed them; and the couple involved in the case, who had brought along their three noisy children.

Conditioned by the solemnity of Western courts, I was embarrassed that we should have arrived a minute or so late, and that we made so much noise sitting down and getting settled. Only the clerk took any notice of us, and since the mullah seemed unconcerned he turned away. The mullah was just posing his first question to the husband:

'Seven months ago, you filed for a divorce from your wife here, and an appointment was made for you both to appear in court again today to let us know whether you wanted to carry on with the divorce. What is your opinion now?'

The husband was in his late twenties, with a quick, humorous face in a frame of carefully combed, curly hair. He had the look of a jack-the-lad: the sort of person who would give you a good rate for black-market goods. In fact he was a taxi-driver. He presented an unlikely picture as he sat there feeding a ten-month-old baby from a bottle. The baby's lips slurped from time to time and the rubber teat slipped from its mouth, but its father rarely noticed immediately. Maybe he had offered to take the baby in order to impress the judge with his loving family ways; the awkwardness with which he fed it seemed to show he was unfamiliar with the operation.

'Yes,' he replied. 'We've tried to get along together, but it doesn't work.'

The sharp features of the judge were turned towards the wife.

'I don't want a divorce, with these three children. I want to live with my husband.'

She was about ten years younger than he was, wrapped in a *chador* but with black high heels showing underneath it. Her discontented expression seemed to have become a fixture; she was like a piece of delicate fruit that had been bruised. The two older children played around her, pulling at her *chador*. She pushed them away with unconscious irritation, as she set out the rest of her case:

'The trouble is, he doesn't pay me a proper allowance. And he's taken another wife now, and I've got to live with my married sister.'

I leaned across to our 'minder' from the Ministry of Islamic Guidance and asked him in a whisper how old the wife was. Embarrassingly, he interrupted the proceedings to ask the judge. For the first time the judge acknowledged our presence, inclining his head with great courtesy, and asked the girl herself. Eighteen, she said.

'Would you like to put any questions to them about the case?' the mullah said to us.

His expression was mildly ironic, but he seemed to mean it. For us, though, it was as hard to join in the cross-examination here as it would have been at the Old Bailey in London. I shook my head and the duel continued.

Insects buzzed occasionally through the open window, and the noise of children playing in the streets outside filled the room whenever there was a moment of silence. The electric fan whirred away, stirring the dove-grey robes which the judge was wearing over a white shirt with its collar buttoned like a surgeon's. His hands were together in the Christian attitude of prayer as an aid to more concise thought, and the sunlight glittered on his silver ring set with an engraved cornelian.

'I've gone back to her time and again, but it doesn't work. We can't get along. And now I've got this other wife...'

The husband's voice trailed off in embarrassment; there was nothing against his taking a second wife, or even a third and fourth wife, in an Islamic society, but the judge was perfectly well aware that the marriage had occurred after the beginning of the present divorce case, and that it represented a form of escape for the taxi-driver. And since the seven-month wait had been imposed on him by the judge in order to give the original marriage a chance, it was clear that the husband had ignored the spirit of the ruling.

'The house needs looking after,' said the wife, pressing her advantage. 'But he doesn't do that, and he doesn't pay me an allowance to look after the children. She won't let him.'

'His other wife?'

'Of course. She tells him not to do the work, and not to give me the money.'

'I'll pay you when I get it. But things are difficult nowadays. You can't find passengers easily, and it costs a lot to run the cab.'

He looked at me, as though sensing a potential customer; there was a jaunty resilience about him which was his most endearing quality. It might, I reflected, make him an amusing companion, but it was unlikely to make him a good husband to either woman for long.

'It's your duty to look after her and your children,' said the judge. 'There is no need for you to divorce her just because you've married another woman.'

He looked at me.

'We have divorce laws here, but we prefer to keep families together if it's possible.'

It wasn't quite what I expected; and when he looked back at the erring husband his eyes had a noticeable glitter in them.

'If you don't pay her the proper amount of maintenance, I'll make sure you do.'

The wife wasn't prepared to leave it there, however, and she interrupted the judge sharply.

'I don't accept that. He won't pay up. Even if he says he'll pay, he won't do it.'

The judge did not seem at all angry that she should have challenged his authority like this.

'Anything else you want to say?' he asked, ironically. She shook her head sourly, a shrew at eighteen.

The clerk interrupted his scribbling to push a piece of paper across to the judge with an obsequious inclination of the head. The judge studied it carefully, and jotted a few calculations in the margin.

'You'll have to pay her 30,000 *rials* a month to take care of her expenses and those of the children.'

The couple bickered among themselves about the amount, and the bickering turned into a row. The baby started crying, the bottle fell unnoticed to the ground. The mullah scarcely seemed to be listening; he played with his cornelian ring and looked out of the window. No one rapped the desk with a gavel or cried 'Silence in court', even when they started shouting at one another. Eventually the shouting died away in embarrassment.

The judge seemed to have allowed the scene to continue for two reasons: partly in order to see what the state of the couple's relationship really was, and partly to edge the case on to its next stage. In the sudden silence, he gave his ruling:

'Come back together in a month's time, and we'll see how you both feel about getting a divorce, now that we have discussed it here in court. In the meantime,' he turned to the husband, 'you must come here every ten days and pay 10,000 *rials* for her maintenance.'

Now that he was one stage closer to getting his divorce, the taxi-driver's old jauntiness had returned.

'You bring home your day's earning to one wife,' he said, 'and before you know it you've got to pay half of it to the other one.'

But his all-men-of-the-world approach drew no sympathy from the judge, and his wife pulled her *chador* around her with irritable tightness and took the baby from him sharply. It had no further use to him as a prop now. They all trooped out together: the tired, bored children, the straying father, the discontented spoiled wife. The taxi-driver's sharp voice could still be heard long after the door had closed behind them.

The Islamic Republic took the family seriously. Its Constitution said:

> Considering that the family is the fundamental unit of Islamic society, all relevant laws, regulations and planning provisions should serve the purpose of facilitating the establishing of families and safeguarding the sacredness of the family institution and strengthening family relations on the basis of Islamic Law and morality.

The laws of the Islamic Republic about divorce are predictably brief, and mostly concerned with the dowry the wife brought to the marriage, and whether or not she is menstruating at the time of the divorce; if she is, it is usually invalid. The business of the divorce is simple enough: it has to be witnessed by two just men, and the husband has to use the following formula: 'I make my wife free, upon remittance of her dowry.' Yet there is a genuine examination of the way both partners have behaved, with no particular bias in the husband's favour.

A woman can initiate a divorce only if her husband is impotent or does not provide for her. But she is not therefore a disposable item of her husband's property. The mullah in Rey was not acting as an agent for the husband: he was trying firstly to keep the family together, and secondly to establish a balance between the couple which took the interests of the wife and the children into account. 'Irreconcilable differences' are grounds for most of the divorces in Iran. Adultery, however, is not: it is a criminal offence and something to be punished by the courts.

In the empty courtroom the judge explained these things to us in his thoughtful yet somehow mocking fashion, using the previous case as his example.

'You see the less attractive side of human nature in your court,' I suggested. He inclined his head in agreement.

'The next case,' he said, 'will show that.'

It did. The couple who came in were a generation older than the previous one, having lived together in a bitter, loveless marriage for eighteen years. The husband was a curiously farouche figure with a huge, crooked nose and a disconcertingly bad strabismus. Most of the time, as a result, he looked at the floor. His wife was a sharp-featured woman in her late thirties. They had each calculated their strategy with care: the husband, a builder by trade, had turned up in a ragged shirt and a pair of dirty jeans. 'I am a poor man,' his clothes proclaimed. Anticipating this, his wife had run a calculated risk by coming to court, not in a meek *chador*, but in a loose black *roupush* which opened from time to time, showing an expensive white outfit underneath. The scarf she wore on her head was expensive, too. 'Don't let him fool you,' her clothes replied.

Their divorce was well advanced; the process had begun a year before, and the point of dispute was the financial settlement.

'How much do you earn?' the judge asked.

'About 3000 *rials* a day.' The answer was directed to the floor, and it irritated the judge.

'Those are the wages of a labourer. If you work so cheaply, come to my house and work for me.'

The wife smirked with pleasure that her husband's big act had failed. The first round had gone to her.

The clerk handed the mullah a sealed envelope: it contained the report of two assessors, chosen jointly by the couple from among their respective families to work out the details of the divorce settlement. The assessors' proposal was that, since the husband did not hold any property in his own name, he should settle an income of 7000 *rials* a day upon his wife: seven times the maintenance figure established in the previous case. The size of the amount took the builder by surprise and threw him into a sudden rage.

'I've been betrayed by that stupid cousin of mine. I should never have suggested his name as an assessor. This woman has got at him in some way. I demand a new assessment.'

His voice was loud and harsh, filling the room, but he still glared at the floor, his hands clenched between the legs of the dirty jeans which had failed to make the impression he had hoped.

The judge saw a lever here which he could use to achieve a reasonable arbitration. He looked up at the ceiling, the palms of his hands together again, and quoted from the Koran:

By another sign He gave you wives from among yourselves, that you might live in joy with them, and planted love and kindness in your hearts. Surely there are signs in this for thinking men.

His gaze rested coolly on the builder again.

'Another assessment would be pointless; why should it produce an answer which would be any different? No. If you don't want a divorce on the terms your own cousin has agreed, then you must go back and live with your wife.'

The builder blustered, using the rhetoric of the Islamic Republic against one of its clerical supporters:

'During the Shah's time we were oppressed. There's no reason why we should be oppressed now.'

The mullah took no notice; he was busy jotting down figures again.

'You should pay her four million *rials* as a divorce settlement. Then you will not have to live with her again. But you must take pity on her, and on your three children. They have to live somehow.'

'No! I'd rather go to gaol than pay. I'd rather be hanged. I can't live with that woman for another second – but I can't pay as much as that.'

The judge's quick ear must have detected a deal in the making; but before he could take advantage of it, the woman broke in. It was special pleading, though coming from her, ugly and prematurely old as she was, it had a certain force.

'I came to live with you eighteen years ago, when we only had one room which we had to rent. I bore you three children. Now we have a big house, but you don't want to live with me there. Even when you left me, I still went on looking after your parents.'

The judge, taking advantage of the mood, joined in:

'You say you're ready to go to gaol or be hanged, but you aren't prepared to live with the woman God has given you.'

The homilies had done their work: the builder's anger faded, and he saw the need to play for a little sympathy himself.

'Look,' he said, holding out his dark gnarled hands with their broken nails. 'You can see my hands. You can see for yourself that I've worked hard all my life. This is my money, and I've earned it. I've had it up to here with this woman.'

'A wife is not like a labourer you hire. She's not just a housekeeper and cook. She has the right to be supported by you; that's the Islamic interpretation of marriage. If she bears you children, and cooks and works in the house, that is something extra. When she came to you, she was a young woman – and now she's an old one, who's given her life to you. You must try to make up to her for your neglect, by paying a reasonable amount of money for her upkeep. If you can't bear to live with her, as you say, then you must make arrangements for her to live somewhere else.'

The deal hung in the air, delicately outlined. For a while, nothing was said. The judge himself sat motionless. Then the husband spoke.

'I can't afford four million. I'll pay one million.'

'Perhaps we should appoint just one assessor, who would make a binding arbitration, after looking at all your assets.'

'Two million.'

At this precise moment the telephone rang. The judge seized the opportunity to increase the pressure. The caller was a colleague who was consulting him about some tricky legal point which had arisen in his own court, and the judge seemed to indicate that he had all the time in the world to answer. At one point it looked as though the builder was about to suggest to his wife that they should do a separate deal, away from the court, but she ignored him, brushing an imaginary piece of fluff from the expensive white outfit which had done nothing to make her look younger or more attractive.

At last the call was over, and the mullah pushed the telephone away.

'What were you saying?' he asked blandly.

The delay had done its work: the builder's resistance was crumbling fast now.

'Let's finish this today,' he said.

'All right, but you must sign a statement first that you agree to this divorce.'

The obliging clerk provided the documents and the builder signed. His wife, nervous at the formality of the occasion, agreed eventually to press her forefinger on to an ink pad and made her mark with a fingerprint.

'Now the settlement.' The mullah was inexorable, knowing the builder was in a weaker position now. 'You cannot give her less than three million.'

He was silhouetted against the sunshine in his grey and white robes, monochrome and motionless. It was plain that the deal was about to be done; all that it required was a respectable sum of money from the builder. The gnarled hands gripped the knees of the jeans, the eyes shifted focus. In the silence, children shrieked as they played outside.

'Two point eight million.'

It was just enough. An old man, bent almost double, was allowed to bring in tea, and the judge, pleased with his *coup*, drank noisily through a sugar cube in the approved Persian manner. The builder and his wife drank theirs, side by side, without looking at each other or speaking.

All that remained was to arrange the custody of the children. There were three of them: Mohammed, aged seventeen, Ali Reza, aged ten, and a seven-year-old daughter, Fatima. In the usual way under Islamic law, sons go to the father and daughters, under a certain age, to the mother. In this case the judge seemed to waver. Then he made his final declaration: the builder was to have the sons. The wife said her grovelling thanks to the mullah and swept out triumphantly. The loss of her sons seemed to matter little in comparison with the vindication she had received. The builder said nothing, and if he looked at the mullah before leaving, his strabismus made it impossible to tell. The clerk busied himself with clearing up the papers.

The mullah sat where he was for a little, looking at me in his sceptical, ironic way.

'We try to do our best to expound justice according to God's will,' he said at length, as though he felt that something still required explanation.

I replied that I had been impressed with his even-handedness, and had expected him to favour the men over the women.

'One thing I didn't understand, though. You seemed to have doubts about awarding custody of the sons to the father, and yet you did it anyway.'

'A divorced man with two children will always find it hard to remarry. I didn't want him to get off too easily.'

He got up and walked round the table to shake hands with me. I realised then that he had the heavy, painful limp of a polio victim, and was far shorter than his long face and hands had suggested. The surprise must have shown in my face; there was real mockery in his eyes now.

'Not everything we think beforehand is true,' he said.

9

The Old Enemy

John Simpson

Going along the road one day a bold, witty and well-regarded brigand slipped on a piece of melon rind. Whereupon he drew his knife and stabbed the melon ring. His attendants remarked, 'Master, you are a man of dignity and wit, are you not ashamed to strike at a melon rind?' He replied, 'The melon rind overthrew me; it is my enemy. An enemy must not be despised even though he or it may be worthless.'

A Mirror For Princes

To Celebrate the Birthday of
Her Majesty Queen Elizabeth II
The Chargé d'Affaires of the British Embassy
Mr David Reddaway and Mrs Roshan Firouz Reddaway
request the pleasure of the company of

....

at a Reception in the Embassy Gardens in Gulhak
on Monday 14th June 1993 from 5.30 p.m. To 7.30 p.m.

Please present this card at the   Regrets only
gate on Dr Shariati Street   Telephone 675011

The embossed invitation with its royal crest in gold was a reminder of a grander era, when prominent overland travellers would stay at the British residence as a matter of course; when the British community in Tehran would give wisteria parties to mark the moment when their gardens came into full bloom; when British officers commanded the Persian Cossack Brigade, British engineers ran the oilfields, and British archaeologists dominated the study of the Persian past. Every June they would make the long journey from the remotest parts of the country for the Sovereign's official Birthday Party.

Under the Islamic Republic, everything had changed. And yet for one evening, in the British Embassy compound at Gulhak, those days seemed to return. During the first quarter of the nineteenth century the British mission had traditionally spent the hot Tehran summer at Gulhak, a village on the lower slopes of the Albourz, and in 1835 Mohammed Shah handed the place outright to the British minister of the day, together with the powers of taxation and justice over the local population (who quite liked the justice but were less enthusiastic about the taxation, since the British were more efficient about collecting it than the Persian authorities). A hundred years later, when the motor car made commuting possible, many of the British diplomats spent the whole year in the relative cool of Gulhak and drove down each morning to the British Legation in the polluted and congested centre of Tehran.

At five thirty the shadows were starting to lengthen across the lawns at Gulhak. Recently restored to order after years of neglect since the 1979 revolution, the forty-four acres of the compound demonstrated the best of the British and Iranian traditions; for the Persians, a garden is a retreat from the world, and this one was tended with the methodical devotion of a nation brought up on *Gardeners' Question Time*. Majestic plane trees a century and a half old shaded the lush green lawns, and the flowerbeds perfumed the air as dusk approached. Peacocks strutted the grounds, crying out in their harsh voices, and green parakeets swooped between the upper branches of the trees a hundred feet above, squawking in mock alarm. The *jubs*, or irrigation channels, burbled gently as they carried the mountain streams down through the grounds. Farther off, where the gardens were wilder, half a dozen small Caspian horses, descendants of the ancient breed which appeared on the bas-reliefs at Persepolis, cropped the grass quietly and ignored the noise of the party.

A queue of diplomatic representatives was waiting to be greeted by the British chargé d'affaires and his wife. Some wore national costume: turbans, *kfirs*, robes and gowns. Most of the women were in short dresses, with their hair uncovered and their arms bare. This was British territory, and *hejab* did not apply. Many of the guests were elderly Iranians, longtime friends or business contacts of the British, who had never accustomed themselves to the changes since the revolution. There were also many younger Iranians, sociable and instinctively more receptive to the West in their attitudes, who had gravitated towards the British Embassy and its chargé, David Reddaway: a man who spoke Persian fluently and had married a member of the Qajar dynasty which preceded the Pahlavis: a direct descendant, therefore, of the Shah who had presented Gulhak to the British.

Various representatives of the Iranian government moved uneasily around the lawn: men in dark suits, tieless, their shirts buttoned at the collar. For some reason, while ties are regarded as unacceptably Western, suits and shirts are not. A dozen waiters, all of them Iranian and all wearing black ties, circulated constantly with trays of soft drinks, especially the translucent red *Ab-hendevaneh*, the juice of ripe water melons; even on British territory the Islamic Republic's ban on alcohol had to be observed. The invitation had specified 5.30 to 7.30 and the government officials in the dark suits and blank shirts had long since left, but the party was still going strong at 10 p.m.

'I love these romantic Persian nights,' an elderly Iranian guest murmured as he looked across the lawns, dark now, and heard the peacocks calling.

The British may forget their imperial past, but Iranians do not. They have long memories, and Britain bulks large in their view of history, even though Iran was never a British colony. According to a Persian proverb, 'If you trip over a pebble on the ground, you can be sure that an Englishman put it there.' The notion of Britain's hidden hand in Iran, which is almost universal among Persians, constitutes an alibi for everything wrong or disturbing in Iranian public life. It is an intensification of the powerlessness which every colonised country feels towards the controlling power: that all the decisions which affect everyday life are taken at the imperial centre.

This view has long outlasted any conceivable justification for it. Britain effectively abdicated its influence in Iran to the Americans in 1953; but the Iranian mind decided that the subtle and worldly-wise British had merely decided to control Iran by means of the naïve, unsophisticated Americans. London was, in Iranian eyes, the place where the real decisions were taken, whether it was the arming of the Shah (a British agent, according to Ayatollah Khomeini) or the return from exile of Khomeini (a British agent, according to the Shah). In September 1978 Sir Anthony Parsons, the then ambassador, found the rumour was going the rounds in Tehran that the British Airways flight which had brought him back from his leave in London had made an unscheduled stop at the Iraqi city of Najaf to allow him to discuss with Ayatollah Khomeini the progress of their joint plot to bring down the Shah. Not even the most intelligent and best informed Iranians seem to be entirely free of this delusion about the hidden hand of Britain in their country's affairs; indeed, the more intelligent and better informed they are, the more convoluted their fantasies about British power are liable to be.

It all derives, of course, from two hundred and fifty years of political and military domination by Britain. In the eighteenth century the senior British representative in Persia was appointed by the East India Company and had instructions to protect the route to India from other European predators. A treaty was successfully negotiated under which the Shah declared all previous treaties with European powers null and void. In return, Britain undertook to send an expeditionary force or pay a military subsidy if any European power invaded Persia.

The government in London took longer than the East India Company to appreciate the strategic value of Persia, and the first British ambassador to Tehran did not arrive until 1810 in the wake of the successful visit of the first Persian Minister Plenipotentiary to London. The distinguished Persian ambassador, Mirza Abul Hassan Khan, delighted fashionable London with his exotic style. He was fêted by the best hostesses who were charmed by his wit and interest in English life, as well as by his imposing appearance: a huge beard and magnificent robes. Hassan Khan recorded his impressions in a delightful journal, *The Book of Wonders*. James Morier, who had served in the British mission in Tehran, recalled in his diaries the social success the Persian visitor enjoyed, and made him the model for the hero of *Hajji Baba of Ispahan*. The book is a sharp satire about Persians; it was an immediate hit with fashionable London, but Persians who read it found it distinctly offensive.

Situated as it was between the British sphere of interest in the Middle East and its Indian Empire, a compliant Persia was strategically essential. British pressure increased throughout the nineteenth century, as the Qajar dynasty became progressively weaker. When the demand for constitutional government arose in the first years of the twentieth century, the British, who had long regarded themselves as the upholders of liberty, did little in practical terms to support it. They had developed a certain contempt for the Persians, believing them to be, in the phrase of the day, 'played out' as a nation. They gave only lukewarm support to the alliance between the educated élite and the clergy which was demanding a constitutional monarchy. The weak and corrupt Shah, Muzaffar-ud-Din Shah Qajar, received heavy encouragement (and bribes) from the Russians to resist.

In the grounds of the grand British Legation building, fifteen acres of magnificent gardens in the heart of Tehran, where nowadays a colony of green parakeets screech in alarm from the tall plane trees, one of the great occasions of modern Iranian history took place in 1905. It was the peaceful equivalent of revolution, and became known as the great *bast* – *bast* meaning sanctuary. Nowadays it might be called a sit-in, though it was on a huge scale. A crowd of sixteen thousand, led by a number of mullahs, took over the British compound, arranging their own food and sanitation, and stayed there without threatening anyone until they had compelled the Shah to dismiss his chief minister, grant a constitution and establish a parliament.

The British were not enthusiastic, but by allowing the demonstrators to stay they gained a certain limited amount of credit. When the Shah, at Russia's urging, went back on part of the agreement, another *bast* took place, again entirely peacefully, in the Legation grounds. The Shah was obliged to agree to hold elections, and the *bast* came to an end once more. It is strange to look at photographs of this extraordinary, Gandhian affair: thousands of men standing quietly, mullahs in their black or white turbans in front and their followers behind, stretching as far as the camera's lens reaches, silently and peacefully exerting their will on the Shah and on the great Powers.

The first Majlis was convened in October 1906. The Shah died two months later, and was replaced by a much more reactionary figure, Muhammad Ali Shah, who did his best to suppress the Constitution. The Russians supported him in this; the British, though they did not favour his removal, did not. Imperial Russia had already expanded to touch Persia's northern borders, first on the western side of the Caspian Sea and then on the east; and as the Russians competed more and more strongly with the British for influence in Central Asia, Persia became an important pawn in the so-called 'Great Game' between them. Finally, in August 1907 an Anglo-Russian convention was signed in St Petersburg dividing Persia into zones of interest, with the northern part abutting the Russian border adjudged to be in the Tsar's zone and the southern part, with its oilfields and its Gulf ports, in Britain's. Neither government bothered to notify the Persians. The 1907 agreement was the basis for a similar one in 1942, which divided up the country in much the same way. Both documents insisted that the independence and integrity of Persia would be strictly observed; neither power meant it, in 1907 or in 1942.

Three years later, in October 1910, Britain sent an ultimatum to the Shah, demanding that officers of the British Army in India should be placed in charge of policing the roads of southern Persia, at Persian expense; and in the same month, when the minister of foreign affairs in Tehran proposed to stop the pension of a former Shah, who had been a supporter of Britain and Russia, the ambassadors of the two countries ordered their uniformed servants to follow the foreign minister through the streets of Tehran and wait outside his house until the pension was paid.

After the Bolshevik Revolution, the Russian-trained Persian Cossack Brigade passed under British control. Maj. Gen. Sir Edmund Ironside was particularly impressed with a colonel in the brigade, Reza Khan, who had risen through the ranks. It has always been believed in Iran that Britain played an essential part in encouraging the coup of Reza Khan. Ironside's diary entry has been much quoted:

> I fancy that all the people think I engineered the coup d'etat. I suppose I did strictly speaking.

Faced with the threat from the Bolsheviks, Britain certainly provided the conditions and encouragement for a coup. In 1926 Reza Khan crowned himself Reza Shah, and founded an imperial house which he named Pahlavi after the script in use in Persia before the Islamic conquest. Twenty years later, in the Second World War, British and Soviet troops moved into Iran to overthrow Reza Shah on the grounds (which were accurate enough) that he sympathised with the Axis powers. The BBC's Persian language section was founded in 1941, partly in order to prepare public opinion in the country for his forced abdication. He was replaced on the throne by his son, Mohammed Reza, whose suspicions of Britain and the BBC during the revolution of 1978–9 had a certain historical perspective, even if they failed to take into account the way Britain had changed in the years between his elevation to the throne and his removal from it.

In the first half of the twentieth century the oil concession granted to the Anglo-Iranian Oil Company (AIOC) became central to the relationship between Britain and Iran. First formed in 1909 as the Anglo-Persian Oil Company, it had always managed to secure extremely favourable terms for itself. After the Second World War, Iran had become more unified and nationally aware, and was increasingly resentful of the AIOC. The company was criticised for taking the lion's share of profits, not providing jobs and training for Iranian workers and behaving as a sovereign power in southern Iran. Iran received less than 40 per cent of the net profits after British taxes, foreign exchange differentials and dividends were calculated. As the taxes increased dramatically in the post-war years and the value of sterling fell, Iran's share of its own oil money diminished.

Demands in the Iranian press for a fifty-fifty sharing agreement resulted only in lectures from the British Treasury that 'the Iranian government has benefited greatly from the victory of the Allies, in that it has enabled us to develop the concession and bring progressively larger revenues to the Iranian government from our expanding business'. As it seemed that the only side of the business that was expanding was the British one, the controversy over Iran's oil profits soon ceased to be about economic power and instead became about political power. Yet the young Shah had no desire to antagonise the British, and took no part in the fight for increased profits.

The man who led the political battle was Dr Mohammed Mossadeq, who became prime minister in 1951. It was clear that he would not accept the kind of deal with the AIOC which Britain had negotiated with the governments of Saudi Arabia and Venezuela. A memo written by the British civil servant involved in negotiations, Sir Donald Fergusson, gives a flavour of the British view:

> In the case of a mineral like oil they are of course morally entitled to a royalty. But to my mind the Asiatic idea that morally they are entitled to 50% . . . is bunk.

Mossadeq felt that even 50 per cent was not acceptable and nationalised the oil industry in May 1951. The British regarded this as outright theft.

Mossadeq's victory was brief. All British oil technicians were withdrawn from Iran and a British-inspired boycott of the oil that the few Iranian technicians were able to extract brought the economy to its knees. Political instability followed. In 1953 the Shah, alarmed by the demonstrations and by his loss of support in the Majlis, fled the country. Meanwhile the British had persuaded the new administration of President Eisenhower to mount a CIA coup against the democratically elected government: a suggestion which President Truman had earlier rejected.

The plan was devised by MI6, and involved large-scale demonstrations against Mossadeq, together with a series of attacks on him by a leading cleric, Ayatollah Kashani. Mossadeq's hold on power was fatally weakened, but the resulting bitterness against the British was still evident, decades later. The Shah, who benefited at the time, never forgot what had happened. During the last months of 1978 he asked the British ambassador more than once if the Americans were stirring up the crowds in the street, and the American ambassador if the British were encouraging Ayatollah Khomeini. Until virtually the day he died, the Shah believed he had been the victim of a conspiracy originated by the British. Earlier, he had been quoted as saying: 'If you lift Khomeini's beard you will find printed under it, "Made in England".'

After the revolution, diplomatic relations between Britain and Iran were scaled down to the minimum. A large part of the British community had left during the winter of 1978–9. Most of the rest of the diplomatic and business community were evacuated by the British Embassy in February 1979, together with thousands of British expatriates who had worked alongside Iranian colleagues in all walks of life. David Reddaway, on his first posting in the country, played a prominent role in the evacuation. His flair and courage earned him an MBE. (In 1993, when he returned to Iran as chargé, he added a CMG to his honours for completing even more delicate and difficult tasks.)

Trade between the two countries after the revolution was a tiny fraction of its level in the days of the Shah, and Britain was as much a target for political hostility as the United States. The British Embassy was officially closed down and Britain's interests handled by the Swedes. British Airways stopped its flights to Tehran. For the British, meanwhile, Iran had shrunk radically in importance, both as a market and as a regional power. Throughout the 1980s, relations worsened.

In December 1985 Roger Cooper, a British businessman and journalist who had continued to live in Tehran after the revolution, was arrested. After being denied consular visits and legal representation, he was charged with espionage. Seventeen months later, an Iranian vice-consul in Manchester, Ahmad Qassemi, was accused of shoplifting. The total value of the unpaid goods he was carrying was £7.55. The police were called, and he was questioned and charged. Directly he claimed diplomatic immunity he was released. He agreed to present himself at the police station seventeen days later.

On the appointed day Qassemi did not appear. He was arrested and held for nine hours, during which he seems to have been assaulted by the police; at that time such a thing was not unknown in Manchester. An independent medical examination several days later found that he had been kicked hard in the testicles. Iranian consular officials in London complained to the Foreign Office that he had almost died of his injuries, though this was an absurd exaggeration. Some days later Tehran Radio warned that 'the barbaric treatment' of their diplomat would cause anger among Muslims throughout the world.

In Tehran, three hours after Qassemi had finally been released by the Manchester police, a car being driven by a British diplomat was stopped on a Tehran motorway by four *Komiteh* men. The diplomat, Edward Chaplin, was pulled out of his vehicle, and when he resisted the *Komiteh* beat him up. One of the *Komiteh* men climbed into the Range Rover with Chaplin's wife Nicola and their two children, and drove off at high speed in the direction of Gulhak. On the way there, the driver was stopped by another security vehicle which had been ordered to look for a Range Rover with British diplomatic numberplates. Neither group apparently knew that the other was involved in the hunt. Nicola Chaplin and her children, shaken but unhurt, arrived safely at the residence.

Edward Chaplin was taken, hooded and bound in the back seat of his attackers' vehicle, to a private house in north Tehran. Once there, he was allowed to wash and was given clean clothes to replace his own, which were stained with his blood. The guards became less hostile and (a touch which anyone who has lived in Iran will recognise as authentic) one of them asked him for help in getting a visa to Britain.

After an unpleasant night, confined to a chair with his hands bound, Chaplin was questioned repeatedly. In the end he signed a statement which he had succeeded in watering down considerably. That afternoon he was taken out to a car with a hood over his head, and driven around for some time. Then the car stopped and he was pushed out. When he took the hood off, he found he was in Shemiran Road, a short way from the compound at Gulhak.

The Islamic Republic had decided, as ever, to apply the principle of an eye for an eye, even though Qassemi had undoubtedly been shoplifting, whereas Edward Chaplin was a senior diplomat in a country which was a signatory to the Vienna Convention, and had done nothing. In the end the British government ordered the closure of the Iranian consulate in Manchester, which had been used to spy on the relatively large number of Iranian students in the north of England. The staff of five, including Qassemi, were told to leave. The Iranians then ordered five British diplomats to leave Iran. In the days that followed there were more expulsions. After the dust had settled, each side was left with a single diplomat each in the other's capital.

Iran was unwilling to break off relations with Britain completely, since it stood to lose too much. London was a major centre of the international arms trade, and a full diplomatic break would have been followed by the closure of the Iranian arms-buying commission in the National Iranian Oil Company office, a few hundred yards from the Houses of Parliament. At a time when the Iran–Iraq war was at its height, Iran needed access to world arms markets. The government in Tehran wanted to save face, but not to sever relations entirely.

Throughout this period there was one British organisation which continued to function in Tehran: the British Institute of Persian Studies. The Institute was located in part of the embassy compound at Gulhak, but there was little contact between the two; British Embassies are rarely enthusiastic about helping British citizens who are outside the charmed circle of diplomacy. Nowadays the Institute is empty except for a caretaker, and the garden with its ornamental trees and rosebushes is badly neglected. Once the seven rooms were filled with extra beds for the archaeology students who had gathered for the season's dig, and even the lecture hall had to be turned into a large dormitory. But after the revolution a visa system was introduced for Westerners and it became almost impossible to get into Iran.

The library at the British Institute of Persian Studies is the heart of the building. It has the smell of leather and paper, and of the peculiar dust which books generate. There is an air of bare, white neatness, like the atmosphere in a college library at Cambridge. Its coolness is the perfect antidote to the heat and the madness of the Tehran traffic. There are a few rarities on the shelves: an early edition of Sir Richard Burton's *Pilgrimage to Al-Medina and Mecca*, a first edition of Howard Carter's *Tomb of Tutankhamen*. But it is the books on Persia which are unrivalled outside the great collections: from a splendid volume called *Merv and the Man-Stealing Turcomans*, with a gilt Turcoman charging across the spine, to *Aramaic Ritual Texts from Persepolis* and a full bound set of the *Journal of the Royal Asiatic Society* from 1877 to the present day.

Martin Charlesworth, an enthusiastic, angular, wiry English archaeologist with a Persian wife, kept the Institute going single-handedly during most of the difficult years. In 1980 he was given the cliff-hanging title of temporary acting assistant director, and was then promoted to acting director since he was the only member of staff left. There was very little money, but Charlesworth maintained the buildings and ensured that the three pre-revolutionary Land-Rovers were still roadworthy. Above all, he continued the Institute's work. When he could, he would travel around the country, sometimes with his wife Helen, who was also an archaeologist. Part of his duties involved checking out the state of various sites where the Institute

had worked in the past: among them Shahr-i-Qumis near Damghan
and Nush-i-Jan in the west of the country.

For many years the Iranian government seemed to value Charlesworth's
knowledge of their country's history. During the Iran–Iraq war, when
foreigners were forbidden to travel to areas affected by the fighting,
Charlesworth was invited on a ten-day tour of the country, in order
to photograph and catalogue the damage which Iraqi bombers and
missiles had done to sites of archaeological and artistic importance.
When his articles were printed abroad they alerted academics and
others to the destruction which the war was causing. In Iran itself
Charlesworth was introduced as the 'great learned professor' on Iranian
television, and there were hopes of a long-term partnership between the
cultural authorities and the Institute.

From the roof of the Institute, Charlesworth could see most of Tehran
laid out on the plain below, and he watched as the notoriously inaccurate
Iraqi Scud missiles came overhead and hit the centre of the city. In one
of the last missile attacks of the war a Scud landed only a hundred yards
from the Institute. The house shook, and he and his family were thrown
on the floor. Fortunately, though, the windows and doors took most of
the damage. The next day, the government sent men round to measure
up all the damage. Within a week everything had been replaced.

The Institute might not have had many practical links with the
Embassy, but it was still part of the remaining British influence in Iran.
The authorities must have watched it with some care, and concluded that
it was neither a nest of spies nor a tool of imperial interests, but exactly
what it seemed: a small, underfunded organisation with a useful part to
play in preserving Iran's archaeological sites. Martin Charlesworth gave
the Institute's annual course of lectures, which were attended by any
English-speaking diplomats in town, together with a few Iranians: young
archaeologists and older Anglophiles with academic ties. For them, the
lectures and the Queen's Birthday Party at the Embassy were all that
was left of the imperial connection.

In 1989, as part of yet another round of diplomatic retaliation, Martin
Charlesworth was expelled from Iran. The Foreign Office had ordered
eighteen Iranian students to leave Britain on the grounds that they were
involved in spying on, or threatening the lives of, Iranian dissidents in
Britain. In Tehran, the authorities looked around for British subjects to
expel in turn. They could find only eleven Englishmen living in Iran,
all of whom were married to Iranian women. Martin Charlesworth
was one of them. All eleven had stayed on there because they loved
the country, but in Charlesworth, particularly, Iran lost someone who
had worked hard to promote its culture and care for its heritage.
He was given five days to leave the country. Neither he nor Helen
Charlesworth has been able to go back to Iran. Nowadays he makes a
living selling insurance in Liverpool. In his spare time he teaches Persian

history and archaeology at the university there and in Manchester, in readiness for the day when the political climate changes and a new generation of enthusiasts fills the dormitories of the Institute building in Gulhak.

In June 1988 a group of four British politicians visited Tehran. It seemed like a new beginning. The following month the Iranian and British governments agreed on the levels of compensation they would each pay the other for damage to its Embassy. (The Iranian Embassy in London had been burned in the aftermath of a terrorist attack in 1980; the British Embassy in Tehran had been burned by a mob in 1978.) Iran was to pay £980,000, Britain £2,020,000. Finally David Reddaway, by then a first secretary at the Foreign Office, visited Tehran in August 1988 to see if it would be possible to reopen the Embassy, and to obtain assurances that if diplomatic relations were improved, British officials at the Embassy would receive better protection than Edward Chaplin had. He also wanted to see whether the Iranians would allow him to visit Roger Cooper in Evin prison.

The visit was a delicate one. The British were worried that it might look as though the improvement in relations was part of a price they were paying for the release of the British hostages who were still being held by pro-Iranian groups in Lebanon. In Iran, meanwhile, many senior government figures were worried that they might be leaving themselves open to political attack at home if they were too enthusiastic about restoring relations. Some Tehran newspapers, notably the English-language *Tehran Times*, which spoke for the pragmatic faction in the Iranian leadership, welcomed Reddaway's arrival. But the full paranoia of the hardliners was aroused. The newspaper *Jomhourieh Islami* called the British initiative 'a filthy handshake ... we can do without. London wants to open its Embassy in Tehran in order to reorganise its shattered intelligence service and revive Freemasonry.'

It turned into a full-scale political battle in Tehran. The hardliners demanded that Britain should apologise for its support of the Shah and for its actions over many years. Since Britain had less reason than Iran to want a resumption of relations, that was out of the question. But in the end the Foreign Ministry in Tehran prevailed. It argued that since Britain was a permanent member of the United Nations Security Council it could, if approached correctly, use its influence to help Iran in the peace talks with Iraq.

The war had at last come to an end in July 1988 when Iran accepted a cease-fire sponsored by Britain and the United States: a victory for Rafsanjani and his pragmatic allies over the radicals. A rethink of most of Iran's foreign-policy links followed. Relations began to improve with the Gulf Arab states which had backed Iraq. There was even speculation about an approach to Washington. In the meantime, Iran wanted a proper diplomatic base in London which would spearhead the campaign for post-war reconstruction. There seemed no reason why the relationship between Iran and Britain should not quietly prosper.

In late January 1989, a British diplomat in his late thirties, Nick Browne, set out for Tehran to become chargé d'affaires. He took over the Embassy from Gordon Pirie, who had run the Union Jack up the flagpole at the British Embassy on 4 December 1988. Browne had been looking forward to his posting; he had served in the British Embassy in Tehran before the revolution. Both he and his wife Diana had affectionate memories of the country and the hospitality of the Persians. They had even given their daughter a Persian name. Browne settled into the ambassadorial residence in the main Ferdowsi compound and began a wearisome round of meetings with the Iranian Foreign Ministry. He also started organising the repair and maintenance work that was badly needed on the compound. He enjoyed the chance to speak Persian again, and to see the changes which had come about in post-revolutionary Tehran. There was every reason to expect that he would stay there for a normal tour of three or four years.

Some months earlier, the writer Salman Rushdie had produced a new novel, *The Satanic Verses*. His publishers, Penguin Books, had been nervous about it, since it seemed to take elements from the life of the Prophet Mohammed and present them in a devilish, contorted form. It could be interpreted as a satire, not just on Muslims but on Islam itself. Eventually, however, the publishers had been sufficiently reassured to allow the novel to appear. The feeling may have been that even though it might cause something of a scandal, sales of *The Satanic Verses* would not suffer. It was duly published towards the end of 1988, to a mildly favourable critical reception. Only those who knew something of the way the Muslim world had developed during the 1980s thought it would create trouble; especially since it was written by a man whose family was Muslim.

The protests followed almost immediately in several parts of the Muslim world; and especially those countries, like India and Pakistan, which had close links with Britain. The Egyptian and Saudi Arabian governments banned *The Satanic Verses* immediately. Soon the translators who had worked on it, the publishers who had produced it and the bookshops which sold it were under threat. Opinion in the West was strongly in support of Rushdie's right to freedom of expression; in the Muslim world there was incomprehension that anyone should publish or defend a book which was believed to be deliberately insulting. Few of Rushdie's attackers bothered to read *The Satanic Verses*, though, if they had, their anger would probably have increased; to some people it seemed to go out of its way to be offensive to the followers of the Prophet Mohammed.

By mid-February 1989 Muslims everywhere were taking up positions on the novel. In Pakistan six people had been killed and a hundred injured in a violent demonstration against *The Satanic Verses* at the American Cultural Centre. It was typical of the Islamic Republic in Iran, inward-looking and self-obsessed, that the controversy should have attracted almost no attention at first. The radicals were in disarray, and the pragmatists were mostly concerned with attempts to revive the economy and make openings to the West. Then pictures of the demonstration in Pakistan were shown at length on Iranian television news. For any politician opposed to the resumption of relations with Britain and the West generally, they offered a perfect opportunity to obstruct the 'pragmatists'. Britain was 'The Little Satan' to America's 'Great Satan', and now *The Satanic Verses*, by a British writer, showed the extent of British collusion in the campaign to undermine Islam.

At this point Ayatollah Khomeini had less than five months to live. He had never recovered from his bitterness over the ending of the war with Iraq; but although he was close to death his mind was clear. His son Ahmad, a leading radical who was one of the few people with access to him at this stage, gave him a lengthy briefing on *The Satanic Verses*. He may also have shown him translations of some of the more offensive passages. Khomeini was incensed, and declared Rushdie, whom he regarded as a Muslim, guilty of apostasy. According to the Koran, this carried an automatic death penalty. Khomeini's judgement constituted a religious decree, or *fatwa*. *Fatwas* may be pronounced in any number of cases, and most of them concern lesser matters than the ultimate religious crime of apostasy. A sentence of death is a very considerable rarity. Tehran Radio carried a report of Khomeini's words:

> The author of the book *The Satanic Verses*, which is contrary to Islam, the Prophet and the Koran, together with all those involved in its publication who were aware of its content, are hereby sentenced to death . . .
> I call on zealous Muslims to execute them promptly on the spot they find them, so that no one else will dare to blasphemise (*sic*) Muslim sanctities.

This was not merely the standard rhetoric of the Iranian demonstrator: '*Marg bar . . .*', 'death to' someone or something. Here, Rushdie's actual death was intended. A day of public mourning to protest against 'the Great Satan's new plot' was officially declared; demonstrations were held throughout Iran. In Tehran, an angry crowd gathered outside the British Embassy, as one of the people inside later recalled:

> At midday a crowd of around eight thousand people started gathering outside. They were chanting 'Death to America', 'Death

to Britain', 'Death to Thatcher', 'Death to Rushdie', death to just about everybody. Then they started throwing stones. Several windows in the office block, near the embassy walls, were broken. We retreated to the residence, some way from the street.

When we vacated the building, communications had to be closed down. Foreign news organisations were taking up all the phone lines into the country to find out what was going on, and the Foreign Office in London were in the dark. If they wanted to know, they would have had to listen to the *World at One*. James Naughtie rang us up to do an interview, and asked us to hold the phone out of the window so the listeners could hear the baying crowd. But I have to say that the security which the Ministry of Foreign Affairs had provided did a very good job. They held the crowds back and controlled the situation. It was a demonstration which was not allowed to go beyond a certain point.

A huge reward, $2.6 million, was offered to anyone who killed Rushdie by one of the semi-autonomous agencies, or *Bonyads*, founded by the Iranian government: the 15th Khordad Foundation. Government agents had been murdering Iranian dissidents and political enemies ever since the revolution, so it was a threat that had to be taken seriously. The European Community condemned Khomeini's *fatwa*, and the member countries recalled their ambassadors. British Airways cancelled its plans for resuming the London–Tehran route. The Iranian government demanded that the British government should publicly condemn *The Satanic Verses*. This was an impossibility: public opinion in Britain would not have accepted it. The most that the Foreign Secretary, Sir Geoffrey Howe, would do was to issue a statement regretting any offence that *The Satanic Verses* might have caused Muslims. All the British staff were withdrawn from the British Embassy.

Salman Rushdie, who was now under the protection of the Security Service, MI5, spent most of his time in hiding at different military bases. Eventually he issued what seemed to be a qualified apology for any offence that his book had given. It went almost unreported in Iran, but it would not have changed matters anyway. His waverings did, however, upset some of his supporters, who felt that they were now stronger defenders of his freedom of expression than he was himself. Over the next few years Rushdie's attitude varied from courageous defiance to self-pity, and it was some time before he felt able to appear in public. By this stage he was better protected than almost anyone else in the country, including the Queen and the prime minister. Eventually, after one of the British right-wing tabloids had pointed out the criticisms which Rushdie had once made of Britain and its security services, he offered to pay a proportion of the high cost of his protection. *The Satanic Verses*, meanwhile, continued to sell well, although at least three people involved in the translation and editing of the book around the world were murdered. The assumption was that this was the work of agents of the Iranian government.

The Majlis treated the withdrawal of the British Embassy staff as an insult, and passed an immediate resolution calling for a break in diplomatic relations. The pragmatists who now dominated the government were in no position to resist. Indeed, some of them seemed as strongly opposed as the radicals to *The Satanic Verses*. On 7 March 1989 diplomatic relations were duly broken, and the Iranian ambassador and most of his staff were withdrawn from London. As for Nick Browne, he had left a witty, slightly melancholy letter in his desk drawer, for the next person who would sit there. It would be some time before anyone arrived to open it.

The pragmatists, and Rafsanjani in particular, would certainly have preferred it if the crisis over Salman Rushdie had not arisen, since it put off a *rapprochement* with the West yet again. Rafsanjani even tried to close down the 15th Khordad Foundation, which had put a price on Salman Rushdie's head, but he was frustrated in this as in so much else by his former ally, the country's religious leader Ali Khamene'i. Nevertheless, at a time when Khomeini was welcoming the affair as a chance for Iran to give up a 'naïve foreign policy', it enabled the regime to reassert its revolutionary credentials. It also diverted attention from the worsening economic situation inside Iran.

The attitude of the Iranian government to the *fatwa* remained ambivalent for years. On the one hand, it clearly had a great deal to lose if Rushdie were murdered. On the other hand, it was politically impossible for the government to declare the *fatwa* null and void. As ever, different factions within the regime followed their own line. Over the years several officials at the Iranian Embassy in London were implicated in attempts to discover Rushdie's whereabouts; and while they may have been working for different factions back in Tehran, there was a very definite ambiguity about the attitude of even relatively moderate figures like Javad Larijani, who was an adviser to the foreign minister, Ali Akbar Velayati, and had a better understanding of the West than most other figures within the regime. He told a Western news agency in an interview:

> I think in this case perhaps the government in London is being manipulated . . . The issue of Salman Rushdie is sometimes inflated by circles connected to Israel. They are very unhappy with relations between the West and Iran. I do not believe in conspiracy theories, but I cannot ignore that Israel does have a good apparatus for making some issues known to public opinion.

But anyhow, it is the perceptions which are so different. The West considers the case like this: the head of a government is

pointing his finger at a man in a foreign country and saying that
this man should be executed because he wrote a book.

From our side the picture is quite different. We consider
[Rushdie] as a man who tried to betray Islam, to downgrade
Islam and to downgrade the sentiments of more than a billion
Muslims. So we said only what Islam expects for that man: that
he does not deserve to exist. It's like, for example, you pointing
your finger at Hitler when he was alive and saying that this man
should be tried and executed a hundred times. This does not mean
that you are sending paratroops to execute him . . . It is not right
for Britain to put all the blame on Iran.

When even a rational man like Larijani finds it hard to understand
what all the fuss is about (and blames it, characteristically, on the secret
machinations of Israel) it is not surprising that a radical newspaper like
Kayhan should have taken a far less reflective and more excitable line:

The West's aim undoubtedly was to destroy a culture whose
growth endangered all its colonialist goals. Western animosity
towards Islam has been the main cause of this culture's growth . . .

Yet despite the difficulties over *The Satanic Verses*, Iran's relations with
Britain and the West in general started to improve quickly following
the *fatwa*. Ayatollah Khomeini died less than three months later, on
4 June 1989, and Rafsanjani seemed at last to have a free hand. The
other EC ambassadors returned to Tehran, and Rafsanjani seemed
to want to seek a formula for reopening relations with Britain. A
natural disaster helped him in this.

In June 1990 Iran was hit by a devastating earthquake, and the
dimensions of the tragedy demanded more resources than Iran possessed.
Aid quickly arrived from dozens of countries as well as the Red Cross
and the Red Crescent. The acceptance of help from political enemies
became an issue among the radical clergy, who preached sermons against
'tainted aid' during Friday Prayers. But Rafsanjani was adamant. He
insisted that Iran would accept help from any source, even the United
States, and he gained the backing of public opinion when he challenged
those who 'lectured the people in their shattered villages and houses
from air-conditioned offices in Tehran'. The issue of earthquake relief
itself became a political battleground, and the moderates won. Britain
was among the many Western countries that sent specialised teams,
food and materials for the victims.

Six weeks later, in August 1990, Saddam Hussein invaded Kuwait.
To secure his border with Iran he accepted Tehran's territorial and
other claims which had been the pretext for his invasion of Iran back
in 1980: the Iran–Iraq war, with its million deaths, need never have

taken place. Within days the two former enemies were discussing the possibility of resuming diplomatic relations. Other countries too saw the new situation in the Middle East as a reason to come to terms. Soon after the invasion of Kuwait British and Iranian representatives met in New York and attempted to solve the difficult question of *The Satanic Verses* with an agreement that neither Iran nor Britain would interfere in one another's internal affairs. Britain agreed to respect Islam, Iran agreed to observe international law. A month after the successful end of the talks in New York, on 27 October 1990, five British diplomats headed by David Reddaway as chargé d'affaires arrived to take over the Embassy in Tehran. It was he who opened Nick Browne's letter in the desk drawer, written nearly eighteen months earlier.

Everything was made a great deal easier because international perceptions of Iran had changed. Before the Iraqi invasion of Kuwait, Iran had been seen as a difficult and dangerous country which threatened the rest of the world with its brand of revolutionary fundamentalism. Now there was a new and more pressing enemy, and Iran was suddenly recognised as a key regional power which had fought Iraq to a standstill and knew better than anyone how Saddam Hussein's army planned its campaigns. The government in Tehran was unlikely to become an ally, but it could perhaps be persuaded to maintain neutrality. David Reddaway's task was a considerable one, therefore. He was instructed to improve bilateral relations to the point where a number of difficult problems could be tackled: among them, the continuing threat to Salman Rushdie, the imprisonment of the three British hostages in Lebanon, and the plight of Roger Cooper.

When Cooper had been arrested in December 1985, ostensibly because his visa had run out, he had lived in Iran for twenty-five years. Such small infractions of the law are not uncommon in a country where officialdom is often both incompetent and indulgent, and in similar cases all that was required was to pay a bribe to some local official. It probably did not help that soon after the revolution Cooper had written a courageous pamphlet for the Minority Rights Group in Britain about the sufferings of the Baha'is under the Islamic Republic. Some officials within the Intelligence Ministry found it hard to understand that someone could be a freelance journalist and a businessman at one and the same time. Similar suspicions on the part of the SAVAK had led to his arrest during the Shah's regime, and the files seem to have been inherited by the revolutionary regime.

Now, after Cooper had spent several months in captivity and there had been many requests for information about him from the British, the Iranians seem to have decided that they must do something to justify the long delay. Accordingly, they charged him with espionage, tried him and

found him guilty. The sentence was death plus ten years' imprisonment;
Roger Cooper, with his usual sardonic wit, asked the court which would
come first. He was transferred to Evin prison, which he described in a
letter to the present authors in the terms of a hotel brochure:

> Set in its own spacious grounds in the cool foothills of the
> Albourz, this modern caravanserai captures the spirit of The
> Thousand And One Nights . . .

Helped by his extensive knowledge of the Persian language and
Persian history, culture and religion, Roger Cooper kept his equilibrium
and his sense of humour. He sometimes found himself explaining Persian
traditions to his guards, many of whom were uneducated young men from
south Tehran or the countryside. He loved the country unreservedly. On
a postcard of the Khajou Bridge in Isfahan, which he also sent to the
authors, Cooper wrote:

> In its heyday in the 17th century this bridge must have been quite
> a sight with all the little alcoves used as shops, and the jugglers
> and mountebanks rubbing shoulders with Safavid courtiers and
> European adventurers.

Yet it was Cooper's knowledge of Iran that made his gaolers so
suspicious of him. In January 1987, after many months of interrogation
(which he turned, characteristically, into a complex game), Cooper
appeared on Iranian television and made a statement which his captors
intended to be his confession of espionage. During his interrogation
Cooper had negotiated interminably about what he would and would
not say, and in his television performance he managed to avoid a direct
admission that he had been a spy. He put in several references, indeed,
which would make it clear to any informed observer that he was innocent;
though unfortunately only the BBC, of all the foreign media who reported
his broadcast, seems to have spotted the deliberate errors he made. The
'confession' took the part of a carefully choreographed interview:

Q: According to your own statements, Britain used an intelligence system
in order to control Iran. What role did you play in this connexion?
A: Well, I must say that I had links with the BIS – the British
Intelligent [sic] Service – and co-operated with it in supplying and
carrying out analyses of political and other problems. From my earliest
days in Iran, I was friendly with British Intelligent [sic] agents, both in the
embassy and outside it, and helped them in several ways. As I mentioned,
it was easy for me to gather information, because my friends in many
organisations were like a private intelligence network. Apart from this
form of co-operation, I also did my best to promote British interests in

other ways. If, for instance, I met people who I felt could be useful to Britain, I introduced them to the embassy or the BIS.

Q: There is no doubt that your services were very valuable to your own intelligence agency. How do you evaluate these services?

A: Well, I believe my co-operation with the BIS was somewhat unusual. Apart from the reports which the British Embassy sent to London, the authorities there also received my reports and analyses of current problems. So you might say that my co-operation wasn't ordinary espionage, but perhaps was on a higher plane.

Roger Cooper said he had links with British intelligence, but denied that this constituted 'ordinary' espionage. Choosing his words with great care, he gave the name of the organisation for which he supposedly worked as 'the BIS – the British Intelligent Service'. No one whose English is fluent would fall for an espionage organisation called 'Intelligent' as opposed to 'Intelligence'; Iran's Intelligence Ministry, however, did. In reality there is no intelligence agency called 'the BIS'. The organisation which bears these initials is the British Information Service, an entirely non-secret agency which supplies facts about British life and industry. It says a great deal for Roger Cooper's nerve, and for the ignorance and gullibility of his Iranian interrogators, that they never spotted his deliberately misleading references.

During the period of almost a year during which he was interrogated, Cooper played on the weaknesses of his questioners, capitalising on their instinctive belief that Iran must be of critical importance to Britain and that the British government was determined to manipulate events in Tehran. He refused to make any reference to it in his public confession, but during the interrogation he invented a powerful secret committee, headed by Margaret Thatcher in person, which gathered any and all information on Tehran. The Intelligence Ministry believed it. Fortunately the Iranians knew as little about English literature as they knew about the reality of British intelligence; Roger Cooper found himself inventing more and more characters for 'the British Intelligent Service', and he wrote long reports on their characteristics and doings:

To titillate Hosein and his masters [Cooper wrote later] I needed to spice my otherwise bald and unconvincing narrative with rumour and speculation. To help with this, and to justify my writing as a confession, however feeble, I introduced them to Colonel Dick Hooker, the man I claimed was my first and most influential contact in the British Intelligent Service. His name is based on Brigadier Ritchie-Hooke, a character in Evelyn Waugh's 'Men At Arms' trilogy.

Other characters who appeared in his 'confession' were drawn from
Brideshead Revisited and *Decline and Fall*. The Iranians lapped it up;
and Roger Cooper privately composed a crowing little clerihew:

> *Brigadier Ritchie-Hooke*
> *Is a character in a book.*
> *My Colonel Dick Hooker*
> *Should have won me the Booker.*

The Cooper case was an embarrassment for the more moderate
elements in the Iranian government, including the Ministry of Foreign
Affairs, once diplomatic relations with Britain had been resumed. But
the more radical elements had linked Roger Cooper's fate with that of
Mehrdad Kowkabi, an Iranian student who had been arrested in Britain
in December 1989 on charges of conspiring to plant incendiary devices in
bookshops which sold *The Satanic Verses*. Kowkabi's trial had been
adjourned several times, but finally in March 1991 the case was heard
in the Old Bailey.

Kowkabi had requested as witnesses several other Iranian students
who had since been expelled from Britain and were back in Iran. They
were reluctant to return to London to testify, but David Reddaway
arranged visas and promises of safe conduct for them. At the last
minute the students changed their agreed travel plans and arrived
unexpectedly at Heathrow. There they were delayed and apparently
closely questioned by immigration officers about the evidence they
intended to give. Alarmed, they insisted on reboarding the plane which
had brought them, and returned to Iran without having left the airport.
When the judge at the Old Bailey learned of this he stopped the trial.
Kowkabi was subsequently expelled from Britain.

The Iranians, characteristically, assumed that the British government
had organised an elegant way out of the Cooper–Kowkabi problem. It
is not clear even now whether they were right or wrong. A few days
later, in great secrecy, Roger Cooper was taken out of Evin prison and
driven to Mehrabad Airport. He protested, characteristically, that he
didn't want to leave Iran quite yet; he had bills to settle and people to
say goodbye to. He even tried to persuade the mullah who was escorting
him to drive him to the cemetery where his father-in-law was buried, so
that he could pay his last respects.

'Couldn't I stay on for two or three days?' he asked.

'No,' said the mullah. He must have found Cooper's reluctance to leave
the country which had sentenced him to death deeply puzzling.

Cooper was escorted on the flight to Frankfurt and London by
David Reddaway, and arrived at Heathrow the following morning.
His half-brother George later described the scene for the benefit of
the organisation set up to lobby for Cooper's release:

Roger's appearance was shocking. He looked thin, pale, stooped and tired. Close up, his face had a paper-like quality, without expression, but his voice was strong, full of vigour and pleasure. He telephoned his father, posed with a glass of champagne, but had a sip of tea. The Foreign Office told him of the enormous interest from the media and he chose to hold a press conference there and then. The room was so full that the family couldn't get in, and the noise of cameras, questions and laughter drowned out most of Roger's answers for us. From the news bulletins it was clear his performance had been a great success. His most quoted remarks were 'sheer bloody-mindedness' (in reply to how he had survived) and 'Anyone who has been to an English public school and served in the ranks of the British army is perfectly at home in a Third World prison.'

Partly on the strength of that remark, which he admitted with typical frankness that he had worked out on the plane beforehand, Roger Cooper was honoured alongside General Sir Peter de la Billière, the British commander in the Gulf War, at the 'Men Of The Year Awards' for 1991.

His release removed one of the impediments to a better relationship between Iran and Britain, but there remained the question of the British hostages still held in Lebanon. Britain had evidence of Iran's influence over the captors of Jackie Mann, John McCarthy and Terry Waite, although Iran had never admitted it. The view was growing in Tehran that whatever value the hostages might once have had for them had long since evaporated. The holding of hostages was seen as a disadvantage rather than an advantage at a time when Iran needed Western trade and investment. In the end, the necessary pressure was applied to the group which held the hostages. John McCarthy was released in August 1991. Jackie Mann, the eldest, followed in September 1991. Finally, Terry Waite was freed in November 1991.

British businessmen had begun to arrive in Tehran in increasing numbers. Trade rose to £500 million in 1992, though that was a small fraction of its real value before the revolution. At the International Trade Fair held in Tehran that year a record number of British exhibitors advertised themselves and their services, from Rover cars to British universities. Britain even won the prize for the best foreign stand. Yet the Intelligence Ministry, no doubt still excited by Roger Cooper's revelations about the British Intelligent Service, clung to its suspicions. A consular official at the British Embassy was ordered to leave Iran 'because of acts violating diplomatic norms'; he had arranged a game of squash with a pilot from Iran Air. This may also have been part of the Intelligence Ministry's continuing battle with the Ministry of Foreign Affairs. In such cases of infighting within the administration, the hardline elements always seemed to prevail.

Against this background, a series of events damaged relations with Britain still further. On 28 April 1994, the Foreign Office accused Iranian intelligence agents of having had contacts with the IRA and offering to provide it with money and weapons. The Foreign Office maintained that this had been proven by what it called 'primary' evidence. Iran denied the charges, but the IRA admitted that it had been approached by Iranian agents who had offered money in exchange for help in murdering the political opponents of the Islamic Republic: in particular, members of the Mojaheddin-e-Khalq organisation. The IRA maintained that it had turned this offer down.

Next, the Foreign Office revealed that Gerry Adams, the head of the IRA's political wing, Sinn Fein, had visited Iran in the late 1980s. The IRA claimed that it had not wanted to become involved in Iran's political war with its enemies, and this was no doubt true. Nevertheless it seems to have accepted money from the Iranians, and the British government was worried that it might have accepted weapons from them as well.

The government made its revelations about the IRA's links with Iran when it did to cover a considerable diplomatic embarrassment. Several days later Iran announced that it had discovered a listening device in its London Embassy, which was undergoing a general refurbishment. The deputy foreign minister, Mahmoud Vaezi, said that the device, which weighed about half a kilo, had been discovered when an interior wall was demolished.

'It is composed of several parts and had a battery inside,' he declared vaguely.

President Rafsanjani insisted that the accusations about links with the IRA had been made on the very day the bugging device was discovered. The British had made them, he said, in order to deflect attention from its discovery. This was true: the British security service, MI5, and the Secret Intelligence Service, MI6, had been collecting evidence about Iran's links with the IRA for many months, and MI5, which presumably planted the listening device, would have known the instant it was discovered. To distract attention from their chagrin, the British authorities decided to leak the news about Iran's links with the IRA immediately. By contrast, Tehran waited as long as two weeks before making the announcement about the bugging device, and even then did not produce it as evidence. When an official at the Iranian Embassy in London was questioned about it by journalists, he too seemed deliberately vague:

> I'm not aware when and how it was discovered . . . It's very difficult to make a judgement when I have very little information other than what Mr Rafsanjani and Mr Vaezi have said.

Perhaps this was just another example of Iranian official carelessness; but it might have sprung from something very different: a determination on the part of the pragmatists to avoid too serious a row with Britain. Certainly President Rafsanjani fought hard to ensure that diplomatic relations with Britain would remain broadly unaffected:

> We see no need to take the first step in severing relations ... severing ties will not change anything. We will not benefit from cutting them.

Instead he blamed the British press for inventing the whole business.

'There are no links between the IRA and Iran,' he insisted blandly. 'This [the Irish question] is an issue between the British and the Irish governments.'

Yet there was to be no respite. Britain no longer had much faith in Rafsanjani's political strength, and was no longer inhibited by the presence of British prisoners in Iranian or Lebanese gaols. It went on to the offensive. Within a fortnight of Tehran's announcement about the bugging device, the Iranian chargé in London was summoned to the Foreign Office and told that his first secretary, Vahid Bolourchi, should be withdrawn from Britain. There was strong evidence, the Foreign Office said, that he had been involved in forging documents about British policy in the war in Bosnia. Similar documents had been circulating in the Middle East for some months, and had done a certain amount of damage to Britain's reputation there. When the Iranians responded by requesting the withdrawal of the first secretary at the British Embassy in Tehran, Hamish Cowell, the Foreign Office released copies of two of the forged documents.

One of these purports to be a letter sent by the Foreign Secretary, Douglas Hurd, to the Defence Secretary, Malcolm Rifkind. The letter suggests that Britain favours the Bosnian Serb forces in former Yugoslavia and is conducting an anti-Muslim policy:

Foreign & Commonwealth Office
London SW*1* 2AH
18 April *1994*

Mr Malcolm Rifkind,
Ministry of Defence
Main Building, Whitehall,
London SW*1* 2HB

Dear Malcolm,

Following our conversation in the Committee, I believe what has been done in recent days in Gorazde shows that General Rose and the British forces have been successful in implementing our policies. These achievements are indeed creditable, and we should continue to give our full support to our troops. To keep the lead that we took in the United Nations in co-ordinating that effort, and to continue our policies, I think it is the appropriate time to respond to the [sic] General Rose's request for more troops.

As you have observed on your recent visits to the United States there might be some change of policy by the United States and some other European countries which disagree with our policies to help the Serbs. So I am beginning a new effort to persuade the United States Administration on [sic] our objectives. Please ensure [sic] the others that we are trying to secure the long-term interests of Europe.

I believe much has been achieved, and there is a lot to be done.

Yours sincerely,
Douglas Hurd
Secretary of State

The lack of care in the writing of this letter brands it as being unmistakably Iranian: the poor grammar ('on our objectives'), the wrong use of words ('Please ensure the others'), and the unnecessary definite article ('the General Rose's request'). That, in particular, betrays the writer's own language: Persian has no definite or indefinite articles, and Iranians often find it hard to know precisely when to use them. Worse still, the hand-written address and signature betray the forger's unfamiliarity with the business of writing in Roman letters from left to right. Vahid Bolourchi, if he was indeed the man responsible, was a bungler.

The covering note, signed 'A Sympathizer ... in the Foreign & Commonwealth Office', purports to be from a British official outraged by his country's perfidy over Bosnia. It is even more carelessly drafted, and uses typically Iranian phraseology:

TO ALL PEOPLE that still have a 'voice' within the Western World's Democracies and the United Nations (UN), that feel that 'EVIL' must be opposed, please read these documents by the so-called 'civilised' leaders of the UK.

I myself have served this & the previous government over many years, but I feel that I must leak this document to those that will listen to its pure evil contents in the context of the world situation today.

Despite their crudity, the documents were widely believed in the Middle East, by those who wanted to believe them at any rate. No government was taken in by the documents, however, and no reputable newspaper quoted from them.

In the month when all these things happened, an Iranian economic magazine, *Iran Exports*, carried an article which tried to explain the historical ties and the continuing antagonism between Iran and Britain. Printed in English, it was as honest and as free from rhetoric as anything published on the subject in Iran; it also had more than a touch of affection in it. This, as close as anything could be, is an Anglophile Iranian's view of a long and complex relationship:

> Political differences notwithstanding, deep curiosity has underlain both sides' attitudes towards each other. The desire to understand one another's culture is reflected in the systematic approach of the British to collect and analyse all things Iranian, which has happened to offend Iranians' sense of nationalism, and charged their sense of intrigue into thoughts about conspiracies and colonialism, and has stimulated tales about the old political master trying to manipulate the underlying cross-currents of the world political system. British regard for Iranian culture, poetry, theosophy, and history is very real, and indeed determines much of their élite's attitudes toward Iran.
> Iran's bias against the English stems from British oil policy in Iran, past colonialist attitudes, interference in Iran's political affairs, and recently the Rushdie episode. Nevertheless, there's also a certain awe and respect to the political manipulator who can even, according to Jawaharlal Nehru, set the fish off against each other in the oceans.

Britain has not played an impressive part in Iran's affairs during the twentieth century. It has often stood in the way of its efforts (which nowadays seem perfectly legitimate) to manage its own affairs, and it has twice intervened to give Iran the government it wanted, regardless of the wishes of the Iranians themselves. Time and again the line-up has been the same: the educated élite who, together with the clergy, demanded a Constitution in 1906 were much the same as the educated people who, under Mossadeq's leadership, demanded a more equitable return from their oil industry half a century later. The revolution of 1979 was once again carried out by a combination of the educated élite and the clergy.

Since Iranian political life has followed such a clear pattern this century, it is hard not to sympathise with the assumption of most Persians that Britain, too, must have maintained a constant attitude towards their country: intervening from time to time, and constantly, subtly, undermining Iran's efforts to run its own affairs. It seems difficult for Iranians to grasp the degree to which the outside world has changed in the last part of the century. Neither Britain, nor the United States, nor Russia are the powers they were in past decades. Britain, in particular, has become a different country altogether. The fact that so many Iranians still believe that the pebble on the ground must have been left there by the old enemy nowadays says more about Iran than it does about the British. And yet what is remarkable is that there is still a degree of respect, and even occasionally a certain affection, in the relationship.

10

The Great Satan

Tira Shubart

However weak the enemy may be, attribute no weakness to him and take as great precautions with him as you would with a powerful foe ... Never neglect to send out spies and to inform yourself of the dispositions of the enemy; let there be no neglect either by day or night of putting out sentinels.

A Mirror For Princes

As they drove through the crowded streets Tehran buses carried a familiar red-and-white logo on their sides which had not been there the night before. The wording read: 'Celebration of the first anniversary of production in Iran. Exceptional price. Drink Coca-Cola.'

There is probably no other country in the world where a Coca-Cola advertising campaign has prompted so many editorials in the press.

'Just when the *rial* fell to its lowest price against the US dollar in recent days, people suddenly saw American Coca-Cola marketed with a 20 per cent price cut. Could there be a bigger PR coup?' asked the leading radical newspaper *Kayhan*. Taking the moral high ground, it explained why it had not joined most of the other Tehran newspapers, which had accepted Coca-Cola's advertisements. 'We are not dazzled by dollars,' the paper intoned.

The aggressive marketing campaign had been very successful, but *Kayhan* felt the product carried too much political baggage. The solution was for Iranian soft-drink manufacturers to improve the taste of their products. And it believed there could be worse to come: 'The Coca-Cola fans' celebration will peak when they can have McDonald's hamburgers with their American Coke.' The newspaper *Resalat*, read by the more conservative mullahs and bazaar merchants, asked, 'Does a country which is as short of foreign currency as Iran *need* Coca Cola?'

'I don't know what the big deal is about Coke,' said a wealthy merchant in the bazaar. 'Pepsi is much better. Why don't they open a factory here? I have to bring in all my Pepsi from Dubai. It costs a lot more than Coke, but I started drinking Pepsi before the revolution and I want to go on drinking Pepsi.'

His friend rolled his eyes and smiled.

'You're crazy, there's no difference between them.'

'I tell you there is.'

I found it hard to believe that I was listening to an argument about the rival merits of American soft drinks in the fabrics section of the Tehran bazaar, beneath a disapproving picture of Ayatollah Khomeini. Khomeini had condemned the United States of America as early as 1963, calling it 'the Great Satan'. Since 1979 American culture and American political influence had been considered a threat to the purity of the revolution, and had been excluded as far as possible from everyday life. Since Khomeini's death, however, the Great Satan had appeared again in the form of a Coca-Cola bottling plant operating under licence in the holy city of Mashhad.

Outside the mosque at Tehran University, midday prayers had just ended. A group of students, who would not be buying Coke even at its specially reduced rate, were trying to burn the American flag. Demonstrators in Iran had had plenty of practice at this over the years, but now there was an embarrassing false start; the cigarette lighter would not ignite in the crisp breeze. The chanting continued: 'Death to America, Death to Britain, Death to Israel.' At long last the Stars and Stripes caught light. Someone intoned through a megaphone:

'We believe that to break the teeth of criminal America, US goods must be strictly barred and US firms such as Coca-Cola should be prevented from operating in this country. Coca-Cola advertisements are the starting point of an offensive by Western luxury goods.'

The crowd of two hundred students cheered. It was a low turnout. A decade earlier a hundred times as many demonstrators would have been here; in those days Tehran University was highly politicised. Iranian television would have sent a camera crew, and stills photographers would have covered the event for the Tehran newspapers. Now dozens of students, no doubt secret Coke drinkers, ignored the demonstration as they headed out for lunch. The man with the megaphone suggested one reason why they weren't interested.

'There is a contradiction between our slogan of "Death to America" and the action taken by the authorities,' he shouted.

He was right. President Rafsanjani's enemies nicknamed him 'the American President' and, following his line, welcomed the growth in trade with the United States. In the spring of 1994, after the Iranian New Year when the annual budget and economic forecasts are announced, the Iranian press published reports that the United States might eventually be Iran's top trading partner again some day. The deputy speaker of the Majlis, Hassan Rowhani, said increased purchases of Iranian oil by the US had pushed the figures up:

'Economic relations with the United States were never cut, even though political and cultural relations were severed.'

It was something else for Rafsanjani's growing band of political critics to attack him over. *Kayhan*, in another editorial, questioned the presence of 'US-led Western decadence and corruption in the form of trade'. *Resalat*, a newspaper read by the more conservative mullahs and bazaar merchants, directed a series of questions to Rafsanjani:

> Trade has never been separate from politics and diplomacy . . . Why do we need trade links with the US when the markets of Europe and Asia are open to us? Why should we have any link with the Great Satan when our delegations are humiliated at American airports and the US is promoting an embargo against Islamic Iran?

Yet much of the anger, like much of the enthusiasm, was misplaced. Trade between Iran and the United States had indeed grown steadily during the 1990s, but there was a very long way to go before the US could again become Iran's largest trading partner. American imports from Iran had grown to approximately $4 billion a year by 1993, though precise statistics were impossible to find because the American oil companies, who buy varying amounts of Iranian crude, have never been entirely open about the country of origin of their imports.

As for American exports to Iran, which consisted mostly of equipment for oil-drilling and engineering, they increased dramatically in the wake of the post-Gulf War 'new world order', going up from a few million dollars in 1989 to $1 billion in 1993. Much of this trade reflected the fact that the United States supplied virtually all the equipment for the oil industry during the Shah's reign. When the rebuilding of the oilfields started in earnest, the only source for spare parts was the US. There was no real alternative: Iran badly needed the revenue that its working oilfields alone could provide.

Yet it was politically embarrassing for both countries; Iran did not want to be seen to be profiting from a relationship with the Great Satan, and the substantial American trade with Iran undermined Washington's efforts to force other Western governments to reduce their economic links with Iran. The United States had complained most strongly about those countries which had arranged loans on favourable terms to Tehran, or were purchasing Iranian goods with hard currency, yet it continued to buy Iranian oil with dollars. And although Washington had no diplomatic relations with Iran, it was doing much better business than many European countries which staffed their embassies in Tehran with commercial officers.

After almost half a century of containing the Soviet threat, the United States had a new enemy. Iran, the would-be exporter of anti-Western

Islamic revolutions, was the target of Washington's strongest suspicion and dislike. The 444 days in 1979–81 during which that America was held hostage had not been forgotten. They had left an almost Vietnam-sized impression on the American psyche. According to the US State Department, Iran was the deadliest and most active state sponsor of terrorism with a worldwide reach. In 1993 the Secretary of State, Warren Christopher, stated that Iran was an international outlaw, 'and we're trying to persuade the other nations of the world to feel as we do'. The fight against terrorism had been presented in some quarters as a crusade against the radical tendency within Islam: almost the equivalent of declaring a second Cold War. Perhaps it helped to fulfil the needs of big bureaucracies like the CIA and the Pentagon which were faced with a sudden need to justify their budgets. Iran's revolutionary brand of Islam began to be presented in the same kind of terms as the old Communist threat; and by many of the same people. Critics of the American position pointed out that, as so often in the past, Washington's approach in the Middle East seemed to follow that of Israel. In 1989 and early 1990 Israel had identified Saddam Hussein's Iraq as its direct enemy and the US followed suit. After the Gulf War, Israel declared that Iran was now the enemy. Soon Washington was saying the same thing.

Officials in Washington maintained that Iran had planned many terrorist actions against American citizens and interests around the world, even if not all of them had come to fruition. The State Department pointed to the clear evidence of links between Iran and Hezbollah in Lebanon as well as other terrorist organisations and governments. There were worries, too, about Iran's rearmament programme which involved purchases worldwide, especially from Russia and China, and which introduced submarines into the vital Gulf waterways. Worse, there were serious questions about the nuclear programme which Tehran was pursuing like the other regional powers: Israel, Pakistan, Kazakhstan and Iraq. If Iran called the United States 'the Great Satan', the United States thought of Iran in very similar terms.

The one-time centre of American power in Tehran was marked on the map of the city as 'The Previous Embassy of the USA'. There was no listing for it in the telephone book. The Swiss, who had the awkward task of looking after American interests in Iran, kept as quiet about it as they could. Often, when countries break off relations with each other, they quietly allow one or more of each others' diplomats to work in the interest sections of the protecting power; not, however, in the case of Iran and the United States. Revolutionary Guards were posted every few yards along the walls of the old American Embassy, in what had once been Roosevelt Avenue and was renamed after a former student of Khomeini's, Dr Mohammed Mofatteh. It was extremely risky to take a photograph there. The talk on the streets of Tehran was that the former Embassy had been turned into a training school where Revolutionary Guards could learn terrorist techniques; though it was a very public place for future secret agents to assemble. The Embassy walls were covered with slogans, some dating from the period of the hostage crisis: 'We will make America face a severe defeat', 'US is angry with us, and will die of the anger'. For many years the Previous Embassy of the USA was a desolate and forbidding place.

Over the gateway on the corner entrance to the compound a sign read 'Centre of Publication for US Espionage Den of Documents'. There was a little shop, next to the entrance, where the published documents could be bought. John banged on the window. An old man shuffled forward from some inner refuge and pushed the window open.

'*Bale?*' he asked, with an air of resignation. He was wearing pyjama trousers and slippers: we had interrupted his afternoon siesta. John explained that we wanted to buy the books of American documents which were on sale. The old man sighed, and called over his shoulder to someone.

A much younger man with large cow-like eyes which matched his brown uniform came out and gave us a typewritten list of the volumes which were available, together with an expensive-looking catalogue in an approximation of English which explained the documents:

The books about the US espionage deb [sic], mentioned in the list show overall ploitical [sic], military and economic dominance of great satan on our country.

The catalogue listed the various categories of document which were captured on 4 November 1979 when the revolutionary students swarmed over the wall of the Embassy and took its occupants hostage. These included reports, memoranda and despatches in clear or in cipher, which dealt with American policy towards Iran; with contacts between the Embassy and Iranian politicians, before and after the revolution; with American assessments of the activities of the Soviet Union in the region; and with American involvement in other parts of the Middle East. In all, according to the catalogue, they amounted to over seventy volumes; others were still in production. Each book was the size of an ordinary paperback, reasonably well produced, with a Farsi translation at the back, and carried the same words on the cover: 'Documents from the US Espionage Den' at the top, and 'Muslim Students Following the Line of the Imam' at the bottom.

'Are you one of the Students Following the Line of the Imam?' John asked.

The brown eyes of the young man behind the glasses were clouded with suspicion.

'Why do you want to know?'

'No reason, really; just interested.'

The suspicion faded.

'I used to be,' he said, with a certain pride.

'You were there when everyone went over the wall, in 1979?'

'Yes.'

Slowly we drew out of him the fact that the documents were no longer pieced together and published here in the former Embassy. It took much longer to publish each volume nowadays, he said, and was much less fun than it used to be. He made us out a splendid receipt, rather like a storekeeper in a Victorian grocery, and the old man wrapped up our volumes in magnificent wrapping paper, along the lines of something you might get at the Victoria and Albert or the Metropolitan Museum. The paper was grey, with white lettering, and a photograph of the Students attacking the Embassy gates. Slantwise across the paper is a CIA document in vivid red which said 'SECRET. This is a Cover Sheet'. I thought it was much too good for wrapping paper, and asked for a sheet of it as a memento. An American journalist who visited Tehran and took back several volumes wrapped in their 'secret' covers was stopped at Dulles Airport when he returned to the US, and the books were confiscated from him. He was warned that it was an offence to be in possession of classified government documents.

The documents which the Iranians reprinted should never have been captured in the first place. The lapse of security and the absence of ordinary common sense were considerable. The previous February, soon after the revolution had taken place, there had been a brief attempt to take over the compound. Because it had been anticipated, the staff had been thinned out, most of the classified documents had been shipped back to Washington, and the remaining files had been collected in the code room. During this attack, all the documents had been efficiently destroyed, together with the cryptographic material.

Nine months later, in November, the staff numbers had been allowed to increase once more, and Washington had sent many of the sensitive documents back to the Embassy. When the attack came, diplomats and secretaries crowded round the shredder machines and a specially designed furnace, cramming documents into them by the hundred. Few of the machines worked properly. Later, it suited the Students to give the impression that each of the documents they published had been painstakingly assembled over a period of years. In most cases, though, they were spared the trouble. The vast majority of the embassy documents were taken intact, including nearly all the classified material. The job of destruction was botched: the shredders jammed and the furnace was overloaded and failed to burn properly.

No attempt was even made to destroy many of the most important documents. They had not been stored in the code room with the shredder, as in February, but were merely kept in the office of Bruce Laingen, the chargé. When the attack came, Laingen was at the Foreign Ministry, asking for better protection at the Embassy. The Marines failed to break down his door, and the Students were able to take the files off the shelves and out of the safe without any effort on their part. These documents contained the names of all the Embassy's CIA officers, and of virtually every one of their local contacts.

One of the American diplomats who was taken hostage is still indignant at allowing such material to fall into the revolutionaries' hands.

> There were a number of us who viewed with great disquiet the proliferation of paperwork in the months before the takeover. Some people were careless about using the proper names of local contacts in their reporting. In the end there were so many documents and files thrown on the burner that only a handful on the bottom had actually been destroyed when they were taken.

This diplomat maintains that he never used full names in his reporting. When he was released, one of the first things he did was to find out what had happened to his Iranian friends. He learned with great relief that they had all survived and were still living and working in Tehran. It was, unfortunately, rare.

For a large number of Iranians who had had contacts with the Embassy, the capture of the documents had a devastating effect on their lives. The documents were used as powerful weapons to discredit the moderate, liberal politicians in the first revolutionary government: the Students denounced anyone unfortunate enough to have been mentioned in a favourable, or even a neutral, way. It was the start of a witch-hunt at a time when the country was already in the grip of anti-American hysteria. Many innocent people were arrested, questioned, tortured, and sometimes executed. Some prominent moderates had already left Iran, but others fled when the Embassy was taken over and went into exile abroad. At least one person who returned, after what he thought was a safe interval of two years, was arrested and shot.

To a Western reader, the documents show United States policy towards Iran in a sorry rather than a criminal light: poorly informed, influenced by sycophantic and dubious figures in the Shah's hierarchy, and woefully lacking in a clear awareness of real American interests. The US Embassy proved to have no sources of information independent of the Shah's government. Any thought of cultivating contacts in the opposition was dismissed; it was assumed that the SAVAK would find out and embarrassment would follow.

The introduction to one volume of the reprinted documents shows, however, that the supporters of the Islamic Republic saw the documents in an altogether different light.

America, Superdevil of the 20th century, has for so many years exerted intense effort to expand its hegemony and impose its policies worldwide. Pigheadedly, she continues her seditious campaigns to exploit, tyrannize, intimidate, spy, assassinate . . . It is our sincere hope that [the publication of these documents] will help expose the true visage of this bastion of evil, at present hidden under a mask of sophistry, misleading propaganda and deceiving policies.

A less excitable examination of the documents demonstrates, on the contrary, that far from being the puppeteer running the Shah's regime, the United States was in fact its prisoner. By the end of his reign, Washington was so tied to the Shah that its interests were destroyed with him.

It is clear that the US Embassy had painfully little idea of what was going on during the months that led up to the revolution; it also seemed incapable afterwards of appreciating the full implication of what had happened. Even during the months of political upheaval and fierce anti-American rhetoric which followed Khomeini's return, some embassy staff were reporting back to Washington that relations with the United States and the American business community would soon return to normal. The views of other officials in the Embassy who spoke Persian and knew Iran better were usually ignored. Months after the capture of the documents, one of the Students, who had been educated in America and had been given the task of reading them, came to the realisation that America's perceptions of the revolution had been completely false. It disturbed and intrigued him so much that he sought out some of the higher-ranking American hostages to discuss what had gone wrong with their political intelligence. His discussions with them confirmed his view; but it was so much at variance with the official approach of the revolutionary government that he had to keep quiet about it.

In one of the documents published by the Students and written as late as 30 November 1978, a mere six weeks before the Shah left Iran and two months before Ayatollah Khomeini took power, Ambassador William H. Sullivan reported to the Secretary of State, Cyrus Vance, as follows:

While we realize distrust which most opposition leaders have in Shah's promises, we believe it is unrealistic for them to insist on Shah's abdication . . .

We . . . believe [Khomeini] has implacable hatred for Shah and for the Pahlavi dynasty. His only program seems to be a negative one, designed to serve his personal revenge. His concept of an 'Islamic Republic' is nebulous, and in the face of the power controlled by the armed forces, is unrealistic. Therefore, we believe politicians must make their choice based on prospects for retaining the integrity of the country and without reference to the probability that Khomeini would renounce it.

In any event, we doubt Khomeini personally commands all the power that is often attributed to him. We feel many groups, which are far from religious Moslems, accept Khomeini as a symbol and use his rhetoric because it serves their own purposes and coincides with their own aims. We doubt he would have much concept of how to organize the govt of a nation.

We consider time for beginning of realistic negotiations with Shah is now.

There is no doubt that this document, like most of the others printed by the Students, is genuine: it contains all the misunderstandings and miscalculations which marked American policy during this period. But by no means all the documents have the same stamp of authenticity. Some of those which the Students claimed to have assembled from thousands of tiny bits of paper are much more questionable; for instance, these supposed instructions to a CIA agent:

TOP SECRET
To be mentioned in passport:
According to the information given about your identity in your passport, you are a bachelor born on the 8th July 1934 at Anthorp [Antwerp?] in Belgium; eyes: blue; without any particular sign; height: 1.88; profession: Commercial representative. A Belgian can have Flemish as his mother tongue and live on the French territories of Belgium, in the region of G.T. for example. You can equally claim to have been born at Anthorp where you have worked for a society. And that you have later been transferred to the central office of this society in Brasel [Brussels?]. Though Anthorp is only a 90 minute ride from Brasel, you have decided to settle in the suburbs of the latter ... Your address is as follows: 17th, G.T. road, Belgium.

That is obviously not genuine. But most of the documents about clandestine activity as well as about policy matters are real enough, and the most convincing thing about them is the growing awareness within the Embassy of the predicament in which US policy found itself.

The United States had come to put all its regional eggs in the single, ultimately fragile basket of the Pahlavi dynasty through a series of miscalculations which began in earnest in 1953. The Students who occupied their time in the patient piecing together of their interminable documents believed they were constructing a unique archive of evil; instead, they merely added to evidence which demonstrated how a great power managed to misunderstand completely where its own real interests lay.

'I owe my throne to God, my people, my army – and to you!' The Shah was speaking to Kermit Roosevelt, the Central Intelligence Agency representative in Tehran. Roosevelt quotes the remark in his book *Countercoup: The Struggle for the Control of Iran*, which was reissued in 1979 at the height of the political turmoil in Iran, much against the wishes of the CIA itself. The book is a highly selective and not entirely accurate account of the 1953 countercoup which reinstated Mohammed Reza Pahlavi. In 1978–9 the Shah was convinced that the CIA, together with the British, had engineered his downfall. That was not the case; the CIA's own documents, as published by the Students, show this clearly enough. Yet he certainly owed his throne to the success of Operation AJAX on 19 August 1953.

Faced with a powerful constitutional threat from his prime minister and political enemy, Dr Mohammed Mossadeq, the Shah briefly lost his nerve and fled the country when the soldiers sent to arrest his prime minister were overpowered and captured.

Kermit Roosevelt's book, together with recently declassified documents, have revealed further details about the coup. Using money that had been brought into Iran a few months earlier by General Norman Schwarzkopf, Snr, the father of the American commander in the Gulf War, Roosevelt set about buying the support he needed. Bribing the key officers in the police and army, and organising partisan crowds from the bazaar with the help of British intelligence agents, he instructed them to attack mosques and pull down statues of the Shah while shouting slogans in support of Mossadeq.

Two weeks later, Roosevelt used the same crowd of soldiers and bazaaris to demonstrate their revulsion against such 'communist' actions. Obediently, they demanded Mossadeq's overthrow and chanted slogans in favour of the Shah. Meanwhile the Imperial Guards attacked the prime minister's house, killing around three hundred of his supporters. General Zahedi, who had been chosen by the Americans and the British to take over from Mossadeq as prime minister, waited in the safety of the American Embassy until the fighting ended. Then he made a suitably triumphant appearance on a Sherman tank. The Shah, his courage and his throne restored, flew back to Tehran to crowds of thousands of cheering demonstrators. It was one of the most cost-efficient operations the United States ever conducted in Iran: a mere $100,000 was needed to bribe the crowd and the security forces, and the remainder of the million dollars which General Schwarzkopf had brought into the country was not required. By 1954 the oil consortium was dominated by American companies.

And so the United States bought the post of chief protector to the Shah at a bargain rate. Britain, which had held the post for a hundred years, had handled the crisis over Mossadeq's nationalisation of Iran's oil so maladroitly, and was anyway so much weakened by the Second World War, that it had no chance of regaining its old position. For the Americans, Iran was new territory; they had had little to do with the country in the past and at first lacked the background knowledge to make their own assessment of United States interests there. Washington, however, came to share Britain's assessment that Iran occupied an important strategic position and that the Shah was the figure who would best preserve Western interests.

In 1953 the Soviet Union was a serious threat. The Western Allies, with great difficulty, had forced Stalin to withdraw his troops from Iran after the end of the Second World War. Washington now accepted the inaccurate British assumption that Mossadeq's campaign to nationalise Iran's oil was inspired by Soviet Communism. Mossadeq had certainly received support from the Communist Tudeh Party, among other groups, but he was a nationalist in the tradition of the 1906 constitutional campaign.

The powerful Time-Life empire of Henry Luce, in its newsreel for March 1952, gave its backing to the view that the man it called 'the ageing, neurotic Mossadeq' was doing the work of the Soviet Union:

[A]ny new instability in Iran might pave the way for Russian infiltration. This in turn could outflank the Turkish bastion, a main strongpoint against communism in the Middle East, and open a Red road to the Mediterranean and to Suez, to the oil of Iraq and Arabia, to the coveted ports of the Persian Gulf, and even to Pakistan and India.

And yet the dangerous, neurotic near-Communist of Anglo-American imaginings was in reality an elderly liberal whose thinking had developed along specifically Western European lines. Dr Mossadeq had studied law at the Ecole des Sciences in Paris and obtained his doctorate in Switzerland, where he was called to the Bar and practised for many years. What made him unacceptable in the eyes of British foreign policy was that he regarded Iran much as western European countries regarded themselves: as independent entities with a right to control their own resources.

The Americans, who in less sensitive parts of the world were starting to support nationalist leaders in British colonies against their colonial masters, chose to regard Mossadeq's challenge as unacceptable also. After the successful operation which put the Shah back on his throne, Washington was committed to keeping him there. By blocking liberal, secular nationalism in 1953, the Americans had unwittingly played an important part in ensuring the rise of fundamentalist Islamic nationalism a quarter of a century later.

Now throve the armourers. From 1950 to 1963 the United States provided the Shah with military assistance worth $829 million and weapons systems worth $1.3 billion. The Shah, who was fascinated all his life by advanced weaponry, continually asked the Eisenhower administration for more; in this he had the vocal support of the vice-president, Richard Nixon, who had met the Shah and was impressed by him. It was the beginning of a powerful friendship. Eisenhower, from the basis of real military experience, resisted the Shah's demands on the grounds that better training, not more expensive weaponry, was required to deal with any threat from across the Soviet border.

President Kennedy, elected in 1960, was less interested in the threat to Iran from the outside, and more in the possibility of internal revolution. He made a loan of $35 million contingent on a programme of social reform, and urged the Shah to appoint Dr Ali Amini, the Iranian ambassador to Washington, as his prime minister. For a century and more, Iran's rulers had been told to run their country in the interests of outside powers; now the Shah was being ordered to run it in the interests of his own people – as defined by the theories of liberal economists such as Barbara Ward and W. W. Rostow.

The White Revolution which the Shah launched in 1962 ('white' as opposed to the 'black' revolution of the religious conservatives or the 'red' revolution of Marxism which he maintained were the alternatives) concentrated on land reform. That, indeed, was a liberal measure which was to have a profound effect on the prosperity of the country; but it also brought Khomeini, who had recently become an ayatollah, to national prominence. In 1962 and 1963 he took a leading part in the resistance to the Shah's refusal to exempt religious endowments from the programme of compulsory land purchase, and to the plans for the emancipation of women. When Khomeini was arrested in June 1963, there was serious rioting in Tehran.

But however advantageous the White Revolution was to many Iranians, it came complete with traditional colonial trappings. There was an influx of thousands of American technicians, support staff, military men and their families; and they were accorded the principle of extra-territoriality in a bill which passed through the usually tame Majlis by a majority of only 74 to 61. One deputy asked why a foreign refrigerator repairman should have the same legal immunity as Iran's ambassadors abroad. In his sermons, Ayatollah Khomeini characteristically couched it in terms that were stronger, more personal and more ominous:

> If the Shah should run over an American dog, he would be called to account. But if an American cook should run over the Shah, no one would have any claim over him . . . If the men of religion

Right: Ayatollah Khomeini's tomb at Behesht-e-Zahra in south Tehran opened in 1990 a year after his death.

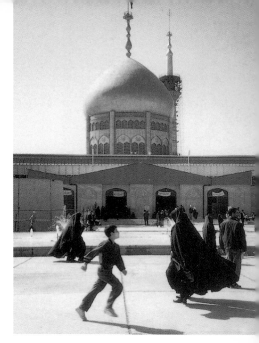

Below left: Mahmoudi, our driver and companion from the revolution onwards.

Below right: Street scene in Tehran with portrait of President Rafsanjani.

Above left: Street scene in Tehran with portrait of Ayatollah Khamene'i who succeeded Ayatollah Khomeini as the country's spiritual leader.

Above right: Family on a motorcycle: the population explosion.

Below left: Keepers of the revolution: a Pasdar (Revolutionary Guard) and Gendarme.

Below right: Pasargardae: Cyrus's tomb, two and a half millenia old with, in the foreground, the disintegrating remains of the Shah's saluting base of 1971.

Above: Friday Prayers: prayer leader flanked by Ayatollahs.

Below left: Worshippers at a shrine.

Below right: The theocracy: mullahs in Qom.

Bottom right: Islamic Justice: the mullah presides over family court in Rey.

Left: Den of Spies: the walled compound of the former U.S. embassy.

Left: A bazaari transports his masters' goods.

Skiing in the Albourz Mountains.

Cooked beets for sale: fast food in the Tehran bazaar.

Top left: Shopping for food at one of the smartest markets in Tehran.

Above left: Visiting the mullah: John with Sayeed Tehrani.

Above right: Islamic Marriage: a wedding party at the Hotel Persepolis.

Below: Persepolis: the ruined palace and the tents erected by the Shah for the 2500th anniversary of the monarchy.

Above left: The toll of the Iran-Iraq War: graves at Behesht-e-Zahara.

Above right: Persepolis: Tira at the ceremonial platform.

Below: Marking the 40th day after death.

Above: Picnic in Isfahan.

Below: Khajou bridge at Isfahan.

Bottom: Under the Khajou bridge: people relaxing under the arches.

Above: Isfahan: Al Qapu Palace.

Below left: An enthusiast at the front.

Below right: War of the cities: a Scud missile hits Tehran.

had any influence, it would be impossible for the nation to be at one moment the prisoner of England, the next of America.

The debate, and the rioting which accompanied it, went largely unnoticed in the United States, even though several hundred people were killed. The exiling of Ayatollah Khomeini was not mentioned in any major American newspaper.

The presidential election of 1968 brought the Shah's friend Richard Nixon to power. When they had first met, in 1953, they had taken to each other and found they shared the same anxieties about the Soviet Union. Now Iran was the dominant regional power, and President Nixon was in a position to give the Shah what he wanted. The number of uniformed American military advisers was greatly increased, and the Shah was given almost unlimited access to the non-nuclear military technology of the United States. When Nixon visited Tehran in May 1972 he looked across the negotiating table at the Shah and said simply, 'Protect me.' The meeting placed the Shah on a new level: no longer the leader of a client state but an equal, regarded by Nixon and Henry Kissinger, his National Security Adviser, as a fellow strategist.

Only the Department of Defense, echoing Eisenhower's reservations, resisted the idea of opening the American arsenal to Iran and tried to introduce a note of caution. But Kissinger issued a memorandum in July 1972 that arms sales to the Shah were to be encouraged. In the four years that followed, Iran became the largest importer of US-produced arms in the world, at a cost of $4 billion. At that level, the United States was becoming as dependent upon Iran as Iran was on the United States.

After Nixon's fall as a result of the Watergate scandal James Schlesinger, as Secretary of Defense, asked President Ford in September 1975 for a review of US arms sales policy to Iran, doubting 'whether our policy of supporting an apparently open-ended Iranian military build-up will continue to serve our long-term interests'. But Kissinger was still in control of policy towards Iran and backed the continuation of the arms sales. The review took years to produce anyway; and only two months later Schlesinger was replaced as Defense Secretary by Donald Rumsfeld.

By 1976 there were 24,000 Americans working in Iran; 1270 of them were retired military men, hired by US manufacturers to work in Iran as arms salesmen. The American Embassy and its military mission employed 2000 US citizens. Two years later, in the months that led up to the revolution, the figure for US citizens living and working in Iran had risen to more than 40,000. Americans were paid much more than Iranians who were doing the same jobs for the same companies, even when those Iranians had received equivalent degrees from the same American universities. On oil projects in Abadan, Iranian technicians were housed in quarters which were separate from, and inferior to, the American quarters; air conditioning, for instance, was standard only for the Americans.

In Isfahan, where Bell Helicopters employed 1700 people on a forty-five-acre site near the city, there were regular complaints about the behaviour of American workers. Some of them were in the habit of roaring at speed around the city on motorbikes late at night. Street fights took place there between groups of Iranians and Americans. As in Abadan, anti-American feeling was high, and it was noticeable later that both cities played a significant part in the events leading up to the revolution. In Abadan the Iranian oil workers went on strike in the autumn of 1978, and workers in the civil service throughout Iran began to follow their example. In Isfahan, the Islamic Republic was in full operation before the final act of the revolution took place in Tehran.

The Americans, having adopted the British colonial pattern in Iran in 1953, found themselves facing a full-blown independence movement along colonial lines by 1978. And like one of the less experienced colonial powers of Europe, the United States found itself with no time in which to create some more popular alternative Iranian leadership to support. Within six years of being asked to be the protector of United States interests in the region, Iran had become its worst enemy there.

The man who was to pay the price for Nixon's and Kissinger's unheeding dependence on the Shah was President Jimmy Carter. The Shah himself was unenthusiastic about Carter's election to the presidency in 1976: under a Democratic administration there might be less chance of obtaining what he wanted in the way of weaponry. The Shah had felt most comfortable with the approach of the previous Republican administration.

Carter, by contrast, had campaigned on a promise to link American arms sales to a country's record in human rights. Nevertheless, his incoming administration was quick to exempt Iran from any prohibition on the grounds of its strategic importance; and when the Secretary of State, Cyrus Vance, visited Tehran in May 1977 he promised the Shah that the United States would honour all the arms contracts that had already been signed, and offered him the AWACS airborne early-warning system and 160 F-16 fighters. The Shah's response was to ask for another 140 F-16s.

Carter was also prepared to sell Iran the technology for generating nuclear energy, and approved a $1.1 billion package of military equipment. But the AWACS deal ran into trouble with the House International Relations Committee, on the grounds, later fully justified, that 'the security of advanced electronic devices could not be assured in Iran'. The subject was debated for three months, in terms that the Shah found deeply humiliating.

The subject of Iran's internal policies was less of a problem. The Shah, remembering the measures he had taken under President Kennedy in 1963, had introduced some modest social reforms and had done something to limit the use of torture by the SAVAK. Carter accepted the changes the Shah was trying to make, as he later wrote in his memoirs:

> My intelligence briefings revealed that despite the Iranian standard of living from the distribution of oil revenues, the Shah's single-minded pursuit of his own goals had engendered opposition from the intelligentsia and others who desired more participation in the political processes of Iran. SAVAK was notorious for its ruthless suppression of any dissent and I was informed that there were 2500 (the Shah said 'below 2500') political prisoners in Iranian jails. The Shah was convinced that immediate suppression was the best response to opposition, and he was somewhat scornful of Western leaders (including me) who did not emulate his tactics.

In November 1977 the Shah visited Washington. His meetings with Carter went well; but 60,000 Iranian students had gathered to demonstrate against him, some of them carrying pictures of Khomeini. A counter-demonstration, using military cadets, had been rather ineptly organised by the Iranian Embassy, and while the President and Mrs Carter greeted the Shah and his Empress on the White House lawn the two groups clashed. The tear gas which the Washington DC police had been using drifted across the lawn and affected the eyes of the visitors and their hosts as they stood to attention for the two national anthems.

It seemed trivial enough; but in Iran, where the new mood of mild liberalisation enabled the pictures of the tear-gas incident to be shown on television, it demonstrated to people what they had not previously been told: the degree of hostility to the Shah which existed outside the country. With the Persian's ready enthusiasm for detecting hidden messages, many of those who watched their televisions that night assumed that the entire incident could have been allowed only with President Carter's agreement: in other words, the television pictures were a sign that Carter had implicitly withdrawn his support from the Shah. It was a significant success for the opposition, at a time when the Shah himself believed his position had never been stronger.

In the aftermath of the fall of the Shah, almost exactly a year later, every government with an embassy in Tehran examined its reporting during the difficult months of 1978 to see whether the revolution had been predictable; and the general verdict was that no one had forecast it with any accuracy. Neither the Israelis, the French, the British, the Russians nor the Americans – the embassies with the best connections in Iran – correctly anticipated what would happen. As late as August 1978 the CIA, in its National Intelligence Estimate, reported that Iran could not be considered to be in a 'pre-revolutionary' position, because

... those who are in opposition, both violent and non-violent,
do not have the capacity to be more troublesome. There is
dissatisfaction with the Shah's tight control of the political process,
but this does not threaten the government.

The CIA, by this stage, was working extremely closely with the SAVAK,
and was influenced by the SAVAK's own, moderately optimistic view of
events. The US Embassy did not share that particular set of blinkers,
but it was equipped with others.

Part of the price that the United States paid for its close relationship
with the Shah was that it was obliged to bow to the imperial wishes and
avoid any link with the opposition groups or with individual political
dissidents. Although relations with the military and with security
organisations were extremely good, there was virtually no contact
with the bazaar. Only one political officer apparently had contacts with
the clergy, gained on an earlier Peace Corps posting. As for the locally
employed staff, the majority were Armenians or Baha'is; there were very
few Shi'ite Muslims. The ambassador himself came to rely heavily on
the gossip provided by his Armenian driver. Apart from him, the only
Iranians whom William Sullivan spoke to at any length were army
officers, the Shah's ministers, and the Shah himself.

American journalists gained a far more accurate picture of what was
going on, as did British and French ones, since they were often in daily
touch with demonstrators and the leading ayatollahs. By the autumn,
having witnessed the strength of feeling on the streets, and watched the
draftees in the army wavering in their loyalty to the Shah, a number of
American and British journalists were openly questioning his chances
of political survival; but on 28 October Ambassador Sullivan was still
reporting:

... the Shah is the unique element which can, on the one hand
restrain the military, and on the other hand, lead a controlled
transition ... I would oppose any overture to Khomeini.

Sullivan, like President Carter himself, had inherited a bureaucratic
machine which was capable only of viewing the situation from one
direction. His Embassy had become an office for selling equipment and
weapons systems, and its political reporting role had been heavily reduced
long before he was posted to Iran. He faced hostility from Zbigniew
Brzezinski's National Security Council, which tried to undermine his
influence and that of the US State Department. Brzezinski, indeed,
seemed convinced that the Russians were behind the trouble in Iran:
not a mistake which Sullivan made. Above all, Sullivan was reporting
to an administration which for much of 1978 had been concentrating
on the Camp David negotiations with the prime minister of Israel and

the President of Egypt, to the exclusion of almost everything else.

On 9 November, without any prior warning, Sullivan broached the issues that had been raised by the demonstrators on the streets and by many journalists. His telegram, entitled 'Thinking the Unthinkable', suggested that the Shah, far from being the unique restraining element, might actually leave the country and Khomeini might return to Iran and take up 'a Gandhi-like position', choosing a leader who would be acceptable to the Iranian military. In the telegram there was no suggestion of the role which US policy might play with either the military or the Islamic forces, nor did it recommend making contact with the people who might possibly take over from the Shah. There had been no attempt to communicate with Khomeini in exile.

Sullivan later omitted the embarrassing expression 'Gandhi-like' when he quoted the telegram in his memoirs, and it is hard not to sympathise with him for leaving it out. As late as February 1979 a writer in the *New York Times* was suggesting that Khomeini might provide the Third World with a model of humane governance. But then journalists are used to making public mistakes and having to live with them. Ambassadors also have to live with their mistakes, but they are usually made in private. The telegram was used as ammunition between the State Department and the National Security Council and further eroded Sullivan's position in the bureaucratic infighting over Iran.

It is doubtful whether it would have made any difference to the situation at all if Sullivan had recognised the dangers to the Shah earlier than he did. After the Shah's overthrow, his reporting to Washington was often more accurate than that of other observers: he forecast both the weakness of Bakhtiar and the intransigence of Khomeini. But it made no difference whatever to US policy, which was rudderless now that the Shah had left. Departmental infighting worsened; but the view of the Iran Country Director at the State Department, Henry Precht, prevailed. Precht insisted, up to the day of the embassy takeover, that Iran was really being run by moderate elements who were gaining strength daily: Khomeini was just a figurehead. This view had been vigorously opposed by many in the Embassy, but Precht had brushed them aside.

One evening in 1986 an announcer on Iranian television warned viewers that they should watch an important programme later that night, but gave no indication of the subject. When the programme began, it proved to be about the takeover of the American Embassy, seven years previously, which had been the beginning of the hostage crisis. There had been programmes on the subject before, but this one differed in that the pictures which were shown had not been taken by people in the crowd outside; they were recorded by the fixed security cameras which the Americans themselves had installed on the main buildings of the Embassy.

Soundlessly, in black and white, the waves of attackers came swarming over the walls and gates and charged towards the embassy entrance. The pictures showed a few of the Marine guards trying to stand in the crowd's path, but they disappeared under the sheer weight of the attack. The pictures lasted for a matter of minutes only, but they were an extraordinary record of an incident which led to the humiliation of the United States and the ending of the political career of its President.

The great majority of the hostages who were taken at the Embassy that day were to remain prisoners for 444 days. But Marine Sgt. William Quarles, who had been out jogging when the attack took place, was released early. He was black, and the Students of the Imam's Line who were in control of the Embassy decided to free him and the other blacks and most of the women, thirteen Americans in all, as a gesture to people whom they believed to be oppressed by white American society. When Quarles had finished jogging he had gone back to his flat on the other side of the street from the Embassy, and had heard the security officer give the order over the walkie-talkies they all carried: 'Don't fire your weapons. When they come for you, give up.' A photograph taken by one of the Students immediately after the storming of the Embassy shows Quarles, who stands head and shoulders above everybody else, resisting while a blindfold is tied round the eyes of one of his fellow-Marines.

Quarles was an intelligent man, who had joined the Marine Corps because he wanted to see the world. Like one or two of the other Marines, he had learned a little Farsi. He also spent his free time out of the confines of the Embassy, which was unusual for Americans. He had Iranian girlfriends who were politically aware and had warned him some days earlier that there was going to be an attack on the Embassy. Quarles seems to have reported this to his commanding officer, but no extra precautions were taken. There had been similar warnings in the past and nothing had come of them.

The disaster was complete. Yet there was worse to come: in particular the botched attempt to rescue the hostages. This was forced on President Carter by some of his advisers and military men, and by the sense in the United States as a whole that not enough was being done. The plan was a risky one and if it had gone ahead many people, including most of the American hostages, would probably have died. As it was, the entire operation was aborted through a combination of bad luck and incompetence: a helicopter crashed into a tanker aircraft, eight men died, the necessary margin of logistical support (which would probably have been insufficient) was eroded. There was always something faintly make-believe about the plan anyway: two Iranian women I know happened to be walking past a football stadium about five minutes' drive from the American Embassy that day, and glanced into it. Every pillar and upright that they could see had yellow ribbons tied to them. The plan envisaged taking the hostages there on their way out of the country, and some

CIA agent in Tehran had clearly decided to make them feel welcome. The women knew nothing at that stage of the rescue attempt, but they guessed at once that something was going on. They hurried off, anxious not to be associated with it in any way.

When the 444 days were over, it was President Carter who received the entire blame for everything; and in particular for the original cause of the attack: the decision to allow the Shah to come to the United States for medical attention a few days before. The Shah's strongest supporters in Washington, Henry Kissinger, David Rockefeller and Zbigniew Brzezinski, had urged Carter for months to let him go to New York for treatment of the cancer from which he was suffering. Since equivalent medical facilities were available in Mexico, their purpose seemed less to do with the treatment than with a signal to America's friends that it would not desert them, whatever happened. Carter reluctantly agreed.

When the hostages were eventually released in January 1981, one of them, Moorhead Kennedy, an economic officer at the Embassy, was scathing about the lack of forethought which he maintained had characterised American policy:

[W]hat happened in Tehran was the diplomatic equivalent of Pearl Harbor. It was bad. We totally missed the significance of the Revolution. We supported the Shah much too long. We couldn't cut loose from him. We felt we owed him a debt of honor, and we sacrificed an embassy so he could have an operation. It was laziness, sheer intellectual laziness.

When I was facing execution, one of the things that occurred to me was that I and a group of us had reported honestly, the embassy had done a very good job. But our warnings were not given the attention they should have in Washington. The same people [who had supported the Shah] blindly thought everything would be onward and upward in our relations with Khomeini. Of course it wasn't.

The hostages were freed only minutes after Ronald Reagan was sworn in as President. There was a powerful rumour in Washington to the effect that Reagan's campaign team had done a deal with the Iranians to delay their release until Carter was out of office. The Reagan team was certainly extremely nervous about the possibility of an 'October surprise' in the run-up to the 1980 election, in which Carter's diplomacy would win the hostages' freedom and he would be re-elected on the strength of it. The notion that Reagan's officials would have negotiated secretly with their country's enemies for the sake of party advantage was something that most American newspapers dismissed without investigation. The mood of the first Reagan presidency was not one that encouraged reporting that was critical of him. It was only after his re-election in 1984 that American journalists began to realise that his officials had entered into relations with Iran which were morally dubious and sometimes questionable constitutionally. Reagan himself, with his fading selective memory and frequent inability to sort out fact from fiction, was not perhaps the best witness about the truth or otherwise of the 'October Surprise' concept. Nevertheless, when he was interviewed about it on a golf course in California in June 1991 his answers seemed highly suggestive, even though he was trying to deny any wrongdoing:

REAGAN: I did some things actually the other way, to try to be of help in getting those hostages . . . I felt very sorry for them and getting them out of there. And this whole thing, that I would have worried about that as a campaign thing, is absolute fiction. I did some things to try the other way . . . The only efforts on my part were directed at getting them home.
QUESTION: Did that mean contacts with the Iranian government?
REAGAN: Not by me, no.
QUESTION: By your campaign, perhaps?
REAGAN: I can't get into details. Some of these things are still classified.

Gary Sick, an academic and specialist on Iranian affairs who served on the National Security Council under President Carter, examined the question of illicit contacts between the Reagan team and Iran and decided that there was evidence that these had taken place. Sick's book, *October Surprise*, was carefully researched and far from excitable; yet when it appeared in 1991 there was still little interest in the notion on the part of the American media. Sick himself writes:

The critical question is whether representatives of a political party out of power secretly, and illegally, negotiated with representatives of a hostile foreign power, thereby distorting or undermining the efforts of the legitimate government. Even today, more than a decade later, it is still difficult to imagine that an opposition political faction in the United States would employ such tactics, wilfully prolonging the imprisonment of fifty-two American citizens for partisan political gain.
    Nevertheless, that is what occurred: the Reagan–Bush campaign mounted a professionally organized intelligence operation to subvert the American democratic process.

If Carter believed that his chances of re-election had been destroyed in this way, he did not show it. Soon after Reagan had been inaugurated in January 1980, Carter boarded a plane for Wiesbaden in Germany where the hostages had been taken for medical treatment and debriefing. The visit was in the nature of a personal pilgrimage, and it must have taken a good deal of courage. Most of the hostages felt that Carter had personally let them down, and was responsible for their long imprisonment. Shortly before he arrived in Wiesbaden the more hot-headed of the young Marines were taken aside by their commanding officer and told to control their tempers and behave properly towards the man who had been their commander-in-chief. When Carter spoke to them, however, his obvious emotion won over a number of people who had previously regarded him as their worst enemy.

Few of them extended the same forgiveness to Iran. When they were interviewed before their return to the United States, many of the hostages reacted bitterly. Donald Hohman of the US Army said: 'All I want to see is a scorched earth policy in Iran. I want to make it clear to them they don't have the right to treat people the way they treated us.' Malcolm Kalp, an economics officer, who had spent 373 days in solitary confinement after trying to escape: 'I'd give them eight billion dollars' worth of bombs.' Bruce German, from the budget and management section: 'I'd only want to go back in a B-52.'

Marine Sgt. William Quarles, who had joined the military to see the world, had a different perspective; partly, no doubt, because he had been released early.

I hear people say 'Send in the Marines', or 'Let's nuke the hell out of them', so that the United States can look good in the eyes of the world.' But I don't think Americans really understand. [The Iranians] began showing me official US classified documents. I realized that the US has been doing things there that these people didn't like. It makes you see that there are two sides to every story, and seeing what I have since I have been home, the media doesn't tell Americans all the things that are going on, all the things this country has participated in over there.

Quarles's insights were not shared by most ordinary Americans. There were many interviews on radio and television with people who wanted to turn Iran into a parking lot. In California, Texas and New York, businessmen and students who had come to the United States to find sanctuary from Khomeini's revolution were attacked and beaten up in the streets, merely for being Iranian. An Iranian student who was badly injured in an accident which was the fault of the other driver was advised by his lawyer not to sue for damages. 'In this climate,' the lawyer said, 'no court will give you a sympathetic hearing.'

* * *

Seven years after the revolution and the takeover of the US Embassy there was a secret, highly questionable, and at times ludicrous attempt by a handful of men in the Reagan administration with a taste for covert activities to reach agreement with Iran.

Shortly after 8 a.m. on the morning of Sunday, 25 May 1986, a Boeing 707, painted black, landed at Mehrabad Airport in Tehran. As it taxied across the runway it was the most conspicuous object in the entire airport. The men on board, who included President Ronald Reagan's National Security Adviser, Robert McFarlane, and a conspiracy-minded, boyish-looking figure from the White House staff, Lieutenant Colonel Oliver North, waited for nearly an hour and a half before anyone came across to the plane to speak to them. It would have been difficult to select a worse time to come. It was Ramadan, when nothing very much gets done in Iran and the attention span and temper of government officials is noticeably short. Worse, a serious battle was going on between several of the leading figures in the Iranian hierarchy over policy in the war with Iraq and in the economy, and it was going to prove extremely difficult to find anyone to negotiate with. The faulty timing was only one of a series of mistakes and misunderstandings which had gone into the planning of the venture.

The plane had been supplied by Israel. On board was a kosher chocolate cake in the shape of a key which the Israelis had also supplied as a goodwill gesture; the key was supposed to represent the opening of a new era in relations between Iran and the United States. The cake became a symbol of the whole absurd endeavour; later it was eaten by the Revolutionary Guards at the airport. Lieutenant-Colonel North, at the suggestion of the CIA director William Casey, had equipped himself with a poison capsule, in case the Iranians decided to kidnap him.

In fact the Iranians took very little notice of him or of the others. They were eventually taken to the Esteqlal Hotel, which had formerly been the Hilton and was now owned by the government and used partially as a post for Revolutionary Guards. They were installed in several suites on the top floor, each of which was thoroughly equipped with listening devices. That night the first high-level meeting between American and Iranian officials took place. It was not, however, nearly as high-level as McFarlane had been led to expect. He and North later described the man who came to the hotel to see them as a deputy prime minister, but he was in fact an assistant to the prime minister, and not a very senior one at that.

McFarlane and the others had come in the expectation that a deal could be agreed fast: the United States would supply Iran with the weapons it needed for its war with Iraq, and Iran would use its influence in Lebanon to hand over the American hostages. But over the next two days it became clear that the groundwork which the American side thought had been done had scarcely been started; and the Iranians, expecting that the Boeing 707 had brought half the weapons which had been agreed as part of the overall deal, were taken aback to discover only a quarter of that amount. To make matters worse, the Hawk anti-aircraft missiles which North had arranged to be delivered to Iran the previous year were painted with Israeli Star of David markings.

The high-level meetings which North believed had been promised with Rafsanjani, Khamene'i, and Mussavi, the prime minister, did not materialise. Perhaps this was because the meetings had been arranged, not by the Iranians but merely by the intermediary with whom McFarlane, on North's urging, had been dealing. Manucher Ghorbanifar was an Iranian businessman living in France, and he had good connections with the arms trade. The CIA had once used him, but had dropped him six years before because of what they called his 'bravado and exaggeration'. They had issued what is known as a 'burn notice' on him, warning other US agencies to beware. McFarlane and North, who had failed to take the CIA's advice, sat in their hotel suites, virtual prisoners. Frustrated and angry, McFarlane sent a message back to Washington:

> It may be best for us to try to picture what it would be like if after a nuclear attack a surviving Tartar became Vice-President, a recent grad student became Secretary of State, and a bookie became the interlocutor for all discourse with foreign countries.

The second evening a more senior figure, an adviser from the Ministry of Foreign Affairs, came to the Esteqlal. He quoted an old Persian saying: 'Patience will bring you victory.' North, however, made a hard-and-fast offer: ten hours after the release of the American hostages, an aircraft would land in Tehran with the spare parts which Iran needed for the Hawk anti-aircraft missiles it had already received from the United States, together with two sophisticated radar systems. The Iranian foreign affairs adviser countered with a list of weapons Iran would also want, including Tow anti-tank missiles complete with technicians. At one point the official said they had been in touch with the Hezbollah leaders in Lebanon, who were assumed to be holding the American hostages, and that they would agree to release them if Israel withdrew from the Golan Heights and southern Lebanon, and seventeen Muslim fundamentalists held in prison in Kuwait were freed. These demands had all been made publicly; they scarcely suggested the prospect of serious negotiation.

At 9.30 that evening the Americans handed over a document outlining a draft agreement, and told the Iranian side that they had until 4 a.m. the following morning to free the hostages. At 2 a.m. the Iranians asked for a delay until 6 a.m., but the official did not return until 7.50. When he did, he said they thought they could get two hostages out. McFarlane's patience snapped. 'It's too late,' he said. 'We're leaving.' The black 707 took off an hour and five minutes later.

In the months that followed, more Hawk spares and more Tow missiles were sent to Iran, and two hostages, Father Lawrence Jenco and David Jacobsen, were released in Beirut. The day before Jacobsen was freed, the Lebanese magazine *Ash Shiraa*, which had close links with Syria, broke the news of the deal. Jenco and Jacobsen were presumably the two whose release had been offered during the final meeting in Tehran. But in the intervening period, early in 1987, Terry Waite was kidnapped because of his alleged involvement with Oliver North in attempting to negotiate hostage releases; and two more Americans, Frank Reed and Joseph Cicippio, were taken hostage as well. The freedom of all the American and British hostages only came after the Coalition powers had gone to war with Saddam Hussein.

The Tower Commission, which was established to investigate the whole affair, was scathing about the operation's unprofessional quality, and about the contrast between the Reagan administration's public condemnation of negotiating with terrorists for the release of hostages and of supplying arms to Iran, while in private the administration had done both. Soon, however, the issue became subsumed in the more general question of how much the President had known about the payment to Contras in Nicaragua of the money which Iran had spent to buy American missiles: a 'neat idea', North had described it.

On 4 July 1988, after a series of small-scale attacks by Iranian gunboats (which were often little more than rubber dinghies with a powerful engine), the United States naval forces based in the Gulf were on full alert for an all-out assault which would coincide with American Independence Day. The USS *Vincennes*, commanded by Captain Will Rogers, mistook an Iran Airbus A300 passenger plane taking off at a scheduled time from Bandar Abbas and following an internationally agreed flight path across the Gulf to Dubai, for an F-14 fighter aircraft making an attacking run. A video, shot on the bridge of the *Vincennes*, showed the delight of the crew as their missiles hit the mark turning to disbelief and horror as they realised what it was they had shot down. Two hundred and ninety-eight people died on board flight IR 655, many of them not even citizens of Iran.

The United States apologised quickly, but there were attempts to provide a form of justification, and the American public – unlike the members of the Reagan administration and the *Vincennes* crew

– exhibited few signs of remorse. Indeed, even after it had become clear that the disaster was entirely the fault of the ship and her commanding officer, an opinion poll found that 75 per cent of Americans thought Captain Rogers had made the right decision in shooting the airbus down. Iran filed a suit against the United States at the International Court in The Hague, demanding compensation for the families of the victims. But in 1993 the US Supreme Court ruled that a state of war had existed in the Gulf at the time and that there was no requirement to pay any compensation.

Ayatollah Khomeini, who had always preached the creed of an eye for an eye and a tooth for a tooth, seemed by contrast to be remarkably forgiving. Nevertheless, suspicion inevitably fell on Iran when a Pan American jumbo jet was blown up over the Scottish village of Lockerbie five months later, in December 1988. Two hundred and seventy people, mainly American and British, were killed on the airliner and in the village where the wreckage landed. The question of guilt was clearly a complex one, and it was never clearly established who had drawn up the original plan. Meticulous police work identified two Libyans as the men who actually ensured that the bomb would go off, and a legal and political battle lasting many years was waged against Colonel Qadaffi's regime to obtain the extradition of the two accused men. Iran's name was scarcely mentioned, though Tehran made a point of supporting Libya against American and British pressure. President Rafsanjani met the Speaker of the Libyan parliament when he visited Tehran, and called for 'unity and co-ordination among Moslem states with regard to the recent US propaganda campaign against Libya'.

There are times, as you drive through the rubble and decaying garbage of south Beirut, or the small mountain villages of southern Lebanon, when you could easily imagine yourself to be in Iran. The portraits of Ayatollah Khomeini, of his successor Ali Khamene'i, of other leading Iranian clerics living and dead, are everywhere. So are the heavily-bearded young men of Hezbollah, lounging at road blocks in their dark olive camouflage, guns at their sides. Hezbollah, which models itself closely on the Iranian *Pasdaran*, or Revolutionary Guards, and is advised and probably funded directly from Iran, gradually wrested control of most of southern Beirut from the more moderate Shi'ite group Amal, led by the old-fashioned Lebanese warlord Nabi Berri, in the mid-1980s. It wasn't merely a matter of Iranian money and influence; the revolution in Iran had galvanised the Shi'ia Muslim population of Lebanon and gave them a pride in their Shi'ia origins as nothing else had ever done. The Shi'ites had always been regarded as uneducated peasants by most of the other Lebanese population groups. With the exception of a few wealthy families they had formed the under-class of

Lebanon: the hewers of wood and the drawers of water. When they left their hill-villages in the south of the country to settle in Beirut, their suburbs were the poorest in the city.

The Iranian Revolution changed all that. It was a revelation of Shi'ite power, and their various political and military organisations took advantage of the new mood of self-confidence and pride. Hezbollah, the Party of God, was the strongest and most feared of them all, thanks mostly to its Iranian links; and when it started capturing Western hostages, there was a strong suspicion immediately that this was on the instructions of Tehran. Nevertheless, in reality the precise details of the connection with Iran remain uncertain: for instance, which part of the Iranian government or leadership (and they were not always the same thing) supported the hostage-takers; whether funds were sent to them by Tehran, and by whom; whether the kidnappers were under specific orders from Tehran when the hostages were picked up, or were simply acting on impulse. There was certainly something of a patron–client relationship between Hezbollah and its Iranian contacts, but the patron did not necessarily control the transactions. A political client always has a certain power over the patron as well.

Hostage-taking was nothing new, especially in Lebanon during the 1970s, but it seems as though the inspiration for capturing Western hostages came from the takeover of the American Embassy in Tehran. The daily spectacle of Washington's anguish and embarrassment during the 444 days during which the people from the Embassy were held was a revelation to those in Lebanon who supported Iran or wanted to humiliate the United States. But as Iran changed, so did the relationship with its Lebanese client. The ending of the Iran–Iraq war in July 1988 was the first big step. The moderates were now in the ascendant in Tehran, and they knew that Iran would need better links with the West if the slow process of reconstruction were to start in earnest. Still unresolved was the issue of several hundred million dollars' worth of frozen Iranian assets held by the US; and in guarded terms that enabled him to deny direct complicity with the hostage-takers, Rafsanjani offered his help in arranging the release of the captured Americans in exchange for these disputed assets. Washington rejected the offer, but the need for stronger links with the West remained.

In the final analysis, Iran's revival depended on oil money, and the industry had always been dependent on American and Western technology. Slowly and uncertainly, Iran re-established full diplomatic relations with Britain, its other big Western trading partner in the days of the Shah and a key member of the European Community which Iran wanted to cultivate as a counterweight to the United States. The improvement in relations would always be in doubt, however, while the British and American hostages were still being held in Lebanon.

The precise terms on which the groups which held the Western hostages might be prepared to release them were always vague, but some elements in the demands came up again and again. The basic deal on offer might have been framed for its impossibility: the hostages would be released in exchange for the seventeen Shi'ia militants held in Kuwait for planting bombs there in 1983, and for three Iranian diplomats and an Iranian journalist who disappeared in Lebanon in July 1982 after stopping at a road block manned by the Israeli-backed Christian militia. It was generally accepted that the four Iranians were dead; according to a persistent report, they were held by a particularly violent Christian faction leader, Samir Geagea, and one of his men threw a hand grenade into the room where they were being held. For years, the Iranians refused to accept this without being shown the bodies, or the graves, of the four men. It seemed a complete impasse. The British government sent special representatives to try to find out precisely what had happened to their bodies, but without success. As for the seventeen Shi'ite prisoners, the Kuwaiti government refused point-blank to give them up, and neither the British nor the United States governments felt able to put pressure on them to do so.

What changed everything was the Iraqi invasion of Kuwait in August 1990. The seventeen Shi'ia fundamentalists, who had been of major significance to both the Iranians and Hezbollah, were freed from prison by the invading troops, and were therefore no longer part of the deal. The West's attitude towards Iran changed in something of the way the Iranian authorities had wanted: for a time, at any rate, Iran (as Iraq's greatest enemy) was regarded as a surrogate friend. The West tacitly accepted that since Saddam Hussein's invasion of Kuwait was illegal, his invasion of Iran in 1980 had been unprovoked as well: a recognition that Iran had demanded. During this brief period of *rapprochement* the Iranian government accepted that its three diplomats and the journalist in Lebanon were indeed dead. So the most difficult aspect of the quid pro quo had simply evaporated in a matter of months; now all that was necessary was a practical negotiation.

For President Rafsanjani, the benefits of a deal suddenly outweighed the difficulties, and he could afford to ignore the wilder demands of the kidnappers, such as the immediate withdrawal of Israeli forces from the Golan Heights. The benefits seemed very real to many other people too. The Iranian business community understood that the link between their government and the hostage-takers was seriously affecting profits; and since most businessmen in Iran had the backing of a mullah for political reasons, many of the clergy wanted to see an end to the hostage crisis as well. And since the link with the hostage-takers was the Iranian radicals' most important asset, Rafsanjani would be dealing them a serious blow by bringing the crisis to an end.

The negotiations, when they came, went remarkably smoothly. On the Western side no money seems to have been paid over, and the

promises of better relations were equally vague. The Iranians agreed
to pay the various Lebanese groups for the expenses they claimed to
have incurred during the years the hostages had been held, together
with bonuses for everyone involved in capturing and holding them. In
other words, the criminals were at last reaping some of the benefits
of their crime. But at least the innocent were freed. Slowly, with some
difficult pauses, the releases started, both of the American hostages and
of the British. The hostage question, which had made relations with Iran
so difficult since the mid-1980s, was over.

In the summer of 1993 a member of the Iranian Majlis made a speech,
probably with the approval of President Rafsanjani, in which he argued
that Iran should resume diplomatic relations with Washington. Iran
would then be able to receive financial credits which it badly needed,
recover its frozen assets and have access to technical expertise. It was
a risky speech to make; political moderates in Iran who supported the
notion of a deal with the United States have often paid a high price.
Many were executed or murdered or forced to live abroad, and many
others had to undergo a form of internal exile and wait quietly for
times to get better. President Rafsanjani might use his waning powers
to press for an improvement in relations with Washington, but his
former ally, the country's religious leader Ayatollah Khamene'i, made
his views clear. Anyone who wanted to deal with America was, he
said, 'naïve, ignorant, and unfamiliar with political issues and with the
dangers that such negotiations entail'.

And yet there was no question that the violent feelings about the
United States had mostly subsided. November 4, the day the US Embassy
was overrun, became enshrined in the Iranian revolutionary calendar
as 'Hate America Day'. In the 1980s the date was the occasion for
huge rallies at Azadi Square, at which President Ronald Reagan was
usually burned in effigy. By 1993 it was marked only by a handful of
hardliners. At a demonstration outside the former American Embassy
in central Tehran a dozen banners were on show, with the words
'Death to America' written on them in skulls and crossbones, and
various insulting songs were blasted out from loudspeakers attached
to the embassy walls. But the self-confident slogans of the early days
of the revolution, once painted so boldly on the walls, had long since
begun to fade. The years of sun, snow and rain had done their work on
them, and no one ever bothered to repaint them. The day of powerful,
virulent anti-Americanism in Iran had long gone.

For thousands of Americans, their view of the awfulness of Iran was
fixed not merely by the revolution and the hostage crisis, but by a book

written by an American woman who married an Iranian and eventually escaped from him and from Iran with their child. *Not Without My Daughter* by Betty Mahmoody is execrably written, but it reinforced a view of Iran which many Americans held: that it was a country of violent, unreasoning cruelty. By the early 1990s there were only two hundred American women left in Iran, almost all of them married to Iranians. For the great majority of them, their experience has been completely different from Betty Mahmoody's, and they tend to have nothing but contempt for her book.

Nancy grew up in the Midwest in the 1980s, an adventurous and independent-minded young woman who was always interested in the world outside the confines of Middle America. She met her future husband Bijan at university. He came from a well-to-do family in north Tehran, and was finishing his medical studies.

'On my first date with Bijan he cooked me a Persian meal. It was great chicken *Khoresht* with fragrant saffron rice and it seemed so exotic to me. I didn't know any men who could cook and I hadn't travelled outside America then. He had to show me where Iran was on the map. But his cooking worked and later that year, right after we graduated, we got married.

'My parents didn't know anything about Iran, and I suppose neither did I. They were really charmed by Bijan and impressed by his generosity, and very, very happy that I was marrying a doctor. When we told them we were moving to Iran, my mother was terrified; a friend had just given her that ridiculous book *Not Without My Daughter* and she was practically hysterical. Bijan's parents tried to talk to her on the phone from Tehran and tell her not to worry, but when I got on the plane I discovered she had put that book in my bag. Bijan was really disgusted and threw it away. It was months later that I read it in Tehran, and there were not many things in it that I believed; especially about how dirty Iranians are. That's so dumb. And I know people who were friends of Betty Mahmoody's who were very unhappy about how they were portrayed.

'All the American women who live here come and go with our children to America. We get together for tea sometimes and just chat. Some of the women are good friends, and some are very different from me. Just because we are Americans in Iran doesn't mean we are going to be best friends; my closest girlfriends are two Persian girls that I ride with: our horses are at the same stable. But I haven't stopped going to America and I spend at least a month there every summer. It's nice to get out of the heat here for a bit and walk around in skimpy T-shirts and shorts outside, but Iran is my home. I've given up even trying to explain it to most Americans I know; they seem to think it's like a prison and I'm crazy.

'Yes, I hate *hejab* when I really think about it, and sometimes I get

angry if I get hassled by the *Komiteh* or something. But we have a
beautiful home and my boys are safe, not like where I grew up where
you're nervous every time your kids walk out the door.'

Nancy speaks good conversational Persian and is learning to read and
write the Arabic script it is written in. Unable to pursue her work in the
field of sociology, a field which scarcely exists in Iran, she has turned
to other things. She helps with local children's groups and has acquired
dozens of books on Persian art.

'Bijan always gives me some Persian craft or carpet for my birthday
and Christmas. Whenever there's a holiday we will go to some new part
of the country, depending on what I've been reading. We've been to
the city of Bam and set up our tents to just breathe in the atmosphere
of the place. I should have taken some photos and sent them to the
L. L. Bean catalogue. And then there's Luristan and the bronzes. And
of course Isfahan alone is like a Ph.D. course on Persian arts from
crafts to architecture. I'm not a Muslim but I love the mosques there,
especially the Friday mosque. My new passion is tiles; I'm beginning
to learn more about them and I've just ordered some books from
London on them. This could develop into a serious addiction. And then
of course there's water-skiing.'

A day or so later Bijan was sitting in a motorboat, watching the driver
revving up the engine and waiting for the figure in the water to give a
thumbs-up sign. Rising above us were bare red cliffs which reflected the
sun back on to the lake. Beyond them lay the stark Albourz Mountains,
the last green of the spring burned out by mid-June. The tang of diesel
rose in the air as the motor purred.

'OK, hit it!'

The boat took off from a standstill and the figure in the water was
pulled up by the towrope, perfectly balanced on a slalom ski, weaving
curving turns back and forth in the wake of the boat. Nancy is an expert
water-skier, and she has not given it up in Iran; merely modified her
clothes. The contrast between her graceful style and her dripping wet,
all-encompassing *roupush* and black leggings, topped by a bathing cap,
was ludicrous. Nancy said it took her some weeks to get used to the
different balance because of the weight of wet Islamic clothes. After
twenty minutes we slowed down. Nancy's momentum carried her close
to the boat and she sank down in the water, loosening her ski to hand
it up to us.

A few hundred metres away on the shore, a *Komiteh* patrol watched us
carefully. Nothing improper had occurred and we had strictly observed
the Islamic rules on dress. The men in the boat couldn't give Nancy a
hand up, not even her husband; so they lowered a clumsy rope-ladder
and moved a few feet away towards the bow to make it obvious to
the moral guardians opposite that no physical contact had been made.

Nancy grinned as she climbed over the side of the boat: she knew her water-skiing had improved.

'My face is burning up. That's the trouble with sports here, unless you cover your face with lotion, you end up with a tan face and white body. It's just too weird, so I always use factor 25.'

She turned to her husband.

'Bijan, please hand me the sun lotion.'

As she smoothed it on, she started smiling again.

'Bijan tells me that when I write my book on Iran I should call it "Not Without my Coppertone".'

11

Life with Allah

Tira Shubart

Be well aware, my son, that riding and hunting are the occupation for gentlemen, particularly in youth. Yet there must be bounds and measure to every occupation, and one cannot hunt every day. In the week of seven days hunt for two days, devote yourself to the fulfilment of God's commands for three days and to your own domestic affairs for the remaining two.

A Mirror For Princes

'One Thursday night at a family dinner, my little cousin Ziba, who's fourteen, begged me to please, please take her out; she knew I had a car and there was someplace she badly wanted to go.

'"Of course," I said, because I was rather intrigued. "Where would that be?"

'She named a park in Tehran and asked if I'd pick her up and take her there at six o'clock the next morning.'

Shari is a young professional woman with a good business career in Tehran. Smartly dressed and witty, she manages to coexist with a system she dislikes intensely. One of her great pleasures is to observe the more absurd ways in which the regime persists in trying to suppress the indefatigable nature of the Persian.

'We arrived at the park and before I got out of the car, Ziba was off like a streak, and I was practically jogging to keep up with her. I wondered if maybe she had decided to get into the whole fitness thing. Then we turned the corner and I saw the reason she had wanted to come. There were about five hundred teenagers, dressed as though they were going to a party in their smart shoes or leather jackets, showing themselves off at their best. They walked around, trying to be casual, which isn't easy when there are hundreds of kids around and you're in a park at six or seven in the morning. They were checking each other out. They went around in groups, the boys separate from the girls, occasionally stopping and asking for each other's telephone numbers.

'You see, Fridays, early in the morning, they felt safe, trying to meet up that way. Even so, the *Komiteh* turned up and they started grabbing a bunch of the kids. Some scattered, others were caught and got thrown in the car and were taken away. It really got out of hand. But Ziba and I were okay because we were far enough away not to be bothered.

'So that's what the kids do, whenever and wherever they can. Three girls go to the pizza joint and check out three guys on the other side of the restaurant. That's why we don't have any real cafés here, like the ones you get in Europe for people to meet. If you did, the authorities would have to close it down, so it would be a bad business to invest in. Some teenagers meet in each other's houses if their parents are liberal and let them have parties. My little cousin was once picked up by the *Komiteh* when they found out about one of these parties; unrelated boys and girls together. For two or three nights all the kids were held in Evin prison. Some of the boys were even beaten. But it's not like it would be for us. For the kids, it's all a big adventure, going to the prison together overnight and getting the chance to hang out some more. Then their parents pay a little fine and tell them off. How ridiculous! These crazy laws don't have much impact any more; for the kids, the fear element just isn't there. If it were, they wouldn't be dressing up the way they do, looking fashionable all the time and thinking up new ways to have dates. I really admire them for their spirit.'

More than half the Iranian population is under twenty-five, and has never known any system other than the Islamic Republic. But they are not the inheritors of the revolution, as the original revolutionaries hoped.

'Most of these kids have never left the country,' Shari says, 'but they have pictures of all the pop stars on their walls. And of course the music. I think the more the authorities force people to be a certain way, the more they react against it.'

Many of the old social strictures have loosened in the Islamic Republic. The attempt to eliminate Western influences in the country became less of a priority as the revolution established itself; at first a behavioural self-censorship did the authorities' job for them. It was easier to obey the new rules than have to deal with the *Komitehs*. Western videos, pop music, traditional Persian music, love-affairs, wine and vodka could still be enjoyed, but only in secret and behind closed doors. The wealthy, with their swimming pools and tennis courts, continued to sunbathe in bikinis and play mixed doubles; they simply built their garden walls higher in order to do so.

Yet the westernised middle classes who were educated abroad represent only about 5 per cent of the population. The more traditionally-minded men and women felt that the revolution had restored their dignity to them after the decades during which their values, both religious and secular, were devalued and considered old-fashioned by their rulers. But the rulings by which Ayatollah Khomeini tried to create his Islamically pure society often flew in the face of tradition, and brought disillusion to many who had at first supported the revolution wholeheartedly. Many of these rulings were petty as well as vindictive: in the decade which followed the revolution, board games such as chess and backgammon, which had been played for centuries in Iran, were banned. Buying a chessboard was a clandestine activity, and foreigners had their travelling sets confiscated at the airport.

Popular Iranian singers like Googoosh were forbidden to give concerts, and Persian popular music could not be played in public. Yet it still commanded a huge following. In July 1994 one dealer tried to smuggle in 200,000 photographs of Iranian singers and musicians to sell on the black market. The caravan of three camels which were carrying them was stopped by the Iranian security services near the border with Pakistan. They also found 1,580 key-rings bearing 'depraved signs'.

Those who controlled the programmes on state radio and television had a serious problem. There were no strictly Muslim songs available, and it was felt that recordings of Koranic chanting could not be used in case this gave the impression that the only value of religion was to act as a buffer between secular programmes. During the first year of the revolution, at one of his regular press conferences, Ayatollah Khomeini was asked what he thought about Western pop music. It was, he replied, totally decadent and unworthy of being played in the Islamic Republic.

'And what about Western classical music?' the questioner persisted.
'If it is good, then it is acceptable.'

The television authority's problem was solved; Vivaldi, Mozart, Schubert and Beethoven were all pressed into the service of Islamic entertainment, though nothing more modern than Tchaikovsky was heard. As for the gentle, exploratory, intelligent music of the *tar*, the Persian stringed instrument related to Western stringed instruments like the guitar (whose name derives directly from it), it was almost entirely banned from the national airwaves for nine years.

Finally, towards the end of the Iran–Iraq war, the decision was taken to allow a greater cultural breathing space, a sort of Islamic *glasnost*. Perhaps it was an attempt to appeal to the ancient Persian feelings which ran deeper than the new revolutionary mores, rather as Stalin had invoked the image of Mother Russia when Hitler invaded the Soviet Union. In the spring of 1988, in the centre of Tehran, a concert of traditional music was staged in a hall which had rarely been used since the revolution. The concert was broadcast live, and a series of individual musicians, choirs and orchestras played to a packed auditorium. To underline the significance of the occasion, the Minister of Islamic Guidance appeared on the television screen, embracing and kissing each of the musicians in turn. It happened during the run-up to the Majlis elections, and it was no coincidence that large numbers of foreign journalists were visiting Tehran at the time.

The cultural thaw continued. One of the great Persian epics, *Shahnameh* – the Book of Kings – had never been staged since the revolution because it dealt with past dynasties. It was finally performed in 1989. Since it had a big cast, *Shahmaneh* provided many Iranian actors with their first opportunity to work on the stage again. It was also the first time under the Islamic Republic that actresses were allowed to appear in the theatre. Once again, it had the official seal of approval: President Rafsanjani and half a dozen cabinet ministers were sitting in the front row.

The considerable artistic community in Iran took heart. Until now it had endured a sort of internal exile. Artists had continued to paint and sculpt, private exhibitions were still held and works were purchased by collectors, dress designers still made 'indoor' clothes for their clients; but it had all happened behind closed doors. Now, at last, it seemed as though things were changing.

At the City Theatre, in the older part of Tehran, there was to be a Persian-language production of Chekhov's *Uncle Vanya*. The doors would not be opened until the last moment, to avoid attracting too much notice, but there had been an unspoken communal decision to dress as smartly as possible: as though this were any first night, anywhere else in the world. The women wore their smartest *roupushes*, lipstick and eye make-up, and displayed more hair than usual. The men were dressed in smart suits, the younger ones tieless, following Armani rather than the leaders of the Islamic Republic, and wearing their linen jackets with the sleeves pushed up to the elbows. Several of them had their hair in ponytails. The older men were dressed more conventionally, in ties and suits with wider lapels than were fashionable in the West. Passers-by stared unbelievingly at the display.

The City Theatre had been built in the 1970s by a well-known Iranian architect, Ali Sardar-Afgani, with the blessing of the Empress Farah. The lower ground floor beneath the main auditorium was the preserve of an avant-garde director, who had turned it into a small fringe theatre where a company called The Four Directions presented plays from abroad. It was in this smaller, less conspicuous space that *Uncle Vanya* would be staged. It had not been advertised anywhere.

A couple of security men, bearded and disapproving, unchained the doors which led to the lower lobby, and everyone filed in. The tickets were not numbered. The performance was to take place on a small circular stage, and the audience sat in tiers looking down on the actors. The lights went down. Most people were probably wondering how the actresses would keep to the Islamic rules about dress.

The cast came on, and the solution to the problem was revealed. The women were presented like Russian *babushkas*, with headscarves which looked entirely authentic in the setting. The younger women wore a sort of turban arrangement. Their dresses were floor-length and long-sleeved, but that was right for the period. When the nephew reeled drunkenly onstage, he carried a torch which he shone up into his face instead of a vodka bottle, wobbling drunkenly and stumbling about. Still, *Uncle Vanya* is one of Chekhov's bleaker plays, and the audience seemed a little disappointed in it. Like much of the Western classical music which had been played on Iranian radio and television before the *tar* was permitted again, it was a little too safe, too solemn, too non-Persian.

In the interval, the lobby filled up quickly. The smokers lit up, the non-smokers headed towards the doors for the evening air. The disapproving security men were standing by the doors, glaring at the theatregoers; if it had been up to them, there would have been no performance. The doors behind them were secured with heavy chains, and no one could get in or out. Someone asked what would happen if a fire broke out, as it had at the Rex Cinema in Abadan in the summer of 1978.

'Why should there be a fire?' asked the head doorkeeper suspiciously, as though we were threatening to start one; but, reluctantly, he unchained the doors all the same.

We packed up the Jeep with picnic baskets and flasks of hot drinks, and loaded up our equipment: ski boots, gloves, hats, suntan lotion. The skis went on the roof rack. It was still early in the day when we headed north and started the climb up the winding roads into the mountains. It was spring, and the roads were still icy; but the roaring creek below showed that the spring melt had started. It had been a hard winter in the Albourz Mountains, and the ski season had lasted longer than usual. Above us rose the perfect snow-covered summit of Mount Damavand.

There are about a dozen ski resorts in the Albourz, most of them within an hour's drive of Tehran. The chair lifts, which were built by Italian and Swiss firms before the revolution, run up to 12,000 feet. Our first stop was one of the larger areas; Shemshak, a resort with plenty of black runs and moguls, which is as good as any in the world. But there were long queues of cars there already, struggling to find a place to park in the muddy fields. It was a Friday, and since this was April it was possibly the last weekend of the ski season: everyone wanted to get a final day in. We turned and headed for the smaller resort of Darvansar. It wasn't quite as good, but at least we would avoid the queues.

The skiing that season had been the best in years, with record amounts of snow. Like the Rocky Mountains, Iran has good powder snow, so dry that it cannot easily be packed into a snowball. But this late in the season the apricot and plum trees at the foot of the mountains were

covered with white blossom. As for the skiers, they were startlingly
white as well, covered with sun-block and factor 25 cream below their
mandatory mirror sunglasses. Many of the men had wrapped scarves
around their heads, turban-style, to shield themselves from the effects
of the sun at high altitude.

The women mostly wore ski trousers or jeans and long sweaters, six
inches above the knee, so they would not show any unIslamic curves.
These sweaters were expensive, and carried designer logos or the names
of smart ski resorts in the Alps or the Rockies. They had tucked their
hair into woolly hats and some women had devised an elaborate method
of braiding two scarves together and winding them round their head
in a way that might have observed the letter of the *hejab* law, but
certainly not the spirit: as a style, it would not have looked out of
place in St Moritz. There was only one woman in a *roupush*. She was
still learning to ski, and struggled up the rope-tow on the baby slope,
attempting snowplough turns and sliding back down every time.

Islamic sexual apartheid was maintained: men and women were not
allowed to sit together on the chair lifts, and in the bigger resorts, some
chair lifts were for men or women only. The lift attendant turned into
a moral policeman. The story is told of a man who tried to board the
chair lift with his wife and shouted at the attendant, 'I was in bed with
this woman an hour ago, and now you tell me that I can't sit next to
her!' It was not an issue which worried Iranian skiers unduly; especially
with lift tickets at less than a dollar a day.

The local *Komiteh* was also there to look after safety, and to protect
the morals of the skiers. Many of them had succumbed to the attractions
of the sport, however; and some of the hottest skiers on the mountain
were *Komiteh* members. They specialised in performing high-speed
stops, spraying snow into the faces of the onlookers, and barged in
at the front of the queues; the urge which grips all skiers at the
end of the season, to get in as many runs as possible before the
big melt, applied to them as well.

In the Shah's days, Bahram was a member of the Ski Federation, and
worked as an instructor from time to time. He is still a first-class skier,
and has the winter suntan and the band of white across his eyes to
prove it. Nowadays he rarely travels outside Iran, but his skis and boots
are the latest Western models.

'Right after the revolution, skiing was stopped for a season. Actually
they tried to stop it, but they never really succeeded. The new regime
wanted to pay the workers connected to the industry so they would
change jobs. At first some villagers supported this, and they believed
the government would give them money from the redistribution of
oil and gas money. They wanted to burn the lifts and the chalets,
everything. When things got really bad I came up here and asked the
villagers why they wanted to do it. Some of them said that skiing was

unIslamic and it had been the Shah's sport. I asked them, "What will you do for jobs if you burn everything? Why don't you wait to see if this new government makes you rich before you start?" And I asked them if they liked skiing. Of course they did; who wouldn't? Well, it soon became obvious they weren't going to get rich overnight. And skiers are skiers. So here we are today.

'Most of the skiers are *taght-ut-tee* [literally, idol worshippers]: you know – rich people who supported the old regime. Now I notice quite a few students skiing, more than before. It's cheap enough for them to be able to afford it, and nowadays there's not much else for them to do socially. So it's probably more egalitarian these days than it used to be. Skiing has been going on in this country for forty or fifty years, but around 1970 the Shah started going into it big time, and spent lots of money on it. That became a problem later, because it was seen as a non-revolutionary sort of sport. But the Shah was clever in one way; he declared that all the local people in the villages should be allowed to ski for nothing. So many of them became very good skiers, and they worked at the resorts and on the slopes.'

That day the atmosphere was good: the new moon had been spotted by the religious authorities the night before, which meant that the fast of Ramadan could end a day ahead of schedule, just in time for the Islamic weekend. It was also a day before the authorities in Mecca would see the new moon.

'Miracles of this sort often happen in Iran,' said Bahram sardonically.

The two men sitting in the chair lift in front broke into a cheerful Persian song for the benefit of their friends on the slope below. Those who had observed the fast could now quench their thirst in the heat of the day, and those who had ignored it could eat and drink openly. The sandwich and soft-drink stand at the foot of the slope was doing a brisk trade. Two girls sat in the shade nearby, eating a picnic lunch. They managed to show as much hair as possible without attracting the unwelcome attention of the *Komiteh*, and gold necklaces glinted underneath their braided scarves. Occasionally, as they ate, they would reach down elegantly and make a snowball to throw at the two boys who were sitting an Islamically correct but not unfriendly distance from them. Our group had an end-of-Ramadan snowball fight too; then we carried our skis through the churned-up mud of the car park, took off our boots, and sat on the tailgate of our jeep drinking tea from a thermos and eating cake. Other parties were doing the same, and we shouted our greetings to people we recognised. It was distinctly non-alcoholic for après-ski, but it had still been a very pleasant day.

Sports had become a weapon in the battle for the hearts and minds of the nation's youth. The more traditional and hardline clergy had declared war on the cultural invasion from the West, which they called 'Westoxification'; but since the frequent attempts to stop young people holding hands in a park, going to parties or watching unIslamic videos had invariably failed, it was decided to see if sport could be encouraged as an alternative. Over a period of several months, more and more sport was shown on television: traditional Iranian wrestling, volleyball, badminton, tennis, all played by men. And there was soccer, which has been a major passion in Iran for most of the twentieth century.

There is a national league, though not a large one, and each city has at least one team. There are two big football stadiums in Tehran itself. For the first time since the revolution Iranian television showed recordings of the matches in the 1994 World Cup, even though the tournament was taking place in the United States. There was heated discussion in the Majlis and the Tehran press about it. *Jomhuri Islami*, which invariably takes a hard line, warned that 'football is no longer a sport ... [it's] a tool to serve the interest of colonial powers.' Majlis members were also criticised for spending too much of their business time discussing the merits of the different national teams.

The television broadcasts were a triumph of Orwellianism: the temperatures in the American stadiums were clearly in the nineties, but whenever the cameras cut away to the stands the spectators were all wearing fur coats, gloves and hats. Pictures of the players in their skimpy shorts were unavoidable, but the authorities could not accept the sight of unIslamically-dressed women in the crowd so they had used pre-recorded footage of the onlookers at some unidentified match held in deep winter instead.

Girls' teams play soccer at school, though they have to wear sports *roupush* and no male spectators are allowed. The same rules apply to women's tennis and athletics. Two other sports which are easier for women to take part in are archery and riding: both are politically correct in Islam, since the Prophet Mohammed encouraged them, and they receive a favourable mention in the Koran. These were the skills with which the Islamic Arab conquests spread the word of Allah.

The horse has always been especially valued in the Persian world for its speed and courage. The great figures of Persian myth and folklore often had famous horses: there was, for instance, Rustam's companion Rakhsh, who accomplished heroic tasks with his master. On the ceremonial staircase at Persepolis the reliefs, carved with great zoological accuracy, show Persian horses being offered to the King in tribute: Caspians, Kurdish Arabs, Fars and others. The Persian love of the horse has not diminished, even though some horses were confiscated and sold for meat at the beginning of the revolution. There was also a brief attempt to use horses to stampede across the Iraqi minefields during the Iran–Iraq war. It failed: at the sound of the first explosion the horses turned and galloped back to safety. When the war ended, the

Revolutionary Guards were left with a herd of semi-wild horses, which they often sold back to their former owners.

About an hour west of Tehran is the village of Kordan, tucked below the Albourz foothills. A few years ago the road to it from the highway was unmarked. Now there are signs in Persian and English pointing the way to the 'Equestrian Centre'. More than a dozen livery stables have sprung up as well as boarding stables for those who own their own horses. Close enough to Tehran to be easily accessible, but far enough away to give a feeling of the wilderness, Kordan is a popular weekend retreat for riders. Once the paths here were used only by the shepherds who moved their flocks back and forth along the bare foothills; now they are marked by hoofprints. On any weekend the landscape is filled with mounted figures disappearing up into the hills or cantering alongside the banks of the Kordan River. Away from the eyes of the *Komitehs* and the *Pasdaran*, men and women can ride together. There is a real sense of freedom in the broad landscape. Even the packs of wild dogs which roam the area, racing across country to bark at the horses and snap at their heels, only enhance the feeling of being out in the wilds, a long way from Tehran and the reign of the mullahs.

Closer to the city, the riding club at Evin in the suburbs of Tehran stages gymkhanas and jumping competitions. When women take part, wearing their billowing outfits, the judges are the only men who are entitled to watch. Not even husbands are allowed to be there when their wives perform in jumping or dressage events. In the early years of the revolution, riding at Evin had a special *frisson*. Whatever the political situation, the horses still needed to be looked after and exercised. There were extra road blocks to pass through, and the *Komiteh* were often deeply hostile. And since Evin prison was less than half a mile away, the riders could sometimes hear the sound of the firing squads in the prison yard above the horses' hoofbeats.

Two years after the revolution, horse-racing began again. The penalty for gambling can be as much as six months in gaol and seventy-four lashes, and yet betting continues quite openly despite the ban. Due to past tradition and a love of horses, betting on races has always been allowed. There are said to be racing enthusiasts within the regime who have asked the religious authorities in Qom to legitimise it; but this has not yet happened.

One hot June day we headed west out of Tehran, along the airport road to Nowrouzabad. Once it lay deep in the countryside, but it has now been swallowed up by the city. There was a line of expensive cars ahead of us: a Mercedes, a Toyota Land Cruiser, several new Renaults. Down a side-road a dozen smartly dressed men wearing peaked caps and Ray-Bans leaned against their cars, which were parked on the edge of a field, and gazed at a cloud of dust from which, eventually, eight horses emerged. The animals seemed to pause, then turned sharply and took off in the opposite direction at a gallop. Mallets swung through the air, perilously close to the helmeted heads of the riders. A small white ball shot out between the horses' legs towards the goalpost, and the herd moved after it. It was hard to tell the two teams apart; the days of matching shirts and numbered saddle-blankets had gone.

The whistle blew, and the chukka was over. Eight grooms who had been sitting in the shade dusted themselves off and walked to the edge of the field, ready to take their horses to be watered and cooled down. Polo is not thriving under the Islamic Republic of Iran, but the surprising thing is that it has continued at all; it was once subsidised by the Shah's army, which helped players to buy horses and pay for their upkeep. For several years after the revolution it stopped entirely; but then a handful of players decided to start it up again. They made the point to the Islamic authorities that polo had originally been a Persian game, and that the Prophet had loved horses. Eventually, grudgingly, the authorities agreed.

'A man phones up Rafsanjani in the middle of the night and says, "My television is broken. Can you come over and repair it?"

'Rafsanjani says, "Sorry, you have a wrong number", hangs up and goes back to sleep.

'A few minutes later the phone rings again.

'"Hello, can you repair my television?" the voice asks again.

'Rafsanjani says, "Look, I'm telling you, you have the wrong number. This is Rafsanjani, President Rafsanjani."

'"I know, I know," says the man, "that's why I called you. You are the only person who can repair my television. I want to get the mullahs off the screen."'

Everyone at the table laughs. Amir, an entrepreneur who knew how to work the system to his advantage, always knows the latest anti-government jokes, and any society where a large portion of the population is disenchanted produces plenty of them. Now people start attacking the television service in earnest.

'You see, that's why we call Iranian television MTV,' says someone else. 'It stands for Mullah TV.'

Under the Islamic Republic, television has always had a heavy religious orientation, with a programming schedule that is worthy and more than a little dull:

CHANNEL 1
16.30 Sign On
16.35 Verses from the Holy Koran
16.45 News in English
17.00 Programme for children
18.00 Sports news

18.10 News from around the country
18.30 Sport
19.10 Call to prayer
19.30 Desert architecture
20.30 Iranian and world news
21.30 Economics programme
23.00 Programme in Arabic

CHANNEL 2
10.00 Sign On
10.05 Verses from the Holy Koran
10.10 Children's programme
11.05 Family programme (lessons in sewing, classical comedy, family care)
—
18.45 Sign On
18.50 Verses from the Holy Koran
19.00 Cultural and economic news
19.10 Call to prayer
19.20 Arabic lesson
19.40 Programme for university students
21.20 Cartoons
21.50 The Shrines of Iran
22.30 Iranian and world news

On radio the religious content is just as unrelenting; yet one programme that sometimes attracted quite large audiences for its bizarre content was *Ask A Mullah*. Questions of extraordinary and unlikely complexity were sent in to a panel of religious scholars, who proceeded to give long, unhumorous answers. During the war with Iraq, for instance, a young woman wrote to say that she was unmarried, and lived in a flat above a young man who was also unmarried. Suppose an Iraqi rocket hit their building, and she was precipitated down through his flat, being forced against his body on her way down; if during that moment he impregnated her, would she be liable to punishment for illicit sex? After some deliberation, the mullahs decided she would not.

Ayatollah Khomeini once declared gloomily, 'There is no fun in Islam.' Yet even in Iranian television's most intensely religious phase there was, just occasionally, a lighter programme or two. One was called *Hidden Camera*, and was an Iranian version of the old television standby, *Candid Camera*. A survival from the time of the Shah, it was extremely popular; for days after each edition went out, people would recount the ludicrous incidents in it to each other. In one show a seriously faulty Paykan car is sold to a series of unsuspecting buyers, and falls to pieces the moment they drive it out of the showroom. Another makes fun of the relentless politeness of the Persian: an actor stands by a swing door at the entrance to a big office block at the start of the morning, holding little contests in courtesy with each new arrival to see who will allow the other to pass in first. In this show, one man battled with him for more than a minute before finally surrendering and leading the way through the door. Sometimes there would be criticism of *Hidden Camera* in the Majlis: a member would attack a particular episode for showing unsuitable character traits. It would always have its defenders, however, and was never taken off the air.

Imported programmes on Iranian television, dubbed into Persian, drew the biggest audiences. Several are British: *Miss Marple Investigates*, David Attenborough's nature documentaries, and *It Shouldn't Happen to a Vet*. Japanese children's cartoons are very popular too. The head of the Islamic Republic of Iran Broadcasting, Ali Larijani, acknowledged how boring its programmes were by calling on his producers to create 'joyful and lively Islamic programmes which portray correct Islamic teachings and revolutionary zeal and also promote a spirit of selflessness, sacrifice and public joy'. Even so, Iranian viewers usually prefer to watch videos. For the first decade of the revolution it was forbidden to import video tapes; but they came into the country all the same, hidden at the bottom of suitcases in Mehrabad, on the wooden dhows of smugglers who plied the waters between Dubai and Iran, and in the postbags of foreign embassies. Since blank video cassettes have always been available, a vast illicit trade flourished. Even in the days when video recorders were also banned, a Tehran newspaper estimated that one in six of the capital's households had video tapes and a player.

So keen is the interest in Hollywood movies that you can see new films in Tehran within weeks of their release in the United States, well ahead of their openings in London and Paris. Sometimes a hostess will hold a dinner party in order to show a new film, fresh from the copying machines of Dubai. The dealers who run the underground video-tape rental network are always willing to offer the first viewing of a big film to their best clients. Smartly-dressed Tehranis sit cross-legged on cushions, their plates piled high with Persian food, the servants filling up their glasses, while they watch Robert Redford seduce a beautiful woman or Tom Cruise fight organised crime.

Mehdi is one of two brothers who run an underground video-tape rental network. Their car is their office, videos stored neatly in the boot in suitcases. They drive around to clients' homes with the suitcases they think will best suit their tastes.

'I have all sorts of clients, from the big houses in north Tehran where they like romances and American comedies, to ordinary working guys who want those crazy films from India where everyone sings all the time, and the girls wear those sexy saris.'

Iranian films are the least popular items in Mehdi's suitcases; which is a pity, since Iran's film industry has often displayed considerable talent. Immediately after the revolution the industry found itself placed under severe constraints. It was now regarded as a useful form of government propaganda, actors and actresses were not allowed to touch each other on screen, and everyone had to wear Islamic clothing. It was impossible to portray life in pre-revolutionary Iran or abroad. Films about the heroic defence of Iran during the war with Iraq, with soldiers being martyred in the defence of their country, were deeply unpopular. By the end of the 1980s, however, directors were allowed to turn to lighter themes and films about family life. Even so, foreign films cost two or three dollars to rent, and Iranian ones less than half that amount. Mehdi is a cautious man; he has never been arrested by the authorities, unlike some of his fellow dealers who have had all their stock confiscated and been given fines and short gaol sentences.

The guardians of the Islamic Revolution realised the popularity of Western videos but were powerless to stop it, since they could not raid every house in Tehran. Official wall slogans appeared, reading, 'Video equals inviting the prostitutes of East and West into your home.' The Minister of Islamic Guidance tried another tack: 'In our view, videos are far more dangerous than drugs. They are an ugly trap set by the West to seduce your children.' The Interior Minister, an ally of the more militant clergy, agreed with this notion of the breakdown of society: 'So many wives have betrayed their husbands, men have left their wives and young boys and girls have lost their chastity as a result of watching decadent tapes.'

Despite the political pressure, films like *Dances with Wolves* have been shown in Tehran cinemas, with some scenes involving women edited out. In 1992 a chain of government-regulated video clubs was opened in an attempt to control the type of foreign videos available. They offered plenty of American films, but usually in heavily edited versions. At the same time the state-owned Pars Electric started manufacturing VCRs. The target was to produce two thousand machines a day for the domestic market, and the directors of the company admitted that even this figure would not fulfil the demand.

Newer technology than the video recorder has provided the moral guardians of the Islamic Republic with perhaps their most difficult challenge. Satellite dishes capable of picking up broadcasts from BBC World Service Television, CNN, and all the Gulf-based stations can be bought by anyone able to pay a thousand dollars. As a result, more than thirty European, American and Asian channels can be received in Iran. By 1994 it was estimated by the Iranian press that more than two million people watched foreign broadcasts.

At least fifty government ministries and departments are linked into the satellite network. The BBC is especially popular, partly because the BBC Persian Service on radio has been broadcasting to Iran since 1941. The indelible Persian belief in a 'hidden hand', chiefly American and British, operating in Iran's affairs encourages people to watch and listen, so that they can see it at work. Even those newspapers which condemn satellite television most strongly sometimes use photographs taken off CNN's and the BBC's coverage of news stories abroad. There is a powerful debate still about the rights and wrongs of general access to foreign television. Several Iranian MPs have called for a ban on satellite dishes, and in mid-1994 Grand Ayatollah Araki, at the age of ninety-nine, declared a *fatwa* against the whole business: 'Installing satellite antennae opens the Islamic society to inroads of decadent foreign culture and the spread of ruinous Western diseases to Moslems and is *haram* [forbidden].' Occasionally satellite dishes are seized by customs officials, even when they have been imported legally, and at least three Iranian factories manufacturing satellite dishes have been raided and closed down.

Inevitably, official disapproval merely drives the business underground, and raises the profits. Some liberal critics have argued that an all-out ban would be impossible to enforce, since technological advances are making the dishes smaller and smaller.

'Soon they will be only as big as your hand,' one mullah told the Majlis, 'and since we will never know who has one, it will be pointless to make a law against them.'

His was the authentic voice, not of the Islamic Republic, but of Persian society.

It was *Moharram*, the month of mourning, and a crackdown by the authorities on 'bad *hejab*', or improper Islamic dress, had just begun.

'I got a phone call early this morning from my girlfriend,' said Leila, a woman in her mid-thirties. 'She was crying. She told me that some *Basijis* had stopped her, pulled her over in her car and shouted at her about her clothes. She was wearing her denim *roupush* and a light blue scarf. And they made her take off her sunglasses to check her eyes to see if she had make-up on, which she didn't. Fortunately they didn't notice she wasn't wearing stockings. She said she was shaking so much she couldn't push the clutch down when they finally left her. From today,' Leila continued, 'I'll be wearing a black scarf and a grey *roupush* until this month is over.'

That first night of *Moharram* we were high in the foothills of north Tehran, enjoying a late meal in a friend's garden. The flowers were in full bloom, and now the heat of day was past their perfume was strong. As we sat on carpets that had been carried out on to the grass for the evening, watching the lights of Tehran stretch below us and reach out towards the plains, a sound like low thunder reached us. It was a deep, dull thudding that reverberated strongly enough to make us fall silent and look at one another: the sound of tens of thousands of men beating their chests for the first prayer session of *Moharram*. They chanted, 'Kerbala, we are coming; Kerbala, we are coming.' The hollow thudding sound grew louder. It was more powerful in its emotional intensity than any chanting of slogans. This was the sound that had brought the Shah's regime down.

The first ten days of *Moharram* are devoted to mourning the martyrdom of Hosain, the grandson of the Prophet, in the seventh century. This was the point at which Sunni and Shi'ia divided. Hosain's father, Ali, was married to Mohammed's daughter. After the Prophet's death a bitter dispute arose over the succession, and Ali was assassinated by his political rivals. The Shi'iat Ali or Shi'ia, as they came to be known, were literally the followers, or the party, of Ali, and Hosain led them in the contest for the guardianship of Islam. With a group of only seventy-two followers, Hosain made his stand against the mainstream Sunni army on the plains of Kerbala, in modern Iraq, and chose to fight to the death. The tradition of sacrifice, of martyrdom, of resistance to the death against unjust authority, is therefore at the heart of the Shi'ia faith; and the belief that the Shi'i were the victims of persecution by their fellow Muslims as well as by the rest of the world has stamped itself indelibly on the Iranian character.

During *Moharram*, every city and village in Iran holds a series of plays, or *taaziyeh*, re-enacting the events which led to Hosain's death. They are comparable to the mystery cycles of medieval Europe, or the passion play of Oberammergau, and the emotions they evoke are extremely powerful, even for people who have ceased to regard themselves as Muslims. The *taaziyeh* is planned months in advance. There are local contests over who should play the good and noble characters: who should speak in verse, and the villains who should merely speak in prose. Local farmers vie for the honour of offering their horses for the battle scene. It is a classic duel between good and evil, and is often adapted to include touches of contemporary politics, with evil characters wearing sunglasses or the masks of known villains.

During the ten days leading up to *Ashura*, the main procession day, groups called *hay'ats*, organised by local mosques or bazaar merchants, meet for a series of ritual dinners. These are charitable affairs, providing meals for the less fortunate, and each *hay'at* tries to outdo the others in generosity. In Tehran, hundreds of thousands of meals are given away. Over the years the significance of the *hay'ats* has grown; they are not only religious and cultural groups, but political ones as well. For many urban working-class people they represent the only non-governmental religious organisation open to them, and the regime has no control over it. During the last years of the Shah, it was the local *hay'ats* which smuggled in the audio cassettes of Khomeini's lectures in exile, and played them to neighbourhood groups. The SAVAK found it very hard to infiltrate the *hay'ats*. When Ayatollah Khomeini finally returned to Iran, the *taaziyeh* and *Ashura* processions were celebrated with an extraordinary intensity: the down-trodden Shi'i had triumphed at last. And over the years that followed, the influence and the independence of the *hay'ats* did not diminish.

At *Ashura*, the most important ceremony is held in the Grand Bazaar in Tehran, for centuries, one of the chief centres of political and economic power in Iran. There are around fifty *hay'ats* there, each with several hundred men belonging to it. Foreigners are warned not to show their faces in the bazaar at a time of such emotional intensity, but Helmut, a German businessman who had lived in Tehran for several years and speaks fluent Persian, decided to see the ceremony for himself. Although, being blond and tall, he was highly conspicuous, he found to his surprise that everyone welcomed his interest in *Ashura*.

'It was a hot June day, and the centre of town is always a few degrees hotter, yet it didn't seem so bad. In fact it was easier being there than on a normal day at the bazaar. People were walking around with bottles of rose-water to spray over the crowds, so as to cool the atmosphere and cover the smell of sweat. Everyone seemed to be concentrating hard: the ones who were in the procession were concentrating on their role in it, and the people in the crowd were watching them very intently. The organisation was impressive: not at all the Iran we're used to.

'The different *hay'ats* assembled for the procession. They all have names, usually the sons of so-and-so, some martyr: it all has a lot of historical significance. Everyone was dressed in black. Each *hay'at* had a leader who would go in front of the group, with the elders at the front and children at the end, all following a four-beat movement with complicated steps, while the drums and cymbals beat out the rhythm. There were some men who weren't able to maintain the sequence of the four beats, and they were pushed out of the marching column. Everyone seemed to take this precision very seriously.

'I had been invited to attend by one *hay'at* who carried swords. The men would lift the swords to their heads as part of the four-beat movement of the march. Even the children carried plastic swords: it's all part of the symbolism of Hosain's martyrdom. Other *hay'ats* carried flails, and some simply used their hands to beat their chests. What I hadn't realised is that they weren't allowed to hit themselves during the procession: it wasn't like the pictures I've seen of it on television.

'Another surprise was the participants. They were ordinary businessmen, many of them quite westernised. I recognised some that I had been at parties with in north Tehran, Western parties with Western behaviour. But there they were, in the procession. You could see it had a deep meaning for them. It was more than a religious ritual, it was cultural and traditional.

'The re-enactment of the battle of Kerbala was really impressive; the tents were set on fire with kerosene and whoosh – they went up in flames. Men dressed as soldiers ran about and there were horses cantering everywhere. When the flames shot up, everyone who had been crowded around just stepped back together, there wasn't any panic. Some people even had cameras and were taking photos. No one minded. I looked at the people next to me. It was as if they were seeing it acted out for the first time. Many of them had tears streaming down their faces.

'We went inside, the men only, to watch the culmination of the ceremony. On the streets there had been a few people wearing bandages, which is a status symbol to show that you have shed your blood as Hosain did. Inside, the blood-shedding was very controlled – there was even a doctor standing by. Some people had shaved the crown of their head, and many people had bruised themselves on that part of the skull beforehand over the previous two or three days, according to the men I spoke to. You aren't allowed to cut your head yourself, it's done for you; the blade of the sword touches your crown and the blood spurts out, if you have done the bruising properly. And of course scalp wounds always bleed a lot. As soon as the blood appears, the wounded man wipes it off with a little white towel. Some people consider it an act of faith-healing. But not many people volunteered for it – fewer than one in four. Then the men of the *hay'at* put dirt on their heads and shoulders to symbolise what had happened to Hosain and Hasan. They chant "We have dirt on our heads," which means in Persian that they have been tricked and betrayed.

'Some men were crying with emotion, quietly, but it remained very businesslike, very organised. There were no scenes of hysteria. What I found fascinating was the anti-government feeling, seriously anti-government. There was only one *hay'at*, out of the fifty or so, that was pro-government. There were no *Pasdaran* or security presence. They probably felt that they should stay away. *Ashura* is way beyond the power of any government to control. My friends in the *hay'at* told me that after the first year or two of the revolution it was forbidden to hold the whole thing. But the big businessmen, the *bazaaris*, sponsor it now, and they set down rules. The regime may not like it, but it has to go along with it.'

The year after Helmut attended *Ashura*, the country's new religious leader Ali Khamene'i warned mourners to refrain from 'superstitious or illogical' practices such as slashing themselves with swords: 'It is wrong for people to beat themselves on the head and make themselves bleed. What has this got to do with mourning?' He went on to accuse 'hidden hands in our society' of being involved in the *hay'ats*. But the *hay'ats* defied the call to change their traditional practices; the next year's *Ashura* was celebrated in exactly the same way, and the Revolutionary Guards stayed out of the Tehran bazaar. Even in matters of religion, it is Persian tradition which dominates, and the Islamic Republic is powerless to change that.

12

The Non-Conformists

John Simpson

Human beings cannot be known except by the science of physiognomy and by experience, and the science of physiognomy in its entirety is a branch of prophecy that is not acquired to perfection except by the divinely directed apostle. The reason is that by physiognomy the inward goodness or wickedness of men can be ascertained.

A Mirror For Princes

According to Article 13 of the Constitution of the Islamic Republic, not a document noted for its liberal values, 'Iranian Zoroastrians, Jews and Christians are the only recognised minority religious groups who, within the limits of law, are free to perform their religious rites and ceremonies, and in personal status and religious teaching, they may act in conformity with the dictates of their own creed.' The most notable group left out in the cold by this grudging formula are the Baha'is: a faith born in Iran, and much respected in most other parts of the world. Under the Islamic Republic, however, the Baha'is were treated as apostates and heretics. Khourush, who saw the treatment some of them received in prison, now lives in exile in London.

'It was towards the end of 1981 and I was in my cell in Evin. I had been arrested for leftist activities, but a year later I got out and managed to leave the country. I was very lucky. But I still remember the Baha'i prisoners. They were decent people and carried themselves with pride. Before that time I had never really thought about the Baha'is, but I was impressed at how they maintained themselves. We all knew that they would probably be killed; they had always been hated by the mullahs. When Khomeini's people started turning on those of us who had fought for the revolution, what chance did the Baha'is have?

'We always knew when people would be executed because they were asked to pack up and take their belongings with them. And one day that happened to the Baha'is who were in cells near to some guys I knew. The guards came for them and nobody ever saw them again. I don't know which day they were executed, we heard the gunfire quite a lot then. It was just like the noise of steel girders being thrown off a lorry. Maybe their families were given their belongings afterwards. Maybe not.'

It is hard for Westerners to understand the depth of feeling that exists in Iran against the Baha'i faith. It is a religion of peace and tolerance, it has never advocated violence in Iran or anywhere else, it avoids any forms of political involvement, and the Baha'is, who are under instructions to obey the laws of the country in which they live, have maintained their beliefs with great courage in the face of torture and death. And yet twenty thousand followers of the faith in its earlier form were killed in Persia in the nineteenth century, while since the revolution of 1979 more than two hundred Baha'is have been executed, and nearly one thousand have been imprisoned.

Part of the reason lies in the origins of their religion. It began in the southern Persian city of Shiraz in the 1840s as a development of Shi'ia Islam, just acceptable within the boundaries of Muslim teachings, and preaching the imminent coming of the Hidden Imam. But it was very soon accused of heresy, and its central figure, Sayyed Ali Mohammed, who was styled the 'Bab', or Gate (that is, the gateway to communications with the Hidden Imam), was sentenced to death as a heretic in 1848. His execution took place in Tabriz in 1850. In his classic, *A Year Amongst the Persians*, Edward Granville Browne, the Persian scholar and traveller who was fascinated by the Babis and their faith, relates the much-repeated story that the Bab vanished unhurt after the first volley from the firing squad, though he was found and killed at the second attempt.

In 1863 Mirza Hosayn Ali Nuri announced that he himself was Baba'ullah, the Universal Manifestation of God foretold by the Bab. He was exiled to Acre, which was then part of the Turkish province of Syria, and laid the foundations of the modern Baha'i faith in his writings there. Its Shi'ite origins had long since ceased to be recognisable, and although the Baha'is teach that all revealed religions are true, they maintain that theirs is the one most suited to the modern age. That in itself is total heresy in Islam, which believes that Mohammed is the 'Seal of the Prophets' and that Islam is the final revelation: to suggest that it can be improved upon is the worst form of spiritual error.

The Baha'is, however, pressed on with their faith, stressing the need to improve society through universal education, world peace, and the equality of the sexes, and through living pure and loving lives. They have no priesthood, and no public ritual. Anyone can become a Baha'i without ceremony, and the choice is a free one; but once made, it is adhered to. There are few, if any, cases of Baha'is in Iran giving up their religion, even under torture. Their courage in the face of persecution has always brought them new converts; nowadays there are believed to be up to 350,000 of them in the country. But they are greatly disliked by most Iranians, who refuse to accept that their faith constitutes a real religion. It seems to be widely accepted in Iran, despite all the evidence to the contrary, that the British instigated and encouraged the Baha'i religion in order to undermine the authority of the Islamic clergy; that the Baha'is were especially favoured by the Shah and were linked with the corruption which existed under his regime; and that they are today under the control of Israel.

The Shah certainly allowed the Baha'is a greater measure of protection than previous rulers had. This made them dependent upon him, and he often put them in positions where they would act as buffers against any possible disloyalty: for instance, as controllers of military communications and as military attachés in foreign embassies. Several of his doctors, too, were Baha'is. The Shan's long-serving prime minister, Amir-Abbas Hoveyda, who was executed after the revolution, was always regarded as a Baha'i because his father had been one; but each individual Baha'i is required to affirm his membership of the faith, and Hoveyda did not do so, regarding himself instead as a Muslim.

Many members of the faith received wealth and privilege under the Shah's rule; yet there were times when he turned a blind eye to their persecution rather than risk confrontations with the Shi'ia clergy. In 1955, for example, a campaign of incendiary sermons was followed by widespread violence against the Baha'is. Photographs from the time show mullahs wielding pickaxes to help destroy the National Baha'i Centre while officers from the Shah's army look on approvingly. When the Shah turned Iran into a one-party state in 1975, the Baha'is, being forbidden to associate with political groups, were often penalised for their refusal to join his Rastakhiz Party.

The notion that Britain fostered the Baha'i faith is fictitious, despite the interest which various British scholars took in it. Abdul-Baha, the son of the Baha'ullah, was given a British knighthood in 1920 for having supported the British cause in Palestine against the Turks during the 1914–18 war. But the Baha'i faith owed nothing to British help or involvement. It arose as an independent entity. The choice of site for the Baha'is' international headquarters in what is now Israel was an historical accident; when Baha'ullah was obliged by the Turks to settle in Acre in 1868, the foundation of the Israeli state still lay eighty years in the future. Before the revolution Iranian Baha'is, as well as being expected to travel to Israel to visit their World Centre in Haifa, were required to send donations there; after the revolution this constituted a capital offence.

Only weeks before Ayatollah Khomeini returned to Iran from his exile in France, an American academic, James Cockroft, asked him, 'Will there be either religious or political freedom for the Baha'is under an Islamic government?' Khomeini replied, 'They are a political faction; they are harmful. They will not be accepted.' Encouraged by Khomeini's pronouncements, revolutionary mullahs portrayed Baha'is as corrupt and treacherous. But Khomeini's supporters were not unleashed on individual Baha'is in the first year of the revolution; instead they systematically attacked the symbols of the Baha'i faith. In 1979 the Revolutionary Guards destroyed the House of the Bab in Shiraz, one of the Baha'is' holiest sites. A few courageous Baha'is recovered pieces of tile and brick from the wreckage. Soon afterwards, several Baha'i cemeteries were bulldozed and graves were broken open. In the following year, 1980, when revolutionary power had been consolidated and the regime's confidence was high, the real persecution began.

Baha'is, under Muslim law, are *mahdur al-damm*: those whose blood can be shed with impunity. Not being 'the People of the Book' – Jews, Christians and Zoroastrians, who are all mentioned more or less approvingly in the Koran – the Baha'is were condemned as 'unprivileged infidels, at war with the Muslim nation'. They were accused of apostasy, and of being agents of Zionism: two of the most serious offences in the Islamic Republic, each of which carries the death penalty. Ayatollah Khomeini denounced them as 'a subversive conspiracy'. Even so, a large number of Baha'is chose to stay in Iran at a time when they could have left without difficulty. Hundreds of others who were living or working abroad decided to return home and stand by their co-religionists.

The National Spiritual Assembly, which constituted the leadership of the Baha'i faith in Iran, and the Local Spiritual Assemblies, which were based in every region of the country, became particular targets. In August 1980 all nine members of the National Spiritual Assembly were arrested and disappeared without trace. Since membership of the Spiritual Assembly was listed as a capital offence, they were presumably executed. In 1981 two members of the Local Spiritual Assembly of Shiraz were arrested and executed. By then revolutionary courts no longer felt it necessary to couch the arrests in political terms, and cited purely religious reasons for the execution of Baha'is.

A second National Spiritual Assembly had replaced the first, through elections which were held by the Baha'i community under conditions which were extremely difficult. In December 1981 all nine members of this second Assembly were also arrested, and all were executed. The arrests were facilitated by the fact that, during the Shah's time, the SAVAK had obtained the full records of the Baha'i community by breaking into their offices. These records were now in the hands of the secret police of the new Islamic Republic.

The persecution continued; in 1982 six members of the Local Assembly of Tehran and the woman in whose house they were meeting were shot. In June 1983 seventeen Baha'is, including seven women and three teenage girls, were arrested in Shiraz. The primary charges against the girls were that they had taught children's classes in the Baha'i community. Several of them, both men and women, were tortured in an attempt to get them to renounce their faith or provide video-taped confessions that they had been spies, and that the Baha'i faith was controlled by Israel. They refused, and all seventeen were hanged. The first year after the revolution when no member of the Baha'i community was executed was 1989. But the respite was brief; in March 1992 a Baha'i businessman was summoned to Evin prison. A few days later, when his wife visited the prison to bring him food and clothes, she was told he had been executed. Some Baha'is believe that the arrest and execution were timed to coincide with the Majlis election campaign; it was an easy way for Rafsanjani to appear tough when he was being criticised for liberal tendencies. Not long before his death in 1989, Ayatollah Khomeini repeated his charge against the Baha'is. 'Reagan,' he said, for once varying the paymaster, 'supports the Baha'is in the same way the Soviets control the Tudeh [Iranian Communist Party]. The Baha'is are not a religion but a secretive organisation plotting to subvert the Islamic Republic.'

Yet several hundred Baha'is, usually those found guilty of possessing Baha'i books and literature, survived their imprisonment and were eventually released – often on the exact date their sentences expired. For the most part these people were not beaten or tortured. Behzad, an elderly Baha'i who now lives in the West, describes his brother's experiences in gaol: 'My brother was surprised that the hygiene conditions were quite decent, perhaps it was because there were so many shifts of prisoners who cleaned the latrine. And he also told me that the food was well worked out in terms of calories and nutrition. Each day the prisoners were served different food groups. There was always one *khoresht* dish (rice and stew) and then cheese and bread for another meal. And for breakfast tea and sometimes fruit.'

Conditions became more oppressive, however. Behzad's brother was at first held with nineteen other Baha'is in a large, almost spacious cell.

'But then after a few months of what they later called their luxury time, all the men were transferred by the prison authorities to a cell intended for two people. Imagine that: twenty people in a two-man cell. They would manage by seating five men on the top bunk, five on the lower, five more sitting on the floor and then five standing, or usually leaning against the cell walls. Every few hours they would change places, but of course some of the older men could not stand up for so long, and the younger, healthier ones suffered as a result.'

Their behaviour seems to have earned them the grudging respect of their gaolers. Because of the emphasis their faith lays on education, the Baha'is in gaol were likely to come from a wide range of professions. They would organise courses in languages, astronomy, history and so on. Baha'i doctors were often asked to run the prison hospitals, despite the common Muslim belief that the touch of a Baha'i was unclean. One prison official told the Baha'is under his control that he had been impressed with their morale and organisation. They were, he said, model prisoners. At the end he seemed sorry to see them leave, though the feeling was not reciprocated.

By July 1982 the government had dismissed all Baha'is from the civil service, and no longer paid their pensions. In 1985 it went further: every civil servant who was a Baha'i would be required to repay in full the salary he or she had received during their entire working lives, or face imprisonment. Most of the people who had been sacked from the civil service found it impossible to get jobs elsewhere, and officially Baha'is are not allowed to start their own businesses; as a result, most were obliged to pay back their salaries from their savings.

Although the children of Baha'is in Iran are allowed to go to state schools, they cannot attend university. Those who want further education are told to apply for a passport in order to attend a foreign university. The problem is that the forms for an Iranian passport contain a question about religion; and the paperwork for Baha'is tends to disappear. A whole generation of Baha'is, the religious faith which lays more stress on schooling than almost any other, is being denied access to higher education.

'Being a Baha'i must be like being a black in America.' The feeling of being discriminated against, of being despised, of being perpetually in danger of random attack, was real enough, though the analogy would have been more exact if the speaker had likened himself and his family to Jews in a medieval city. All his life he had been treated by ordinary Muslims as an outcast: as someone to be avoided where possible, and a convenient scapegoat at moments of social and political tension.

'I remember one time when we were in a village. I was seven or eight. We had a driver, and we gave him some ice to take home to his family because it was a very hot day. I went with the driver when he took the car home and gave the ice to his wife. She threw it out, and started shouting something about Baha'is.

'Sometimes my father would come home and say he had met so-and-so, and after they had shaken hands he had seen him go off to wash his hands. It was a ritual washing, like when a dog passes a Muslim in the street before prayers. Other times when you went to someone's house you knew that after you left they would wash out the chair you had sat on, and the cup you had used. It was always worse in smaller places where there was more ignorance and the mullahs had more power. Some people used to tell their kids not to play with us. I remember that.'

The man who is speaking is young and serious. His family is from the *haute bourgeoisie*, but their money has been heavily depleted by exactions and losses during the years of public and private pressure. These are not the first troubled times the family has been through – the young man's parents both knew poverty when they were young – but, as Baha'is often do, they started again. His father obtained a government job in which, as a result of hard work and intelligence, he did well, but he was continually passed over for promotion, and in the end he decided to give up and become a farmer.

'The first day in 1968 all you could see was stones and desert. The mountains were up there and the village was down there. But my father made a success of it. He was one of the few people who did make a success of farming there.

'By 1978 all you could see round about was other people's property. The boom had come, and people had made a lot of money in building. So they wanted to turn my father's farm into a residential area, because it was more profitable for the developers. They didn't like us being there anyway. We weren't welcome in the village, and sometimes they'd turn all the loudspeakers from the mosque in our direction.

'Then the revolution came, and the company that supplied us with our animals couldn't send them to us any more, because they'd all died. After that we had to try to import our animals, and that meant we needed permits. But the permits took a long time coming. That meant we weren't earning much money, and the bank wanted its loan back.

'In the end they took the farm away from us, and our furniture got stolen. All my father's clothes went, and all the things from my childhood: you know, toys and books. And that was how we lost our heritage.'

The father's problems grew. He was always being stopped and arrested. He could not obtain a ration-book since they were distributed by the local mosques, and the family had to buy their food at top prices on the black market. They moved to their house in Tehran; and in 1982 they decided they would have to leave Iran altogether, since the farm had gone and they had no money except what they could get from selling their furniture and jewellery.

'The time when they confiscated things or you could just pay money to keep out of gaol was over. Now they wanted people. Father went into hiding for two months, and he didn't contact my mother the whole of that time – it was too dangerous. The plan was for her to get out to Pakistan, and then he would join her a week later.

'Well, she made it. You could get out quite easily then to Pakistan through Baluchistan, if you paid money. They don't like Baha'is much in Pakistan now, because they're pretty strong Muslims too; but she got out all the same. It wasn't until she was safe that she found out my father had been arrested. There'd been a raid on the house, and they took him away. She wanted to go back, of course, but it would have been suicide. They'd have executed her for sure.'

The father was charged with helping his wife to escape, with sending money out of the country, and with being a Zionist agent. The case dragged on for several years, and has now fallen into abeyance. The father has to live on the generosity of his relatives. His wife and son talk to him occasionally on the telephone, they in their new life and he in the old one. The only way they have of judging whether he is in any trouble is from the tone of his voice.

'It's difficult to understand, maybe, if you aren't a Baha'i. It's a system of living. For us, working in a spirit of service isn't any different from praying. Being a Baha'i is a progressive thing – kind of like going to school, except it never ends. It doesn't matter how many Baha'is are in gaol, or even killed, it'll carry on. And we certainly don't want to convert anybody. We just want to make them understand.'

The building was solid, simple, peaceful, a quiet haven in the racket and heat of Tehran. Above the doorway was carved, in Persian, the phrase *'Pendor-e nik, Goftor-e nik, Kerdor-e nik'*; 'good thoughts, good words, good deeds'. Usually the only representational art works you see in Iran are the obligatory, standardised posters of prominent ayatollahs, but here the external decorations were bas-reliefs of angels with gentle faces. This was a Zoroastrian house of worship; a fire-temple, built in a place of concentrated energy, or 'power point', by the followers of the first monotheistic religion to reach the Persian plateau.

Zoroaster was its first prophet. He may have lived somewhere between 1000 and 800 BC in the eastern part of Iran, though there is no certain evidence that he was anything more than a figure of legend, and no mention of him on the inscriptions of the period. He is, however, credited with developing the conception of the universe as the battleground between the powers of good and evil, light and darkness: that is, between the spirit of wisdom, Ahuramazda, and the spirit of evil, Ahriman. Man has the freedom to choose between these two principles, and is judged in the afterlife according to his choice. Zoroastrianism is a profoundly moral religion.

Fire represents the principle of goodness and light, and is therefore central to the religion. It seems likely that the original flame from which all the fires in all the temples of Zoroastrianism have been lit sprang naturally from the ground in the oilfields of south-western Iran. Worship took place at altars in significant places – mountaintops, the craters of extinct volcanoes – and at traditional Zoroastrian sites, it is still common to see the traces of recent fires. Even non-believers often experience a sense of considerable natural and spiritual power in these places. Originally, Zoroastrians were forbidden to defile the elements of fire, water or earth with the bodies of the dead. Instead, corpses were exposed on mountains or on wooden towers until there was nothing left except the bones. In recent centuries, under Islam, this was forbidden; and in Tehran and Yazd (a particular centre of Zoroastrianism even today) cemeteries were set aside for them to bury their dead. To compensate for defiling the earth in this way, Zoroastrians plant a cypress tree for each body they bury.

Inside the fire-temple in Tehran, half a dozen men and women were sitting in quiet contemplation. One man walked up to the embers of the fire on the altar and stood facing it briefly. His lips moved and he dabbed his finger in the ash, then touched his forehead with it, leaving a grey mark. There was none of the chanting and choreographed movement of Islamic prayer rituals. The fire of sandalwood and charcoal burned on a large brazier in a central cell of the temple. It must always be kept alive, either as a flame or smouldering ember. If the flame is extinguished, a replacement must be brought from another fire-temple, as part of a chain from the original source thousands of years ago. Some of the worshippers had come to recite their prayers, the Avesta; others were here simply to experience the quiet and spiritual peace for an hour or two.

The Zoroastrians of Iran are a small island in an Islamic sea, a passive minority tolerated only because they have accepted a diminished place after the long centuries of persecution. They have not suffered as other minorities in Iran have. No one accuses them of receiving foreign backing, and they do not offend the religious hierarchy by attempting to convert Muslims. As followers of a faith far older than Islam, they have been granted limited rights and an uneasy place in society. There are thought to be 30,000 Zoroastrians in Iran, and the majority of them live in Tehran. About 10,000 have left since the revolution. Because of the excellence of the Zoroastrian schools and the cohesiveness of the community, they tend to be relatively rich. Through private donations they have built up various charitable institutions, several of which – hospitals, for instance – were open to all Iranians. This, together with the Zoroastrians' prosperity, inevitably attracted attention and criticism when the Islamic Republic was established.

Jamshid is a Zoroastrian who makes a living as a writer. After living in Iran for the first ten years of the Islamic Republic, he gave up the unequal struggle and left to join his family in Europe. It was difficult and expensive to get out, but at least he was free of the Islamic thought-police.

'After the revolution, people of means were targets and wealthy Zoroastrians were even easier targets. I know the stories of dozens of illegal confiscations of property – houses and land – and demands for huge payments, sometimes disguised as back taxes and other fiscal demands, but essentially it was pure extortion. There are far worse things than losing money, though; there has been tremendous job discrimination, particularly in the academic world or any state-controlled organisation.

'In some cases Zoroastrians have been driven out of business by prejudice. One man in our community ran a sandwich shop. For years he had a good business – as other Iranians will tell you, we have a reputation for honesty – and his customers were loyal. The government then introduced the requirement that he had to say on his food licence, which was up on the wall like a sign, that he was a member of a religious minority. Some people who didn't know him personally would see this and wouldn't come in as a result, but others in the neighbourhood continued to support him. One time a real Hezbollah type ordered some food, but when he turned around and saw the sign he stormed out. Soon the first hints of intimidation began to appear. And when times are rough, and the *Komiteh* are hanging around on the street, people have to make a decision. Do you want to attract that kind of attention just in order to get yourself a meal? What price can you put on friendship and decency? Not enough people seemed to feel it was worth it, so eventually he went out of business.'

Zoroastrian schools, which had been carefully built up over decades, were taken over by the Islamic Republic after 1979 and filled with Muslim students. 'Islamic Guidance', the study of the Koran, is an obligatory subject for all the students; Zoroastrianism is ignored. One particularly distinguished school, a symbol to the community, was destroyed by a fire, the cause of which official investigations were unable to establish. To the Zoroastrians, it all seemed part of a pattern, a low-intensity campaign to undermine their cultural heritage.

In the 1920s Reza Shah was the first Iranian leader in Islamic times to move beyond mere toleration of Zoroastrianism. He encouraged Zoroastrians to take their place fully in Muslim society. No doubt it was part of his need for historical legitimacy: the Pahlavi dynasty which he had proclaimed lacked any real roots in Persian history. Since he was unable to claim an historical continuity, he looked to the past, before Islam, to the original glories of the nation. He insisted that the country should be called by the ancient name of Iran and fostered an interest in the empires of the Achaemenians and the Sassanians. The official architecture of Reza Shah's Tehran was inspired by the art of Persepolis. This was a past which he could shape to his political needs, and the Zoroastrians were central to it. They became a significant part of the new, secular Iran and flourished accordingly; the Islamic edicts which had controlled their behaviour, their clothes and sometimes even the jobs they were allowed to do were overturned by modern laws. This did not escape the notice of the conservative clergy.

Throughout the 1960s and 1970s, Mohammed Reza Shah continued his father's policy of invoking the symbols of Iran's distant past. It culminated in the opulent and excessive celebration at Persepolis of the 2500th anniversary of the establishment of the Persian monarchy. There was more than a hint that Zoroastrianism, as the religion of ancient Persia, had a particular legitimacy. As for the country's Islamic tradition, it was almost completely ignored. This, and the feeling that Zoroastrians received special favour from the monarchy, created a good deal of resentment against them among the Muslim clergy. It was made even more acute by a thoughtless act.

As the Pahlavi dynasty entered its final years the Empress, who had always been an enthusiastic patron of Persian culture, arranged a Zoroastrian Congress in Tehran. Delegates came from all over the country, and from the various Iranian and Parsee communities abroad. It was done, naturally, on a lavish scale, and received extensive coverage by the state-controlled press and television. But the congress was held during Ramadan, the Muslim month of fasting and contemplation when meals can only be taken before dawn or after dusk. Even so, the Congress concluded with an afternoon champagne reception at one of the royal palaces. The diplomatic corps was invited, but all the Arab ambassadors felt obliged to boycott it on religious grounds. It would be hard to think of a better way for the Shah's government to have shown its contempt for traditional Muslim values.

Nowadays, the Zoroastrians are a quiet and no longer particularly wealthy minority, tolerated only because the Islamic authorities regard them as harmless. It helps that Zoroastrian priests are traditionally little more than the servants of the community, exercising no great social or political influence (unlike the mullahs of Shi'ia Islam) and serving only to officiate at prayers, and at the rituals of birth, marriage and death. They do not interpret their God to the believers, and offer no guidance to them. There is only one official representative of the Zoroastrian community in the Iranian Parliament, a single deputy who holds his seat through the favour of the Islamic government. If this was intended to keep the Zoroastrians happy, it has failed. They instinctively dislike the intrusive system which the Islamic Republic has introduced. Yet they know there is nothing to be gained by complaining openly. They keep their heads down, and hope for better days.

The carpets inside the shop off Manacheri Street in central Tehran were barely visible through windows that hadn't been washed for years. Somewhere at the back was the figure of a grey-haired man, at a desk piled high with paperwork. There was nothing grey or dull about the place inside: rich reds and blues glowed from the pile of silken Kashan and Isfahani carpets on the floor. There was a pile of modern carpets too, machine-made and coloured with industrial dyes, but that was left unceremoniously at the side of the shop. On the wall above the desk was a little sign in Hebrew.

'Is this a prayer?' I asked in English.

The grey-haired man did not look up from the paperwork.

'Maybe,' he said. 'Why not? Are you from England? Would you like to see something?'

We began to talk about carpets, and about religion. It did not seem to worry him. There was, he said, a synagogue 'not far away', but he did not elaborate. As the small sign above the desk showed, Iranian Jews have neither denied their religion nor advertised it. Like the Zoroastrians and the Christians, they have their own representative in Parliament, sworn in on the Scriptures. The Constitution recognises their civil rights; though in the Islamic Republic this cannot be said to guarantee anything.

Ayatollah Khomeini made his position on the Jews clear in his writings from exile in Najaf. 'From the very beginning, the historical movement of Islam has had to contend with the Jews, for it was they who first established anti-Islamic propaganda ... They are wretched people who wish to establish Jewish domination throughout the world.' He also accused Jews of printing 'distorted' versions of the Koran in the Occupied Territories. In 1979 three Jews were executed for allegedly collaborating with Israel. Dozens more were arrested and imprisoned on lesser charges, but were released some years later. There was systematic confiscation of the property of Jews who were accused of supporting the Shah. The ferocity of the persecution faded as the 1980s wore on, but there is no guarantee of safety even now. A death sentence on one Jew who had been accused of collaborating with Zionists was commuted to only three years' imprisonment. In February 1994, however, his family was summoned to Evin prison to say goodbye to him. He was executed the next day.

In spite of the rights promised in the Constitution, the Iranian press seems to make no distinction between Jews, Zionists and Israel. As the Middle East peace process developed, the attitude seemed to harden. Trivial yet offensive gestures are commonplace; for instance, the issue of a postage stamp showing a boy throwing a stone at the Star of David. The best protection for the Jewish community in Iran seems to be the interest and awareness of the outside world; the Iranian government knows that too much repression of the Jews will draw unwelcome attention. For this reason, and perhaps because the Islamic Republic's Constitution does clearly promise the Jewish community the protection of the law, most Jews prefer to be open about their religion.

Iran's Jewish community started leaving in substantial numbers in 1978. After the revolution, its leaders were forced to renounce any support for Israel or Zionism and there was a further migration. Now there are fewer than 25,000 Jews, out of a community which once numbered 80,000. For the most part, it is the wealthier people who have left, and most of the exiles now live in Los Angeles. The Jewish Community Council helps to administer a number of community services in Tehran: a nursing home for elderly Jews and a nursery school for the dwindling number of Jewish children born every year. Now fewer than ninety children attend the school, and the Jewish hospital, with its 120 beds, is mainly filled with Muslims who have a high regard for the skills of the doctors there.

The shopkeeper carefully, lovingly piled up the carpets he had pulled out to display. They were more to him than merely a way to make money.

'You ask about the sign. I see you have questions, but we are Persians and my family has always lived here. We are not a political people. I have many cousins in America, but I have my business here. And my carpets. Now there are more carpets than Jews in Iran.'

From time to time, when a marriage is being celebrated in one of the few Christian churches which are permitted to function, the bells ring out; but only if both bride and groom are Christians by birth. But the calculated repression of the 310,000 Christians in Iran has not ended. Iranian officials usually deny that there are restrictions on the practice of Christianity, but they exist. There is, for instance, a prohibition on the sale of Bibles in Iran, and the Iranian Bible Society was closed down after the revolution. Many church leaders were pressured into signing letters stating that they enjoyed full constitutional rights as Christians in the Islamic Republic.

The largest part of the Christian community is Armenian Orthodox, but there are also Assyrian Orthodox, Roman Catholics and various Protestant churches. The Armenians and the Assyrians have been in Iran the longest and have their own member of the Majlis. The Catholics have also been in Iran since the eighteenth century, and enjoy the additional advantage of having a diplomat, the Papal Nuncio representing the Holy See, to keep an eye on their position. As a result, the Iranian authorities have always been wary of antagonising the small Catholic community.

Ever since the Armenians were brought into the country by Shah Abbas, they have been allowed to get on with making money. Sometimes circumstances have changed radically for them: after the revolution all the Armenian men who styled women's hair went out of business. Their restaurants, like the charming Café Naderi in Tehran with its beautiful garden, still offer a bohemian atmosphere for directors and artists. Armenian butchers, bakeries and sandwich shops provide top-quality products at good prices. But as with the Zoroastrians, every Armenian business which handles food must display a sign which says '*Agaliat-e-dinee*': 'Minority Religion'. It has to be displayed prominently, and it costs 5,000 *toman* (50,000 *rials*, or about $18). Apart from this, however, the Armenian community is mostly left alone.

The six Protestant denominations represented in Iran, with about 15,000 followers altogether, formed a unified Council of Protestant

Churches in 1986. Among them are the Anglicans, with their base in Isfahan, who have always been suspected of being fifth columnists for Britain. Unlike the Armenians and the Catholics, many Iranian Protestants come from Muslim backgrounds; and they and the various Protestant evangelical groups, which believe strongly in proselytising and conversion, and preach in Farsi, are particular targets for the Islamic authorities.

In 1993, after the ministers and priests in the Christian community had been ordered to sign declarations promising that Muslims would not be allowed into their services, Revolutionary Guards appeared in several churches and took up positions in the aisles. More were positioned outside. On each occasion a dozen or so members of the congregation were arrested. They were taken to a *Pasdaran* centre in south Tehran, held for several hours, and then released. It was intended as a reminder of the realities of life for the religious minorities in the Islamic Republic.

Some months later, at the beginning of 1994, Mehdi Dibaj – a Muslim who converted to Protestantism in 1953, at the age of nineteen – disappeared after leaving his house in Tehran. His body was found on 5 July in a forest to the west of the city. Only three days before he vanished he had been released from prison after serving a nine-year sentence for 'offending the Prophet of Islam'. There were suggestions that he might have been murdered by militants from the Ministry of Information, which has become a particular stronghold for radicals. These people own a number of safe houses in Tehran and are not under the control either of President Rafsanjani or of the country's religious leader, Ali Khamene'i, who are regarded as more tolerant in such matters. Dibaj may therefore have been a victim of the vicious factionalism within the Iranian government.

The man who did most in Iran to bring the imprisonment of Mehdi Dibaj to international attention was the bishop of the Pentecostal church he attended, Haik Hovsepian Mehr. Bishop Hovsepian Mehr was an outspoken defender of the freedom of worship, and while he was superintendent of the various Pentecostal Assemblies of God churches in Iran he helped to found five more churches. He refused to sign a government-drafted statement that Christians enjoyed full rights in Iran, and he compiled a detailed report for the United Nations on violations of the rights of the religious minorities which were supposedly guaranteed by the 1979 Constitution.

Bishop Hovsepian Mehr disappeared in Tehran on 19 January 1994, soon after the release of Mehdi Dibaj from prison. He was killed the next day. The Tehran police denied that they or any of the security forces had detained him; and it is possible that he, too, was killed by one of the death squads operated by officials from the Ministry of Information. He certainly lost his life because of his stand for the freedom of religion which the Iranian authorities claimed to protect.

And yet it is not necessarily any protection to take a more circumspect line in a society where only one religion is regarded by the government and its servants as true, and the rule of law is not properly secured: Tateos Michaelian, the acting chairman of the Council of Protestant Ministers in Iran, was persuaded in December 1993 to sign the declaration that proper religious freedom existed in the country. Six months later, on 29 June 1994, he too was murdered. The government maintained that he was a victim of the opposition group, the Mojaheddin-e-Khalq. It seems much more likely that the Islamic death squads were responsible.

These cases demonstrate clearly that the guarantees which the Iranian Constitution claims to offer to those religions which the Islamic Republic accepts as being worthy of protection are largely valueless. There is no evidence that the police or the Revolutionary Guards have tried to curb the activities of the death squads. Religious extremists who claim to be operating according to the Koran invariably occupy the moral high ground in a state whose ethos is itself Koranic. Iran is a remarkably homogeneous society, especially in religious terms. It has little interest in, or sympathy for, people who fall outside the vast Shi'ite majority. They may pay special taxes, they may give their wholehearted allegiance to the government; but they will always remain separate and unequal.

13

Trading

Tira Shubart

You observe that the life of a lamp is generated by oil; if you pour oil into the lamp without measure and limit, so that it overflows the spout of the container and passes beyond the tip of the wick, it immediately extinguishes the lamp. Thus is demonstrated the fact that oil, which is the means of keeping a lamp alight, is also, if used without moderation and to an extravagant extent, the means of extinction.

A Mirror For Princes

The centre of Tehran is best avoided in the afternoon heat. The pollution from car fumes reaches its zenith then, and you can feel the grittiness of the dust from the streets between your teeth. The pavements radiate heat, and the temper of the Tehran drivers grows shorter than ever. By mid-afternoon the volume control of the city has been turned up to maximum. Sensible people look for somewhere quiet and shady to relax.

This summer's afternoon, however, a small group of middle-class Iranians, well dressed and slightly self-conscious, were standing in an orderly queue by the gate which led to the side door of the Bank Markazi in the centre of the city. According to the lopsided sign posted on the gate, there was no need to queue: the bank vaults should have been open to visitors already. Instead, the guards made an elaborate show of ignoring them. One of the older Iranian men in the queue pointed to his watch and shrugged his shoulders, but he was unwilling to attract attention to himself or question the guards' authority. The four of us were, however, obvious foreigners: two adults and two blond children. I had dressed carefully for the occasion; I did not want our outing to be spoiled because of bad *hejab*. We had no such inhibitions, and made an elaborate show of pushing at the gates, appearing surprised that they should still be locked, and shouting to the guards about the opening time. For the first time they looked up, regarded us all silently and disappeared. A few minutes later, through the curious logic of revolutionary Iran, the four of us were waved in while the middle-class Iranians, whose national treasure we had come to see, still waited uncomplainingly outside.

The vaults of the Bank Markazi contain Iran's crown jewels: in the past, they were the basis of the royal family's wealth and the chief guarantee of the country's economy. Now they are a museum piece for the Islamic Republic, which can neither capitalise on them, use them, pawn them nor sell them. They represent immense, but completely unrealisable, wealth. As we walked into the dark hallway from the bright sunlight, the guards inside watched us each in turn and pointed to a desk in the corner, on which stood a sign: 'The Collection of the National Jewels of Iran. 2500 rials.' The bearded young man who took the money warned us four times not to touch the glass cases in the exhibition ourselves, and not to let the children touch them. We promised four times, and were allowed through.

The men who guarded the national treasure of Iran were dressed in street clothes, with open-neck shirts and regulation stubble. They had revolvers strapped to their hips in leather holsters worn Wild-West fashion, and stood at intervals of ten feet throughout the hallway and down the stairs leading to the subterranean vault. The temperature was becoming cooler with each step we took downstairs. Then we turned a corner and caught our breath: thousands of jewels shimmered under spotlights mounted in the ceiling and walls.

Behind the first glass case was a throne made of precious metals and encrusted with jewels; the Naderi Throne, made in 1798 with 26,733 precious stones. On the footrest of the throne, emeralds and rubies were set in a field of gold. The back was a peacock's tail of sapphires, pearls and turquoises. At the base, the throne was guarded by an imperial lion in gold and diamonds. The next case held the great diamond known as *Daria-i-Nur*, the Sea of Light: 182 carats, and one of the largest diamonds ever found. Square-cut, it sat in a frame of five dozen smaller diamonds guarded and crowned with two lions, ruby eyes blazing, and surmounted by an imperial Persian crown, also in diamonds.

Each object seemed more fantastical than the one before: robes of gold thread embroidered with pearls, a snuffbox made of 92 matching emeralds, necklaces of pearls which were each several inches across and were overshadowed by emeralds which were even larger. It was ludicrously ostentatious, unthinkably vulgar, and completely fascinating; and the most ostentatious, vulgar and fascinating object of all was an enormous globe, five feet high, made in 1869, and set with 51,363 stones. The equator was delineated by diamonds, the seven seas composed of sapphires and emeralds, the continents outlined in rubies. The hub of this 24-carat globe was, of course, Iran: the centre of the universe.

For ten minutes we were the only visitors in the vault. The guards watched us in silence, following our movements, listening to our reverential whispers. When we pointed at something, they grew especially nervous, as though they thought we were about to touch the glass, contrary to instructions. Then a wave of noise came down the steps; the gates had opened for the other visitors, and the strongrooms filled with loud Persian exclamations and excited chatter. We found ourselves, like them, drawn towards the huge dishes filled with loose gems; a salad bowl heaped with diamonds, golden caskets overflowing with pearls, soup tureens red with rubies and green with emeralds. It went on and on; amber, beryl, jade, lapis lazuli, opals, topaz, turquoise, garnets and tourmalines. It was an orgy, a gross excess, an immoderation of riches. The Persians could not restrain themselves as we did. They repeatedly reached out and touched the glass, and an ear-splitting klaxon went off each time, reverberating through the small dark vaults. But the guards' pistols always stayed in their holsters and the alarm would stop after half a minute. Directly the nervous laughter had faded away the noise would be forgotten. Then somebody else would reach out longingly ...

After hundreds of years of conquests, purchases and gifts, the crown jewels of Iran are, by both aesthetic and monetary standards, one of the world's greatest accumulations of treasure. It was Reza Shah who took them from the private collection of the Qajars and handed them over to the nation. During the Pahlavi years they were displayed, at set times, to the diplomatic community and important guests. In the 1970s they were properly catalogued and a book devoted to the collection was written to coincide with the 2500th anniversary ceremony. But after the revolution, the jewels were withdrawn from show. The usual Iranian rumours abounded: some people believed that they had been sold off, bit by bit, to finance the purchase of weapons when the oil industry almost ground to a halt during the Iran–Iraq war; the gold was said to have been melted down and the jewels replaced by paste. The most widely believed story was that the Shah and his family had taken the collection abroad with them when they had fled. It was only after the tenth anniversary of the revolution that the crown jewels appeared on public display again; all that was changed were the imperial titles. The new nameplates describe Reza Shah as Reza Khan, his son as Mohammed Reza, and the empress as merely Farah.

The time when the Iranian crown jewels were the guarantee of the country's currency had long passed. The new wealth which would turn a backward country into a rich one began to flow at 4 a.m. on 26 May 1908 at Masjid-i-Suleiman near the Persian Gulf. An oil gusher 1180 feet high shot into the air, watched by the British officers and businessmen who had invested eight years and nearly half a million pounds in finding new sources which would allow the Royal Navy to convert from coal to oil. This oil had a profound effect on the Royal Navy and the British economy over the next half-century; but it was to revolutionise Iran.

The revenue from oil gave Reza Shah the first chance in Iran's history to build a modern economy and restructure society. It also turned the state into the dominant force in the economy. The revenue was used for Reza Shah's programmes on education, health and enforcing aspects of cultural change. Nevertheless, the agreement which the government signed with the British-owned Anglo-Iranian Oil Company, giving Iran less than 40 per cent of the oil revenue, was deeply resented in the country as a whole. In 1951 Iran's oil wells and refineries were nationalised by the then prime minister, Mohammed Mossadeq; but in the political chaos which followed, when countercoup followed coup, Mossadeq lost power. The position of the Anglo-Iranian Oil Company had become untenable, and when it withdrew from Iran the country was left for the first time in full control of its oil wells and the revenue from them.

In the years which followed, oil became an increasingly valuable commodity and by the 1960s the government was Iran's largest employer. In 1973, when the Organisation of Petroleum Exporting Nations (OPEC) quadrupled its prices as a result of the urgent lobbying of the Shah, Iran became one of the richest countries in the world overnight. The Shah's intention was to transform this wealth into industrial power as quickly as possible. It never happened. The policy of industrialisation merely introduced a series of factories which assembled cars and other consumer items designed and often produced abroad. The country was awash with cash that had nowhere to go. While living standards improved everywhere, the income gap between the rich and the poor grew wider than ever. Rising expectations brought discontent and disillusionment. Inflation reached 17 per cent, and by 1978 the boom had turned to recession. The Shah's government even had to borrow to finance the large amounts of military hardware which were being purchased from Europe and the United States. Even the middle class and the wealthy grew discontented with the old regime, and looked for something better. As for the people who had been drawn to the cities in huge numbers by the prospect of work and had found only dislocation and misery, they were the natural material for revolution.

The constant strikes, and the flight of capital and of skilled labour which the revolution brought with it, affected the oil industry badly. Far greater damage was done, though, when Iraq under Saddam Hussein invaded the weakened country in 1980. Much of the fighting took place around the oilfields and the ports where the tankers loaded. Iran's economy was placed on a war footing, and the drastic cut in oil revenue was matched by a sharp decrease in imports. That, at least, had its benefits: after the ceasefire in 1988, Iran had virtually no foreign debt and its first priority was a rehabilitation programme for the oil industry and petrochemical plants; the policy paid off within a year and production began to rise steadily. Once again, Iran had a reliable source of foreign currency and could at last afford to invest and expand elsewhere in the economy. The Islamic Republic became known as a sound risk, paying its debts promptly.

Still, its dependence on oil income was considerable; oil exports now accounted for over 10 per cent of gross domestic product and the largest share of foreign exchange income. The good times were brief: some unrealistically optimistic assumptions about the oil price between 1991 and 1993, combined with lax control of imports and the growing corruption, created severe economic problems as it became clear that hopes for an economic upturn were misplaced.

By mid-1992 Iran's financial position was visibly deteriorating, and foreign companies and merchant banks were no longer enthusiastic about doing business with it. Iran paid slowly or not at all, and many European and Japanese companies refused to sell to the country except on a cash basis. In 1993, in the course of a reform of the exchange rate, the Iranian government ended the practice whereby importers could pay by cash. In order to import consumer goods or, more vitally, capital goods for light manufacturing, businessmen had to go through a lengthy and expensive process. First, they had to deposit cash with an Iranian bank in order to open a letter of credit. Second, the importer needed to obtain Central Bank approval for the letter of credit and the import order. Sometimes the Customs Administration rejected imports on the grounds that they were 'non-essential'; at other times the Central Bank simply appropriated the cash deposit because the government itself happened to be short of funds. Although the Central Bank was supposed to pay within three months, businessmen found themselves waiting up to two years before foreign suppliers received what was due to them. So, therefore, did their Western suppliers. Not surprisingly, Iranian letters of credit became generally unacceptable to Western companies. In 1994, according to one British bank, Iran's external debt was around $20 billion dollars. Around 80 per cent of that debt was short-term, and most of it was in the form of letters of credit with deferred payment terms.

Commercial banks in the City of London with long experience in the Middle East agreed with various Western export credit agencies that until Iran's financial situation improved there was little point in trading there. Most of the major infrastructure projects for which contracts had been awarded in 1990–92 to European companies seemed unlikely to go ahead because of the almost total lack of external finance. A senior British banker who knew Iran well said it would take several years for Iran to bring its overdue payments fully up to date, and it could be longer.

'We continue to travel to Iran periodically to keep an eye on the situation,' he said, 'but we have no plans for any projects. Our confidence in the future of the Iranian economy is not helped by the

fact that the bureaucrats we meet are unfamiliar with the basics of
international finance. They are not technocrats with real experience,
just men with the title of "engineer" which is a catch-all phrase given
to anyone with a degree, it seems.'

As for the oil industry, the situation was made even worse by production problems, lack of investment and continual political interference
in the workings of the Ministry of Oil. By 1994 Iran's inability to pay
foreign subcontractors on time for parts and equipment had severe
consequences; the number of operational oil rigs had been reduced from
several dozen in the previous year to fewer than ten. The economic
slowdown brought galloping inflation and a renewed financial crisis.
More and more of Iran's oil revenue was going directly to pay off
foreign debts, payments under rescheduled or overdue letters of credit,
export credit loan repayments and for food and medicine. By the end
of 1994 the proportion of oil money which could be invested in Iran
was actually less than it had been in the days of the deeply unpopular
agreement with the Anglo-Iranian Oil Company.

Nadir is a dealer in electronic goods who returned to Iran from California
at the end of the Iran–Iraq war. He has done his best to provide for his
family without using up his savings, but it has not been easy. He is
particularly gloomy about the outlook for the economy.

'We are all suffering because there are no economic policies, just
political ones. The technocrats who knew what they were doing mostly
left after the revolution. A few remained during the war and they
were allowed to function properly under Moussavi and Khamene'i, who
directed the war effort. Of course no one wanted to invest during the
war years, so anyone who had money used it in land and currency
speculation. That helped create the huge black market. After the ceasefire
people thought that a kind of Eldorado had arrived. The state-controlled
economy vanished and a laissez-faire Thatcherite system opened up
before us. Because there is no Islamic economic system, or rather there
are many different theories that have been put forward, it was possible
to make this big jump without damaging the regime. In fact, it proved
very popular and fitted the mood of the people who were tired of the
restrictions of the war economy.

'It started in 1988–89. It was a fantastic relief when imports of
consumer goods were allowed once again – cars, computers, clothes,
televisions – and the number of dealerships shot up. There was good
money to be made, though a large part of it had to be handed over
to the suppliers in Europe and Japan and elsewhere. Plenty of people
made a profit, and of course there was a lot of money paid in bribes for
allowing goods to come in and for paperwork to be done. And business
licences had to be purchased from the proper ministries, not to mention

the thousands of dollars to get a phone connection and a fax line. Very little went where it should. I can tell you that nobody I work with paid more taxes when their incomes went up, because cheating on taxes is a kind of religion here. The people on salaries lose out; but the big guys, the entrepreneurs, can pay a smaller amount under the table. I'm speaking from personal experience.

'Meanwhile good Iranian products, and let's face it there aren't many, mostly food and petrol, were being subsidised. Market forces were just ignored and still are. Petrol is incredibly cheap and people used it in all the new cars they were buying. Did you see that the Deputy Oil Minister [Ardeshir Fathi-Nejad] said the other day that Iran uses almost one-third of its own oil production? That's the population boom and the car boom together. Now the farmers have started using bread as cheap animal feed because the price is kept so low.'

The government found it very difficult politically to move away from the old welfare state approach to the new conservatism. Basic foods such as meat, cooking oil and rice were available at artificially low prices in exchange for coupons. The system was essential during the war with Iraq, when so many working-class men were fighting at the front. When the war ended, the government lacked the political will to get rid of the coupon system and merely cut down the range of goods available, even though the World Bank made one of its larger loans to Iran contingent upon the ending of the system. In 1994 coupons were still available to anyone who applied for them, though the banks would issue them (on production of a *daftar ke bassij*, or identification book) only three times a year. In the meantime, trading in them had become big business. Outside most big government stores in Tehran, groups of men would stand around calling out '*Kupon, kupon!*' and trying to buy coupons off the shoppers. Poorer women who could not afford to give their children pocket-money would hand them the coupons they didn't need, and the children would sell them to the dealers.

When the war ended, a million servicemen returned to civilian life. There was no possibility of finding jobs for more than about a third of them, except in government. As a result, the payroll of the civil service rose alarmingly. Ministries took on people on the basis of their war service and their faithfulness to the Islamic cause, rather than their experience or efficiency. Businessmen like Nadir blamed the disappointingly poor performance of the economy on the influx of unseasoned civil servants, who lacked the proper background to make the correct economic decisions, and tended to plan only for the short term.

'It's hard, though, to put all the blame on them. After all, the Majlis is passing budgets that assume Iranian oil will sell at $20 a barrel when the real price is $11 a barrel.'

One of the results of this unrealistic forecasting, as well as of the overmanning which followed the ending of the war with Iraq, was that individual ministries were unable to pay realistic salaries to their employees. As in Russia during the final stages of Marxism–Leninism, civil servants had to find other ways of making a living. Corruption was one natural way. The other was to take one, two or even three other jobs in order to earn a decent wage. A civil servant would spend only part of the day at his desk. The rest of the day he might be a taxi-driver, using his own car or one he shared with a colleague in the same position, while in the evening he might sell the things he had bought in the daytime, or work in a hotel or a restaurant. His civil service work would receive the smallest part of his time and attention.

Nadir, as ever, had a true story to illustrate the problem.

'A foreign diplomat who believed in following the correct procedure, had to have a large tree cut down on his Embassy property. Apparently it was endangering some power lines which were underneath. So he sent his deputy to the correct ministry for cutting down trees. After finding the right department, the deputy was led into an office with an official sitting behind his desk drinking tea. Let's call him Mr Ali. The problem was explained and Mr Ali said that he understood and appreciated the concern for safety that the diplomats had shown but the ministry was not in the business of cutting down trees; they preferred to contract out work of that sort. But he could recommend a good private company that would do the job competently. He handed over the details and suggested that the deputy visit the company in the afternoon at about 2 p.m. and somebody would help him. At 2 p.m. the deputy from this Embassy went along to the private company that undertook tree-cutting and gardening contracts for the ministry. He was shown in and then taken to an office. He opened the door and there, sitting behind the desk, was the very same Mr Ali. It was his second job. So he spent his first job recommending his services in the private sector. And that is how Iran works nowadays.'

The Tehran bazaar is the economic heart of Iran: a great block of shops and businesses in the city centre where a third of the country's commerce is carried on. Every year, as Tehran expands, the bazaar's share of overall trade is a little diminished, but it is still the most important business centre in Iran, controlling two-thirds of the domestic wholesale trade and 30 per cent of imports into the country. When it closed down in the months before the revolution, the Shah's hopes of survival came to an end: losing the confidence of the bazaar merchants was the equivalent of a disastrous flight of capital from the country.

The entrance to the *Bazaar-e Bozorg*, the Grand Bazaar, has never been grand: a dirty earth-coloured archway simply merges with the

buildings around it. Both the architecture and the attitude look inward.
By the start of the 1990s even the unprepossessing archway was hidden,
and the main approach to the bazaar was through the building works
for the apparently endless construction of the Tehran subway system.
Inside, though, it was a different world. The goldsmiths' shops line the
main alleyway, each window hung with gold chains glittering in the
light. Women wander from shop to shop in search of gold for a dowry,
an investment, or merely decoration. This is the most impressive part
of the bazaar, and it sits suitably enough at the top of a slight incline,
looking down on to the shops selling goods of lesser value. From here
you can see perhaps a hundred yards down the alleyway: the start of
eight miles of lanes and corridors.

It could be the entrance to an ancient city, and a constant, restless
flow of *chador*ed women, mullahs and men in open-necked shirts moves
through the Grand Bazaar, elbowed aside by old men bent completely
double under burdens that they carry like donkeys, or making way
for goods being dragged along on heavy trolleys by men who whistle
loudly to signal their approach. The sun's rays cut sharply downwards
through the holes in the grimy glass panes above us, bright enough to
make the hoops of neon light which hang everywhere seem pale and
weak.

A few minutes further, and you cross an unseen frontier. The gold
has come to an end, and the shops are selling white bridal gowns
indistinguishable from Western ones. Others specialise in *chadors*, and
cloth on enormous bolts which they fling out and display with practised
skill. Another frontier: the area of herbs and spices, with great open
panniers of turmeric, saffron, nutmeg, sage, tiny red *zereshk* berries,
coriander, chillies, dried roots, peppercorns, cardamoms, ginger, rock
salt, dates, raisins, heaped and overflowing so that the shopkeeper
and his customers tread the yellow, red and green dust underfoot
and further enrich the pungent smell of the alleyway. Next are the
shops that sell tacky plastic goods: a thousand strings of cheap *taspih*,
or worry-beads, in primary greens and yellows and reds; or tens of
thousands of buttons of different designs; or key-holders with cars
and Persian rock stars and ayatollahs on them. Not far away are
the stalls devoted to women's make-up, with pictures of Rafsanjani,
Khamene'i and Khomeini staring out grim and disapproving above
the racks of rouge and mascara.

Nearby are the fast food vendors. A man stands behind a brazier
selling cooked red beets which simmer in their juice. He keeps up a steady
patter of jokes, criticisms and personal comments about passers-by.
People stop to listen and laugh, and he bayonets a juicy beet from
the pan and wraps it in a screw of paper so it can be eaten like
a toffee apple. The beet man is competing with the new attraction:
bananas, imported from the western hemisphere since the lifting of

import controls. The Asian and African varieties have far more flavour and interest, but the unblemished yellow variety from Central America, produced by the American-owned United Fruit Company, still have a rarity value and people seem to want them most.

As my Iranian friend and I penetrated deeper into the bazaar, we found ourselves regressing in time. Here the shoppers and the merchants dressed traditionally, and the mullahs were more numerous. We were the only women here who were not wearing *chadors*. Since I was obviously a foreigner and an outsider, no one took much notice of my blue denim *roupush*. It was my friend who received the heavy treatment: she was wearing a pink *roupush* and a brightly patterned headscarf, and men would deliberately bump into her, and the handlers of loaded carts did not bother to shout out and warn her. She was lucky not to be knocked over, though she insisted that no one, even here, would attack a woman physically. But the bazaar is a place of traditional values. Modernity is not appreciated, especially in women.

It took us a long time to find the shop we were looking for. We were received hospitably: chairs were brought up, tea and soft drinks were set in front of us. Mr Saderi was the father of a friend, and he treated us as if we were in his sitting room rather than balancing on rickety chairs in the confined space of his shop. He was a little man, stooped from a lifetime of leaning over counters showing fabric to his customers. His clothes were old and baggy, and he looked as though he rarely saw the sun. Mr Saderi would not even consider talking about business until we had finished our tea and spoken of our mutual friends. Nor was it possible to get his undivided attention. A constant stream of merchants, mullahs and acquaintances passed by, and most of them stopped to speak to him, turning courteously to us before telling him the latest gossip and prices. Mr Saderi would listen quietly, smiling slightly, leaning forward, clicking his *taspih* in time with the chatter.

His shop was entirely filled with rolls of fabric and boxes of lace and trimmings. There was scarcely room to display his goods to the customers, though his stock seemed small. I knew he was a rich man: his sons all drove new cars, and he had a large family house in north Tehran. It was hard to reconcile all that with this little box of fabrics. But appearances are deceptive in the bazaar; the most obvious thing about it, the daily selling of goods across the counter, is the least important of its functions. Mr Saderi had a storage warehouse on the other side of Tehran where he kept a large amount of stock, and also had shops in Mashhad and Qazvin. In the Grand Bazaar, business lies not in sales across the counter so much as in the large-scale deals between its merchants. The shops are merely a front: they provide their owners with a place to carry on the day-to-day, hour-by-hour contact with suppliers, agents, contacts and customers throughout the whole of Iran and further afield. Through exports like carpets, nuts and dried fruits the bazaaris have access to foreign exchange which is rarely channelled through the official system. The bazaar provides a banking system of its own, and when private banks were abolished in 1979 this function increased. Loans and investments are arranged swiftly and easily for customers and fellow retailers. No guarantees are required for these transactions, no matter how large; a man's reputation is all that counts. The Grand Bazaar offers most of the financial services you could obtain in the City of London or in Frankfurt. It is a stock exchange, a commodities market and a banking network on a large scale; and all the while it masquerades as a collection of hucksters' stalls.

In the brief intervals between greeting his friends and ordering more tea for us, Mr Saderi described the life of the Tehran bazaari in terms that showed how proud he was of it.

'My sons look after the other part of the business. Me, I don't like to leave the bazaar. Why should I? My friends are here, my business is here, everything I need is here. My wife has been asking me for years to take her on a holiday and I have to tell her that if I was one day away from the bazaar I could not breathe.'

Soon it would be time for the midday meal, and he invited us to join him. But it was far too hot and noisy by now, and we had other people to see. He accepted our thanks politely, though I thought he seemed a little relieved; perhaps lunching with two women whose clothes showed little respect for the traditional norms would have been a strain for him. We said our goodbyes, and he sent his assistant, one of the old men who pushed the loaded carts, to show us the way. With him to guide us we had no more problems from the bazaaris: no one pushed us or shouted at us, and we didn't even seem to attract the hostile looks we had noticed before. Mr Saderi's social credit had been extended to cover us, and that was good enough. On the way the old man clucked at us for missing the chance of a really good meal. It would certainly be better than anywhere else we might go, he said. When we reached the main gate he stopped in the shadows, as though he felt he didn't belong in the sunlight. He watched us to see that we were safely on our way. Then he turned and headed into his darker, sheltered world again.

The Grand Bazaar is an entire community within itself. In its maze of alleyways there are mosques, religious schools and even public baths for men and women. It is also a political centre as crucial as any in the country. Information is a commodity as important as any other here: more important, often. At times of tension the bazaar seethes with rumour and speculation. The merchants reflect the mood

of the entire country, and when the bazaar is 'in disorder' – *bazaar
naaraam*, in Persian – the government has to be careful. A shutdown
of the bazaar is a serious matter, and it has happened at all the
pivotal moments of Iranian history; in 1905 during the campaign for
a constitution, when the bazaaris were punished for not lowering their
prices to suit the government; during the staged pro-Shah demonstrations in 1953 and when the results of the rigged elections of 1960
were announced; and, most significantly of all, in 1978, when the
revolution against the Shah was building up in earnest. It had always
before been possible to buy peace by making concessions; but not in
1978.

Traditionally, the bazaaris have always had close links with the clergy.
This is partly a matter of enhancing the reputation of an individual
business. A merchant pays his tithe to a mullah in much the same
way that a Western company contributes to charity: it shows goodwill
towards the community. But the link with the mullah also provides the
merchant with a certain moral authority. After the revolution and
the establishment of the Islamic Republic, the link between the bazaaris
and the mullahs became even stronger. It suited both sides, but was
deeply resented by businessmen outside the bazaar.

Kourush is an economist from an academic family. After living
abroad for years he has come back to study the Iranian economy
for an international institute. Although he often visits the bazaar, he
is not part of it. He finds many of its mechanisms admirable, but he is
critical of it in a number of ways.

'The bazaaris are only out for themselves; they have always judged
Iran's governments by the advantages it offers them. They disapproved
of the Shah for several reasons. He wanted money placed in long-
term investments, whereas they like to make a deal and turn over
the profit quickly, then put as much of it outside the country as
possible. And then the Shah didn't consult the bazaaris, and that
hurt their pride. It turned into a contest between the Shah's circle,
who controlled access to so many ventures, and wanted to modernise everything, and the bazaaris who wanted to keep things as they
were.

'When the revolution happened, it was total victory for the bazaaris:
no more rivals, no more attempts to modernise everything. But they're
short-sighted. They still won't invest in production, and as a result there
isn't enough manufacturing in this country. In one way I can't blame
them: it's hard to invest if you can't be sure of getting the imports you
need, when you need them. And the labour laws in this country mean
that it's almost impossible to fire people once they're hired. Go to any
factory and see how many people are working there. Then go back on
pay-day: you'll notice the difference. They all turn up then, even though
they do other jobs the rest of the week.

'This question of investment, or the lack of it, is really important. Yes, it's a gamble, but most bazaaris have money outside the country, enough capital to take a risk. They don't do it because they're always looking for quick returns. The mullahs are the other problem. There's usually a mullah behind each bazaari, and these mullahs like the good life; they don't want to risk their steady income, so they encourage the bazaaris to stick to making deals. So what you see around you in Iran is the result: no new investment in the country at all, and it's getting poorer and poorer as a result. But in the meantime just to buy a stall and a business in the bazaar will cost you 500 million *toman*, that's 5,000 million *rials*. It's the market price, you see. It works perfectly in there. It just doesn't work for the rest of the country, outside.'

14

Lunching with the Mullah

John Simpson

In your discourses and sermons let all your utterances inspire either fear or expectation; but never allow men to despair completely of God's mercy, nor yet unfailingly admit them to Paradise without regard to their goodness. In general, speak on those matters in which you are properly versed and of which you have a good knowledge, for the result of unsubstantiated pretence is disgrace.

A Mirror For Princes

The holy city of Qom is famous for many things: its shrine, its domes, its carpets, its blue pottery, its curious sweetmeat *soghan*, its unpleasant salty drinking water. And its piety. It has never been a popular place among Persians who are not religious: a proverb, much-quoted, says that a dog of Kashan is better than the nobles of Qom.

Mahmoudi put it less epigrammatically as his Paykan rattled along the desert highway from Tehran.

'No good sleeping tonight in Qom, Mr John.'

'Why is that, Mahmoudi?' I always enjoyed his judgements on people and places.

'Getting their water from here, Mr John.'

He laughed wolfishly and jerked his thumb at the extraordinary lake of salt which lay on our left: a white inland sea with the shadows of cloud travelling over its surface and the brilliance of the sunshine on its poisoned waters. The beach around it is crusted with salty residues, and nothing grows within a quarter of a mile. The only greenery is in the rocks: geological layers of some greenish stone, running through the hills for a mile or more. It is not, of course, true that Qom gets its water from this great inland sea, the *Daryache-ye-Namak* or Salt Lake; but every water source in the entire area is tainted with saltiness.

Qom itself begins among low hills and the clustering of power-lines across the open desert, and its outskirts are signalled by an enormous steel sculpture of the 'Allah' symbol which the Islamic Republic has adopted, and which resembles a sword in brackets. It suits the ethos of a state which has committed itself to cutting off the hands of foreign agents. The sculpture is so designed that it can be appreciated from every angle, and it stands prosaically in the middle of a traffic roundabout. A bus with the words 'My God' on a strip of clear green plastic on the windscreen wobbled past us at speed and the driver waved and smiled a gappy yellow smile in answer to our shouts of anger and alarm. 'Kerbala, 1125 km', said a signpost optimistically; one of the chief shrines of Shi'ia Islam, the Iraqi town of Kerbala was among the places Iranians would most have liked to capture in their war with Iraq. A mullah sat under the sign, guarding a mound of suitcases, cardboard boxes and plastic bags which seemed to have been dumped off by some passing bus. Perhaps he was on his way to Kerbala.

Qom is indeed scarcely attractive. It is flat and dun-coloured and dusty. It presents much the same aspect as it did a century ago, when travellers like Lord Curzon and Edward Granville Browne passed through, and a small group of British engineers and their wives lived at the telegraph office. Apart from a large modern hotel block, built to accommodate the tens of thousands of pilgrims who come to visit Fatima's shrine, and a vast new mosque on the edge of the city, the skyline looks much as it always has, the golden, green and blue domes rising from the mud-brick buildings.

A river, also called the Qom, runs through the heart of the city. It rises outside the town of Khomein, the birthplace of Khomeini. But in the summer the waters dry up altogether, and the river ceases to exist. Its bed is as broad as the Thames at Richmond or the Seine at the Pont Neuf, and instead of water there are only stones. Bridges cross it, piers jut out in it, gulleys and drains open on to it – but in August it is a river of colourless shingle, heaped up into banks or hollowed out into channels by the action of water that disappeared months ago and has left only its dry bones, like the skeleton of an animal in the desert.

Qom is utterly devoid of the pleasures which make other cities attractive to westernised Persians. There are no fashionable stores, no video rental shops, no fast-food restaurants. It is one of the few places in Iran where women appear in the street entirely veiled, a black covering over their faces as well as the *chador* which covers their heads and bodies. Under Reza Shah, the decree of 1936 which ordered the compulsory unveiling of women was enforced more severely in Qom than anywhere else. As for men, they had to wear suits and a curious peaked cap named after Reza Shah. Nowadays another set of laws on clothing applies, and is enforced with the same determination. Where the Pahlavi dynasty of Reza Shah and his son tried to make Persians modern, the Islamic Republic is trying to make them pure.

We had come to Qom to do some filming, accompanied by a rather impressive Iranian cameraman whom we had hired. The best cameramen dress and behave like insurance salesmen or librarians, and Ali Torabi could have been either. By the time he had set up his tripod, a crowd of about fifty boys had gathered in front of him to watch. They were neither hostile nor noisy; they were, indeed, perfectly friendly. But they could not be made to understand that they could watch us just as well from behind the camera as in front of it. Neither reason nor aggression in English or Farsi had any effect on them; they stood there just as silently and respectfully, sometimes moving a pace or two in obedience to our furious demands, but never clearing the shot.

A policeman came along and ordered them to leave. They dispersed, then re-formed directly he had swaggered off. A *Komiteh* man turned up, his walkie-talkie wrapped in a copy of the Qom newspaper like fish-and-chips; he talked into it for effect (there seemed to be no answering voice from inside the newspaper) and cleared the onlookers rather less effectively than the policeman had. This time they did not wait for him to go away before clustering round us again, in numbers which had grown by now to more than a hundred. All we wanted to do was to film people walking naturally in and out of the mosque that overlooked the river of dry stones, and we had become the biggest crowd attraction in Qom. Finally we enlisted the help of a middle-aged man in khaki pyjamas (two words which originated in Farsi), a man in an Adidas sweatshirt with long Qom-length sleeves, and an old character with five days' stubble who looked like any bazaari hanger-on and asked us in good American English, 'Who are you shooting for? NBC? CBS?' As a result, Ali Torabi managed to get a few shots that were reasonable; but not many. We had to get away from the crowd, so we called up Mahmoudi, who looked as though he had more radical and physical suggestions for dispersing them, and drove off faster than they could follow us.

The inhabitants of Qom are descended mostly from Arab settlers. They fled there from what is now Iraq to escape from the victorious enemies of the Prophet's grandson Hosain, killed at the battle of Kerbala. At that stage Iran was still mostly Zoroastrian in religion, and the Arab refugees converted the Persian inhabitants to Shi'ia Islam, while becoming converted themselves to the use of the Persian language. A little over a century later Fatima, the great-great-granddaughter of Hosain, died in Qom, and her tomb became one of the holiest shrines in Iran.

The square in front of the great mosque is a magnificent place, open and clean. Afghan refugees lay their brightly coloured blankets along the wall of the shrine, and the women annoy the faithful by wearing their red and blue tribal clothes and not being too particular about *hejab*. Various neat religious stalls were set up close to the grand entrance, selling beautifully woven linen shrouds which the pious could take into the shrine for blessing. I bought one from a large, engaging man with a curious wall eye, and as I put it away in my bag I asked if he minded selling such a good shroud to a *Firanji*.

'My friend,' he said, and I could see the joke coming from some way off, 'the more shrouds I sell to *Firanjis* the better I like it.'

He laughed uproariously, and Mahmoudi was torn between laughing himself and being offended on my behalf.

'You won't find a shroud holier than mine,' the seller of shrouds added, as I fumbled for the money. 'That's why I've got my stall here, right by the mosque.'

He took the money, and then handed me several of the optional extras – a cloth to cover my face, a strip to bind my jaw, and various other pieces of linen whose use I couldn't work out – and refused to charge me for them. I was, he said, his guest in Qom.

Any number of more secular hucksters were at work in the square as well. In the photographers' booth you can have your picture taken by putting your head through a hole in a screen, on which has been painted a figure in full religious garb. The result is to make you look like an old-fashioned ayatollah, even though you are wearing only a shirt and trousers. Women, too, can have their photographs taken there, though they have to keep their *chadors* on. Other stalls sell crudely printed T-shirts, plastic knick-knacks, and the *sohan* which is one of Qom's claims to fame. Packed in a round, flat metal can about the size of a can of film, *sohan* is a flat disc of caramel with squashed pistachio nuts baked into it. The shops in the city pile the cans one on top of the other till they reach the ceiling, and look like a veritable library of film; and if you go in, as I did, with someone the shopkeeper knows, he will go to great pains to pull down a can for you from the top, where they are fresh. Mere passing pilgrims are given cans of less recent vintage.

We sat down in the park outside the mosque and drank from cans of sickly orangeade. Behind us in the bushes there was a sudden rustling, and an outburst of giggles. I peered round. Three soldiers were having their fortune told by an elderly man with an equally elderly canary. It used its beak to pick out a card from a rack he held up in front of it: the card contained the fortune. I asked Mahmoudi if he would get the man to tell my fortune as well, and for a few *rials* the canary was invited to size me up with its tiny brown eyes. It put its head on one side and seemed to take especial care over making up its mind which card to choose. Then its head plunged down decisively, and it pulled out one of the tattered range of twenty or so. But it was a disappointment. 'Love conquers all,' the card read.

Beside the great gate of the mosque a notice in Farsi and English reads: '1. Photography is strictly forbidden. 2. Nobody except Muslim is allowed into the shrine.' I would dearly have loved to see and smell the vast frame of sandalwood that covers the tomb, and watched as visitors kissed the doorposts of the tomb chamber and inspected the extraordinary silver and crystal furnishings of the outer chamber, now adorned with a large photograph of Ayatollah Khomeini. When Ali Torabi, the cameraman, and his fat, unhandy sound-recordist went inside, the mosque guards, seeing the camera, rushed over to stop them entering, and there was a brief scuffle; but Ali pushed his way past them with a couple of well-aimed punches. Tira and I were left standing in the doorway, examining the gravestones which were set in this particularly holy ground and gleamed like alabaster in the sunlight. The square was noisy with the laughter of the Afghan refugees and the shouts of the hucksters, while *rowzeh-khani*, or preachers, offered to recite improving tales. This was Persia as the travellers of the past had known it. We sat in the hot sun and waited, as doves perched on the tops of the minarets, and mullahs in white and grey moved majestically through the crowds like so many pigeons.

One particular mullah strode into view, an elegant, clean, imposing figure in the midday heat and the noise of the square. The people he passed deferred to him and moved aside to give him greater room. He was clearly a figure of consequence. He did not, however, lord it over them; indeed, he scarcely seemed to notice them. I was reminded of a biblical pharisee: with his crisp robes and his head at a grand but not necessarily boastful angle, he could have been walking to a meeting of the Sanhedrin.

The mullah's spotless white turban presented an imposing frontage, but as it only covered part of his head, it could not hide the fact that his hair was thinning. The pate gleamed through the carefully-combed brown covering of hair like earth through worn grass, and his beard had a reddish tinge which wasn't natural. He was something of a dandy, then, as well as a figure of significance. His gown, which reached almost to his ankles, was black like that of some fastidious Oxford or Cambridge don, thin enough for the light to shine through the fabric and fine enough for the slight breeze to catch in it and billow its folds about him, so that he had to catch them with his white, ringed hands (the engraved cornelian catching the sunlight) and rearrange the lie of the gown on his shoulders. There was power in the way he walked, his hips swinging, his shoulders moving masterfully. He knew exactly where he belonged in the scheme of things, and what duty other people owed him.

Not far away, her back against a wall, sat a blind woman, a little bundle of bones and rags and *hejab*. She could have been any age from fifty to ninety, and had probably never seen in her life. There were no eyeballs behind the lids, and her face was skull-like, the sharp unfleshed bones catching the sunlight, which made the empty eye-sockets darker and emptier than ever. A crude wooden bowl was set out in front of her, with a couple of small-denomination coins in it. She swivelled her head as the mullah approached, her heightened hearing able to detect a soft footfall in the surrounding noise. Maybe she could even tell how much it represented in the way of alms.

The mullah passed her by, his head still held at an angle that made the insignificant things of life invisible. Her claw of a hand, the colour of earth, followed the faint breeze of his passing, and remained outstretched towards him as he walked on. She could probably smell the faint odour of rose-water. She said nothing, but the way she followed him with her claw showed that she knew his exact position still.

He was eight or ten paces beyond her before he stopped: maybe he was so deep in thought that he needed time to register her presence. The white turban turned towards her, and, more pharisaical than ever, he fished in the depth of his robe for a coin. He pulled out a twenty-*rial* piece with the name and superscription of Allah on it – Caesar's head disappeared from the coinage after the revolution – and walked back grandly to place it in the outstretched claw. Then he sauntered away. The claw turned the coin over experimentally, and hid it away. The old woman's lips moved a little, but whether in gratitude or in expectation of something to eat it is impossible to be certain. Then the claw went out again, searching for more coins from other passers-by.

The use of the term 'mullah' is first recorded in the English language in 1613. It was picked up by Sir Anthony Sherley during his Persian travels and used by him in *A True Discourse of Sir Anthony Sherley's Travel into Persia* which was published that year. It is in use in Farsi, Turkish and Urdu – the languages spoken in Iran and the neighbouring countries – and was originally a corrupt Persian pronunciation of the Arabic *maula*, meaning 'master'. To the ear of a Persian, it still sounds like slang; something like the word 'boss' in English, perhaps. A mullah is not the precise Islamic equivalent of a Christian priest or minister; since Islam is a religion of the Law, it is passed on to each new generation by teaching. Shi'ia Islam is more hierarchical than mainstream Sunni Islam, yet even Shi'ism does not have the kind of hierarchy that Christian denominations do. A Shi'i ayatollah does not stand in the same relationship to a mullah as a bishop does to a priest; and a *hojat-ol-Eslam*, the halfway stage between the two, is not the equivalent of a dean. The gradations of the Shi'i clergy relate to study and teaching, rather than to promotion within a spiritual career structure. An ayatollah receives seniority and respect because of his scholarship.

The meaning of the titles indicates this. *Hojat-ol-Eslam* means the 'proof of Islam': that is, a mullah who has given evidence of his learning but has not yet achieved the status of an ayatollah. 'Ayatollah' itself means 'sign of God'; there are about two hundred mullahs who have reached the rank of ayatollah and can teach and interpret Islamic law. There are five Grand Ayatollahs, who are the leaders of the Shi'ia faith. Yet they are not comparable with, say, a college of cardinals: they have almost as much in common with a country's Supreme Court, or even with the heads of its main universities.

As for the mullahs of Iran, they collectively form the *ulema*: an Arabic word which means 'men of religious learning'. To find a parallel for the extraordinary range of their involvement and activity it is necessary to look at other near-theocracies – medieval Europe, say, or Cromwellian England. Mullahs in Iran can be found in the Majlis or parliament, in the universities as teachers, in the courts as advisers and judges, in government ministries as political directors, in the welfare offices attached to their mosques as supervisors of the rationing system. During the war with Iraq their role was rather like that of Stalin's political commissars, who were supposed to maintain the morale of the men at the front and lead them by example rather than precept. The bravery of many mullahs during the war won a grudging respect even from those who dislike the clergy.

Mullahs are not usually regarded as being sexual hypocrites, as were the clergy in late medieval Europe; for one thing, they can marry, and for another they do not set themselves exaggerated moral standards then fail to live up to them. Many mullahs do, however, have a reputation for being grasping, and there have been notable examples of outright corruption. When Hojat-ol-Eslam Sadeq Khalkhali, the infamous 'hanging judge', could not account for several million dollars' worth of goods which he and his men had confiscated from so-called enemies of the regime, he was openly described as corrupt. There are many mullahs who drive Mercedes and live in large houses in north Tehran. Their links with the bazaaris, and the opportunities available to them to put businessmen in touch with government ministers and senior officials, have made them rich. They have become precise equivalents of the grasping, corrupt officials of the Shah's time.

'The Imam Khomeini said recently that you always exaggerate everything, and make it worse than it really is. Why do you do this?'

We were sitting in the back of our car, with Mahmoudi at the steering-wheel and a handsome, prematurely grey-haired man in his late thirties in mullah's robes beside him. The mullah's face was turned towards me soulfully, as though he would have liked to understand my Western perversity but found it incomprehensible.

The Imam Khomeini did not, needless to say, mean me as an individual; the 'you' was plural, and meant the Western news media in general.

'In hot weather and on bad roads,' I replied, 'I think these subjects are difficult to discuss.'

The pleasant face with its wide-set grey eyes over a badly broken nose continued to look at me. With his colouring and that nose he looked less like a Persian mullah than a Welshman: possibly a Methodist clergyman

who had played a good deal of rugby in his time. Only the black turban
which proclaimed that he was a *seyyed*, a descendant of the Prophet,
placed him squarely in his real context. I did not like him very much.
Tira, dressed modestly from head to foot in a *chador* made specifically
for this trip, nudged me warningly. As for the mullah, he swivelled
round in his seat and looked enigmatically out of the car window at
the mean streets and the mud-brick buildings which surrounded us.

We drove in near-silence until we reached his house: a desolate
development in a flat khaki landscape, draped with electricity cables.
In front was a small high-walled garden where a few tendrils of plants
struggled with the natural disadvantages of their environment. I found
it touching, and praised the efforts at a garden as highly as I could. A
new mildness entered the atmosphere, as though a small fountain had
suddenly sprung up in the dry earth in front of his door.

Inside, the house was unfinished: he had moved in about three months
before. The stairs to the main living room had an incomplete look to
them, and the plastering of the walls was sketchy, so that here and there
the grey blocks from which the house had been constructed showed
through. The living room itself was large and spacious and light, and
furnished with little more than the big cushions, *nazbalesh*, which
Persians prefer to chairs. Thick factory-woven carpets overlapped one
another on the floor. The mullah, Hojat-ol-Eslam Seyyed Zade Tehrani,
was clearly not a poor man but he preferred his carpets bright and
new. A pleasant, stuffy odour of new wood and hessian arose from
them, and mingled with the faint smell of fruit and rose-water which
permeates most Persian houses.

He left us there to look at the large photograph of Ayatollah Khomeini
in a recess in a wall, and the pictures of a man in uniform who
was sufficiently like the mullah to be his brother. The man wore
an open-necked shirt and, with his grizzled beard, could have been
an ageing rock-and-roll star. Birds sang fitfully outside, and the heat
seeped in. Flies buzzed around us, settling on our hands, our necks, our
lips. From the kitchen on the floor below us there came the encouraging
sounds of cooking, but we had seen, and were to see, nothing of the
woman who was doing it.

After ten minutes, Tehrani came back, padding across the thick new
carpets in his socks. His mullah's robes were gone, and he was wearing
a grey shirt and grey trousers. Without the garments that set him apart
from the rest of the world, Tehrani seemed quiet and self-contained
and rather defensive. His little daughter, a girl of about seven, came
in carrying a bowl of bright red and yellow apples that was almost
too big for her, and set it down in the exact centre of the carpet. The
apples were sweet but much attacked by worms. She stood beside her
father with her arms around his neck as he sat with his back resting
against the big red *nazbalesh*, presenting her hands so that she, and

we, could admire the red varnish on her fingernails. It was a pleasing domestic picture: The Mullah at Home.

'As a nation,' he said, 'we enjoy explosions. Please ask me any questions you like, and I will answer them as truthfully as I can.'

For my part, I saw no need for explosions. I simply wanted to know why a man chose to be a mullah, and how he went about it. It was not always easy to draw the basic information from him because he remained defensive, and seemed certain that I was looking for something I might regard as damaging to him, or to Iran, or to Islam itself. Yet, like most of us, he gradually warmed to his theme because it concerned himself.

In 1964, when he was sixteen, he had decided that he wanted to join the clergy. He was a good deal older than most boys who take that decision.

'My reason was simply that I wanted to guide people, to help them live their lives correctly, as the Holy Koran dictates. You should remember that this was a time of great upheaval in Iran: the Imam Khomeini had been sent into exile, and the Americans and British gave the Shah his orders, and told him what policies to follow. Everything was so materialistic then, and the people were being diverted into corruption and they were oppressed.

'No member of my family had ever joined the clergy before. I don't think they really approved of my decision: they didn't give me that impression at the time. But they never tried to stop me, and now they are very proud of me. They come and listen to me, and bring their friends to hear me, and they know that my decision, taken when I was so young, was the right one.'

It was Tehrani's preaching that reconciled his family to his choice of career. If he had had ambitions to become an ayatollah, he would have needed to study for upwards of forty years in Qom or Mashhad or one of the other centres of Shi'i learning. But as a *rowzeh-khan* he was able to bring himself to public attention relatively early. *Rowzeh* in Arabic means 'garden', and in the sixteenth century, under the Safavid dynasty, when graphic and bloody depictions of the sufferings of Hosain and the other martyrs of the Shi'ia faith were common, a book entitled *The Garden of the Martyrs* was published. It became extremely popular almost at once, and preachers began using it for their texts, thus becoming *rowzeh-khani* – 'readers of the Garden'. This is not always a very elevated profession; in Qom, in particular, *rowzeh-khani* wander around the city, competing with one another in the violence of their emotions and hiring themselves out to work on the feelings of the faithful.

Tehrani was, however, a good deal more dignified than that. He was well-educated and restrained, and his handsome face and quiet, confident bearing had attracted patrons who were wealthy and had good taste. He would preach in private houses, or in schools, or at the headquarters of big organisations, as well as in mosques. He could, no doubt, work on people's feelings with the best of them, but for the most part his sermons were about the duty a Muslim owes to his faith, his family and his country.

'You have to have the talent to speak in public, and the ability to learn your material well: that takes a good deal of research. And you have to have the will to do it well. No one can teach you that, and you cannot read about it in a book. It has to come from inside you. I never read my sermons from notes, because that makes you slow and lifeless. I know how I will say it; that comes from the inspiration of the moment. Before I give a sermon I find out about the people who are hiring me, and what kind of subjects they are interested in. Sometimes, if I can, I go to see the hall where I will be speaking. Mostly, I find, they prefer to hear about the way to become a better Muslim, and how politics and religion go together.'

I asked him if his work was well paid.

'I have enough. The money is not important to me anyway. It is Islam that is important.'

'But this house is an expensive one. Did you pay for it from your fees for preaching?'

'Allah is generous.'

'Are the authorities in Qom generous too? By which I mean, do they pay you a stipend?'

'No. The only money that the authorities in Qom pay out is for study. I do not study nowadays, I preach. And for that I am paid by the people who hire my services.'

The seminal period of his preaching had been the year that preceded the revolution.

'We followed the Imam's guidance from the start,' he said, his grey eyes straying now to the forbidding picture of Khomeini in its recess on his wall, an inscription of Koranic praise at the foot of it. The Ayatollah's own eyes were fixed questioningly on a point just over the photographer's right shoulder, one eyebrow raised, as though someone had walked in unannounced at the moment the picture was being taken. Tehrani had run into a certain amount of danger by following the cause of the Ayatollah. On several occasions when he was preaching he had received notes warning him that SAVAK agents were waiting outside to arrest him. On all but one occasion he managed to slip out with the crowd of worshippers, hiding his distinctive, prematurely grey hair under a hat. The one time he was captured, he was held in a cellar overnight, and threatened with death by the SAVAK if he continued to preach. He took no notice.

'Later, I was arrested in August 1978 with several other members of the clergy. We were told to take off our clerical robes, but we refused. We said to them that only those who had given us our clothes, at the theological school, could take them away from us. They tried to make us sign a paper saying that we would never preach again. And they asked us questions continually, just as you are doing. But they let us go in the end. It was nothing more than intimidation. They wouldn't have dared to do anything serious to us. Things were so tense in Iran then that it would have caused a real upheaval.'

I asked him about the man in the photograph who looked like a rock star. As I thought, it was his brother, who had been in the Revolutionary Guards and was missing in action during the war with Iraq. He had last been seen after a battle in 1981, shortly after being seriously wounded, but Tehrani thought he might have recovered and be still alive as a prisoner. Even if his brother were dead, Tehrani said, he would not be unhappy: the revolution needed martyrs, and it was an honour to be one.

It made him sound smug and self-satisfied, and as he lay against his cushion sipping the tea his daughter had brought in, my irritation flared up again: wrongly, as it turned out. I had seen him as an elegant, plump despatcher of others to the front line, remaining behind himself because his duty of preparing would-be martyrs was more important than fighting. It was not like that at all.

'I had hoped to be a martyr myself,' he said, with great matter-of-factness, as though he were talking about a transfer to another parish; which was, presumably, rather as he would regard it. 'I never had the chance, though. I was a major in what we called then a People's Unit. It was before the *Basij* – the Volunteers – were organised. This was at the start of the war, when nothing much was organised and we were fighting for our lives. I was the operational commander, and most of the time I wore military uniform. The only time I put on my clerical robes was at the time of prayer – if I got the chance. But we were very hard pressed a lot of the time: so hard pressed we didn't always have time to pray, which caused us a great deal of concern and anxiety. I was at Abadan and Khorramshahr for more than three years, and we were fighting for a lot of the time.'

'Were you ever injured?' I asked, knowing the high rate of casualties. For the first and only time in our meeting he laughed, and it was the laughter of self-amusement. He had, he said, been invalided out of the army. He had dived into a foxhole when his position came under fire from a machine gun in the Iraqi trenches opposite. Only his feet had been sticking out, and he received a bullet in the ankle. Later I noticed that he still had a slight limp.

We sat for a while looking at his album of war photographs: Tehrani with his friends, many of whom were dead; Tehrani at the controls of his anti-aircraft gun; Tehrani holding a large piece of shrapnel which had nearly made a martyr of him after all; Tehrani preaching in the open air with hundreds of volunteers hanging on his every word; Tehrani lying in his hospital bed with his leg in plaster, managing a brave smile.

'We find it amusing that you in the West should accuse us of forcing young boys into the minefields. When I think of the problems we used to have, stopping them from volunteering, that makes me angry. It's wrong to let people expose themselves needlessly to danger; that's completely against Islam. No, I'm not saying that young boys never went out. They did, and we lost quite a lot of them. But I always tried to stop them. It's a good thing to give your life for Islam, but suicide is something altogether different.'

A white cloth had been spread over the carpet, and Tehrani's three children had all appeared now, bringing in the dishes for lunch. The efforts of Tehrani's wife, whom we heard but never saw, had resulted in a marvellous *morgh pulao* – a dish with chicken and saffron rice, spiced with *zereshk*, redcurrants with a sharp taste, which added colour as well as flavour to it. Even the little daughter sat with us, eating and being fed from her father's plate: she was regarded as being young enough not to need protecting from adult male eyes. But the woman who had prepared the meal had to eat her share of it in the kitchen; and although Tehrani was extremely hospitable to everyone, including Tira, and answered her questions as readily as he answered mine, he seemed uncomfortable that she was there.

The meal, however, helped to mellow all of us, and as we ate our apples and sipped our tea at the end of it, we were able to turn back with less hostility than before to the question of how Iran appeared to Western eyes.

'If people in the West were told the truth about Iran, they would realise that it was much more favourable than they think,' Tehrani said.

I did not find it impossible to agree with that, but tried to make him understand that the barriers were erected by his own government, rather than by people like me; I, after all, had tried for months to come to Iran, without success. We argued for a long time, hampered on either side by the host–guest relationship, which made it difficult to be blunt about the way we felt. Several times I saw a hurt look in his grey eyes at the things I was saying, and I found myself withholding some of my best arguments. The atmosphere slowly became more friendly, and finally the cameras came out, his as well as ours, and he took photographs of Tira and me without apparent qualms, and allowed Tira to take some of him and me together.

Five years later we were in Shiraz, travelling to Persepolis. Our hotel was the Homa: dirty, expensive and unfriendly. That evening the staff went out of their way to hide us at a table in a far corner of the mostly empty restaurant. Tira guessed it was because of her, and she pointed out a mullah who was sitting at the other end of the restaurant.

'I'm sure they've done this so he won't be offended,' she said.

I stared at the mullah in a particularly hostile way for a long time. 'He looks awfully like the mullah we met in Rey back in eighty-six,' I said.

'Maybe all mullahs get to look that way,' Tira answered, and we turned our attention to the flavourless *chelo kebab*.

The following morning we walked out of the lift and almost knocked into the mullah. It was Tehrani, just coming back from breakfast. He recognised us at once. More than that, he put his arms round me and kissed me. Then he looked directly at Tira, in a way he had never done five years earlier. He was more handsome than ever, and looked more prosperous. He was also distinctly less reserved. We talked a little, then he reached into his robes and extracted the plastic concertina of photographs which he had shown us in Rey. He held it out to me, and I opened it. There we were, sitting together in his sitting room in the photograph he had taken, with the picture of Ayatollah Khomeini glowering down at us from behind. I showed it to Tira. All this time, I thought, she and I had been carried next to a mullah's heart.

The following spring we saw him again: this time by appointment. Now he was living in an outer suburb of Tehran called Poonak, a place where much of the land had been confiscated soon after the revolution from wealthy supporters of the Shah. Tehrani had bought one of the two-storey houses that had been built there, and left his hot, dusty house in Rey. He was moving up-market.

We rang the electronic entry phone on the outside gate and were greeted by his six-year-old son. Here he had a little cement courtyard with a few parched flowers and shrubs planted around the edges. Then to our surprise his wife appeared in the door of the house, dressed in a *chador* but with a gold necklace visible underneath. Tehrani was still in the bath, she told us apologetically. He emerged a few minutes later in bare feet, wearing a white shirt under his black cloak. It looked very much as though he had kept us waiting on purpose. Still, he was extremely friendly.

We were shown into a room with better carpets than before. There was the same big photographic poster of a snow-capped Alp and a green valley with a stream where a herd of cows was grazing: Switzerland in Tehran. Below that was a loyal photograph of Khomeini and Rafsanjani, much as people in Russia once had photographs of Lenin and Stalin in their houses. On either side were portraits of Tehrani himself. Near the large television set was the familiar picture of his brother, who had died in the war.

His son brought us a tray with cups of tea, pastries, apples and cucumbers, and as we drank and ate, Tehrani showed us more photographs. He seemed genuinely proud of the ones he had taken when we last visited him. He asked politely about my work, and whether Margaret Thatcher's fall from power would be bad for the BBC. He had seen my reporting on television during the Gulf War. When it was my

turn to ask him about his work, he described his new flock and told us
that he now had to preach to them about birth control and the importance
of having only two children. But as the local people all knew he had five
children himself, he said, none of them seemed to take any notice of him.
He seemed more jovial than before, and more sure of himself.

All this time, a copy of the first version of this book, with a photograph
of Tehrani and me on its back cover, lay on the low table near us. He
was consumed with curiosity about it. I explained to him as pleasantly
as I could that there might be things in it which he didn't agree with.
He beamed.

'There are things in every book that one does not agree with,' he
said. Then he asked if we would read out the passages about him.

There was an awkward pause: I had not, after all, been entirely
flattering about him. I handed the book to our friend Robert, whose
Persian was matched only by his tact and quick thinking. He read a
paragraph or two, then looked at Tehrani, laughing.

'Mr Simpson says he didn't like you much when you first met. What
did you do to him?'

The direct approach proved to be the best. Slowly the stunned look
on Tehrani's face – for mullahs are not spoken to like this – changed
to laughter.

Tira, meanwhile, was being shown around the kitchen by Mrs Tehrani.
It was hot and windowless, but full of life. Her youngest child was
crawling on the floor, looked after by an older brother and sister.
Everything was a little chaotic, but rather charming. Tira sat on the
floor, and remarked in her rudimentary Persian that it was hot. She
shook her *roupush*, in the hope that the mullah's wife would invite
her to take it off. She did; it was clear she was curious to see what
Tira's 'indoor' clothing looked like. Tira was wearing loose trousers
and a pink T-shirt with a picture of two monkeys swinging from palm
trees. The children were enchanted when she came up with the word
for monkey – *maymoon* – which is also the term used for a naughty
child. Mrs Tehrani took off her *chador*: underneath she was wearing a
bright red dress covered with sequins, over which were her prized gold
chains. Her son, who was learning English at school, came to the rescue
of their halting conversation, and he and Tira wrote out the Persian and
Latin alphabets and drew pictures of apples and houses and dogs. As
a game, it was a great success, and they were almost at the end of the
alphabet when there was a polite cough outside the kitchen door. The two
women pulled on their Islamic coverings, and Tehrani put his head round
the door and invited Tira to rejoin us in the sitting room.

By this stage another guest had arrived: an older mullah, who seemed
not to have been warned that Tira would be with us. He looked distinctly
shocked. Tehrani, who had earlier seemed to want to show how liberated
he was, was now formal and distant. If we had any theological questions,

he said, sounding like a university lecturer, we should ask them now. It was difficult to think of anything particularly sensible.

'Why are dogs considered unclean in Islam?' Tira asked. She liked dogs.

There was a slight sense of strain in the room.

'Because they are in dirt everywhere.'

'And cats?' She liked cats too. But she was avoiding our eyes, guessing that we might think this a frivolous line of questioning. The mullah, however, seemed rather pleased.

'Once,' he said, 'the Prophet – peace be upon Him – was about to wash before his prayers and he saw a cat drinking from the same water. He continued washing anyway. But if you have a cat hair on you when you pray, all your prayers will be invalid.'

After that the mullah took us through the animal kingdom: why donkeys stand in midstream and pollute the whole river, why pig meat is unclean (it contains exactly 150 microbes per cubic centimetre) and so on.

'What about the differences between Muslims?' Tira asked. 'Are Shi'is and Sunnis equal in the eyes of Allah?'

A glint came into the old mullah's eyes, and his voice took on a harsher note.

'You must remember that Sunnis are not real Muslims,' he answered, 'especially in Saudi Arabia because the Wahhabis [a fundamentalist Sunni sect] were the creation of Britain; and Britain also encouraged the split between Sunni and Shi'i.'

There followed a long account of British interference in Islam. When at last the mullah fell silent, I remarked that the British must have been very busy. If he had been on his own, Tehrani might have laughed at that. Instead, he nodded solemnly. So did the old man.

When he left, the atmosphere improved markedly. By the end of the afternoon Tehrani was speaking to Tira exactly as he spoke to Robert and me, asking her opinion on all sorts of subjects. She had become an honorary man. He invited us to make his household our home, and to come over every night for dinner as long as we stayed in Iran. The evening ended with the taking of more ceremonial photographs: this, after all, was what had brought us closest together. I promised to send him copies of them.

'You won't do a mullah on me?' he asked, grinning.

I said I didn't understand.

'You know,' he said, 'act like a mullah – like we are always doing: promise something and never deliver.'

15

Journeys

Tira Shubart and John Simpson

*The Arabs say 'Were it not for venturesome men, mankind would perish.'
What is meant by these words is that merchants, in their eagerness for
gain, bring goods from the east to the west, exposing their lives to peril on
mountain and seas, careless of robbers and highwaymen and without fear
either of living the life of brutal people or of the insecurity of the roads.*
                                                            A Mirror For Princes

We were heading south on the road Alexander the Great took when
he invaded Persia. This was the high plain where the kings of Persia
made their homes and ruled their empires in pre-Islamic times. Except
for the narrow ribbon of black tarmac, two lanes wide, the dry yellow
landscape of the plain of Fars had hardly changed since Alexander's
day. The long stretches between the infrequent towns and villages were
uncultivated and wild. Reddish cliffs rose up in the distance. Mahmoudi's
white Paykan rattled along, and John and I found ourselves dozing in
the heat. Suddenly there was a loud roar and a dramatic change of
air pressure like a passing freight train, and we sat bolt upright as
the car shook in the backwash. In the rear-view mirror I could see
Mahmoudi's amused eyes watching our reaction: we had almost been
forced off the road by a huge truck which had thundered past at high
speed in the opposite direction.

The main roads of Iran are unquestionably dangerous. The drivers
of big long-distance trucks seem particularly careless and fatalistic.
Still, the decoration which is lavished on the trucks is one of the
great attractions of the country. There is a distinctively Iranian truck
art: the vehicles are tricked out with coloured light-bulbs (the red, white
and green of Iran's national flag predominate), and plastic stickers often
cover the windscreens with decorated arches, making the trucks look like
monstrous travelling mosques. The faces of ayatollahs, stencilled on to
the bodywork, glower at the passing traffic. Giant eyes, sometimes

accompanied by a tear-drop, appear on the back mudguards to keep watch. The more religious drivers replace their red brake lights with ones that are Islamically green. Many trucks are painted with warnings, religious slogans, appeals to Allah. Some say nothing more than 'Mohammed'. Others proclaim *'Mash'Allah'* [God is wonderful] or *'Insh'Allah'* [If God wills]. A few say, apparently in desperation, 'My God'. We often felt the same.

Mahmoudi found our long drives exhilarating and a chance to match his wits against those of other drivers on the road. He rubbed his hand over his short grey hair and bared his teeth in pleasure when we reached our top speed of about 70 mph; slightly alarming in the Paykan, whose tyres had only the faintest trace of tread left on them. All the same, we had total faith in Mahmoudi's infallibility behind the wheel. We had travelled thousands of miles with him up and down the country, and had never had a puncture or an accident. *Insh'Allah.*

It was rare for us to find a road that Mahmoudi hadn't travelled on before. When we did, he would remark on it and memorise the appropriate landmarks and distances. Driving had always been his profession and he was a great authority on Iranian roads. As a long-distance truck driver, he had worked first out of Isfahan and then, in the mid-seventies, settled in Tehran where the work was better paid. He had married there, and now had three sons and a daughter. His wife, who was also from an Isfahani family which had settled in the capital, was proud of what he did, but persuaded him to give up trucks and turn to driving taxis. He obviously missed the independence of the road, the companionship of other men as resourceful as himself and the responsibility of looking after a huge Mack truck or a Leyland. But Mahmoudi had bowed to his wife's wishes. 'She wanted me to be at home at night-time,' he said expressionlessly.

The plain was slowly becoming greener, and in the distance, a mile or so from us, we could see tents. This was the country of the Qashqai, Falqani and Khamseh tribes who had wandered the rich land of the Persian steppe for centuries, following their livestock from one grazing-place to the next. There was room enough for everyone on the Plain of Fars: for the settled villagers who cultivated fruit and corn and for the nomads. Now the traditional way of life was disappearing. The great migrations of sheep, goats, camels, horses and men no longer took place each spring. The tribesmen mostly worked as labourers and all that was left of an entire way of living was the collection of a few dozen tents on open ground. The Pahlavis had tied the tribes to the land in order to control them better; the Islamic Republic was suspicious of Sunni tribesmen, who disliked officialdom, and it took away even more of their freedom of movement.

Mahmoudi pulled off the road and parked at a respectful distance from the group of tents, black and made of goat hair. We headed towards them. A dozen small children stared at us silently, while the goats they had been tending were left to look after themselves. The men were squatting on their heels in front of their tents, watching us. The women were bent over large buckets filled with freshly cut green grapes, which they were sorting and cleaning.

They were dressed in bright reds and blues, their dresses decorated with embroidery. The scarves they wore were tied behind the neck rather than under the chin, revealing the whole face and neck. These women were obviously proud of their hair, and plaited it in long braids which hung down at angles the Shi'is of the town would have regarded as scandalous. To us it was a great relief to see them. Their complexions were weathered and their smiles were open and broad.

We stopped at the first tent we came to. The man who had been sitting on his heels in front of it stood up and shook hands with Mahmoudi and John, and smiled in my direction. Mahmoudi got into conversation with him at once. His wife gave up washing clothes in a shallow pan and brought over a large bunch of grapes which she presented to us in a bowl. The offer of hospitality gave her the right to ask us questions, which she directed to Mahmoudi. Where were we going and who were we? Mahmoudi told her that we had driven from Tehran but that John and I had come from a long way away; he didn't say where we lived, perhaps because it would have involved over-complicated explanations.

The couple looked at us with renewed interest. Yes, we had obviously come from a long way away, they said, looking at our clothes. My *roupush*, a garment which is rare outside the larger cities of Iran, was made of a light blue denim and had buttons that looked like the rivets on Levis. As for my trousers, I had bought them at a street market in London. They were violet and blue, and very baggy, and they were fastened at my ankles with an elastic band. They might look as though they came from a Christmas pantomime, but I liked them because they were cool and loose and colourful. The couple were baffled; they could only think of one group of people who wore baggy trousers. '*Kurdi*,' the man said to her, and his wife nodded sagely. For them, we were Kurds.

We wanted to see a little of Shiraz before it was dark, and we also had to find a hotel. We reached the last mountain pass, which is called Allah-u-Akhbar (God is Great) because that is what travellers say when they catch their first sight of the city below. It was a glorious setting: and the rose-coloured hills surrounded Shiraz in the soft afternoon light. But it was no longer the place which Hafez had celebrated:

Right through Shiraz the path goes of perfection,
Anyone in Shiraz knows its direction.

Forty years ago it had had the charm of an overgrown village, but now it was grossly overpopulated and a layer of smog which often took weeks to clear hung over it. We looked down and wondered, like two thousand years of travellers before us, how easy it would be to find a hotel there. Mahmoudi assured us that he knew a place we would like; it was in the centre of town, and had a garden. He himself would be staying with one of the network of friends from his truck-driving days.

Mahmoudi took us into the very centre of the town and drove through the complicated streets to the Park Hotel. Getting a room took some effort of will; John had left his passport behind in Tehran, but I knew that he relished the challenge of being without official documents in a country which has a passion for demanding them. In Shiraz and everywhere else we went, the hotel clerks were genuinely puzzled that he should 'be so cavalier about something so important. We came to judge each hotel by the length of time the clerks held out before they succumbed to our insistence that a passport was not necessary to secure a room.

'Did I cross some international border when I came in here?' John would ask blandly.

The hotel clerk in Shiraz was particularly stubborn; but in the end the prospect of the foreign currency we would be spending convinced him to overlook the rules.

The next morning Mahmoudi appeared just as we arrived in the breakfast room; he prided himself on being early, a most un-Iranian trait. When we had finished our breakfast of tea, stale bread and white cheese he showed us the tiny garden which gave the hotel its name. At one end of it was a swimming pool which, like so many others at Iranian hotels since the revolution, had been converted into a very large and unnecessary ornamental fountain. A sprinkler, set up in the middle, sputtered away feebly. No one would be allowed to tempt the dormant sexual feelings of the other hotel guests by taking a swim.

As we walked through the streets with Mahmoudi as our guide we could see why Shiraz had changed so. It was bursting at the seams with people; they filled the pavements, crowded the streets and spilled out of the shops. It was far busier than Tehran, and was more like an Indian city with its sheer density of population. During the Iran–Iraq war, waves of refugees, more than a million people in all, had been sent here when the towns of Khorramshahr and Abadan were largely destroyed by the Iraqi invasion and the Iranian counterattack. Shiraz had the misfortune to be the city which was closest to much of the fighting. Many of the refugees, especially farmers and unskilled labourers, had become street traders on a small scale, and spread out their cigarette lighters and plastic kitchen goods on worn cloths on the pavements. It was difficult even to find somewhere to walk.

We followed Mahmoudi obediently across the hot, busy street between the gridlocked cars which shimmered in the intense heat haze rising off them, and headed for the entrance to the bazaar. I had expected it to be quieter and cooler, but I was wrong: here too there was a vast crush of people, and it was hard for the three of us to keep together as we battled our way through. It was only the determination to find some rugs or clothes made by the nomadic tribes of the Fars plain that kept us going. Eventually, we found a small display of dark Qashqai saddle-cloths. Yet even with Mahmoudi doing the bargaining for us it was clear that the bazaari had marked us out as people with more money than sense; his lowest price was more than double what we wanted to pay, and we walked away. He didn't come after us.

We headed on to the section of the bazaar devoted to spices. Here there were just as many people but it seemed a little cooler. Great vats and barrels of spice lay open for our inspection, and we bought several packets of pungent-smelling saffron, one of the essential ingredients of Iranian cooking. Honour was satisfied, and we could at last head for the hotel again. But as we turned back we noticed a stall selling Western hats, unusual in Iran. There was a selection of peaked caps, and another of cowboy hats. The incongruity was irresistible. I tried on several cowboy models, allowing for the thickness of my headscarf, before I found one to fit.

It was a great relief to leave the noise and heat of Shiraz behind and join the road which took us up over the surrounding hills to the high plain where the Achaemenid kings had lived. A sign in Persian pointed off the road to the left. 'Direction of *Takht-i-Jamshid*,' Mahmoudi said: the Throne of Jamshid, who was a legendary Persian hero. It was in fact the seat of Persia's ancient kings, and the Greeks under Alexander the Great, who captured it, called it Persepolis.

I brought out our increasingly dog-eared copy of Sir Roger Stevens's *The Land of the Great Sophy*. Published in 1962, it is still the most engaging guide to Iran. Sir Roger had started gathering material for his charmingly eccentric book when he served as ambassador in Tehran in the mid-1950s, but he continued travelling in Iran for years afterwards. To read him is to enter an older tradition of gentlemen archaeologists and travellers, the kind of men who came to Persia well versed in the classics and ancient history.

'A first view of Persepolis, seen from the south-west, is disappointing,' Sir Roger Stevens warned us; and, indeed, from a half-mile away Persepolis had a distinctly industrial look, like a collection of abandoned smokestacks at a deserted oil refinery. But as we drove along the main avenue the splendours of the ancient palace began to reveal themselves. The huge stone blocks, nearly sixty feet high, rise above the double-flighted grand staircase which was, according to Sir Roger Stevens, 'so beautifully proportioned that a horseman can ride up or down them with ease'. Above the staircase the wonders of the constructions on the terrace itself could be glimpsed: ruined gateways and huge columns which had seemed insignificant from a distance. The white marble of Darius's palace shimmered in the midday heat. Even from the car we could see that after 2500 years it had survived in remarkable condition.

The biggest threat to Persepolis since ancient times had come in the early months of the revolution in 1979, when a group set out from Shiraz with bulldozers to knock down the ruins because of their link with the Shah and the imperial past. Fortunately the arguments of the watchmen at the site, combined with the sheer difficulty of the task, dissuaded them. Another group of zealots headed for the Sassanian ruins at Bishapur to destroy the large rock reliefs which were carved in the third century AD by Roman prisoners. They were saved by the quick thinking of a guard, who announced that one of the figures who appeared in them was the man who married the daughter of Hosain. What sort of Muslims was it, he asked, who wanted to destroy the representation of the Prophet's grandson? There was no answer, and the crowd of Islamic iconoclasts melted away.

Mahmoudi left his Paykan in the huge car park, built in pre-revolutionary days when Persepolis was a regular attraction for European and American tourists on the overland route. Now there were only half a dozen cars in a place that could hold hundreds. On a stretch of the empty tarmac a Persian man offered rides to visitors on his black Arabian stallion. He only had one customer: a little girl who was lifted on to the horse's back by her father. The horse allowed itself to be led up and down the roadway, while the small passenger shrieked with delight. I would have preferred to hire the horse to verify Sir Roger Stevens's statement about the grand staircase.

Instead, less theatrically, we walked through the wire entrance gate to pay our admission fee to the gatekeeper in a little wooden hut.

'I don't suppose you get many people from England here,' John said to him. 'Oh yes, they're always coming,' he replied. We were rather crestfallen, having thought we had been given the first visas for British tourists in more than a decade. He produced the visitors' book for us, and we started paging through. There were recent Japanese entries and dozens of Slavic names from eastern Europe. A party of eight Italians appeared to have visited the previous spring (there was an Italian industrial project in Isfahan, a day's drive away). We had to do a lot of searching to find the last British entry: it was in 1978.

We went on foot up the massive staircase to the platform where Darius had built his palace in 514 BC. At the top of the stairs you begin to appreciate the vast size of Persepolis: the buildings and ceremonial rows of columns stretch for hundreds of yards towards the hills to the north. Winged bulls and creatures with human heads and the bodies of giant animals guard the gateways which have survived where the state rooms of the palace have long since vanished. Later additions have been carved on the walls: 'Curzon', 'Stanley, NY Herald, 1870' and, with intolerable pomposity, 'Lt. Col. Malcolm J. Meade, HMB Consul General 1898 and Mrs Meade'.

While we examined the graffiti, a handful of Iranian tourists examined us. For the women in their black *chadors*, moving between the columns, we must have seemed as exotic and remote as the winged bulls and the sculptured rows of envoys and slaves on the ancient reliefs. They looked away quickly when we turned and saw them, but the children were more frank and went on staring at us. I was, after all, scarcely dressed conventionally for rural Iran: my blue denim *roupush* and lavender headscarf provided the one point of colour in the marble ruins. Because the sun's rays were so fierce in all this whiteness, I pulled my headscarf off and tucked my hair into my new cowboy hat. I was scarcely conforming to the spirit of *hejab*, but I felt it was only reasonable in this pre-Islamic place. In the absence of the solar topee that Stanley, Curzon and even Mrs Meade undoubtedly wore, a cowboy hat would have to do. Mahmoudi was delighted; especially when I told him I was wearing cowboy *hejab*.

Darius, who built Persepolis, never had to endure the intense summer heat here. He used the palace only in the spring and autumn; the court migrated north to Ecbatana in the hot weather, and wintered in Susa. The magnificent carvings on the staircases and doorways show scenes from the life of the court: King Darius stalking past on built-up shoes, his braided beard sticking forward at an angle, with two servants behind him, holding a large umbrella over his head to shield him from the sun; soldiers standing stiffly to attention, eunuchs from Babylon guarding the private rooms of the household, noblemen fingering the rich decoration of their clothes. Elsewhere the tone is more magical and legendary: lions fight bulls, the King defeats a fierce winged beast with the tail of a scorpion; Ahuramazda, the supreme god of Zoroastrianism, covers walls and great archways with his wings. Perhaps the greatest of the royal ceremonies which took place here were at *Now Ruz*, the Persian New Year, which is celebrated at the time of the spring solstice.

One of these ceremonies is shown on the staircase of the Apadana, the palace of audience. Because it was covered up by sand and rocks from the hillside above for almost two thousand years, the carvings are wonderfully preserved. A procession is paying tribute to the King of Kings, who is guarded by soldiers from the Susa regiment, ninety-two identical figures. Up the steps are the queues of tribute bearers from everywhere in the Persian Empire bringing offerings: Aryans, Egyptians, Armenians, Indian Brahmans, Medes turning casually to talk to one another as they climb the great staircase, Scythians from the region of Samarkand in their long pointed caps, Syrians with horse-drawn chariots, Phoenicians with vessels of chased gold, Cappadocians carrying the cloth they were famous for, Arabs leading a dromedary and Bactrians with a two-humped camel. Our custom of giving presents at Christmas, celebrating the gold, frankincense and myrrh of the Magi who were themselves Persian, is a faint, distant memory of all this gift-bearing.

Altogether two dozen subject peoples are depicted with their New Year offerings, their gifts and their costumes shown in extraordinary, loving detail. The animals they have brought are equally faithfully rendered, and there is a real sense of life about them which is often missing from the idealised human figures. Vast inscriptions, the cuneiform characters marching across the stone as purposefully as the soldiers on the reliefs, proclaim the praises of God and the King of Kings:

> A great god is Ahuramazda, who created this earth, who created yonder heaven, who created man, who created the welfare of man, who made Xerxes King, one King of many, one Lord of many. I am Xerxes, the great King, the King of Kings, the King of the countries with many different peoples, the King of this wide earth, the son of Darius the King, the Achaemenian . . .

We walked to the top of the staircase to look across the plains: the view that Darius and Xerxes saw when they received these tributes. From there you could see the ceremonial constructions of a more recent King of Kings: the tented village erected by Mohammed Reza Shah for the guests who attended his celebration of the 2500th anniversary of the Persian monarchy in 1971. This is where kings, emperors, presidents and prime ministers, many of whom were to be overthrown or discredited in the years that followed, gathered for one of the gaudier and more expensive occasions of the decade. Nowadays the tents, in beige and blue, are almost hidden by the pine trees which were planted at the time of the anniversary. The tents, which were supplied by a French firm, seem to have lasted extraordinarily well; during the 1980s each new wave of volunteers from Shiraz camped in them as they did their basic training for the war with Iraq. Now the tents still seem to be army property; when John tried to get close to them to take a photograph, a soldier came out menacingly and ordered him away. As for the Shah who built the camp, he lost his kingdom like the rulers of Persepolis before him.

Alexander the Great captured the Persian homeland in 330 BC, his light cavalry and small army outmanoeuvring Darius III's Immortals in their heavy chariots. From the time of Darius I, five great kings had ruled from Persepolis. After the royal city of Susa surrendered to Alexander, Alexander took the road to Persepolis, the richest of the Persian cities, and captured it almost unresisted. He had spent four months in the palace when a fire broke out and consumed the roof timbers, the panellings and the carvings within the palace and halls. There has been much speculation about whether the fire was deliberate. Alexander's supporters say that it would have been completely out of character for him to have burned Persepolis on purpose; and they ascribe his haste in leaving the ruins to a feeling of profound depression for the destruction caused.

Less than three miles across the valley was the site, called Naqsh-i-Rustam, below the mountain ridge, which Darius and his successors had chosen for their tombs. Huge Sassanian bas-reliefs adorned the cliff-face. Some archaeological work was still being carried on at Persepolis, and there was a certain amount of restoration too: damaged columns were supported by metal cages, and there was the occasional sound of a hammer and chisel on stone in the hot sunshine. The place is looked after with indolent but reasonable care. What Iran has lost is the assistance of foreign archaeologists. German and British specialists were once particularly active here, and a Frenchman, André Godard, was director of the Archaeological Service of Iran under the Shah. Many of Iran's own archeologists, experts in a field of which the Islamic Republic now disapproves, have left the country. Those who remain have only small amounts of government money to spend, and most of it has to be directed towards preserving the site rather than exploring it further. Yet even in ruins, Persepolis is magnificent, as its creator justly claimed:

Darius, Great King, King of Kings, King of Lands, King Upon the Earth, says, By the grace of Ahuramazda I built this place. And I built it secure and beautiful and fitting, just as I had intended.

We had wanted to stay and see the sunset from the platform where Darius had received his tributes, but the heat drove us out a good two hours before the gates closed. We were the last to leave; the more sensible Iranian tourists had left by mid-afternoon, seeking the shade. As we walked down the beautifully proportioned double staircase, the gatekeeper was sitting on his heels in the shade beside his wooden hut fingering his *taspih* patiently and he shut the gate firmly behind us. Persepolis was closed for the day.

We wandered across to a little hotel beyond the parking lot which we had only noticed that morning. A sign, barely visible through an overhanging tree, read 'Persepolis Hotel'. It must once have been a pretty and lively place, with a garden, a terrace and a swimming pool. Now it was crumbling. The concrete frontage was cracked and the brickwork showed underneath. Nobody had done anything about the garden for years, but it still provided a certain amount of shade from the sun. As for the swimming pool, it contained about three feet of water covered with thick green scum: a useful breeding ground for mosquitoes.

The place seemed deserted when we walked in, but somewhere a television set was blaring away and we tracked down the noise. It came from the reception desk, where an elderly man was sitting with his young grandson, watching the indistinct images on the screen. He stood up courteously and greeted us, and told us we could take our pick of his rooms.

'Don't you want to see my passport?' John asked, unwilling now to give up his daily struggle with the Iranian hotel industry.

'Why? You are here,' the old man replied with a certain logic.

The room rate was $22, and I started extracting the right number of bills from my handbag. He waved his hand; we should only pay when we left in the morning. The young boy led us through the dusty corridors to the rooms. They were pretty basic, and home to a variety of insects; but the friendliness of our reception made up for all of that. We chose the room which seemed to have a lavatory that worked, and the boy darted off. He came back with some clean sheets, obviously a rarity, and a vase of plastic flowers. Then he started sweeping the floor. We went to the dining room and were served a cool drink of *sekanjebeen*, composed of sugar, vinegar, mint and water: a Persian speciality.

Mahmoudi reappeared, having chosen a room himself, a more modest one somewhere at the back of the hotel. We took our drinks and sat on the little terrace looking at the swimming pool filled with slimy water. The garden had a certain wild charm, and was peaceful and cool. The three of us sat there until the brilliance of the sunset had faded, and the boy brought us *juje kebab*, or grilled chicken and rice.

We had just finished eating, and were trying to decide whether or not to go to bed, when we heard the sound of cars approaching. A convoy of beat-up Paykans and dusty trucks turned into the gravel drive of the Persepolis Hotel, and their headlights caught us as they swept to a halt. Each car was carrying at least six people, men and women, small children, old people with walking sticks. They were noisy, cheerful and boisterous, calling out, singing, chattering excitedly. They scarcely noticed us on our terrace above them. Instead, they turned to face the drive and started clapping in unison as another car, a little newer and better kept than the rest, drove up and stopped. The doors were pulled open by several young men, and a bride and groom emerged, happy and slightly embarrassed.

The bride was dressed in a Western wedding dress with white lace and abundant frills. It was low-cut and tight-waisted, and she had the right figure for it. She was the centre of attraction, and revelled in it. On her head she wore a wedding veil made of translucent lace which only made the slightest pretence of covering the crown of her head, and her black curls danced around her face. Like the other women in the party, she was wearing rouge and lipstick. It was as unIslamic a sight as we had seen during our time in the country. The groom looked ill at ease, but that seemed to be on account of his new and badly tailored blue suit. His hair had been slicked down like a Brylcreem advertisement.

The women went rushing into the dining room, and the men were left standing in groups, rather silently now, around the swimming pool. The hotel manager and his young helper appeared with tables and chairs, and served them with soft drinks and bowls of cucumbers and nuts. Three musicians started playing traditional music. Out here there was a distinct air of glumness, as though no one really knew each other but everyone realised that the interesting things were happening indoors. We could hear the women's laughter and shrieks reverberating through the night air. Islamic convention insisted that the wedding parties had to be separate; only the young children were allowed to move between the men's group and the women indoors, and they would come running out every now and then to get their fathers' attention or snatch some food.

After a while one of the older women, with a grandmotherly air, marched out and spoke to the musicians. Two of them rose obediently and followed her inside. A few minutes later there was dancing and clapping and music inside, so loud we could feel the vibration of it on the terrace, while the lone musician played his *tar* dutifully for the silent groups of men outside but was thoroughly drowned out. I couldn't resist it any longer, and went and peered through the curtains. Several of the women looked up and saw me, and pointed me out to the others. They smiled broadly, and beckoned me inside.

The scene in the dining room was dazzling; all the women had shed their *chadors* and the profusion of colour and jewellery made me feel almost giddy. The two musicians were sitting in the middle of the room, playing their hearts out. The older women danced with their arms in the air, swaying to the beat. The younger ones were much less restrained; they swirled and turned and wriggled their hips suggestively. As for the children, they were on the tabletops, spinning and hopping to the music. The moment I walked through the door, I was swept up in the crowd, and two women helped to pull off my *roupush*. My T-shirt and baggy trousers were obviously a disappointment to everyone, but they insisted that I had to dance.

At that moment two teenage girls, who had made a daring foray into the men's party, brought back their quarry; a young, strikingly handsome man looking extremely sheepish was being pulled into the room by his arms. The girls giggled and turned their faces away, but wouldn't let go. Outnumbered, resisting feebly, he found himself pushed into the centre of our circle. The two girls, encouraged by their friends, danced around him, still a little shyly; but the married women were less reticent and looked at him boldly, laughing at his confusion. In a few minutes he had joined in the mood and danced from girl to girl, his eyes sparkling. Perhaps a little romantically, I thought he looked like one of the figures carved in relief on the walls of the palace close by; a true descendant of the rulers of Persia, surrounded by his adoring court. It reminded me of Christopher Marlowe:

> *Is it not passing brave to be a King*
> *And ride in triumph through Persepolis?*

Tira and I found that driving with Martin Charlesworth, on his travels for the British Institute of Persian Studies, was a very different proposition from driving with Mahmoudi. It was, for a start, about thirty miles an hour slower, since the elderly grey Land-Rover of the British Institute was a great deal heavier than the white Paykan and Martin had not contracted the Iranian desire to live dangerously on the road. It was also a good many decibels noisier, since the Paykan at least belonged to the same family as a limousine, while the Land-Rover is still in essence an adaptation of a military jeep. Everything makes a noise in an elderly Land-Rover, driving at 40 miles per hour along an Iranian freeway.

We were heading north-westwards in the direction of Qazvin, along the road which would eventually lead to Rasht, near the Caspian Sea, and on towards Azerbaijan and the former Soviet Union. Tira and I sat alongside Martin on the bench-seat of the Land-Rover, listening to its primitively effective cooling system. Martin was a fountain of information about everything from the Elamites and Kassites of the second millennium BC to the ownership of the estates we passed: the difficulty was keeping track of it all.

We were accompanying him on what was in his terms a tame and relatively local expedition, and one that was somewhat outside his area of specialisation: an investigation of the state of repair of the Assassins' castles, in the westerly reaches of the Albourz Mountains between Qazvin and the Caspian. This is the territory explored by Freya Stark in the 1930s, and there was a vast difference between her rough and perilous journey on horseback up into the mountains from Qazvin, and our trip down a good road in a Land-Rover. Yet hardship, though unquestionably romantic, is not the only criterion of interest in life. Given the small number of Westerners who had been able to travel to Iran since the revolution, even the freeway we drove along had the attraction of unexplored territory. Everything we passed seemed to possess a mythic quality about it.

There was for instance the immense housing estate of Shahrak-e-Apadana on the western edge of Tehran, close to the airport at Mehrabad. It is composed of more than forty great blocks of flats, most of them uncompleted when we first saw them in 1986. The reason was prosaic enough: the private consortium which had started the project fell apart at the time of the revolution. But the subtle mind of the Persian had developed an attractive conspiracy theory about it. The estate, Martin told us, was rumoured to have been laid out in the form of the words *'Javid Shah'* – 'Long live the Shah' – in Arabic letters, designed to be seen from the aircraft taking off at Mehrabad nearby. The revolutionary authorities, according to the legend, naturally wanted to change this to *'Javid Khomeini'*, but the cost of building the additional blocks of flats to make up the extra letters proved too great, and the entire construction was left unfinished. None of this was in the slightest degree true, of course. What had really happened was that during the Iran–Iraq war there were no resources available for building public housing. Once the war was over the estate was duly completed. And the buildings had no slogans, revolutionary or otherwise, to proclaim to those passing overhead.

The expressway heads on towards an enormous belt of trees – part of the government programme of afforestation – past the place where the Shah, carefully isolated from the populace, would review his troops, and the main factory where the Paykan is built, and the old studios which the Iranian film industry used to hire for its features. From the road the sets still look real enough, with a mosque and a pleasant, rundown village around it. But it is only a set: the buildings in the village are merely fronts, held up at the back by poles. On the highest mountaintop to our right a radar installation which the Shah bought in the 1970s is visible for miles. It was this radar installation which had the responsibility of watching for Iraqi missiles and sounding the warning and the all-clear during the war.

A broad expanse of plain between the mountain ranges thirty or forty miles apart, and the smooth expressway, and the white radar golfballs above us: we could have been in Utah or Colorado. Overhead there was even the clatter of a police helicopter, keeping watch on the build-up of traffic this summer afternoon. Freya Stark may have discovered the oriental strangeness of Persia here, but for us, sixty years later, the discovery was the hidden progress of it all, largely unknown outside Iran itself because of the deliberate secrecy of its regime. The strangeness and the sameness had merged together.

Three o'clock on a Thursday afternoon in August was the time when the rush to the beaches of the Caspian started to build up. From time to time we passed ambulances posted by the side of the road, waiting for a radio message to direct them to the scene of an accident. The radio in our Land-Rover blared out the traffic news:

'There are jams on the main road to Nowshahr and Sari, and the police report a four-mile tailback at Gachsar. A family of five was killed early this afternoon near Tajrish when their car was hit by a truck loaded with building materials . . .'

Familiar, yet unfamiliar: just about every one of the cars flowing out
of Tehran with us contained women wearing *chadors*, and carried on
its roof the rolled-up carpets for a weekend of picnics. The driving
was distinctly un-Western too. There were notionally five lanes on our
side of this divided highway, but cars swooped in and out, ignoring the
occasional lane markings, as though we were involved in a race to lay
claim to virgin territory: an undisciplined, enthusiastic, and sometimes
disastrous rush to win a little advantage. Beside the road a truck had
halted, a motorbike impaled on its offside. There was no sign of its
driver or passenger; but a piece of black cloth which might have been a
chador hung from the wreckage. All along the side of the road, mile after
mile, lay fragments of shredded tyres and pieces of chrome-plated metal.
Stranded groups stood gloomily beside broken-down cars watching as
someone struggled with the wheel or dived into the engine. A few miles
further, near Karaj (a suburb of Tehran that seems to double in size every
few years), we ourselves suffered a clutch failure. But Martin sorted it
out in a matter of minutes, and topped up the leak with the requisite
fluid which he always carried.

In Karaj itself we stopped at a roadside shop to buy fruit: small, hard
pears, heavy peaches, grapes, and a handsome melon with delicious
whitish-yellow flesh. We cleaned it off with a hose that was provided
for the purpose outside the shop, and the shopkeeper added up the cost
on a pocket calculator.

'It's no good writing it down in Arabic,' said his assistant. 'These
characters won't be able to read it, they're *faringi*.'

'Of course I can understand it, you clown,' said Martin in Persian,
and the entire shop, assistant, shopkeeper and customers, fell about
with laughter.

A few miles farther along the motorway we came to a line of
tollbooths with red and green lights over them to guide us in the
right direction. There was a fifty-*rial* fee to pay. A friend of ours,
who had a farm beyond the tollbooths and commuted to Tehran most
days, had told us that for an entire year she had tried to make one
particular attendant smile when she wished him good morning. He
neither smiled nor spoke to her, and in the end she decided to use
another booth where the attendant seemed friendlier. One day her new
tollbooth was closed, and she had to go to the solemn, silent attendant
once again. This time he spoke to her.

'Why have you stopped coming to this booth?' he asked her, in a hurt
voice.

'Because you never smiled at me,' she replied.

'You should have told me,' he said. 'From now on I'll smile at you
every day.'

And he did. We tried to spot this particular attendant, but to us
they all looked equally gloomy.

In the layby beyond the tollbooth highway policemen lounged beside their cars in the afternoon heat. Mostly their job was to watch for speeding and deal with accidents, but they occasionally stopped private cars and checked that they weren't overloading their roof racks or packing in too many passengers. They weren't there to check for un*chador*ed women or unIslamic rock tapes: that was a matter for the Revolutionary Guards, and the ordinary police were deeply unenthusiastic about enforcing these social laws. With their black-and-white cars and their dark uniforms they could have been a Highway Patrol somewhere in the United States.

The outskirts of Qazvin declared themselves in various ways: by an unmarked tollbooth, by an obligatory fountain in the middle of a roundabout, and by posters of a stern-looking Ayatollah Khomeini. The town has a reputation, no doubt centuries old and malicious in origin, of being a centre for homosexuality. Freya Stark says nothing about that. Granville Browne finds the Qazvinis 'more pleasing in countenance, more gentle in manners, and rather darker in complexion' than the Azerbaijanis, whose territory he had just crossed. Robert Byron, whose *Road to Oxiana* is one of the best books on travel in the English language, found another advantage in the town:

> Stopping at Kazvin on the way back, I discovered the local white wine and bought the whole stock of the hotel.

If there is white wine in Qazvin nowadays, it will be very carefully hidden, and there will have to be a new regime in Tehran before it is brought out again. All we saw were the local grapes, thick and deep yellow in colour, which were sold for eating rather than treading. We each drank a sober bottle of grape juice, and headed on our way. We wanted to be in the Valley of the Assassins by nightfall, and the sun was shining redly in our eyes.

By the time we had taken the road marked 'To Alamut' and had climbed into the mountains above Qazvin it was half an hour after sunset, and the great central plain of Iran, which could be said to begin there, lay below us in the fading, rose-coloured light. A large animal of some sort bounded across the rocks near us, and we had a long discussion about wolves and their habits. Wolves certainly flourish close to Tehran: a week or so later we encountered a woman building special defences against them around the stud where she bred her horses. She wanted to be ready for the coming winter.

Our plan was to meet up with some friends who would already have arrived and set up camp: one of those 'you won't be able to miss it' arrangements. But as darkness came on, and we rattled our way from hilltop to hilltop, shattering the silence with the noise of our engine, it all became a great deal more complicated than we had imagined. For a start, the valleys extend for twenty-five miles of rough country, and there are at least eight castles there. The Assassins had picked the area because of its inaccessibility. Even with four-wheel drive, it was obvious they had chosen well.

We followed light after light, finding in each case that they came from isolated farms. Will-o'-the-wisp cars which seemed to be flashing signals turned out simply to be going up and down the same kind of hills as we were. Sometimes we would stop the Land-Rover and shout, waiting for some answering sound that was not just the echo of our own voices. And eventually, in an area where we were sure we had looked before, we found them: a small, civilised party on a hilltop, with food cooking on an open fire, good things to drink, and a wide area in which to settle down once the food was eaten and the talking had died away.

We three latecomers could not be bothered to put up tents, and decided to sleep on blankets laid out on the soft stubble. It was a mistake; a species of low-flying mosquito was operating up to a foot or so from the ground. I couldn't sleep, because I was finding the grandeur of the night sky too magnificent; so I got up and pulled a folding bedstead out of the Land-Rover. It was impossible to wake Tira or Martin, and I lay in selfish, guilty freedom for the rest of the night.

The wheeling constellations and the occasional shooting stars of the Asteroid Belt were intoxicating in the clear, thin, warmish night air of the mountains. In the darkness I strove for quotations:

> For I will consider thy heavens, even the works of thy fingers: the moon and the stars which thou hast ordained. What is man, that thou art mindful of him: and the son of man, that thou visitest him?

I thought I hadn't slept, and yet I must have: the Great Wain had disappeared by the end of the night without my realising it, even though I felt I had watched its slow passage across the sky the entire time. The silence of the night beat in my ears.

The next morning, Martin counted forty-four bites on his right forearm, and Tira had a line of them across her forehead, as though the mosquitoes had been drilling test-wells. I was less affected, but as I folded up my blanket a small yellow-green scorpion clambered out of it towards my hand, holding out its sting like a street-fighter holds a knife. I caught the scorpion in a glass and showed it to the others as they were eating breakfast. It clambered around irritably, trying to get out and pay me back. At first I felt I should kill it, but the mood of the previous night had not entirely left me; so I went to the edge of the hill on which we had camped and flicked the scorpion out of its glass, high up in the air. It fell harmlessly on the rocks below me and scuttled away into shelter.

The morning landscape was splendid: the hills we had toiled up and down the previous night were now revealed as gentle undulations of limestone, covered with thorn bushes which gave them a variegated khaki effect, like Iranian army camouflage. White gravel roads crossed the hills here and there, and where the valleys were deep enough and the Shahrud River ran there would be startling patches of bright green, where the villagers grew their rice. Crickets with blue or scarlet underwings burst suddenly out of the dried bushes that looked like the bleached skeletons of small animals, and closer to the Shahrud black dragonflies flashed about like military helicopters. Of the Assassins' castles, which my imagination the previous night had placed on every available hilltop, there was no sign whatever.

We loaded ourselves and the handsome Alsatian dog belonging to some of our companions into the Land-Rovers and jeeps and moved off, leaving a servant (since roughing it had its limits) to take care of the camp and prepare lunch. It took us more than an hour's driving over roads which became mere tracks, and through occasional, scarcely inhabited villages of sun-dried brick. Our objective was Alamut, the most important of the castles in historical terms.

The legend of the Old Man of the Mountains, the leader of the Ismaili sect, who drugged his devoted followers on hashish (whence the name 'Assassins') and sent them out to murder his political and religious enemies, has been a part of the European imagination since at least 1192, when Conrad of Montferrat, king of the Latin kingdom of Jerusalem, was murdered by them. Westerners have always been fascinated and repelled in roughly equal proportions by the concept of blind devotion to an incomprehensible religious cause: that is part of the interest and horror which Khomeini's Iran has aroused in the West. An easily-grasped name has helped; within a century and a half of Conrad's death, 'assassino' was in common use in Italy to mean any murderer, and it spread quickly to France and from there, a little more slowly, to England.

As always, of course, the legend lacks accuracy: we might just as well take our ideas of modern Iran solely from the *Sun* or the *New York World*. For a start, the name 'Assassin' seems to have arisen, not because the Ismailis necessarily used hashish, but because their enemies attributed their fanatical behaviour to drug-taking, and the accusation stuck. Nor is there any evidence that the Persian Ismailis were ever called 'Assassins'; the term was applied solely to the Syrian branch of the sect, which was established later.

Yet the core of the legend is the existence of a body of revolutionaries so dedicated that they could be ordered to undertake often suicidal attacks on the lives of their political enemies; and that is certainly true. The Ismailis are now ultra-respectable, and their leader is the Aga Khan. Even so, their origins were violent, and their aim was the revolutionary overthrow of Sunni Islam, which they regarded as evil and corrupt, and its replacement by a just society based wholly on the Koran. Comparisons with Iran's Islamic Republic are inaccurate in both religious and political terms, but there is a certain resonance there, all the same.

The founder of the Assassins was Hasan-i-Sabbah, who was born in the middle of the eleventh century in the holy city of Qom. A convert to the Ismaili sect and an instinctive revolutionary, he selected the mountain valleys near Qazvin as his base of operations. In particular, he chose the castle of Alamut, built on an inaccessible ridge of rock six thousand feet above sea level. Instead of capturing it by force he infiltrated it in 1090 and offered its owner an immense price in gold for it. The owner, having no alternative, took the money and left.

The first of the Assassins' murders took place two years later, in 1092. Hasan-i-Sabbah, calling his sixty or so devotees to him, asked which of them was prepared to kill Nizam al-Mulk, the all-powerful vizier who represented Seljuk power in Iran. A man called Bu Tahir Arrani laid his hand on his heart as a sign that he was prepared to volunteer for the task. At a place called Sahna, while the vizier was being carried by litter to the tent of his wives, Arrani approached him, disguised as a Sufi, and stabbed him with a knife. 'The killing of this devil,' said Hasan-i-Sabbah when the news was brought to him in his castle at Alamut, 'is the beginning of bliss.'

For the remaining thirty-three years of his life Hasan-i-Sabbah never left the Rock; he remained there, studying in his immense library, administering his province, ordering the murder of his enemies, and leading an otherwise pious and abstemious life. Marco Polo, who travelled through Persia in 1273, knew a good story when he heard one:

> The Old Man . . . caused a certain valley between two mountains to be enclosed, and had turned it into a garden, the largest and most beautiful that was ever seen, filled with every variety of fruit. In it were erected pavilions and palaces, the most elegant that can be imagined, all covered with gilding and exquisite painting. And there were runnels too, flowing freely with wine and milk and honey and water; and numbers of ladies and of the most beautiful damsels in the world, who could play on all manner of instruments . . .

We arrived at the village of Qasir Khan, at the foot of Alamut Rock, in the middle of the morning, and managed to make out the outlines of what is left of the castle on the long ridge of rock from our position several hundred feet below it. The Mongols who captured it in 1256 did a remarkably efficient job of destroying it; so efficient that a British traveller, Colonel Monteith, who reached the Alamut Valley in 1833, failed to recognise the castle at all. As for Marco Polo's tabloid newspaper account of life there, it is impossible, sadly, to believe that the valley, whose sides slope violently down to a single stream far below, can ever have been turned into anything; let alone a garden.

We had parked on the farther side of Qasir Khan, at the start of the path that led to the Rock. The children of the village gathered at a respectful distance to inspect us. The distance was respectful because of our accompanying Alsatian, which seemed to be deeply anti-Persian and kept lunging towards them. The children fell back with shouts of fear, then regrouped to throw stones and perform a goading war dance. Martin Charlesworth gathered together the measuring and surveying equipment he had brought from Tehran, and everyone else loaded up with walking sticks, water-bottles, cameras, and other exploratory gear. The shouts of the village children faded as we struck out for the Rock.

It was steep and distinctly alarming, though we made our way quickly up the slippery scree-slope and along a path which shrank to a few inches' width in several places and often disappeared altogether. At first, embarrassment at the thought of being left behind was all that kept me going. Then there was no alternative but to keep on, since going back was clearly going to be even worse. I was, however, the last by a long way of all those who attempted the climb. As I hauled myself up the final slope I came across a cave, and in it, sheltering from the heat, three Iranians in their early twenties. I stopped and talked to them, in order to rest and to conceal my sense of shame at having covered the last hundred yards or so virtually on my hands and knees. The shame was merited: later I watched as the three ran down a slope which seemed almost vertical and dropped uninterrupted for four or five hundred feet.

They had come out for the day from Qazvin, and were slightly annoyed that their vantage point on the top of the Rock should have been invaded by non-believers.

'*Engilisi?*' the eldest one asked. He was wearing a woolly hat.

I acknowledged that I was.

'*Marg bar Thatcher,*' ('Death to Thatcher') he said, conversationally.

'Don't be so bloody offensive,' I shouted, waving my arms and nearly slipping back down the mountainside. '*Shoma biadab,*' I added, remembering a lesson from my copy of *Colloquial Persian*. This was rather uncolloquial Persian for 'you are being rude', but it was surprisingly effective. Embarrassed by his social gaffe, the Iranian placed his hand over his heart, rather as Bu Tahir Arrani, the murderer of Nizam al-Mulk, had done on this same rock nine hundred years before. Then he made what seemed to be a bow. I was so gratified by having remembered the word *biadab* that my irritation evaporated at once. We all smiled, and exchanged polite words of farewell, and then the three of them ran off suicidally down the precipice while I struggled on to find Martin and the others.

The view was unforgettably wonderful, like being taken up on a pinnacle of the Temple and being shown all the kingdoms of the world.

The mountains and the rivers and the bright green of paddy fields and the slicks of near-desert stretched out into oblivion. Everyone else, having long become accustomed to the view, was watching while Martin, complete with measuring-rods, was lowered by rope together with two of the younger members of the party into a slit in the Rock which contained one of the Assassins' water-cisterns. The three Persians who were doing the lowering were visitors themselves and not guides, and they refused all offers of money for their help or the use of their ropes.

Of the castle itself, there seemed to be very little indeed: one or two low walls of brick and mortar, some steps cut in the Rock, a few pathways. The site of the marvellous library of Hasan-i-Sabbah was destroyed utterly, but not necessarily the books themselves, since the pusillanimous defenders of the place were allowed by the Mongols to leave Alamut with all their belongings when they surrendered. Looking out across the plain of Iran from his library, it cannot have been hard for Hasan-i-Sabbah to decide that he never wanted to leave the place again. Or perhaps, like me, he was simply reluctant to face the appalling climb down.

When we returned to the Land-Rovers, the children of the village were hiding; they had smashed one of the windows and poured water inside, to pay us back for the scare the Alsatian had given them. As we bathed our feet in the stream and ate watermelon, the children emerged and picked up stones again, to throw at the dog rather than at us. We shouted at them, and they hid; but when we drove out of Qasir Khan we had an escort of running children, joking and laughing and trying to jump on the back of the Land-Rovers. Tira produced her camera, and started taking pictures of them: at which about half of them covered their faces and ran off, howling with fear, while the others, more resolutely, stood in the road and watched. Then the Land-Rover picked up speed and the clouds of dust hid the children, and the village, and the Rock of Alamut from us, and we became small objects moving across the marvellous plain we had seen from six hundred feet up, in the unchanged view which the Old Man of the Mountains once saw every day from his library.

16

War

John Simpson

In the course of battle, as long as you are able to advance a foot, never take a step backward. Even when you are hemmed in amongst the enemy, never cease the struggle; you may with your bare fist knock the enemy out of the fight. And as long as they see activity, proving you to be in good fettle, they will stand in awe of you. At a time like this reconcile your heart with death.

A Mirror For Princes

'Land is land – it doesn't matter. It's just earth and rock. We can give it back to the Iraqis after the war. What matters is the victory of Allah. This isn't a war for territory, it's a war for Allah.'

The speaker was a short, intense young man in a ragged uniform, who was educated in the gentle city of Norwich, in England: about as far from this barren shell-blasted waste as it was possible to imagine. Around him, a crowd of twenty or thirty of his fellow volunteers were anxious to make sure the point was not lost on the questioner. *'Allahu Akbar!'* they chanted, having recognised the one word 'Allah' in what he was saying. It was impossible for a foreign journalist to visit the war front without hearing this sort of thing; and it seemed to be entirely genuine.

Still, it was hard for post-industrial, Western man to accept at face value. Who ordered them to say this kind of thing? Were they rewarded for saying it? How, after the enormous losses of so many years of fighting, could they maintain any form of enthusiasm for it? The obvious comparison for Europeans is with the First World War: the mud, the shelling, the trench fighting, the use of gas, the huge offensives bogging down after gaining a few hundred yards – it all has a familiar ring. But the First World War lasted for four years, and by 1917 the morale of each of the main armies was stretched almost to breaking point. By contrast, the Iran–Iraq war began in September 1980 and continued until July 1988. There were no reports of serious mutinies on the Iranian side, no evidence that men were turning on their officers or surrendering voluntarily, no suggestion of any of the other symptoms of war-weariness.

We were driving one afternoon down the curiously-named Hejab Avenue, which used to be called Los Angeles Avenue, when Mahmoudi jerked involuntarily at the steering-wheel and pointed out something ahead of us.

'*Basiji,*' he said. The *Basiji* were the volunteers for the front, established in 1980, and before every major offensive they gathered in their hundreds at centres throughout Tehran and every other town and city to pick up their uniforms and be transported to training bases behind the front line. Several buses were parked by the side of the road, and the *Basiji*, who varied in age from boys of fifteen to men in their late fifties, were streaming across the road to climb aboard. They waved the red or white scarves they had been given to tie round their heads in piratical manner, and were chanting about Kerbala, the Shi'ite shrine in Iraq and their hopes of capturing it. They were mostly working class or peasants; the name of their organisation, *Basij-e-Mustazafin,* means 'Mobilisation of the Deprived'. There were educated middle-class *Basiji* at the front – the man from Norwich was one of them – but their numbers, like those of middle-class Americans in Vietnam, were disproportionately small.

Not long before, an American television team had filmed just such an occasion as this, a detachment of *Basijis* leaving Tehran for the front, and had come across a young boy of about thirteen weeping bitterly. It was a natural assumption for Westerners that the boy was crying because he was being sent to fight in the war, and the reporter said as much in his broadcast. The Ministry of Islamic Guidance in Tehran claimed this was a deliberate distortion: the boy had been told he was too young to fight, and was crying as a result. I had the recording of the boy's voice translated, and it was clear that the Ministry was right. The American report was indeed a distortion, but not a deliberate one. It simply cannot have occurred to the television team that a young boy might weep at being denied the chance of dying for his country.

Similarly, at the start of the war, there were stories of young boys and men running ahead of the main body of troops in order to detonate any mines that might have been planted in the way of their attack. The Western media tended to assume that they had been forced to do it: yet when I started talking to the *Basijis* I met, they confirmed what Tehrani had told us – that the boys and men who did this were volunteers. Sometimes, they said, their officers tried to stop it, and even occasionally had to use force.

One Friday evening, in a cemetery in the city of Qom, I came across a group of *Basijis* who had gathered to honour their dead comrades. Several of them had been injured: one, for instance, had lost his foot. But even he was trying to obtain some kind of dispensation which would allow him to return to the front. Men from Kitchener's Army would have recognised the impulse, and so would young Germans in 1945; yet because the circumstances do not arise for us, we find it impossible to imagine that such instincts can be genuine.

For seven years the working class and peasantry of Iran had been taught by every means at the Islamic Republic's disposal that martyrdom was the ultimate achievement for a human being. Given the poverty and rootlessness of large numbers of the deprived, it is not perhaps surprising that so many should have opted for it. Iran's population explosion was on such a scale that there was no shortage of manpower for the front. Until 1988, the last year of the war, the Iranian armed forces were able to rely largely on volunteers.

Later, when I went to Qom, the leading theologian Ayatollah Mohammed Mespah explained the religious impulse that led people to offer themselves to fight for the Islamic Republic.

> The motivation which makes people fight in a holy war is that death does not represent the end of life for a human being. On the contrary, immortal life begins after death, and the kind of salvation that a man has in the next world is dependent on the kind of life he lives in this world. Taking part in a holy war is a way of assuring oneself that one's immortal salvation in the next world is guaranteed. It's only natural therefore that anyone would wish to be killed seventy times, and still come back to life in order to be killed all over again. It is this kind of perception which creates the desire for martyrdom among Muslims.

Even this is not, however, an explanation so much as a rationale. For people to be prepared to sacrifice themselves over so long a period of time there has to be a culture of sacrifice. Iraq, for instance, is a Muslim country with a strong military tradition and an army with a powerful sense of discipline. This, combined with reliance on superior weaponry, enabled Iraq to continue fighting for so long. But there was no comparable willingness among Iraqi soldiers to throw their lives away for the cause. Indeed, for every Iranian taken prisoner by Iraq there were usually seven or eight Iraqis who surrendered to the Iranians. At the same time, there were probably six times as many casualties on the Iranian side.

In Hejab Avenue in Tehran the last *Basijis* had finally been loaded on to their buses, and the sweating drivers checked that the doors were properly shut. With a great deal of hooting and the blowing of whistles, the convoy moved slowly out into the middle of the road, the cars and trucks keeping a respectful distance. The *Basijis* leaned at dangerous angles out of the windows of the buses in order to wave their scarves at us and chant about Kerbala and Saddam Hussein. Seventy years earlier men like them sang about Tipperary and what they would do when they met the Kaiser; these soldiers saw themselves as heading for Kerbala, then moving on to Jerusalem itself. I watched them head slowly down the hill, the chanting growing fainter, the scarves becoming scarcely identifiable, until the heat haze and the exhaust-laden atmosphere of the Tehran streets hid them from us altogether.

For some years it looked likely that Iran would win the war outright. There would be some major breakthrough, the regime of President Saddam Hussein would fall, and the will to continue the war would evaporate. This didn't happen for a number of reasons. One was the role of the great powers, which were so nervous after Iran had captured the Faw Peninsula in February 1986 that they gave Iraq an increasing amount of help. The United States deployed satellites over the region and passed intelligence to Baghdad through Saudi Arabia. As a result, Iran could never stage a surprise attack of any size again. The former Soviet Union provided the technology and some of the manpower to build the vast network of defensive canals and lakes around Basra, the key to the defence of southern Iraq. The cost, borne by Moscow over a period of years, amounted to more than a billion dollars.

After the Iranian capture of the Faw Peninsula most Western governments had begun to believe that Iran would go on to win the war. The key moment had come when the Revolutionary Guards crossed the Shatt-al-Arab waterway under cover of darkness and launched an amphibious attack against Iraqi positions on Faw which had previously seemed impregnable. It was a remarkable feat of military planning and execution.

The Iraqi defenders escaped as best they could, leaving large amounts of equipment behind them, and the Iranians found themselves for the first time in possession of a sizable amount of Iraqi territory. From now on, the war would be fought at least in part on Iraqi soil: a pleasing thought to a country which had been unable to dislodge the invaders for so long. The Iranians sent out a general invitation to the world's television, press and radio to come to Faw to inspect it for themselves.

The world's television, press and radio were not, for the most part, particularly enthusiastic. Such invitations had been issued time and again by both Iran and Iraq, and huge amounts of money and considerable lengths of time would be invested in sending in correspondents or camera teams, who would spend most of their time at expensive hotels in the capital, waiting to leave for the front. They were rarely allowed to see any fighting, and were usually shown a few unburied bodies and a few trenches. Sometimes an explosion on the horizon would show where the fighting was now taking place. Most news organisations had decided that there were better ways to spend their money.

The Iranians were reluctant to take visiting journalists right up to the front line because if they were killed it would look as though the victory had not been as decisive as Iran had claimed. There were no restrictions on their own people: week after week Iranian television showed remarkable coverage of tank battles, infantry charges and bombardments. Thirty-six cameramen, sound-recordists and reporters had been killed on the Iranian side in battle: a higher figure than in either the Second World War or in Vietnam.

I was keen to accept the invitation, even though we found out early on that Tira, as my television producer, would not be allowed in. 'No women at the war front,' was the principle on which the Ministry of Islamic Guidance operated. I thought I might be able to stay on in Iran for a week or two afterwards, my first trip there since the revolution. Altogether there were only a dozen Western journalists on the trip, and most of them had come with the same idea. It seemed unlikely that we would see anything of interest at the front itself.

We gathered at the military air base in Tehran: a dozen British, American and western European journalists. The only member of the party who did not seem to belong was a short, stout German in a tan-coloured suit and tie. I had noticed him the moment he walked into our hotel in Tehran: he had looked so ill at ease and was so laden down with luggage, that I assumed he was a businessman who did little travelling. As it turned out, he was the Middle East office manager for one of the big West German magazines, and the local Iranian Embassy had refused to allow anyone else to come even though it was obvious that they had invited the wrong man. He was a pleasant man, very nervous and full of forebodings about what was going to happen.

'Don't worry,' said a Frenchman, 'nothing ever happens on these trips. They always make sure of that.'

The German did not look convinced. He was sweating heavily.

We flew down to the city of Ahwaz in a Fokker Friendship airliner which was to become famous within a matter of thirty-six hours, and arrived in the early morning. Ahwaz is an ugly, mud-coloured place under leaden skies, lying along the sluggish Karun River in Khuzestan, the Arab province of Iran. The heavy yellow alluvium of the Karun delta gives the city its tone and clogs its streets, so that the soles of your shoes are heavy with mud after twenty yards of walking. Although the war was being fought a matter of thirty miles away, and Ahwaz had often been attacked by the Iraqi air force, all the lights in the city were blazing and the shops were open for the evening trade as we wandered out in small groups to look around. Goldsmiths drank coffee from small cups and looked hopefully at this sudden influx of potential customers. Our guide told us quietly that the gold in Tehran was much better.

The best hotel in Ahwaz did what it could for us. Before the revolution Western oilmen had stayed here and grumbled about it. Now when you

arrived you had to tread on the Stars and Stripes, the Union Jack and
the Hammer and Sickle, painted side by side on the floor in front of the
main door, and a notice on the door requested you sharply to respect
the rules governing Islamic dress. Outside was a large sign which showed
an Iranian soldier under an apparent shower of blood and bore the words,
'We are all warriors and never fear from war'. We made the best of the
hotel, though we were two or three to each of its small, bleakly appointed
rooms. After a brief and disturbed night's sleep we were roused early
for a military briefing on the situation at Faw.

The arrangements for the briefing were of some political and military
interest in themselves. The men who had captured Faw belonged to the
Pasdaran, the Revolutionary Guards: the highly trained force which
the Islamic Republic had created in order to defend itself from external
and internal attack. The Revolutionary Guards had done the most
difficult fighting, and had been sent to the most dangerous areas; and
by and large they and the *Basijis* had acquitted themselves well. The
regular army, by contrast, had been little more than bystanders at some
of the most significant points in the war. They had fought with distinction
in the early stages of the Iraqi invasion, but never been trusted by the
government. Like the Soviets, the ayatollahs created a parallel army of
their own, and the regular army was obliged to accept the demotion.

'In the name of God,' someone began: it was a tall, serious man in his
early twenties with bad posture and an inadequate tuft of beard under
his chin. He stood in front of a large yellow map and made sketchy,
nervous movements at it. He looked very junior indeed: but as the
briefing went on it became clear that he had, in fact, played an important
part in the planning and command of the attack in Faw.

'The enemy were superior in every way,' he said. The map seemed
to give him confidence. I wondered if he had ever addressed a group
of foreigners in his life before.

'They never thought that a military force would be able to cross
the river here.' He pointed with his stick to the wide wound of the
Shatt-al-Arab, cutting its way through the marshes on either bank.

'Our aim was to cut off Iraq's access to the Persian Gulf, and in order
to do that we had to fool the enemy by staging another operation,
further to the north.' He gestured at some point close to the ceiling,
well off the top of his yellow map. 'As a result of our attack we
captured 800 square kilometres of enemy territory and an Iraqi army
headquarters. Altogether the Iraqi losses were 15,000 dead and 22,000
captured – mostly men of the special Presidential Guard.' Even allowing
for a certain amount of enthusiasm in the reckoning, it seemed to be an
important victory.

Another man took his place before the map: a thirty-year-old, who
was operations director of the Revolutionary Guards. Neither he nor
his colleague appeared to have any military rank, which is one of the

peculiarities of the Guards; their officers, it was explained to me later, simply emerge. This man lectured us about the strategic objectives: how they planned to establish a base in Faw for the capture of Iraq's second city, Basra, while closing the waterways and air corridor to Iraq. He was an enthusiast for military history.

'There were worse tides for this attack than for the D-Day landings in Normandy. Napoleon himself rarely managed to get his own military plans accomplished, because of tactical problems on the ground. We achieved great success in that.'

He paused, as though there was something else he was supposed to say, and it had temporarily gone out of his mind. Then he remembered.

'Our military brothers helped us by providing helicopters and so on. After the initial attack had succeeded.'

I looked round at the representative of their military brothers: a tough, self-reliant colonel, smart in his light green uniform, with a camouflage cravat at the throat. He looked straight ahead, not reacting in any way. It probably took some effort.

At the airport we were issued with blue overalls to protect us against gas attacks; but they were poor quality, and all the same size. I am six feet, two inches tall, and the sleeves came halfway up my arms and the trousers halfway up my calves. A square box with a strap attached to it contained a gas mask of antique design. If our equipment was typical of the consignment, I thought, someone had made a killing from the Iranian government. We tied ourselves up like so many blue parcels and were led out to the three waiting helicopters.

They were elderly American Hueys from the time of the Shah, and were painted a muddy yellow for camouflage. I got into the first one together with an American camera crew. Another five people joined us, making about twice as many passengers as the Huey was supposed to take. It hovered a little, waiting for the other two, then headed south-westwards towards Faw. But soon the pilot was shaking his head as a signal to his colleague, and pointing back to Ahwaz. The early-morning mist was too thick.

We sat for two hours in the airport waiting room, our anti-gas suits heating up and getting slippery on the inside, and drank too much sweet Iranian tea. Soon after eleven there was an announcement: we would take off again soon. The face of the reluctant German fell; he must have hoped to have escaped a second trip.

There were even more of us in the lead Huey this time: so many that the pilot, a big, unshaven, impressive man in his late thirties who spoke good American English, had an argument with his co-pilot about the dangers of taking us. In the end he shrugged and agreed. We were crammed in tightly behind him, sitting on the floor of the Huey with our chins on our knees. If we wanted to shift position we had to ask the two or three closest people for help. The Hueys swooped along in convoy, strung out over two-thirds of a mile. The yellow of the mud flats was turning green with palm trees, and when I could turn my head I could see the Karun curving its way two hundred feet below us. It was a beautiful clear day: too clear to fly into a war zone.

Then we were within sight of Faw and dropped down to seventy or eighty feet. Everyone became tense. The co-pilot pointed to something over the horizon, and then white and grey clouds suddenly erupted out of the ground in neat lines across my field of vision, eight miles or so away. The pilot turned and grinned. The Iraqis were bombing at a distance, not over Faw itself but across the Iranian front line. There was a brief radio conversation with the ground control and the decision was taken. We had to go in to Faw; it was too dangerous to go back.

We flew in just above the palm trees. This was not just another well organised press facility, with the danger neatly edited out: the pilots were worried, and wanted to put us down fast and get their valuable machines away as fast as they could. Ahead lay the landing strip, with a few small gesticulating figures visible on it: a great gold-coloured square, bulldozed out of the surrounding mud and marshland. Our helicopter sank down on to it jarringly, and the pilot started yelling, 'Out! Out! Out!' the instant we were settled.

It was difficult to run at first, with the circulation coming back into my legs, but I followed the others out from under the rotor blades and away from the fierce hail of dust and mud they were throwing up. Within half a minute our pilot was already in the air again, heading south-west as the second Huey came in from the north-east and filled the air with its racket. The third stood off, awaiting its turn; and before it had properly settled the bombing began.

The Iraqis had known we were coming. They had followed the progress of our Fokker F-27 the previous day, and they had tracked our helicopters in their radar that morning. Their bombers, two miles above us in the clear blue sky, had plenty of time to scramble and catch us while the Hueys were setting us down. Sudden columns of earth and smoke heaved up into the air around us, and the heart-stopping noise of the Iranian anti-aircraft guns around the landing zone opened up in an effort to defend us. It was appallingly disorienting, as we tried to get our bearings.

'Get down! Get down!' people were screaming at us, and I threw myself, elbows first, into some dead bushes beside the edge of the zone, hoping they would break my fall. They did, and I rolled over and managed to get my stills camera out of my shoulder-bag – the one that didn't contain my gas mask. Taking photographs, I had always found, was a kind of therapy under fire: it gave me something to do and stopped me worrying. The columns of earth and smoke continued to rise around us, and I snapped away.

The third Huey was only now disgorging its tightly-packed occupants, and the shock and disorientation must have been far worse for them than it had been for us. The bombs seemed to be landing all round us, and the explosions from the anti-aircraft guns were terrifyingly close: it took time to realise that those were the only explosions which were not harmful to us, and the latest arrivals by helicopter didn't have that much time.

Now a new order was being shouted: 'Get on to the trucks! Get on to the trucks!' The trucks were a good fifty yards away, on the edge of the landing zone, and the drivers, in their agitation, began revving up and started to move. I had to wait while the cameraman coolly finished filming the chaos around us and collected his gear. All the television cameramen were behaving in exemplary fashion, standing out in the open to film the explosions, while everyone else was trying to dig into the ground to get away from them.

I didn't notice the reluctant German: too much was happening around us for that. But the heat, the fear, the dreadful noise of the artillery and the bombing, and the fifty-yard run for the trucks in the constricting overalls we were wearing, proved fatal for him. He reached the trucks, almost the last to get there, and was hauled on board as they pulled out at speed: and as he lay on the floor of the truck, with the crash of guns still going on around us, his heart gave way under the strain of it all. He was dead before anyone had realised it; and although the doctors at the field hospital had orders to leave the Iranians who had been wounded in the bombing and look after him, two hours and more of effort failed to resuscitate him. I admired him for agreeing to come on the trip at all. Many bureau managers would have found a way of refusing.

Away from the landing zone, things were easier for the rest of us. We bucketed along the potholed road, through the shattered remnants of the town of Faw, whose mosque tower was the only building of any size to have escaped damage. Now the green flag of Islamic revolution flew above it, and everywhere we went the flag was visible, a symbol of the most important battle that Iran had won in centuries. Everywhere, too, we were cheered on by soldiers in makeshift uniforms, units of the rear who occupied each crossroads and dug themselves into the mud for shelter. Our motorcade consisted of three troop-carrying lorries with Western journalists on board, together with Jeeps, motorbikes and whatever else our escorts could commandeer. And all the time, on the skyline around us, grey and black smoke was going up from bomb explosions, and the thud of anti-aircraft fire could be heard above the grinding noise of our trucks' engines. The Iraqi air force had other targets now.

We stopped in the remains of the town, and soldiers surrounded us enthusiastically. They were simple men who assumed we were there out of solidarity, and they were excited and proud of their achievement. Some were very young indeed, but among them was a man who looked like an Old Testament prophet gone to the bad: with his grizzled beard and bald pate, tied around with a red scarf, he seemed to be in his late fifties. He was the most warlike figure we saw all day, with two bandoleros stuffed with bullets crisscrossing his chest, and a rifle which like him was antique but threatening over his shoulder. It would have been terrifying to have come across him at dusk on a remote mountain pass; but here he was the foghorn voice of God's victory:

'*Allahu Akbar!*' Praise be to God for destroying His enemies! We shall march to Kerbala! We shall liberate the shrines of Hosain and Ali from the hands of the defilers! We shall march on holy Qods itself and capture that in the name of God and the Imam Khomeini! God is great! Khomeini is our leader!'

He was magnificent in his way, the kind of technicolour figure who would look good on any newspaper front page or as the opening shot in a report for television news. He was not, however, a combatant, any more than the teenagers who swarmed enthusiastically about him were. We saw the real front-line troops a little later: exhausted, grey figures, their uniforms thick with dust, trudging back for other duties after the bombing they had received that morning. But they too raised a cheer for us, and chanted about God and Khomeini. These were the Revolutionary Guards who had swum the Shatt-al-Arab a few days before and captured the Iraqi positions, and were now holding off all the counterattacks. Not all the bodies of their dead enemies had been buried. Here and there we saw the huddled shapes of men who lay where the bullets or the shells had caught them, singly or in enough numbers to fill a trench, their faces frozen and inhuman, their eyes half-closed, the flies busily at work on them.

We had already been shown one of the crueller aspects of the war that morning: a bus full of gas casualties. We clambered aboard like tourists, with the encouragement of our 'minders', photographing and filming the appalling state of the men sitting there. Many of them were unable to open their eyes, and were sitting, swaying with the pain and the discomfort. Others held medicated cloths to their faces. There was a terrible sound of coughing, tearing at the lungs and throat. Then someone who was less badly gassed noticed that we were there, and began a feeble chant of '*Allahu Akbar*'. Gradually more and more men took it up, chanting the words slowly and weakly, as if they were talking in their sleep. Then the coughing and the moaning became stronger and the chanting weaker, and the sufferers were left on their own again.

A United Nations team, visiting Iran a week or so later, identified the gas which the Iraqis were using as mustard gas, of a type which showed its First World War origins: Yperite. It was mostly dropped from Iraqi planes, and from the moment we landed in Faw I was aware of a faint irritation in the air which made my eyes water a little: it was the almost totally attenuated tang of mustard gas in the air, like the aftermath of a riot where CS gas has been used.

About a mile away across the Ypres landscape, Iraqi bombs were still falling close to the place where our helicopters had landed. Clouds of white smoke billowed up from the explosions: gas, according to the Iranian soldiers escorting us. The trucks we were travelling in seemed to be heading in that direction, so we pulled out our gas masks and sat there with them on, swaying to the motion of the truck, so many anonymous insect-like faces with long protective snouts. Without warning, the driver jammed the brakes on and we were out of the bus and diving for the ditch: Iraqi bombers were coming in low, almost overhead. But they had other targets to attack and ignored us, and when they were safely past we clambered aboard again. It was a little time before I could work out why the Iranians with us were laughing at me. Then I took my mask off and examined it: the filter had fallen out in the ditch incident. I might as well leave it off, since it wouldn't help me now. I tried to pretend I thought it was funny too, but the memory of the men on the bus with their searing coughs and the chemical eruptions on their skin was not really very amusing. I sat in my seat with my useless gas mask on my lap, and tried to think of something else.

We reached the landing zone, and almost immediately the Iraqi planes turned their attentions to us. For the next two hours or so we were pinned down, out in the open, waiting for a lull that would be long enough for our helicopters to pick us up. Sometimes twenty minutes or more would pass without any action, and we would stroll around, interviewing people, filming things and, in my case, looking out for any useful spare parts for my gas mask.

But the Iraqi bombers always came back. It felt as though they knew exactly where we were: a common delusion of people pinned down by aerial bombing. I would lie with my back against a ramp of bulldozed yellow earth and watch the little silver crosses high above us in the blue sky. And each time, as the crews on the anti-aircraft guns spun around trying to get a decent aim, it would occur to me with uncomfortable clarity that the difference of a thousandth of a second in the pilot's timing as he pressed the button to release his load of bombs might mean the difference between a direct hit and a near miss.

Eventually our minders took a decision: the Iraqis were not going to let our helicopters back in, so we would have to be taken by motorboat across the Shatt-al-Arab. From there, more trucks would pick us up and take us to an Iranian air base. We loaded ourselves clumsily into the boats during the next lull in the bombing, and headed out fast into the middle of the waterway, our helpers and guides waving us goodbye from the rickety wooden pier. As the last boat was pulling away, the bombers returned. We were still only a couple of hundred yards from the shore, and watched as a bomb threw up a column of debris and white smoke precisely where we had been taking refuge a few minutes before.

It was a long drive to the Iranian air base. Late in the afternoon, one fewer in number, we climbed on board an enormous Iranian Hercules. The

Fokker Friendship which had brought us down had been requisitioned at the last moment so that a party of government officials and members of the Majlis could visit Ahwaz and Faw. Our escorts kept telling us that the Iraqi bombardment had been directed at us, but in the relief of having survived a difficult day's experiences that seemed hard to believe. It was only the next day that we heard what had happened to our Fokker Friendship: eighteen miles north-east of Ahwaz, an hour or so before we took off in our Hercules, it had been shot down by two Iraqi jets. All forty-four people on board were killed.

The war took on a life of its own, as Siegfried Sassoon believed the First World War did. The balance between the two sides was finely drawn: Iraqi weapons and money versus Ayatollah Khomeini's refusal to countenance anything short of victory. In the summer of 1987 Iraq managed to alter the entire focus of the war, from land to sea. By staging a series of attacks against tankers using Iranian ports in the Gulf, Iraq goaded Iran into retaliating against the shipping of other nations, especially those which supported Iraq in the war.

The United States was still smarting from the humiliation it had received when a lone Iraqi pilot (later, it is thought, executed after being repatriated) successfully attacked the USS *Stark*. Now it warned that it would use force, if necessary, to protect itself and its Gulf State friends from attack, and to keep the sea-lanes open. The fact that it was Iraq, and not Iran, which had attacked the *Stark* and taken the initiative in the war against the tankers was rarely mentioned in the United States; Americans had become conditioned to the notion that Iran was their natural enemy in the region. The British government, though privately of the opinion that Washington's commitment to 'reflag' Kuwaiti tankers and protect them as if they were American was ill-thought-out and unwise, felt obliged nevertheless to send a quarter of the Royal Navy to the Gulf to join in the exercise. The French, the Italians, the Dutch, and the Belgians joined them. The Russians sent a large fleet as well.

In the early stages of the operation things went embarrassingly wrong. The Iranians used fleet auxiliary vessels and small patrol boats to lay mines of World War Two design and manufacture in the sea-lanes of the Gulf, but the United States Navy, equipped for the Third World War, had no minesweepers on hand to deal with this antique menace. US admirals had, it emerged, always regarded minesweeping as unglamorous because it involved a low standard of technology; as a result the ability to build wooden ships of the right size (wood being required to avoid setting off magnetic mines) had died out in American shipyards. Worse, a 'reflagged' Kuwaiti tanker hit a mine while it was under escort by US Navy ships.

The government in Tehran made the most of Washington's

embarrassment. It denied having planted the mines, insisting that they had been laid by 'hidden hands'; and for a time it looked as though a full-scale war might erupt between Iran and the United States. The Iranians, however, were always careful to prevent that from happening: the Americans were capable of inflicting heavy losses on what remained of the Iranian air force and navy, so Iran's ability to continue fighting its war against Iraq was at stake. And although the attention of the rest of the world was fixed on the waters of the Gulf, Iran's Supreme Defence Council, which controlled the strategy of the war, knew the outcome would be settled on land. The provocations against American ships and those of its friends and allies continued, but never to the point where the United States might be provoked into all-out retaliation.

In August 1987, at the height of all this tension, I went back to Iran, to join one of the largest gatherings of foreign journalists since the revolution. We were to be taken to see for ourselves that Iran, far from laying mines as the West believed, was in fact engaged in an elaborate operation to locate mines and render them harmless. It was a maladroit public relations stunt, intended to create an alibi for Iran in case the Americans attacked. We were flown down to the port of Bandar Abbas, from which much of the military and naval hardware seemed to have been withdrawn, and put on board an American-made Sea Stallion helicopter of precisely the kind the US Navy was using to search for mines, not far away. In appalling temperatures we found the small contingent of Iranian naval ships which were supposedly on mine-clearance duties off the coast of the United Arab Emirates, and after circling for half an hour to allow the cameramen on board to film everything they needed, we landed on the deck of a support ship. It was a relief to get out into what seemed like cool fresh air; though the temperature there was 119 degrees Fahrenheit.

In the ship's wardroom, an Iranian naval captain and commodore had been delegated to brief us about the operation. They were pleasant, professional men who had trained in Britain during the Shah's time, and were as awkward about speaking to journalists as most serving officers are in any navy or army. It was, therefore, almost an act of cruelty to interrupt them as they briefed us and ask who had planted the mines they were hunting.

'We don't know who planted them,' said the captain, looking round desperately for the commodore to help him out.

'No, we don't know,' said the commodore. The captain gave a ghastly grin and tried to continue. But the whole point of the exercise had evaporated in the ferocious heat of the wardroom.

There was a great deal of discussion in the United States about the reliability of the seagoing Revolutionary Guards who laid many of the mines and carried out attacks on shipping: were they acting under orders, or were they, as the vogue phrase had it, 'off the wall' – that is, uncontrolled fanatics capable of any insane action? Many American newspapers carried details of an attack by Revolutionary Guards on a ship which turned out to be carrying Iranian oil; several of the reports presented this as evidence that the attackers were so maddened by zeal they were capable of crazy acts of destruction. It was in fact a foolish mistake; the ships which used the Gulf tend to bunch together for protection, and in the confused conditions one tanker was mistaken for another. The notion of the off-the-wall fanatic said more about the standard Western view of Iran than it did about the behaviour of the Revolutionary Guards.

By the time the war entered its final stages the human-wave tactics had become discredited, and the Iranian generals who advocated them were superseded by men with slightly subtler ideas: though in the attacks on the immense Iraqi water-filled defences in front of Basra, built to the designs of Soviet military advisers, there was no real alternative to trying to storm the canals and lakes by sheer weight of numbers. That too had failed by the beginning of 1987, and the Iranian Supreme Defence Council decided to put more effort into other theatres of war – the mountains of Kurdistan, in particular, where the Iraqi defences were often thin and the quality of the troops facing the Iranians was lower. The intention was to draw Iraqi forces away from Basra, but the difficulties of the terrain meant that Iran's logistical problems in bringing up the requisite tanks and artillery to exploit a breakthrough on a narrow front were far greater. The Iranian offensives became fewer and farther between; each took longer to prepare and its failure took longer to recover from.

The final phase of the war began with the resumption of the missile attacks by Iraq on Tehran and other cities in February, March and April 1988. Iran responded with missile attacks of its own on Baghdad and Basra, but they were rarer and apparently less effective. As it happened, Tira and I were invited to Iran in March together with a large number of other Western journalists, because the Iranians wanted maximum publicity for Iraq's use of chemical weapons in destroying the town of Halabche. Halabche lay inside Iraqi territory, and had been taken over by Iraqi Kurds who were fighting as irregular troops alongside the Iranians. Iraq's response had been predictably ferocious. Five thousand people, possibly more, had been killed.

We arrived in Halabche three days after the attack. The bodies still lay where they had fallen. Most of the victims had been killed by cyanide gas, which acts almost instantaneously. In one house I went into, an entire family lay slumped over a table on which the dried remains of their meal were still set out. A middle-aged man was holding his food in his hand: death had caught him at the instant of putting it to his mouth. Others were a great deal less fortunate: tests showed later that nerve gas had also been used. This kills by what amounts to a form of slow internal strangulation by affecting the respiratory system.

The television pictures of Halabche were shown at great length inside Iran, and this was probably a mistake. Morale slumped, and the fear grew that the Iraqis might convert the Scud-B missiles which they fired every day at Tehran to deliver warheads containing nerve gas or cyanide instead of high explosives. As it was, the missiles created considerable fear. Our hotel, the former InterContinental, now the Laleh, was crammed full with rich people who somehow felt that they would be safer there than in the northern suburbs where some of the missiles had landed. Children were playing, running, and crying in the restaurant and the lobby, while the grown-ups sat around listening for air-raid warnings on the radio. When the warnings came, large groups used to gather in front of the plate-glass windows at the front of the hotel, anxious to see what was happening outside. No one seemed to understand that when bombs exploded most of the injuries were caused by flying glass.

For once the streets were free of traffic. People had extended their *Now Ruz* spring holiday, the Iranian New Year, and stayed out of Tehran in the hope that there would be a truce in the War of the Cities, as there always had been in the past. A surgeon who was staying in the Laleh told us sardonically that more lives were saved, because so few Iranian drivers were on the road, than were lost through the missile attacks. But three, four or more explosions a day were frightening in a way that the more familiar form of death by traffic accident could never be. Air-raids by manned bombers tend to reinforce the will to resist; missiles, as Londoners discovered in the Second World War, tend to create panic. There is an unpleasantly random feeling about missiles: you are unsafe anywhere, because there is no pattern to the places where they land. And when you hear an explosion you feel an instant's guilty, indecent feeling of relief: someone else is being cut by plate glass or buried under falling masonry, not you.

There were occasional triumphs over the missiles. In the second week of March 1988, the air-raid alarms sounded during Friday Prayers. Rafsanjani, at that time still the Speaker of the Parliament, was leading the main prayer session in the grounds of Tehran University. This was always televised throughout Iran. He never paused in his sermon, although the congregation was obviously nervous. Then came the sound of anti-aircraft artillery from the mountains above, and the gunners hit one of the Scuds. It blew up in mid-air. Rafsanjani looked up: 'The power of Allah,' he murmured, and his half-smile made it seem more like a witticism than an expression of piety. It added greatly to his growing popularity.

One young British-educated Iranian official, Kaveh, who had been detailed to help look after the visiting journalists, talked about his feelings to us.

'It's like Russian roulette with missiles. One hour there are six missiles which hit the city, then nothing for a day, then the next day we have twenty-seven alerts with four missiles landing. The missiles have brought home the war to Tehran vividly. We telephone each other up and ask "Have you been missile-ised today?" I think about the guy who fires the artillery at the missiles, sitting above us on that mountaintop. He gives us the warning when they spot incoming missiles. I feel I have a personal relationship with the guy. I want his phone number so I can ring him up and talk to him.'

Up at the northern suburb of Gulhak, with a clear view over the plains of south Tehran, Tira watched as a Scud's warhead detached itself with a small explosion from the main body of the rocket, leaving a characteristic pig's tail of white vapour in the sky, and then plummeted down to hit some building in south Tehran. Some weeks afterwards, one of the last Scuds launched in the War of the Cities landed in the British Embassy compound in Gulhak. No one was hurt, but several buildings were damaged. The municipal glaziers turned up surprisingly quickly to repair the damage. It turned out that they had been given the choice of replacing broken windows in Tehran or fighting at the front. They were anxious to show they were giving good service.

The cemetery of Behesht-e-Zahra, where Khomeini went on the day of his return to Iran, was nearly twice as large by 1988 as it had been that February afternoon in 1979. The war had seen to that. As an ugly graphic reminder of the losses on the battlefield, imitation blood gushed out of the fountain in the middle of the cemetery. The crimson water, unpleasantly realistic, welled up and overflowed like a waterfall into the trough below. Sometimes the wind caught it as it jetted out and blew it in the faces of the people who stopped to watch it.

Nearby were the graves of the leading figures of the revolution who died in the guerrilla campaign of the People's Mojaheddin-e-Khalq (later these graves were moved out of the cemetery). As Tira and I stood beside the grave of Ayatollah Beheshti, several people came and touched the stone. One or two even wept. A young woman in a *chador* stood in front of the grave and, as if she were addressing a living person, said in a loud voice, 'Behesti, doctor in Islam.' Then, seeing us, she shouted, 'Down with America', and walked away quickly. It was one of the very few moments of hostility either of us had experienced in Iran.

There was no hostility whatever from the people who wandered with a kind of aimlessness around the graves in the immense tracts which are set aside for the war dead. The graves themselves are simply small slabs of grey stone set into concrete on the ground, with little grey metal structures like noticeboards over them. Behind the glass of each noticeboard are photographs of the dead man, sometimes as a child as well as in uniform or in a neat suit at some formal occasion. The faces looked out at us seriously, quizzically, sometimes even humorously. Behind the glass might also be a bottle of rose-water to be sprinkled on the grave, or a lamp to signify remembrance. Some graves have been turned into little gardens, with rosebushes and small, feeble trees planted beside them. But it doesn't make up for the spareness and barrenness of the place, as the graveyard stretches for mile on mile with its little grey slabs and its grey noticeboards.

From a long way off we could hear a wailing of instruments, and at last a group of mourners emerged into view: a week's remembrance for a dead Revolutionary Guard. First a small truck, driving at snail's pace, then the four men playing the instruments – saxophone, clarinet, trumpet, drums – then a detachment of thirty or so men in Guards' uniform, slapping their chests in time to the music and carrying a vast banner with the figure of Khomeini weeping on it: the regimental funeral banner. A solid black phalanx of a hundred women followed at a distance. The man they had come to remember gazed out at us cheerfully from a photograph taped on to the truck window. His name was Seyyed Hosain Hashemi, he was twenty-one, and he had died of wounds received in the attack on the Faw Peninsula. He could have been any one of the dusty, exhausted, still enthusiastic soldiers I saw on my trip there.

'He was wounded four days before he was supposed to be married,' one of the mourners said. Somehow that made it more pointless, rather than more tragic: other people had been drawn into the circle of grief unnecessarily. Someone had brought a box of roses and the mourners reached in to take them and throw them on to the grave, while a man sprayed rose-water from a bottle over it, and some of the drops fell across our faces with the coolness of rain. A mullah had started to recite verses from the Koran about the necessity of suffering and the duty to sacrifice oneself, and as his voice grew angrier and louder, cracking on the higher notes, we moved away. Little tattered flags fluttered in the dull breeze beside the thousands of noticeboards, and the echo of the loudspeakers around the grave of Seyyed Hosain Hashemi made the sound of the mullah's voice flutter too: '*Allah-ah-ah-ah-u-u-Akbar-ar-ar-ar...*'

Nearby, five workmen were sitting round a recent grave, covering the grey earth with grey cement. Beside them, an old woman sat on the tomb of someone else's son, her chin on her hands, watching as her own son was sealed in. Everywhere, black figures were moving down the avenues, finding the graves of their sons and husbands in all this sameness with the certainty with which they would find their own front door. As we were leaving, the fountain of blood was switched off for the day and the red water stopped spouting at last.

The real flow took a great deal longer to staunch. When we were at Behesht-e-Zahra, the war graves ended about eighty yards from the road, leaving a wide swathe of rough ground. By the end of the war, that was all taken up with the paraphernalia of death: the noticeboards, the grey slabs, the cement, the little fluttering flags, and the black-robed women moving into the newly claimed ground with equal certainty.

By the second half of 1987 the supply of volunteers for the army and the Revolutionary Guards was beginning to dry up. The following spring Iraq scored a number of important successes, and Iran's will to resist began to fade. Saddam Hussein's regime had been receiving considerable quantities of American satellite and signals intelligence, passed to them via Saudi Arabia, for more than eighteen months. This enabled Iraq to find out which were the weak points in Iran's defences. The critical moment came in April 1988. The American satellite pictures showed how few defenders were holding the Iranian positions on the Faw Peninsula: Iran's one real foothold on Iraqi territory, and psychologically its most important gain of the war. The Iraqis staged a sudden, well-disguised attack and overwhelmed the small number of poorly-trained, often elderly troops in the Iranian trenches.

Rafsanjani and his supporters used the ensuing scandal to change the military command structure. Rafsanjani, who had probably been in favour of ending the war for some time, was appointed sole commander of the armed forces. The military commanders he now controlled mostly shared his pessimism about the likely outcome of the war. On 17 July, the day after an intense and often emotional meeting of the political and religious leadership of the country, Rafsanjani and his closest political ally at the time, Ali Khamene'i, paid a visit to Ayatollah Khomeini's house at Jamaran.

Rafsanjani seems to have used the information and status he had obtained from his new position to warn Ayatollah Khomeini that Iran was now in danger of losing the war outright, and that the effect on the Revolutionary Guards, the ultimate defenders of the Islamic Republic, would be disastrous. He knew how weary ordinary people were becoming with the war, and with the economic austerity it involved. He seems to have argued, too, that the shooting down of the airbus of Iran Air by the USS *Vincennes* over the Gulf earlier in the month showed that the United States was now planning to intervene directly in the war on Iraq's side. Altogether, Rafsanjani warned, the Islamic Republic itself was in serious danger. After a bitter period of reflection Khomeini agreed with Rafsanjani's analysis.

By the beginning of July 1988 the diplomatic efforts had intensified at the United Nations and elsewhere to bring the war to an end through implementation of Security Council Resolution 598. On 20 July, three days after Rafsanjani's visit to Jamaran, Iran announced that it would accept Resolution 598. Two days later Ayatollah Khomeini issued a personal statement supporting the decision but showing the degree of his personal bitterness about it:

> I had promised to fight to the last drop of my blood and to my last breath. Taking this decision was more deadly than drinking hemlock. I submitted myself to God's will and drank this drink for His satisfaction. To me, it would have been more bearable to accept death and martyrdom. Today's decision is based only on the interests of the Islamic Republic.

Perhaps what so many other Iranians had long understood: that his refusal to consider a negotiated settlement with Iraq four years earlier, when the Iranians had the upper hand, had caused immense suffering for nothing.

It was not until 20 August that the fighting came to an end everywhere, as Resolution 598 was implemented in full. In Tehran the black-market value of the dollar dropped by two-thirds. Dozens of businessmen who had to repay loans or fulfil contracts at the pre-ceasefire price committed suicide or fell ill. The main cardiac ward of one hospital in Tehran became known as Ward 598. Most Iranians felt a sense of humiliation, mixed with weary relief. For the civilian population, the renewal of the missile attacks by each side on the other's cities in February and March 1988 had brought terror on a large scale. There was little open rejoicing. The country had suffered heavily from the war which Iraq had started eight years before, and although Iran had often been close to victory it had ended on terms which seemed little short of a national disaster. Yet, in reality, Iraq had not won and Iran had not lost; it had been a long and pointless draw, and the regimes in both countries survived. Six years later, several thousand prisoners of war were still being held on both sides.

17

Paradise

John Simpson

Even though the sons of men of quality and high birth acquired a hundred crafts (provided they did not employ them for gain) it would be no fault; nay, rather, it would be a virtue. Every form of art and skilled workmanship at some time bears fruit; it is not wasted.

A Mirror For Princes

'Here,' announced Mahmoudi, 'is Isfahan door.'

It was said with a certain proprietorial satisfaction: he was himself an Isfahani. In fact there was no gate to Isfahan, just a depressing concrete and steel fountain in the middle of an intersection on the road into the city. But he was proud of it, and proud of having got us there fast and in total safety.

Tira and I looked out of the window at a set of dreary outer suburbs, grey and dusty, dating from the years of enrichment under the Shah. After the dry grandeur of the near-desert around the city, they came as a distinct disappointment. The very names of the suburbs seemed dull and repetitive: Lamjir, Kujan, Marun, Barzan. It wasn't electricity, automobile workshops and tarmacadam we wanted, it was a walled city with domes and minarets; but the walls of Isfahan had long since been pulled down, and although the domes and minarets were there in abundance they had to be viewed through cables and between television aerials. It was like approaching Venice through Mestre: the sight of other people's industrial advancement and material comforts can be a disappointment at such times.

I had been here before with Mahmoudi, when the suburbs were younger and less extensive and the country was waiting for its revolution. In February 1979 the revolutionaries were in control of Isfahan before they took power in the rest of the country, and we were welcomed as the first outsiders to see the Islamic Republic in operation. No matter how repellent the reign of the ayatollahs was to become, I would always remember those early days of efficiency and goodwill and general popular relief which followed the bloodless assumption of power in Isfahan. Most revolutions begin in joy, and end in despair; but we should not altogether forget the beginnings when we deplore the latter days.

European travellers have been coming to Isfahan ever since Shah Abbas I proclaimed it his capital city in March 1598. Among the travellers were, as always, a sizable number of Englishmen; and none of them has left a more attractive description of what he saw than Thomas Herbert who visited Persia in the 1620s. Herbert added to the pleasure of his account of Isfahan by comparing it continually with the London of his own day:

> At the West end of Isfahan is that which is called Nazer-jareeb, a garden deservedly famous. From the Maydan if you go to this garden you pass by Cherbaugh, through an even street near two miles long and as broad as Holborn in London, a great part of the way being garden-walls on either side the street; yet here and there bestrewed with mohols or summer-houses, all planted with broad-spreading chenaer trees, which, besides shade, serve for use and ornament.

In Mahmoudi's battered white Paykan we too passed by 'Cherbaugh', or *Chahar Bagh* ('Four Gardens'), which seemed to me to be a good deal wider than Holborn: a promenade lined with bushes and trees, including many of the '*chenar*' or plane trees which Herbert had noticed, running down the centre of what is now the busiest road for cars, buses and taxis in Isfahan. Old men sat on the benches besides the shrubs and flowers, and boys rode up and down excitedly on bicycles; but the noise and fumes from the lines of cars on either side had blighted the atmosphere and trees alike. Plane trees as a rule thrive in cities, but in Isfahan the twentieth century had been too much for them. Their leaves were blotched with the sooty marks of disease, and their trunks were thin and irregular.

We turned off Chahar Bagh beside the splendid azure-domed theological school built about 1710 by the last Safavid king, Shah Soltan Hosain, and into what, before the revolution, had been Shah Abbas Avenue. We were going to stay in one of the most beautiful hotels in the world, but as we stopped outside the main door its external appearance was something of a let-down. Nowadays it was called the Abbasi Hotel, but before 1979 it was the Shah Abbas. In Iran, as in revolutionary France, every name with royal connections had been changed. The front had been badly modernised in the late 1960s, and the new glass doors were an offence to the eye. No uniformed porters were on hand to greet us and take our luggage as they had been when I first came here, in 1979. But no revolution has ever brought about better service in hotels.

Originally the Abbasi was a seventeenth-century caravanserai on the grand scale; the camels and horses from the big desert caravans would be herded into the courtyard at night while the passengers slept in the rooms overlooking the animals and the goods they had brought with them. During the forty years after the end of the caravan trade in the 1920s it had been turned into a prison; but when organised tourism reached Isfahan in the 1960s, the caravanserai was turned into the best hotel in Iran. It was still the best, though that was partly because of the lack of serious competition. After becoming badly run down during the 1980s, the Abbasi's frontage had been scrubbed and repaired and it had regained much of its pre-revolutionary attraction.

Inside, it seemed a little cleaner but otherwise unchanged. Every square inch of the walls and ceiling in the immense lobby was inlaid with green, red and gold-coloured glass in kaleidoscopic patterns, and the floor was covered with elaborate whorls and curlicues of jasper and green marble. Nothing in the entire place was plain and unadorned; it was the seventeenth century as seen through the extravagant lens of the Shah's last years.

This was my third visit to the Abbasi. When I had been here the first time, in 1979, my colleagues and I were the only guests. But the staff had been charming, if nervous. They told us to forget about the bill, on the refreshingly logical grounds that this small amount of money would do nothing to solve the hotel's financial problems anyway; and they sent us off with a present each from the hotel gift shop, since it seemed unlikely that there would be any visitors to buy anything there again.

In 1986 I paid my second visit to the Abbasi, this time with Tira. Now there was a man with several days' growth of beard and a dirty shirt behind the reception desk. He took no notice of us for some time, although there was no one else around. When I asked for a room, it caused a minor crisis: another man had to be summoned from an inner office to look at us and pass judgement. This man shook his head and looked doubtful. It wasn't because the hotel was full: we found later that only four rooms were occupied. For the moment, almost as a concession, I was allowed to fill in a form.

'*Engilisi?*' asked the grubby man behind the desk, peering at what I had written.

I am, of course, but I am just as proud of the Irish passport which I hold, and on which I do much of my travelling to difficult places.

'That's like my asking you if you're Iraqi,' I replied. 'It says "Irish" here.'

Fortunately everyone – for in Iran crowds gather inside hotels as readily as outside them – thought this was funny. The remark was still being repeated to latecomers some minutes afterwards.

'From Iceland?' the grubby man persisted.

'He thinks Irishmen come from Iceland,' I said, and the crowd liked that too; though they were probably vague themselves about where Irishmen came from, exactly.

At this point Tira handed over her completed form, together with her British passport. Such confusion as had existed before seemed like a faint evening breeze by comparison.

'Two rooms,' the man behind the desk declared.

I wasn't keen on this. Apart from anything else, the rooms were $165 each per night at the official exchange rate. It took another twenty minutes before it was agreed that the holders of two separate nationalities might be permitted to share one room, and we were given the key.

'Isfahan,' says a Persian proverb, 'is a paradise full of luxuries; but there ought not to be any Isfahanis in it.' Nevertheless the grubby man and I parted on friendly enough terms, with the encouragement of the remaining members of the crowd. A moderately polite middle-aged porter and a delightful old chambermaid showed us to our room, the chambermaid tussling with me to get hold of my suitcase and carry it for me, while making disapproving noises at the porter to show that he should be carrying everything anyway.

Things were rather different as we approached the reception desk this time. The lobby was full of well-heeled Iranians, and half a dozen large potted palms were scattered about. A group of women in *roupushes* stood together chatting in one corner and young couples, walking close together but not quite touching, strolled from the garden into the lobby. Honeymoon couples could afford the prices now. A young receptionist looked up at me, his beard neatly trimmed and his shirt clean.

'*Bale?*' he asked, pleasantly. 'Yes?'

'My wife and I would like a room, please.'

He pushed some forms across the desk to us.

'Maybe no rooms,' he said with an apologetic grin, and disappeared through a heavily carved door. When he came back he was smiling more confidently and carried a Yale key on a large brass numbered key-ring.

'Only one room, one suite, price $85,' he announced with pride.

I counted out $85 in dollar bills. As the room key was handed over, an elderly porter appeared and took our bags to the lift. Perhaps it was the same porter as before, and he had finally been shown the rudiments of his job; but I didn't recognise him, and he didn't seem to recognise us. He took the lift, and we preferred to walk up the curving staircase to our room on the first floor. We still got there before the porter. Up here there had been no refurbishment. The pictures on the wall, large, bad copies of Persian miniatures, seemed faintly familiar, and the carpet was old and very stained. The porter opened the door to our room and put our bags down just inside and turned to me, waiting for a tip. He had obviously mastered this aspect of hotel life too.

As I looked round, I realised that we had been given the same room as five years earlier. Or rather, the same five rooms, since the suite contained a bedroom, two dressing-rooms, a bathroom, and another room with no particular function and no furniture but which nevertheless added to the general impressive tally. The suite was probably too big and expensive for the honeymooners and tourists from Tehran who otherwise filled the hotel.

Tira walked through to the bedroom.

'It hasn't changed at all,' she called out.

And indeed it was still furnished grandly and heavily in mahogany and red plush. The bed was in a large alcove, which was protected from mosquitoes by a thin gauze curtain decorated with cherubs and birds and held in place with ties of red satin. The bed had a tendency to sag, and the sheets, though clean and well-ironed, were carefully darned in places. It was like being the guests of a maharajah with a cash-flow problem.

'Amazing,' said Tira lifting up a corner of pink material that had once been red. 'Even the same bedspread. Waste not, want not.'

Our apartment was situated in a corner of the hollow square formed by the hotel building, and I opened the elaborately carved cedarwood doors on to a balcony which overlooked the gardens. Fountains played quietly in the late-afternoon sun, tea was being served in the courtyard, and scrawny tabby cats hunted for discarded chicken bones under the eyes of the black-headed, grey-bodied crows which had stationed themselves in the higher branches of the trees. These were Thomas Herbert's 'chenaers', his plane trees, tall, leafy, cool, 'which, besides shade, serve for use and ornament'. I had not seen a pleasanter sight at any hotel anywhere.

An hour later it was dusk, and from the blue-domed mosque which overlooked us the *muezzin* called the faithful to prayer. We went down to the courtyard and found the only unoccupied table. The choice was limited: tea and 'English cake', which was marbled with chocolate and tasted like no cake I had ever eaten in England, fresh pomegranate juice, 'Islamic' (that is, non-alcoholic) beer, and chicken and rice. Persian *tar* music floated from the loudspeakers through the courtyard; when we had been here last there had only been Beethoven's 'Eroica'. It was stunning, but less appropriate to a Persian caravanserai than the gentle notes of the *tar*. To us the chicken was inedible; not so to the cats, who fought and growled over the remains of it in the bushes beside our table.

'Let me,' says Herbert, 'lead you into the Maydan ... without any doubt as spacious, as pleasant, and aromatic a market as any in the universe.' Five years earlier, as now, the invitation had been irresistible. Mahmoudi had gone to spend the night at his father's house, and we wandered off on foot to find the incomparable monuments of Isfahan. We passed through a park entirely filled with pink and white peonies the height of a man's waist. The children who played on the pathways that led through the flowers were almost swallowed up, their heads showing at intervals like swimmers in a river as they danced along. It was Thursday evening, the start of the Muslim weekend, and entire families were out enjoying the air. People smiled at us and sometimes called out greetings, or posed politely when we took photographs of them. There was something innocent and other-worldly about it all, as though we had strayed not simply to another place but another time as well.

We had penetrated the pungent alleyways that led under arches and through delicately carved gateways to the magnificent Maidan-i-Shah, a vast open rectangle surrounded by some of the finest buildings erected anywhere during the seventeenth century. But we had no time to look about us. Karim, a fierce old man with a vast girth and a nasty case of skin cancer, gathered us up at the very moment we emerged into the Maidan and began, in bad English, to declaim the beauties of the Royal Mosque.

'Shah Abbas One – very old. Four hundred year old. I very old.' He paused to tap me on the breast-bone with a friendly finger. 'You very old.'

'*Khaley mamnoon*,' I said. 'Thank you.'

We were, he said, the first Western tourists he had seen since the revolution seven years earlier, and he wasn't wasting any time in getting down to business. He herded us like a large dog with sheep along the cloisters, past walls of intricate, sensitively-worked marble patterned like monochrome carpets, and through doors of silver shone bright by the rubbing of thousands of reverent hands. He moved fast for a man so fat, and stopped only when we reached a wonderful arched area behind the main part of the mosque. He looked down at five square stones of black marble which glinted in the pavement. A lamplighter was wandering around whistling an intricate little tune, which I would have liked to listen to more carefully. Karim, though, had started his routine.

He took up position on one of the black stones and reached into his vast pockets. A small crowd, composed of the lamplighter, two cripples and various children, gathered round. Tira started to say something, but was silenced with a sign; the performance was in progress. He produced, at length, a box of matches, holding it up between his thumb and forefinger as though it had special properties which required respect. Then he tapped it gently with the dark brown nail of his other forefinger: a slight, clear sound. Instantly seven distinct echoes, each louder than the original, sprang out of the brilliant blue, yellow and white tiled dome thirty feet over our heads. The children danced for joy and the cripples banged their bandaged hands together, but since they were not standing on the black stones there was no answering echo. Karim held the matchbox up triumphantly, as though the skill lay with him rather than the architect.

'*Yek, doh, say,*' I counted in Farsi, and a little murmur of admiration went round the group at the talents of this *Engilisi* linguist; but a much clearer and sharper version from the dome above overtook the murmur, interlaced with it and overmastered it. The lamplighter struck a black stone with his wand, grinning, and the seven echoes from that were so loud that they drove us away from the dome altogether. We wandered off with Karim, past two old women who were praying on carpets the colour and age of the paving-stones they covered. I asked Karim if he would pose for a photograph in what remained of the light, and he hitched up his immense trousers and zipped up his fly; he was the only one who had not noticed them gaping open. He glanced apologetically at Tira, but she was pretending to examine the smooth yellow marble of the walls. The photographs were taken, money changed hands, and the only Western tourists since the revolution passed out of Karim's life.

Outside, the darkening Maidan was filled with the surreal echoes of a mullah's voice, hideously distorted by loudspeakers, as he preached a sermon; he would have done better to have stood on one of the black stones. Tira and I wandered off, among the Thursday night holidaymakers. Women in *chadors* were filling their kettles at taps in the pipe which ran the full circumference of the fountains, and settling down with little gas stoves to make tea. While we watched, two women spread carpets on the paving stones and set out a vacuum flask of soup and several glass pots filled with various kinds of food, and lit their small portable stove. Three children, one of them still learning to walk, played around them, while the husbands, who looked like brothers, strolled up and down, talking and laughing, as they picked their way around the other groups of tea-makers.

Elsewhere, a group of four older and more serious children sat playing Monopoly, in what looked like the French version. Little horse-drawn *doroshkehs* decorated with green and red battery lights drove past with couples and entire families in them; for a few *rials* they would take you three times round the Maidan. For a few yards in front of the Ali Qapu Palace the reluctant, elderly ponies were persuaded to trot while the younger passengers squealed with delight.

The atmosphere now was rich with the smell of cooking, and the lights from the shops all round the edges of the Maidan illumined the gardens in the centre. Thomas Herbert had noticed them:

> Not far thence are cooks' shops, where men use to feed the helpful belly, after the busy eye and painful feet have sufficiently laboured.

In the cooks' shops now, much the same kind of food was being prepared for the helpful and noticeably large bellies of the customers. In others, men were beating copper into cooking utensils, and in an upstairs room as we passed, half a dozen craftsmen were painting scenes from Persian history and literature on to leather, or else hammering tiny coloured slivers of metal and wood to form the decoration on picture frames.

An eight-year-old carrying a blow-up plastic plane in the shape and colours of an Iran Air 747 came running past us, and tripped over a skateboard which flew up and landed on its underside, which was marked 'Thunderbird'. His wailing followed us across the square, where we came across three army volunteers who had lined up and were looking for someone to take their photograph. We were not perhaps quite what they had in mind, but one of them pulled a cheap camera out of a brown paper bag and held it out to Tira.

She made them sit on a low wall, hoisting up her *hejab* in unIslamic fashion in order to get a good shot of them. They lined up close to one another, and tried to keep a straight face as they posed. One of them quickly put on his cap and adjusted it while she was still focusing. The war against Iraq was still on, and they were just about to leave for the front. They glowed with embarrassed martial pride, as though they belonged in a photograph from the time of the First World War: three pals from Kitchener's Army, who would be lucky to survive until 1918. Within a few weeks they might well all be dead, with only a photograph or two surviving as a witness to the fact that they had once sat together on a warm Isfahan evening, looking for a bit of fun.

It was dark by now, and we walked back to our hotel through another public park. Away from everyone else, in the light of a small oil-fired hurricane lamp, an entire family – grandparents, parents and four children – had just completed their evening meal, and the father of the children was puffing away at his *qalian* or hubble-bubble. Directly they saw us the man held out the mouthpiece of the *qalian* to me, and his mother offered us a plate of cakes, and all the others called out to us to sit down and join them. We took off our shoes and joined them on their blue and red carpets.

The husband was a motor mechanic, and although they were not rich they were reasonably well off.

'We come out here every Thursday night. It's our main form of entertainment. We live over there,' he pointed off into the darkness, vaguely, 'and we like to sit and watch people go past, and sometimes we ask them to join us. We are,' he added, 'very honoured that you should be sitting with us. It is many years since we saw anyone from *Orupa* – Europe – in our beautiful city.'

As we talked, we made what replies we could and accepted little green savoury cakes and drank tea, refreshing and very sweet, from small glasses. The grandmother, wrapped in a patterned grey *chador*, kept smiling and peering forward to see how we were getting on with the cakes, and each time we finished one her pretty little granddaughter was sent along with the plate to offer us another. When our polite refusals of more were finally accepted, one of the children placed the *qalian* in front of me.

'I expect they use the *qalian* a great deal in *Englistan*.'

I paused for a moment, not wanting to disappoint him. All I could think of was the Caterpillar in *Alice in Wonderland*, smoking his hubble-bubble on top of a large mushroom.

'It is,' I said carefully, 'famous in our literature.'

The answer was approved, and passed on to the grandfather, who was hard of hearing. He, too, leaned forward and smiled in a dignified kind of way, as though passing on greetings from one great *qalian*-smoking nation to another, and gripped his bare brown feet with his hands as he sat cross-legged on the carpet.

I took a deep breath, and the hot water boiled up encouragingly in the vessel, weakening and diffusing the effect of the tobacco as it was intended to do. But I am not a smoker, and the harsh taste of it caught in my throat and made me cough. The family was divided between amusement and consternation, and it required another cup of tea to restore me.

'I think,' said our host politely, 'that the *qalian* is not much used in *Englistan* after all.'

'No,' I admitted, when I could.

The grandfather laughed a good deal when it was all explained to him, and the wife, who had appeared only occasionally and preferred to stay outside the circle of light on the other side of the group from us, clucked her concern for my throat and refilled my tea glass with her own hands.

Not long afterwards we said our goodbyes. When we were a good eighty or a hundred yards away from them we could still see them waving to us, and for some time after that we were able to make out their hurricane lamp gleaming in the surrounding night, like a friendly cottage on a dark moor.

We were heading through the lobby of the Abbasi early the next morning, hoping to see the sights of Isfahan before the day became too hot, when a tall, elderly, dignified man walked across to us.

'Would you care for a guide to the city, sir and madam?' he asked, his English almost perfect but unmistakably antique, as though he had learned it from a late-Victorian phrase-book. He didn't look like the kind of man who was accustomed to tout for business like this.

I started to say we weren't really interested, but he looked so hurt that I changed what I was saying and pretended that, while we didn't want to do any sightseeing that morning, we would be free in the afternoon.

'Please allow me to introduce myself properly,' he said in his elaborate way. 'My name is Mr Amir. I would be very happy to meet you in the afternoon, here in this very lobby.'

He shook my hand gravely, then turned to Tira and shook hers. Scarcely, I decided, an Islamic zealot.

We spent the morning visiting Julfa, the Armenian quarter of the city.

'The site of Jelphey,' says Thomas Herbert, his ear for names as always a fraction out, 'resembles Pera, which is opposite to Constantinople, or as Southwark is to London, the river Zindarout interposing.'

Julfa does indeed lie opposite the centre of Isfahan on the southern bank of the Zayandeh Rud (*rud* meaning river) just as Southwark lies across the Thames from the City of London; but even in 1600 there can have been few other points of similarity. It was merely that Herbert enjoyed putting things in terms his readers could visualise for themselves.

Shah Abbas I, when he rebuilt Isfahan to his own design, needed workmen with the skill to carry out the intricate work he demanded. There must have been many Persians who were capable of it, but instead he brought in several thousand Christians from Armenia. Perhaps it suited him to create a community of intelligent, able people on the outskirts of his capital city who would be totally dependent on his goodwill and protection. Shah Mohammed Reza did much the same with the Baha'is and Zoroastrians, four hundred years later.

I had been down the narrow streets of Julfa, where the tall blank mud walls hide the architectural splendours of the churches behind, on two previous occasions: once in 1979, and once seven years later, with Tira. In 1986, as now, we had made no appointments to see anyone. The Armenians have not quite been persecuted, but life is not easy for them under the Islamic Republic and few of them are pleased to see Western journalists. There are only about five thousand of them in Julfa nowadays, roughly the number who settled there at the invitation of Shah Abbas, and the streets always seemed unnaturally empty. The few I had seen confirmed Thomas Herbert's description: 'The Jelphelyns are habited like Persians, but differ in aspect, most of these and the Georgians having brighter hair and greyer eyes.'

We stopped outside what looked like the door of a church, set in an otherwise blank wall. The handle turned, and the heavy door swung open on to a compound, like a small Cambridge college, in the middle of which stood an ornate little church. The bright sunlight shone down on the polished paving stones, and the white buildings were dazzling after the shadows of the street outside.

An old man with one eye – whether greyer than that of most Persians I couldn't decide – shuffled out of a room on the far side of the courtyard with a bowl of uncooked vegetables in his hand. The midday meal was being prepared. I asked if he would let us see the church, and he disappeared briefly to put the bowl of vegetables down and pick up the key to the church. He held it up to show us, and the wards shone as bright as silver. We followed him across the gravestones which formed the pavement, grey slabs with Armenian writing and the outline of figures on them, and he unlocked the door for us.

Inside, it was as cool and dark as a cave. The smell of incense and old wood was overpowering. Silver and brass glimmered in the faint light from the doorway, and then the old man, after fiddling around behind a curtain, turned on all the lights in the place. The magnificence sprang out at us and overwhelmed us with its reds and golds and greens and the shock of so much intensely decorated space. We murmured something in our surprise, and the old man laughed mockingly.

The altar was tiered, with the front part covered by an embroidered scarlet cloth and the levels above cluttered with gold candlesticks and dark icons, some of which must have been old when the church was built in the early seventeenth century. Every inch of the walls was painted, in a style that seemed more southern European than oriental. Saints I had never heard of were crowded together, rejoicing in the Almighty or being condemned by infidels to terrible martyrdoms. Tortures were performed, the blessed were received by angels, and God the Father presided over it all like a lord chief justice. An anatomically perfect skeleton in a russet cloak invited kings and emperors to pass along to final judgement, and the worthies of the time looked on in seventeenth-century dress, anticipating a little nervously the moment of their own last judgement.

Anxious to get closer, I came up against a white ribbon tied across the pews, barring the way down the aisle. There was to be a wedding there the next day, it seemed.

'Can I get past?' I asked the old man.

He grinned, in a way that fitted him entirely to take his place in the wall paintings.

'You can do anything if you pay,' he said.

Mr Amir was waiting for us in the lobby of the Abbasi. He looked relieved when he saw us; he probably thought we had changed our minds about a guided tour.

'Would you possibly care to see the Royal Mosque?' he asked, using the pre-revolutionary name. 'Or the Ali Qapu Palace?'

The last time we had come to Isfahan, the palace had been closed for repairs. It seemed an excellent idea. As we walked along, Tira asked Mr Amir a little about himself. Did many visitors want a guide?

'No, you should understand that I am a teacher. But now we are enjoying the school holidays. And, you see, teachers are not rich and quite soon I will retire.'

He had, he said, lived in Isfahan all his life and loved the city.

'I cannot, however, say that I approve altogether of some of the changes the modern world has wrought here.' Wrought, I felt, was particularly impressive. He avoided talking about politics and he never once asked us any questions about ourselves. I put it down to courtesy and reticence, in equal proportions.

We turned a corner and were back in the Maidan. Thomas Herbert had stood here, three hundred and seventy years before, and measured it by eye:

> It is a thousand paces from North to South, and from East to West above two hundred, resembling our Exchange, or the Place-Royal in Paris, but six times larger. The building is of sun-dried brick, and an uninterrupted building. The inside full of shops, each shop filled with wares of sundry sorts; arched above (in cupolas), terrace-wise framed at top, and with blue plaster pargetted . . .

It was a splendid sight; more splendid now, perhaps, than it had ever been. For much of its history part of it had been a polo field, and the rest had been left open and become overgrown. Now there were ornamental trees, fountains and decorative lamp stands; but the buildings which surrounded the Maidan were almost exactly as they were when Shah Abbas played polo here, and Sir Anthony Sherley, another late Elizabethan traveller in Persia, was one of the chief spectators:

> . . . so the King went down, and when he had taken his horse, the drums and trumpets sounded; there was twelve horsemen in all with the King; so they divided themselves six on the one side, and six on the other, having in their hands long rods of wood, about the bigness of a man's finger, and on the ends of the rods a piece of wood nailed on like unto a hammer.
>
> After they were divided and turned face to face, there came one into the middle, and did throw a wooden ball between both the companies, and having goals made at either end of the plain, they began their sport, striking the ball with their rods from one to the other, in the fashion of our football play here in England; and ever when the King had gotten the ball before him, the drums and trumpets would play one alarum, and many times the King would come to take Sir Anthony to the window, and ask him how did he like the sport. (George Manwaring, *A True Discourse of Sir Anthony Sherley's Travel Into Persia*, c.1600)

Since Sir Anthony Sherley had a well developed sense of self-protection, he probably said he liked the sport a great deal. Shah Abbas, though a patron of the arts and of religion, had an extremely quick temper and could be ferocious. Another of Sherley's travelling companions, the Frenchman Abel Pincon, reported that the Shah kept a troupe of forty cannibals who followed him everywhere he went, and that from time to time he would feed his victims to them. There was no shortage of victims: Shah Abbas killed people as a matter of justice, he killed them as a warning to others, and, according to the English travellers, sometimes he killed them simply because he was bored.

We walked with Mr Amir the full length of the Maidan. The traffic was noisy, and filled the air with fumes. There had been a proposal to ban cars here and turn the Maidan into a pedestrian precinct, something which everyone but the taxi-drivers thought was a good idea. Sadly, nothing had come of it. Ahead of us rose the magnificent bulk of the Royal Mosque; to our left was the smaller but more precise Sheikh Lotfallah Mosque, built by Shah Abbas I and finished in 1619; Sheikh Lotfallah was a Shi'ite scholar from what is now Lebanon, and became Shah Abbas's favourite theologian. He died three years after the completion of the mosque which bears his name.

To our left was another superb structure: the Ali Qapu (or 'Magnificent Gate') Palace, where Shah Abbas entertained his noble visitors, and ambassadors like Sir Anthony Sherley. Now the front of it was hung with giant portraits of Khomeini and Khamene'i, looking a little like Marx and Lenin in Red Square under the Soviets. We went through the two-storey archway leading into the palace. Tira, overheated in her *hejab*, sighed with relief as she felt the coolness of the stone building after the Maidan's heat, and Mr Amir turned back and smiled at her. We went through a low door and up a narrow, winding staircase which opened out into a little chamber and then resumed its complex climb in the inner parts of the palace in a different direction entirely. The stone walls were smooth and greasy from the tens of thousands of hands which had glided over them.

After the third narrow staircase we came out on to the enormous great balcony, the height of the third and fourth storeys combined, which is the centrepiece of the Ali Qapu. There are fountains and paintings and extraordinarily intricate carvings here, and a gallery where musicians could play without being seen. This was the grandstand of the royal residence, and offers the finest view across the Maidan to the Sheikh Lotfallah Mosque. From here Shah Abbas and his guests watched firework displays and demonstrations of horsemanship and military parades, and this is where Sir Anthony Sherley would have sat, nervously applauding the Shah's proficiency at polo.

Mr Amir allowed us to walk around the balcony and admire the view in silence. Then he came over and continued his tour.

'This grand balcony contains eighteen pillars, made of hardwood, and a wooden roof. Please notice the embellished designs of birds above us. These are the original, natural colours. It was here that the King would visit during the afternoon to enjoy the spectacle on the Maidan. As you know, polo was played here. Also, contests between men and animals would be held for his enjoyment, and members of his court carried out displays of the military arts, such as wrestling and archery. At those times the square would be crowded with people.'

I turned to Tira.

'I've seen this square crowded with people,' I told her. 'It was during the revolution in 1979. The crowds were a little different then. There were so many of them you couldn't even see them all from this balcony.'

'Yes, and so you had to climb the minaret in the Royal Mosque for your television film,' Mr Amir added quietly.

I hadn't realised he was listening, and turned to him in surprise.

'And I walked behind you up the stairs of the minaret.'

Slowly, it came back to me: the tall figure, darker-haired then, speaking his good English, coming up to us and suggesting that we would get the best pictures of the vast demonstration from the Royal Mosque. He was a man of consequence, it seemed, and the mullahs deferred to him. I remembered the climb up the minaret wall, since it gave most of my phobias something to work on. It was completely dark, and very hot, and a crowd of onlookers pushed us from behind while those going ahead of us were rather slower. At times there was only room to squeeze up the narrow staircase sideways on. In all the darkness and the heat and the crush, I could feel that several of the steps were missing and it seemed inevitable that someone would trip and be buried under the bodies. And finally, as we went higher and higher in this tall finger of brick, we could feel it swaying in the wind.

I mentioned some of these things to Mr Amir, and he smiled.

'I myself took some film of you and your friends when you were filming. I had a camera of my own, if you remember.'

Now I did: it had been a big, whirring, clockwork affair which we had to ask him to switch off because the noise of it was registering on our own soundtrack.

'That was an extraordinary time,' I said. I could see why he hadn't needed to ask me any questions about my past, or my job, or my knowledge of Iran. His discretion was superb.

'What happened to you after the revolution?'

But whatever had happened, he didn't want to talk about it. He looked across at the Sheikh Lotfallah Mosque for a moment.

'Now I think you might enjoy the music room upstairs,' he said. I took the hint.

We entered the maze of narrow staircases to reach a reception hall arched and domed and wonderfully decorated; 'with blue plaster pargetted', as Thomas Herbert rightly said. Niches in the shapes of bottles and vases and musical instruments were cut into the plasterwork. At this point two fair-haired Europeans came into the room with an English-speaking guide of their own: they were a Dutch couple who had somehow managed to get themselves visas to drive across the country in their Volkswagen camper bus. They were, they told us, so much in love with the country that they were going to Tehran in the hope of getting their visas extended. But their guide was becoming bored with all this fraternisation between tourists. He cleared his throat irritably.

'These holes were made for three reasons,' he intoned. 'One, to allow wine bottles to be placed. Two, to create more echoes for the music which was played to the King. Three, because they are beautiful. And it was in this chamber that the King would sometimes meet his wives ...'

The guide was obviously going to give them some reach-me-down version of *The Thousand and One Nights*, and we drifted away.

Mr Amir was a great deal more talkative now, and suggested that we stroll towards the *Chechel Sutun*, the Palace of the Forty Columns, which we hadn't visited before.

'We can have some tea and there are renovations which are now open to the public.'

The *Chechel Sutun* was the official court for Shah Abbas II, and retains the feeling of royal grandeur. The palace itself stands in well-maintained gardens whose centrepiece is a large reflecting pool. Mr Amir faced the wooden portico supported by carved columns, each the height of a medium-sized *chenar* tree.

'This is the Palace of Forty Columns. But you can observe that there are only twenty columns.' He turned towards the reflecting pool. 'There are the other twenty columns.'

The Persians traditionally use the number forty to indicate 'many' or 'a sizable number'; yet here, with the reflections they added up to forty exactly.

Inside, we paid a small fee to the gatekeeper and entered the palace. Before the revolution it had been a museum.

'Last year,' said Mr Amir, meaning 1990, 'an OPEC committee came to Isfahan and held a reception here and the wall paintings were uncovered. We had not seen them since 1978. You can see why.'

He pointed them out to us; they were Safavid frescos from the seventeenth century, and portrayed a series of feasts and parties: Shah Abbas entertaining the King of Turkestan, and Shah Tahmasb (the grandfather of Shah Abbas) offering his hospitality to King Homayun of India. Bottles of wine, in the shapes we had seen cut from the walls in the rooms of the Ali Qapu, lay at the feet of the guests from Turkestan as they sat in a semicircle beside Shah Abbas, who was not only more magnificently dressed but also a little larger than everyone else. They were being entertained by four dancing women.

All four were fully clothed, but their hair was mostly uncovered and the shape of their bodies appeared clearly and their ankles showed under their wide, colourful dresses. One guest stroked his long handlebar moustache, another tilted his head appreciatively. A servant holding a bottle of wine peered in through the door to watch the show. We found it very refreshing, and distinctly unIslamic. Occasionally, it seemed, even in the reign of the mullahs, the traditional arts of Persia received a little of the care they deserved.

Strolling around the reflecting pool as we left was a well-dressed young man leading a half-grown Alsatian. He was obviously enjoying the slight consternation it caused when it lunged at passers-by who strayed too close. Dogs are considered unclean in Islam, and although some middle-class people have them as pets it is rare to see them out with their owners in public. To walk your dog is an assertion of your westernism and cosmopolitanism. Tira went over and called to the Alsatian, which jumped up to her knees to be petted. The owner, thirty-something and wearing sunglasses even though the sun had gone down, was delighted: he had met a kindred spirit.

'Down, Rajiv, down!' he said in English, as though he had met us in Hyde Park. Rajiv took no notice. If the command had been in Persian he would probably have ignored it too.

'I am taking my dog for his daily walk. He is a purebred German Shepherd.'

We praised Rajiv a little more, and then the conversation flagged. I looked round as we reached the gates of the park: Rajiv was nipping his owner's ankles, but even behind his dark glasses the owner looked proud.

In the growing dark the lights in the shops along the *Chahar Bagh* were brilliant and enticing, and turned the workaday things on sale into objects of delight. Mr Amir was taking us to the shop that sold the best *gaz* in Isfahan. *Gaz* is an Isfahani speciality, a kind of nougat made with pistachios. I could smell it even before I caught sight of the piled-up blue and white boxes in the window. Barrels of pistachios, almonds, and cashews lined the counter and the smell of hot nougat drifted in from somewhere in the back of the shop.

The man behind the counter greeted Mr Amir with respect and produced a tin of *gaz*. It was the best quality: as white as plaster with flecks of green pistachios, and packed in flour. He broke off a piece for Tira and wrapped it in wax paper, and then repeated the process for me. We weren't expected to buy anything; we could do that, Mr Amir said, in a day or so. He merely wanted us to sample the best *gaz* from the best *gaz*-makers in the city. I bit into it: dry, firm but not brittle, sweet but not sickly, it began to melt the moment it touched the tongue. "Their sweetmeats are white and exceedingly fine,' said Thomas Herbert. For once he could think of nothing in England to compare it with.

There was one last place to visit, and we had deliberately left it until dark. Now we could hear the river rushing through its weirs and arches. The Khajou Bridge, built in the reign of Shah Abbas II (1642–67), is one of the loveliest constructions anywhere. A hundred and forty yards long, built of greyish brick on twenty-four great piers of stone, it carries road traffic on its upper level, and has walkways above and on the main level, with small shops and booths and delightful hexagonal pavilions at the ends and in the centre. The waters of the river roar through the narrow channels formed by the twenty-three arches, though if necessary each can be stopped and the river dammed. On the downstream side flights of stone steps lead down into the water, and in the daytime people come, as they have for three and a half centuries, to wash their carpets, picnic, watch their sons swimming, and enjoy themselves.

Now it was evening, and the bridge was alive with pleasant murmurings; whole families sat dangling their feet on the lower levels, only a little way short of the rushing water, while the women handed around cups of tea and the children ran in and out of the arches for the excitement of hearing the echoes created within the stone vault. These were modest, gentle, timeless pleasures, and Mr Amir, seeing our reaction to them, did not feel it necessary to tell us how long or wide the bridge was, nor how many bricks had gone into its building. By now we had walked the full length of the bridge and turned to go back. It was darker here, and Mr Amir stumbled over a black shape which none of us had noticed before. The black shape made a surprised noise, but no protest. We looked at it more carefully; it was a black *chador* which covered a boy as well as a girl. They were sitting side by side, holding each other, their legs dangling down over the water.

'Haven't they heard of the Revolutionary Guards?' Mr Amir said. But he wasn't shocked or angry. I looked at him: he was smiling indulgently. We wandered back. Somewhere in the darkness a stringed instrument was being played, and its gentle, complex phrasing gradually merged with the sound of the Zayandeh River.

18

Surviving

Tira Shubart

Understand, my son, that as long as men are alive, friends are indispensable to them; they were better, indeed, bereft of brothers than of friends ... all of a man's faults are hidden from his friends, although his virtues are revealed to them.

A Mirror For Princes

It was *Sizdah Bedar*, the thirteenth day after the Persian New Year festival of *Now Ruz*. Almost everyone in Tehran seemed to be on the expressways heading out of town to celebrate the important holiday in the Persian calendar. *Now Ruz* derives directly from the ancient Zoroastrian celebration of the spring solstice on 21 March. The preparations for it begin on *Chahar Shambeh Suree*, the last Tuesday eve of the old year, and continue until the thirteenth day after the solstice. The first event of the *Sizdah Bedar* celebrations is the fire-jumping. Everyone leaps over a small fire in order to cleanse themselves of problems and illness and to take the energy and the vitality of the fire with them into the New Year. Even young babies are carried in their mothers' arms over the flames.

Every Persian household lays out certain objects on a table which remain there during the celebrations. The names of seven of the objects have to begin with an S-sound in Persian. Some of the more popular are; *seep* (apple), *serkah* (vinegar), *seer* (garlic), *sabzeh* (cress sprouts), *seekeh* (a coin), *somagh* (spice), and *seneh* (mirror). There should also be a bowl with goldfish and some painted eggs. The whole period of *Now Ruz* is a time of parties and celebrations and family reunions. It is the most significant holiday in the Iranian calendar, but it is, of course, completely unconnected with Islam, and at *Now Ruz* in 1979 and 1980, in the immediate aftermath of the revolution, there were determined efforts to stamp it out. They failed, just as the English Puritans failed to stamp out the celebration of Christmas and May Day after the defeat of Charles I in 1648. Schools and government offices throughout Iran shut down, and the Majlis dates its budget and its activities from *Now Ruz*.

On *Sizdah Bedar* every Persian is supposed to take the small patch of *sabzeh*, or cress shoots, which they have grown at home over the New Year, out to the countryside and throw it into a body of moving water. The outing is always accompanied by a lavish picnic. I was in Iran without John and my friend Fatima invited me to join her party for the trip. She had returned to Iran the previous summer; after being educated in England she had stayed on there and worked as a designer for nearly fourteen years. This was her first *Now Ruz* in Iran since she was a girl.

'I felt a tremendous need to come back; it's the emotional pull. To have these holidays and be with my family and friends, this is what life in Iran is all about.'

We slipped into the packed lines of traffic, ten miles long and scarcely moving, on the road to Karaj, Kordan and the west. I had never been in a traffic jam which was so good-humoured. Every car overflowed with people, since no one would enforce the law on a day like this, and most carried patches of turf *sabzeh* sprouting from the bonnet. It looked extraordinary, like a garden cut up for a gigantic jigsaw puzzle.

Our car was packed out too. Fatima and her cousins had prepared baskets full of food and fruit to take to the big party we had arranged to join somewhere in the countryside. After about an hour on the motorway, well beyond Karaj, we turned north and looked for the dirt road that would take us down to the Kordan River. The trouble was, there was a traffic jam even on this narrow dusty lane. The Revolutionary Guards had set up a road block and every car was being checked for drugs or alcohol. Davoud, who owned the car, wasn't surprised.

'The *Pasdars* know that nobody would be crazy enough to carry anything illegal, they just want an excuse to hassle people. This holiday is the kind of thing they can't control and they hate it. Everybody else, ninety-five per cent of the population, we all love it.'

When our car came level with the *Pasdars*, Davoud rolled down his window and asked with pretend innocence if there was anything he could do to help. Fatima and I had pulled our headscarves up and sat demurely, looking straight ahead of us to avoid making eye-contact. Even the children sat quietly and ignored them. The *Pasdars* seemed to find us hard to classify: we didn't fit any obvious category and we didn't seem suspicious. They lifted the lids of a few picnic baskets to see if there was anything hidden in them, then waved us on our way. Davoud swore under his breath as he drove off. Fatima and I grinned at each other and loosened our headscarves.

We continued down the increasingly bumpy road to a modest house where a dozen cars were parked. Streams of people were carrying picnic baskets and flowers and cakes for our hosts. The Rolling Stones blared out of the open windows; we could see people dancing inside. The children jumped out of the car and headed straight for the river-bank, while Fatima's friends and relations crowded round her. Old Persian families have notoriously complex family trees dating back to the days when wealthy men married their full quota of five wives and kept several concubines as well. That means that your cousins can be numbered in the hundreds, and the precise genealogical relationship between one cousin and another is often impossible for a mere outsider to fathom.

Fatima was still kissing and embracing her sixth cousins several times removed while we carried our picnic baskets inside and set them out on a big table which was already overflowing. One corner had, however, been reserved for the traditional *Nowruz* display of the seven 'S's, plus the goldfish bowl and the eggs, and someone had added a wreath of bright spring flowers.

This year Ramadan, the month of fasting, had coincided with *Nowruz*, but it made no difference to the guests at this party. None of them could be accused of being a devout Muslim. For those Muslims who did take their fasting seriously a special formula had been worked out centuries before, to allow Islam and the surviving elements of Zoroastrianism to coexist. It was a characteristically Persian solution, sensible and not too self-sacrificing. You could break the Ramadan fast for *Nowruz* and *Sizdah Bedar* if you simply added an extra couple of days' fasting on to the end. That way, both pleasure and piety could be served. The dancing and music during Ramadan were an unscheduled extra.

Persians make the very most of their social gatherings. All around the house, every corner was full of people enjoying themselves; eating generous platefuls of food, or dancing, or seeking out their friends and chatting and laughing with them, or sweeping up a passing child in a friendly hug. Everyone, from grandparents to infants, mixed with an easy charm, and unattached guests like myself were particularly well looked after and drawn into conversations.

Fatima and Layla, and one of her cousins, called to me to join them in the garden.

'Come down to the river, we're going to throw our *sabzeh* in now.'

We pulled on our *roupushes* (the *Pasdars* were still somewhere in the area, and might have come to check on us) and hurried down to the bank of the Kordan River. It was a wide spit of sand, and the waters of the river flowed fast, carrying little bunches of green *sabzeh*, thrown in by people upstream from us. Fatima and Layla lifted out our patch of turf with its bright green shoots. Layla grinned as she turned to me.

'Fatima and I must tie a knot in the *sabzeh* so we'll both find men to marry this year. That way she'll have to stay in Iran.'

They each tied their knots in one of the shoots, and then the three of us put our hands underneath the *sabzeh* and swung it backwards and forwards a couple of times before throwing it into the Kordan on the

third swing. It hung in the air for an instant, then dropped on to the
surface of the brownish river and was swept away fast, carrying with
it all our futures for the year, marriage knots and all. Soon it was gone.
For Fatima it was an enjoyable piece of ritual and mild superstition; but
she knew it had considerable significance in the eyes of her family.

'I decided to come back home because my family wanted me to. I wasn't
married, and I wasn't entirely established in London professionally. They
said, "Why don't you come home and try it out and see?" So I did.

'When I arrived I was in shock for weeks. The physical thing of
seeing people dressed as they were on the street had the most impact.
Everything looked awful to me, everything looked old. A friend of mine
says everything here looks as though it's got the pallor of death over it.
Cars were old, even the car my father was driving. The houses weren't
painted, and they were in rough shape. But after a while all these things
started to have an interest for me. I've got friends who came back and still
won't step out of their houses because they think it looks so bad, but I'm
not like that. I'd love to wander round the streets and photograph people
and buildings but here in Iran I wouldn't feel comfortable doing that.

'I had many fears when I returned. Not being able to follow a profession
was one of them, and not feeling at home was another. But I didn't want
to get caught up in the exile life, where you feel people are only marking
time until some undefined future point. A lot of the people who left during
the revolution had many difficulties and financial problems. They went to
the West because they found life pretty miserable in Iran, but they're very
Iranian at the same time. It isn't easy for them to fit in with a foreign
culture, and they don't enjoy it. Then you have another group of people
who are dreamers, who had this wonderful life in Iran, and felt they were
forced to leave. They're always looking back and thinking of the old days.
Well, I didn't want to fall into either of these categories and I didn't want
to alienate myself from this country, whatever the regime was. The roots
of the family and culture are very strong here, and in the end I didn't
want to ignore them. However much you disagree with the government,
and most Iranians always do, this is my emotional home and I'm willing
to put up with a certain amount of discomfort because of it.'

The *sabzeh* did its work well. Within the year Fatima was married to
a handsome Iranian architect who had lived in Texas for the previous
fifteen years, and returned to Iran the previous year. She joined his
business and was able to use some of her professional skills. He was,
of course, a distant cousin many times removed.

At the end of the nineteenth century it was fashionable in western Europe
to speak of countries like Turkey and Persia as irrevocably decadent,
sunk so deeply in their medieval ways that they would never be able
to govern their own affairs properly again. This was, of course, quite

wrong: even at the time, Turkey and Iran were both starting to become aware of the fermenting effect of new ideas. Those Western travellers who knew the country best were sceptical of the notion that Persia was too sunk in decadence to be able to re-emerge. George Nathaniel Curzon, for instance, the future Viceroy of India and Foreign Secretary, travelled widely in Persia and published, in 1892, the definitive account of it for his time: *Persia and the Persian Question.*

> ... [T]here remain three attributes of the Persian character which lead me to think that the people are not yet, as has been asserted, wholly 'played out' ... These are their irrepressible vitality; an imitativeness long notorious in the East, and capable of honourable utilisation; and, in spite of occasional testimony to the contrary, a healthy freedom from deep-seated prejudice or bigotry. History suggests that the Persians will insist upon surviving themselves ...

Surviving is a Persian speciality; and just as the Zoroastrian New Year celebrations have survived the advent of Islam, so the people of Iran have discovered an elaborate system of ways to survive the more irksome aspects of the Islamic Republic. This is obviously true of middle-class Iranians, who have not been particularly courageous in standing up to the infringements of personal freedom which the regime has introduced. ('Imagine,' said an Indian journalist visiting Tehran, 'what would happen in my country if we tried to introduce laws like these. The streets would never be free of demonstrations again.') Working-class Iranians are often no happier about the system that has been introduced. In south Tehran, the heavily populated, ramshackle warren of side-streets and squatter camps that spreads further south every year, you find little sign of opposition to the rules of *hejab*, though alcohol is quite easy to obtain. It is the failure of the regime to improve living standards to the degree that the revolution once seemed to promise which angers people here.

'Everyone grumbles,' said a woman who works in one of the more densely populated areas of the city. 'Every time I'm in a shop or a queue or a taxi, people complain that the government have destroyed everything. They often go on to say "God bless the Shah", even in a taxi when you're crammed in with half a dozen people you don't know. At first when I heard that I would keep quiet, thinking it might be a trap. But no, everyone else just agrees. They swear at the regime, saying the mullahs have ruined the good name of Islam, and now they're just lining their own pockets. People aren't afraid of complaining, like they used to be. Even religious people complain. It's the prices, and the inflation, and the problem of making a decent living for yourself.'

Complaining is an important safety valve for Iranians, a way of getting through the restrictions and difficulties of everyday living. But if the poor grumble about prices, the well-to-do grumble about the regime's intrusion into their private lives.

Behzad is in his early twenties, and has recently returned to Iran from Paris. His parents are seriously rich, and have a beautiful house on the northern outskirts of Tehran. When he came back, the old Corvette Stingray which he'd received on his sixteenth birthday was still waiting for him in the vast family garage. Behzad has come back with a string of degrees and diplomas, but can't decide whether to stay in Iran or not.

'I don't worry too much about the incredible bureaucracy here and paying off corrupt *Komiteh* people whenever we give a party or get stopped. I can keep a sense of humour about that, and say it's just part of the price I pay for living in a huge house with servants and being surrounded by my family. What I really find depressing is the Big Brother mentality you get here now. Last month, for instance, I went out with a group of friends of mine for a walk in the mountains. We were going up this path behind Evin village, a group of us, three girls and six men, but we were walking slightly apart from the girls in case we came across any *Komiteh*. It was a really nice early summer's day and the mountainside was still green.

'We were enjoying the scenery and the exercise and just chatting back and forth and laughing about the fact we couldn't walk together. Then we came across this beautiful little wooden *chai-khaneh*, and we all went in to get some tea. The place was full of other young people, all chatting and laughing, having tea and cakes, sitting out in the open air. We were careful to sit separate from the girls, so they were on one table and we were on the next one.

'It was really pleasant and reminded me of outings in my childhood except now the girls had to wear *hejab*. But after about thirty minutes someone pointed out several men a few hundred metres away with binoculars watching us. Almost immediately they started heading for the tea-house, and somebody shouted "They're *Komiteh*". Most of the people got out straight away. It was really unbelievable to see the way they were running for it. Some people were laughing and shouting, like it was a game. Three of my friends got out in time but I got caught inside with one guy and the three girls. We'd been in the middle of the room and we hadn't moved quickly enough.

'The *Komiteh* shouted for all of us to stand still, and they started questioning the girls, asking them what they were doing with us. They said they weren't with us at all. The *Komiteh* were really giving them a hard time but the girls stood up to them and were almost sassy back. In the end the *Komiteh* got impatient and couldn't push them any more, because the girls denied that they even knew us. So they shouted at the girls to leave.

'Then they turned to my friend and me. We were the last ones left.

'"We know you were talking to those girls, we were watching you. Don't you know this is Islam? You can't do that."

'The *Komiteh* man who said all this grabbed my wrist and was squeezing it hard. He was shouting at the top of his voice right in my face about Islam, and why didn't I follow it properly, and that we weren't supposed to be talking to girls. He was so angry that he was shaking, and my arm was shaking too. He wasn't like one of the ignorant ones from south Tehran, he sounded educated and had a good accent. Finally he couldn't think of anything to say, so he practically screamed at us to get out. I was amazed they didn't arrest us.

'As we were walking back down the mountain my friend laughed and said, "That's what you'd call in the West an official warning."'

In the early days of the revolution the *Komiteh* claimed the right to break into private houses if they had reason to believe that people were acting immorally in some way. In a country where the privacy of the home is as important as it is in the West, this was regarded with outrage; but the government did nothing serious to rein in the *Komiteh*. Then, at the end of 1982, Ayatollah Khomeini issued a twelve-point statement declaring that people should be allowed to do what they wanted in private without fear of interference, as long as they did not break the criminal law. It helped to curb the activities of the *Komiteh* a little, though it was not always obeyed implicitly.

Above all, it emphasised the schizophrenic tendency in Iranian society: in the privacy of their own homes people behaved in one particular fashion, and where outsiders could see them they behaved altogether differently. It had always been like this; under Reza Shah, those women who wanted to wear the *chador* had to stay at home to do so; now those who don't want to wear it are only free from it indoors. Persian has a large number of words, most of which have no counterpart in other Indo-European languages, in order to refer to the private, inner aspects of family life and the public, outer ones. Traditionally, the Persian house is itself divided into two: the inner rooms (*andaruni*), and the outer ones (*biruni*) where guests are invited. There is no question of inviting guests into the family's private space. Older houses even have two courtyards, one for the family and the other for visitors. Even now, when space and building materials are limited, modern houses are built with a special room for guests. Most people keep it closed when they do not have visitors.

This too made survival a little easier. You might have to dress in one particular way, or behave meekly and modestly when others were looking (in the lobby of the Laleh Hotel John once greeted an Iranian friend who lived in Europe with a kiss, without thinking; she was called in to the security desk and given a serious warning) but you knew that at home you could be yourself. The Islamic Republic strengthened private life, not by its constant exhortations and moral lectures, but by ensuring that the family was the only institution most people could really trust.

Once you cross the threshold of a Persian household, you have entered a different country: a country where the rules of the Islamic Republic no longer apply. There may be heavy rock music on the stereo, the clothes on display would scandalise a mullah, and men and women kiss each other or hold hands even though they aren't related; and it is all done with a sense of real relief at being free from restriction. Someone might come in from the kitchen carrying a large plastic Pepsi-Cola bottle, full, but not with Pepsi.

'*Sultanieh?*'

Sultanieh (which the drinking classes in Iran affectionately call rocket-fuel) is bootlegged vodka. Sweet, viscous, powerful, with a nutty flavour, it is usually drunk with orange juice or cola. And it is made, distributed and marketed in Iran by Iranians.

Manufacturing alcohol for general sale is a serious crime in Iran. Yet it happens, and the industry – for alcohol is produced in large quantities – is presumed to have powerful protection from the *Pasdaran* and the police. Iranian Armenians, who are Christian, are permitted to drink alcohol and to make it for their own use. This exemption has been turned into a considerable source of profit. *Sultanieh* is made from raisins, and has the reputation of being the best bootlegged liquor in the Middle East. It is said that it is now shipped across the Gulf to Dubai and distributed throughout the Gulf States.

Aside from its quality, *Sultanieh* has two important advantages. The first is price stability. In 1990 a litre cost a thousand *rials*, which is precisely what it had cost in 1980, despite the rampant inflation which affected every other sector of the economy. The second advantage is the distribution network. A newcomer will allow it to be known through reliable contacts that he or she wants a supply of alcohol. Soon there will be a phone call.

'I hear you are looking for workmen for your house. How many will you want, and when should they start?'

The householder might say, two workmen starting on Thursday. In the early hours of Thursday morning someone will come very quietly and leave two plastic jerry cans of *Sultanieh* on the back doorstep. They will be there each Thursday morning after that, and the money which has been left out for the delivery men will be gone. It is probably the best and most efficient form of industry operating in Iran today, and it owes nothing (except in the way of bribes) to officialdom.

The wines of Shiraz, praised by the poet Hafez, were being overtaken in terms of sales and popularity by wine from Azerbaijan before the revolution. *Reza'iyeh* (a white) and *Sardasht* (a red) had the best reputation. The only Iranian wine to be found nowadays comes from private cellars. It is still made, but on a tiny scale compared with the vodka; it is much easier for the *Komiteh* to keep track on the owners of vineyards. The grapes which are grown in great profusion beside the road to Hamadan, for instance, end up either on the table or as raisins. Some of the raisins, no doubt, are later turned into *Sultanieh* in the underground distilleries of Tehran.

In the early days of the revolution gangs of vigilantes forced their way into the nightclubs, restaurants and bars of Tehran and destroyed all the alcohol they could find. At the InterContinental the Revolutionary Guards smashed every bottle of wine and spirits in the hotel's cellars, and became absurdly drunk from the fumes. At least it gave the stricken Western journalists who used the hotel as their headquarters something to laugh at. After that, though, no one served alcohol in any public eating-place in Tehran again.

John and I went with a friend to a quiet restaurant which had once been a nightclub. It was very dark, even though it was lunchtime: there was a powercut, and the windows (which dated back to the nightclub days) were small and heavily curtained. As in the past, the only light came from candles; but the bottles behind the bar contained nothing stronger than Pepsi-Cola and non-alcoholic Islamic beer. The place was filled with people eating poor-quality steaks and fried fish, and talking discreetly, looking round and lowering their voices when sensitive words were spoken.

We did the same ourselves. The man who had brought us here was an old north Tehran figure, dressed in the grand manner: suit, silver tie, expensive shoes. He was a big industrialist with contacts in the present government, in the Shah's regime, in the opposition. He knew everything about getting goods and money into and out of the country. The authorities had discovered that people were smuggling $100 bills and 10,000-*rial* notes rolled up in cigarettes, he said, and he told us in full anatomical detail about the new method of smuggling. He quoted the black-market price for a pair of good-quality blue jeans – 15,000 *rials* – and for a torch battery – 3500. He warned us to be careful when we bought caviar inside Iran (though he was perfectly prepared to sell us some if we wanted it).

He told us of the problems in Qom between the different generations of ayatollahs, and the arguments within the different factions of the Islamic Republican Party. He told us of secret links with the Americans, though when the details came out later they bore little relationship to the things he had described. He told us about the state of Ayatollah Khomeini's health, and his likely life-span (he was wrong, but only by a year). He even told us how, if we were Iranian, we could finance a holiday in Europe.

'It's perfectly easy,' he said. Everything seemed to be perfectly easy to him. 'All you have to do is buy ten large packs of Kellogg's Cornflakes and bring them back with you.'

'And that pays for the trip?'

'Sure it does. Look. You can get eighty *rials* to the dollar on the official rate, right? Multiply that by ten to get the black-market rate: that makes eight hundred to the dollar. How much does a trip to Paris cost? A thousand dollars? Okay, 80,000 *rials*, it's going to cost you. If you pay in dollars you get a discount, say 60,000 *rials*. Right. You go to Paris. You have a nice holiday. Last thing you do before you leave, you go to a supermarket and pick up ten packets of cornflakes. Big ones. How much does that cost you?'

'A dollar each.' (This was 1986.)

'A dollar each. Right. You bring them back, you take them into any grocery store in north Tehran. They're crying out for things like that here. Know how much they'll pay you for them?'

The only thing to say was 'no'.

'They'll pay you 6,000 *rials* a box, and sell them for more. We've got people here, they can't live without cornflakes. How many boxes did we say you bring?'

'Ten.'

'Okay. Ten times 6,000 *rials* makes how much?'

We let him work it out.

'Sixty thousand. Exactly. The cost of your trip to Paris.'

'Does a box of Kellogg's Cornflakes really go for 6,000 *rials* in north Tehran?'

'Check it out for yourself, next time you're up there. See if it's true.'

We did; it was.

By 1991, however, everything had changed. Iran Air demanded payment in hard currency. The *rial* had been allowed to float against the dollar, and although there was an official rate at which foreign embassies and some foreign companies had to exchange their dollars, the black market had virtually ceased to exist. The value of the *rial* against the dollar fell alarmingly, however. In 1991 it was still 1200 to the dollar; by 1994 it was 2700 and showed no signs of recovering. Yet although it was no longer possible to finance a European trip with cornflakes, the continuing fall in the dollar provided plenty of businessmen, like our friend with the silver tie, with ways of making a living.

He was the Surviving Persian: no amount of political or religious upheaval could shake his conviction that what counted in life was mental finesse and fancy footwork. And no amount of contact with Westerners like us could lessen his deep personal faith in the conspiracy theory.

North Tehran is the conspiracy-theory capital of the world. Nothing is what it seems to be: to believe that it is, is to be hopelessly naïve. The British secret service, pulling the Americans by the nose, is still responsible for much of what has happened in Iran; the West is still punishing Iran for raising the oil price in the 1970s; the war with Iraq was imposed by Western interests; the West staged the Gulf War to recoup its losses with the supply of new weapons to all sides, and wanted Saddam Hussein to stay in power in order to keep Iran at bay.

Iran, in all these stories, is the centre of the world, the object of every powerful nation's concern. It was Roger Cooper, the British businessman and journalist accused of espionage, who realised that in his confessions he had to place Iran at the heart of the British secret service's obsessive interest; nothing else would do. In 1986 we compiled a list of current conspiracy theories, of which this is a selection:

The sons of various leading ayatollahs have (a) deserted to Iraq; (b) joined the royalists; (c) been arrested for drugs offences in the United States.
There are still American diplomats living and working in Iran.
There are still Israeli diplomats living and working in Iran.
Ayatollah Khomeini was an Indian by birth.
Ayatollah Khomeini's father was a British employee of the Anglo-Persian Oil Company, named Williamson.
Ayatollah Khomeini died soon after the revolution and was impersonated afterwards by an actor.
A new crisis was about to break because the actor, too, was dying.

The attraction of these stories is not their accuracy or lack of it, but their effect in feeding the common Iranian desire to believe that hidden forces are at work in almost every aspect of life. After the revolution the rumour went around that the museum near the Tomb of Cyrus at Pasargadae had been transformed secretly into a prison and SAVAK torture centre. A Swedish engineering firm was retained at considerable expense to investigate another rumour: that a tunnel had been constructed between the Shah's palace at Niavaran and Evin prison, several miles away, so that the Shah could interrogate political prisoners himself.

This faith in the unseen, in the hidden hand and the secret tunnel, reflects the Persian's lack of faith in the simple, aboveboard way of doing things. There is little belief in the due processes of the official system in Iran, with some cause; most people prefer to seek out private ways of their own. Every Western Embassy in Tehran knows how common it is for Iranians who want visas to refuse to make an application in the normal way, which may involve a delay of between four and six months. Instead they wait until the last moment and then opt for some supposed back-door method or some dubious personal contact which, in practice, involves an even longer wait. In their jokes, the Persians themselves mock their desire to cut corners:

A man arrives at the gates of hell, one joke runs, after having led a sinful life. He is cheered by seeing that one of the gatekeepers is an old friend. The gatekeeper greets him warmly, and tells him that there are two different hells; one is American and one is Persian. 'Can you help

me out?' the man asks. 'Please get me into the American hell. It's got
to be better.'

His friend arranges matters and the sinner gains entrance to the
American hell. After a few weeks, the gatekeeper pays him a visit.

'So how do you like the American hell?'

'It's terrible. Every hour on the hour the devils come round with a
huge funnel which they stick in our mouths and pour a bag of shit down
our throats. That happens twenty-four times a day, just like clockwork.
Please, you must do something. Pull some strings and get me into the
Persian hell, it can't be as bad!'

The gatekeeper arranges things for his old friend, who is transferred
to the Persian hell. After a few weeks he pays him a visit.

'So is life any better on this side?'

'It is, a bit. The devils still come round with a funnel and pour a
bag of shit down our throats but we have some breaks; sometimes
they forget to look at the clock, sometimes they lose the funnel and
sometimes they run out of shit.'

For the Persian, the need to demonstrate one's *parti* – clout or pull –
is as important as the object itself. To a Westerner, it can be infuriating;
to an Iranian, it represents one of a wide range of strategies for coping
with a system which cannot be trusted to work in the general interest.

Altogether there are thought to be a million and a half Iranian exiles in
Western Europe, mostly in London and Paris, and the same number in
the United States. A sizable proportion of them decided to take advantage
of a law which came into force in 1993 making former citizens eligible
for Iranian passports again, even if they had become citizens of another
country. The only exceptions were the outright opponents of the regime
and those still too closely associated with the Shah's era. The response
was immediate and overwhelming: thousands of expatriate Iranians in
Europe and the United States put in their requests for Islamic Republic
passports. The consulates of Iranian embassies were swamped with
applications, and they made a profit from it by charging as much
as 300 US dollars per passport.

President Rafsanjani led the drive to attract some of the three million
exiles back to Iran. Whatever their feelings about the regime, he said,
they would be forgiven and made welcome if they were prepared to help
rebuild the economy. The expectation was that the exiles would bring a
large amount of money back with them. The younger men who returned
would not, however, be exempt from military service; but they could pay
an exemption fee. The war with Iraq was long over, but military service
was still a problem to someone who wanted to start a new life.

A sign on the wall read in Persian, 'It would be a kindness not to
smoke'. We were ordering a meal in probably the only non-smoking

restaurant in Iran, and one of the very few vegetarian ones. The owners were Iranians who had come back after years of living in California and thought that a laid-back, user-friendly, alternative restaurant would catch on. They were right; it has become one of the few public places that well-to-do north Tehranis go to regularly.

Our herbal teas were brought by the polite, English-speaking waiters. If it hadn't been for the *hejab* which all the women were wearing, you might have thought from the stripped wood floors, the soft pastel colours of the decoration and the potted plants that you were somewhere in Paris or London. There were eight of us, six women and two men. All of the others had come back to Iran to live and work, and the conversation was about their experiences.

Bahram had returned from London to see if he could overturn the confiscation orders which had cost his family over half of their properties in north Tehran; his father had put the houses and land in Bahram's name at the beginning of the revolution.

'When I got back I found that I had to deal with the national service requirement. It wasn't that difficult; you are allowed to buy your way out of service at a charge which is linked to your qualifications. The fee starts at about three thousand dollars and goes up to fifteen thousand dollars for people with doctorates or law degrees, although I don't know of anyone who has had to pay that amount. Of course everyone claims they have fewer diplomas than they really do. It's hard for the government to check up on these things. Let's just say that I paid about five thousand dollars, and it was money well spent.

'Actually the government needs the hard currency from people like us. It costs more money for them to take a man into the army for two years or so, and they can't afford it. Look at the population figures; half of the country under the age of twenty-five and half of those are men. It's actually cheaper and better for the government to let people buy their way out of the service; soon they'll be letting the people who live here do it, not just the ones who are coming back from abroad.'

'Let's start at the beginning: just getting a phone and a fax,' said Eskandar, a returnee businessman in his late thirties. 'It takes huge amounts of paperwork and paying the right people and maybe a dozen visits to some government office if you don't have a good contact. It costs about $1200 to get a telephone line. I know of some people who have waited three years for one. And even when you have a telephone, sometimes during peak hours you can't get through at all. As for telephone books, they don't exist. If you try to dial 118 for information, you never get through. So you ask a friend for a number, who asks a friend and so on. It's all about networking here.'

'Sometimes I'm amazed the place functions at all,' said Caren, his business partner. 'There are constant electricity blackouts, especially in summer. The newspapers print timetables to tell you when the power cuts are coming. And if you have a business that needs electricity like ours, you might as well be on vacation every day for half a day in the summer.'

Soraya runs an agency to help people, especially foreigners, find houses and flats, and decorate and furnish them. She spends much of her time going from place to place in Tehran for appointments and viewings. She drives a small van, to carry furniture or carpets for her customers to select. Women drivers are in the minority in Iran anyway, but women who drive vans are extremely rare. Soraya, with her forthright style of driving, gets a great deal of abuse in the streets of Tehran. Now she drives with her headphones on and her Sony Walkman turned up.

'For me, the real problem is the petty corruption. Here you have to bargain and pay for everything, big and small. Even when you see the police patrolling your neighbourhood or when they stop you if you are coming home late at night, you speak to them respectfully to make life easier, and you reach into your wallet and give them 2000 *rials*. At first I thought they might get angry – it's like tipping a porter at an airport – but no, that's what they want. And the postman expects something every time he delivers a letter, so you never know if he has ten letters for you and is holding them to receive a tip for ten days running or he has only one letter. There is no civic pride in being a good postman or a good policeman. To a certain extent things were done like that here before the revolution. But it's much worse now.

'Still, there is a very definite up-side about being back. I feel comfortable here in all sorts of ways that surprised me; I'm not afraid of being mugged or raped here, like I was in the West. You aren't in danger here, and there's no such thing as child murder. None of my friends worry about letting their children walk to the shops. I know a lot of you feel that things are easier in the West, but for me these things are important too. Which of you would let your children out in the street in London or Paris or Los Angeles?'

The place was completely empty: in all the 3500-square-metres of land at Ahmad Abad there wasn't a single soul. Farhad looked around: he hadn't seen this place since March 1967, when two million people crowded in here to pay their respects to the disgraced statesman who had died under house arrest. Farhad cut a dignified figure in the open landscape. At sixty-eight, he was upright in his bearing and well dressed, according to the standards of his generation: dark suit, white shirt, neatly knotted tie. This was a pilgrimage for him. The statesman who had owned the estate at Ahmad Abad was Dr Mohammed Mossadeq, who as prime minister had challenged the British government over the control of Iran's oil, and had been overthrown in the countercoup of 1953 by the British and American secret services. Farhad, like the rest of those who had gathered here after Mossadeq's death, had wanted to attend the funeral.

But there was no funeral, on the Shah's orders. Instead, the body had been buried in a room of the family house. Mossadeq himself had once said, when Reza Shah had declared that no one could visit the grave of someone he disliked, 'Dictatorship is so all-encompassing that it has to assert itself even over the dead.'

Like the campaigners for a constitution in 1906, Mossadeq was a nationalist and a supporter of greater parliamentary democracy. On the day the Majlis elected him prime minister in April 1951, it passed the resolution which he supported for the nationalisation of Iran's oil industry, thus taking it out of British hands. During much of the crisis which unfolded over the next two years Mossadeq was a sick man, giving interviews and press conferences from his bed. The BBC, and especially its Persian Service, played an ignoble role by following the British government's line slavishly. The crisis came to a head in 1953 when the Shah fled the country, and it was resolved by Mossadeq's overthrow. The best historian of the episode, Mostafa Elm, writes:

The two greatest democracies of the world aborted the birth of democracy in a distant land for what they wrongly conceived to be in their self-interest. By doing so, they helped to unleash a chain of traumatic events in Iran and the rest of the Middle East, while gravely damaging their own interests.

Farhad was twenty-five when this chain of events began, and had demonstrated in the streets on Mossadeq's behalf. He was still a firm believer in the idea of an independent Iran which would control its own economy and its own affairs. Now, forty-three years later, he found himself walking up to the unassuming two-storey house where Mossadeq had been kept a virtual prisoner until his death. The prime minister's grandson, Dr Mahmoud Mossadeq, came down the steps to greet him. He was in his late forties, and looked like an Englishman in his blazer, club tie and white trousers. Dr Mossadeq was himself a visitor here: the house was unoccupied still. He came to the estate every week now making sure that everything was in order.

'There's a gardener here, somewhere,' he said, looking round the shrubbery. The gardener doubled as a security guard, and had been hired to protect the grave inside the house as well as to tend the grounds. It was only three years earlier, in 1991, that the house had been opened to the public and the Mossadeq family had been permitted to visit it. Before that they had often been harassed and denied entrance by the *Komiteh* members who had been posted at the gate.

The house is in bad repair, with broken windows and its walls stained with pigeon-droppings, and the estate in general is still something of a mess. Weeds have obscured the fountain near the house, and tall grass covers the ornamental gardens. The vines at the eastern end have grown wild, and the grapes which must once have been carefully tended are tiny and bitter. No trace remains of the tennis court or the swimming pool. Outside the front door is the wrecked car which Mossadeq once rode in: a large fifties Plymouth in pale blue. Now it is balanced on a concrete block.

'The Tudeh Party burned the car in 1976,' Mahmoud Mossadeq explained mildly. 'A lot of them were actually villagers who used to queue for free medicines at the door. Very ungrateful people. My grandfather would give out medicine to them every Friday, and they ended up breaking all the windows in his car and burning it.'

The Tudeh Party were Communist; yet it was because the Americans and British accused Mossadeq of being a Communist sympathiser that they decided to overthrow him. Nationalism and Communism were much confused in the early part of the Cold War, and Mossadeq was an unrepentant nationalist.

Farhad went through the house, looking at the couch where Mossadeq once lay, and the books and medicines laid out beside it; at the photographs of Mossadeq, with his long, intelligent, lugubrious face on the walls; at the extraordinary tomb, nothing more than a casket draped in blue silk with two Korans and two candleholders on top of it, which covered the place where his remains were buried under the floor; at the curious scale model of an oil rig, six foot high, in one corner of the room. As with Mossadeq himself, there was something grand and noble, and yet mildly ludicrous, about the place.

No one in Iran except the remnants of his party, the National Front, which is now illegal, seems to honour Mossadeq nowadays. There is no street named after him in the whole of Tehran. Ayatollah Khomeini, who might have been expected to regard him as something of a forerunner in his opposition to the Shah, ignored his memory: Mossadeq was not regarded as a supporter of the clergy. Yet his resistance to British and American domination of the country sparked a chain of events which led directly to the revolution of 1978–9, and a large number of people who supported Ayatollah Khomeini did so because they had earlier supported Mossadeq.

'This resting place is only temporary,' Mahmoud Mossadeq told Farhad as they left the house. 'Maybe in the future we can move his remains to the place where he wanted to be buried, alongside the martyrs of the uprising of 1951. But we must do everything properly, you know: getting the money together for the renovations so we don't jeopardise everything we are hoping to do here.'

The man who began the revolution has been deliberately put out of mind, first by the Shah and then by the revolutionaries who came after. Moderate, democratic, secular nationalism is no more acceptable during the reign of the mullahs than it was during the monarchy. Yet as Farhad said his goodbyes and drove away from the dilapidated house, it must have seemed clear to him that for all the neglect and the official disapproval, the memory of the man who, as much as anyone else, created modern Iran will somehow survive the revolution.

19

Leaving

John Simpson

If you have the means and fail to make the journey, you have not attained completely the happiness and pleasure of worldly riches; indeed, the perfection of pleasure lies in seeing what you have not already seen, eating what you have not hitherto eaten and experiencing what you have not yet experienced. Only by travel can this be achieved.

A Mirror For Princes

Any writer or journalist knows that each time he or she leaves a country as difficult as Iran, it could be for the last time. The chances of offending a government whose susceptibilities are as tender and whose imagination is as unfettered as the Islamic Republic of Iran's are very great indeed; and the easiest way for it to react is to refuse you a visa next time. It becomes very hard to say goodbye to friends who cannot afford to leave the country, or are not allowed to do so. And you find yourself looking at the things which have become familiar to you, conscious that you may not see them again for a very long time. It is not, of course, a new emotion. George Curzon, when he left Persia after his six-month tour in 1890, found that it was Mount Damavand, visible throughout the city, which he would particularly miss.

The shapely white cone, cutting so keenly and so high in the air, becomes so familiar and cherished a figure in the daily landscape, that on leaving Tehran and losing sight thereof the traveller is conscious of a very perceptible void.

The English scholar of Persia, Edward Granville Browne had travelled around the country three years earlier, from 1887 to 1888. Unlike Curzon, he did not drive himself particularly hard when he returned, with the result that Curzon's monumental book was published first and Granville Browne was obliged to write something much more relaxed and discursive. Curzon's book was greatly respected, little read, and was out of print within fifteen years. Granville Browne's book, humorous, chatty and anecdotal, is still available in paperback a hundred years later. 'Persian' Browne never went back to Persia, but he studied its literature for the rest of his life, and taught it to an entire generation of students at Cambridge. He also gave powerful support to the efforts in 1906 to win greater constitutional freedom in Persia.

None of this has been forgotten in Tehran: the revolutionary regime which changed the name of Shah Reza Avenue to Revolution Avenue, Los Angeles Road to Islamic Dress Road, and Queen Elizabeth Boulevard to Peasant Farmer Boulevard has left *Kuche Porofesor Brown*, Professor Browne Street, exactly as it was. The street is short and unobtrusive, but it runs on the western side of Tehran University, one of the centres of revolutionary support and the scene every Friday of the most important prayer meeting in the country. There is no chance whatever that *Kuche Porofesor Brown* might have escaped the notice of the authorities. It is there because even they appreciate the affection Granville Browne had for their country.

In September 1888, at the end of his year of travels around Persia, Granville Browne reached the coast of the Caspian Sea with his servant Haji Safar, and caught the Russian steamer which was to take him away from the country he would always study but never see again.

> It was with genuine regret that I turned for a moment before stepping into the boat to bid farewell to Persia (which, notwithstanding all her faults, I had come to love very dearly) and the faithful and efficient Haji Safar. He had served me well, and to his intelligence and enterprise I owed much. He was not perfect – what man is? – but if ever it be my lot to visit these lands again, I would wish no better than to secure the services of him, or one like him. I slipped into his hands a bag of money which I had reserved for a parting present, and with a few brief words of farewell, stepped into the boat, which at once cast off from the shore, and hoisting a sail, stood out towards the Russian steamer. The sea grew rougher as we left the shelter of the estuary, but with the sail we advanced quickly, and about 8.15 a.m. I climbed on board the *Emperor Alexander*, and, for the first time in many months, felt myself, with a sudden sense of loneliness, a stranger in the midst of strangers.

By the end of the week that followed the revolution in 1979, the cameraman and sound-recordist I was working with, Bill Handford and David Johnson, were getting very tired. So was I. We had been travelling, filming and satelliting our reports under difficult conditions for up to eighteen hours a day ever since 25 January, when we first arrived at Neauphle-le-Château. There had been four nights during which we had not slept at all. We were no different in that respect from the other people from our organisation who were working alongside us and had been in Iran for longer than we had, nor from all the other journalists; nor, for that matter, from the revolutionaries and gunmen and diplomats whose activities we were reporting on.

In my case, though, there was a difference: my office did not really want me to be there at all. I was needed back in London. I resisted for as long as I could, and it helped that the airports were closed to incoming flights. Nobody could be sent in to replace me. But I knew the office would win eventually. It always did.

It was decided, at last, that we should cover the evacuation of British and Commonwealth citizens from Iran, organised by the British Embassy, and fly out with them. The operation was superbly organised – the British have always been good at retreating in style – and a long line of cars and buses brought the evacuees from assembly points all over Tehran up the Shemiran Road to the embassy compound at Gulhak, next door to the British Institute for Persian Studies.

It made good television pictures: the nervous faces looking out of the windows; the children hugging their toys; the escorts, which the revolutionary authorities had provided, with their beards and guns and mismatched uniforms; and David Reddaway, the British diplomat whom I had seen three months earlier trying to close the embassy gates in the face of a crowd that burned the chancery building. Now he was standing up in the lead Jeep, wearing his pink Leander Club tie and directing the line of vehicles like a tank commander at El Alamein.

The crowd of several hundred refugees filled the gardens of the compound, walking aimlessly about, meeting their friends and exchanging stories. Some of them had had a difficult time; several had been shot at or attacked by crowds, and most had been threatened in some way. Others were leaving reluctantly, for the sake of their families. Three or four large trucks were parked in the driveway, and everybody's belongings, including ours, were loaded on to them. The diplomats had the problem of negotiating with the revolutionary authorities for permission to bring in RAF Hercules transport planes to take everyone out. Two were to be allowed in; four more were turned back while they were in the air. With three million people in the country still on strike, and different parts of the city and administration in the hands of different groups, the confusion was immense.

We had our problems too. The streets were easy enough to get through in big convoys with outriders provided by the revolutionary authorities, but much harder to penetrate if you were driving on your own. We had to deliver the material we had been filming that morning to the television station, which was extremely well guarded after a wild outbreak of shooting that had taken place there a few nights before. That

meant getting in even though we did not have the proper passes, finding
the right person to give the film to, making sure he or she knew when
it had to be satellited to London, and being back at Gulhak in time to
film the first group of evacuees being taken to the airport. Everything
had to be done within two hours.

Somehow, at the expense of a great deal of mental and physical effort,
we succeeded; the most difficult part, predictably, was talking our way
past the guards at the television station, and the second most difficult
part was talking our way back into the British compound at Gulhak
where the orders were similar: to admit nobody. We got in at last,
and did some more filming. By now people had had a chance to relax
and there was less tension. Since there was no chance of satelliting these
new pictures, we could relax too.

I was wandering around on my own, looking for people to talk to,
when I came across one of the younger diplomats, a particularly urbane
figure even in these circumstances.

'I was hoping to find you,' he said affably. 'Your office in London
managed to get a phone call through about an hour ago. It seems they
sent in a new correspondent and crew in a Lear jet, and your people
want you to fly back in it. The pilot's been told to wait at the airport
until midday for you, and then he'll have to take off.'

I looked at my watch. 'But it's eleven-twenty now.'

'So it is,' said the affable diplomat. 'Oh well.'

I found my colleagues and told them about it, and together we
decided that we would try and make it, even though we had no
means of transport, our suitcases and equipment would have to be
retrieved from the three trucks loaded down with baggage, and it
would take three-quarters of an hour to get to the airport in normal
conditions. Conditions in Tehran that day were not normal. While
we were still talking about it, the diplomat sought me out again,
this time a little more urgently.

'If you go, would you be able to take someone out with you?'

'Yes, I suppose so, assuming we can make it. Who is it?'

'I'm afraid I'm not at liberty to tell you.'

'Well,' I said, 'I don't think I could just...'

'It's someone who has to be got out for his own safety. I can't tell
you any more.'

There were executions every day now of military men and government
officials who were accused of working for foreign powers, Britain and
the United States especially. I didn't want someone's death on my
conscience, no matter who they were. I could also see a glimmer of
personal advantage.

'If you let us have the ambassador's car and driver to get us to the
airport, I'll do it.'

There was some diplomatic consultation, and the deal was done. The mysterious evacuee would be sent to the airport by a separate route, and would meet up with us at noon. If he were not there by then, we should leave without him. That was the diplomat's suggestion, not mine: I didn't think we would be at the airport by noon ourselves.

By now my colleagues had become deeply pessimistic. For a start, there was the question of the luggage: we couldn't simply leave it, since it contained a good deal of valuable television equipment. But the three baggage trucks were piled high with a thousand or more suitcases.

'It's no use,' said David Johnson gloomily. 'We'll never make it now.' It was eleven twenty-four.

His gloom made up my mind for me. I was seized with a savage determination. With Bill Handford's help I launched myself up into the most likely of the baggage trucks and started lifting out cases to see if I could find ours. There must be a rough order to the placing of the luggage, I reasoned: the earliest layers must be at the bottom. We had been among the first to hand over our bags; *ergo* they must be in the lowest layer, at the back of the truck. I dug down through five or six layers, then gave a shout of angry triumph: one of Bill's cases was visible. I pulled it out, and the rest of our luggage proved to be buried alongside it. By the time we were fully reunited with our gear, it was eleven-thirty.

The ambassadorial Jaguar had been prepared, and the ambassador's chauffeur was already sitting behind the wheel with the engine gunned up. This chauffeur was a formidable figure. His quick thinking had saved Sir Anthony Parsons on at least one occasion when his Rolls (in which the American ambassador William Sullivan was also a passenger) was being chased down the street by a gang of men wielding clubs. The chauffeur headed into the car park of a bank, and the gates were firmly locked behind them. He was a Pakistani, tall, rangy, fiftyish, with a fiercely hooked nose.

Mildly intimidated by this splendid figure, I said something about needing to hurry. He took no notice, having already received his orders. He drove the Jaguar at speed through the gates and out into the Shemiran Road without pausing. One of the most alarming car journeys of my life had begun. There was a good deal of traffic about, but the chauffeur ignored it as if it didn't exist. When there was no room for us on the right side of the road he switched to the wrong side. When there was no room on the wrong side he mounted the pavement and drove along that. Panicky shoppers threw themselves out of our way.

We raced through the streets of Tehran like a liner through pleasure boats. For many years I thought I remembered that the Jaguar was flying the Union Jack, but I have since been told this could not have been true. Even so, that journey seemed like one of the last imperial acts of the British in Persia. We raced through the last of the road blocks, entered the silent airport, and for the first time I felt able to take my eyes off the road ahead and look at my watch. It was two minutes to twelve.

No one was around, and no scheduled flight had arrived or left from there for days. The airport staff had been purged several times and replaced by different groups of armed men. I had been here twice during the previous week, trying to find a way of sending our film out of the country with the pilot of a plane, and each time I dealt with a different official. The previous one had been shot. We drove fast towards the terminal building. Outside it, in the pale sunshine, stood a man in a peaked cap and a white shirt. He was looking at his watch. When he saw the Jaguar he waved.

'My name's Martin,' he said, and shook hands with us.

No one else had arrived. I told Captain Martin that there might be another passenger who was travelling independently to the airport. He raised an eyebrow slightly, but asked no questions. We agreed that we would wait until twelve thirty, if the airport authorities allowed him to keep the Lear jet on the ground that long. If the other man had not turned up by then we would leave without him. It was longer than the embassy people had asked us to wait, but I wanted to give him a decent chance.

We said goodbye to the magnificent chauffeur, and I stood outside the terminal building alone, watching the Jaguar head off. It was driving slower now. The others took our gear through the customs and loaded it on to the plane. The road was empty as far as the eye could see. The silence remained unbroken.

'It's twenty to one,' said a quiet, tactful voice.

'I know,' I said.

'We're cleared for takeoff.'

I stared as hard as I could down the road to Tehran: whoever it was, he wasn't going to come now.

Alex was an American boy, but he had been brought up in Iran since the age of five and spoke, acted and thought like a Persian. He had been educated at the International School, and most of the better-off pupils there had left the country in 1978 and 1979. He waited until the summer of 1980.

'I had lived through the revolution, I'd seen the demonstrations, I'd watched Evin prison being taken by the revolutionaries, and I still managed to graduate from school. But the plan had always been that I would go abroad to college, and the time had arrived.

'All my friends came over the night before I left and had a big party. Everyone slept at my place. We were a real close group of twelve, and I was the first one to leave. We got up early and went to the airport. It was a gruesome scene. The *Pasdars* were being really brutal to people. There were quite a few people trying to escape even then, and they were being given a terrible time. And there were those awful women in uniform, searching people and throwing things out of their suitcases. It took me five hours to get into the airport, go through security, and check in my luggage. Then I got to passport control.

'I had lived in Iran for more than ten years, but I had an American passport and I must have been one of the few Americans in the country who wasn't a hostage at the Embassy. The *Pasdars* were quite shocked when they saw my nationality and they asked me what I was doing in Iran. My friends had come with me up to that point, to passport control, because they were worried there might be problems. Now the immigration people pulled me out of the queue and took me all the way back to the beginning, where I had been five hours earlier. They started interrogating me and asking about my family. The interrogator was probably ex-SAVAK, but he was a revolutionary now. He was very professional and phoned up the Ministry of External Affairs and other ministries. I didn't think they were going to let me leave. The main problem was that he couldn't find a file on me because I was just a kid: only eighteen.

'Finally he started being friendly to me and complimenting me on my Persian. So then we became great friends and chatted away. I was worried that I would miss the flight, which was supposed to go in fifteen minutes. He said "Don't worry," and picked up the phone and shouted down the line, "Hold the flight for another ten minutes."

'So I asked him if I could go and say goodbye to my friends who I knew were still waiting, one last time. I guessed they must be terribly worried. So he and I went out together and found my friends, and they couldn't believe it: me and this bearded colonel who was being so helpful. He stood back and let me say goodbye and then walked me to my flight.'

We were leaving Mount Damavand, and Tehran itself, behind us, and were heading to the east of the Caspian Sea: that area where Persia melts into the steppes of Central Asia. It was 1992, and what will almost certainly be my last visit to Iran for a long time was nearly over. Tira was with me: we were working together on a television documentary about the competition between Iran and Turkey for influence over the countries of Central Asia, newly independent since the collapse of Soviet power during the previous year. We called it 'The New Great Game' to distinguish it from the long battle between Britain and Russia for influence in the same area, but even as early as that it was clear that the game was going to have an outright winner.

Iran simply had too many disadvantages to be able to compete with Turkey on equal terms: it was Shi'i and most of the Central Asian states were Sunni; it was Persian-speaking and most of them spoke a Turkic language; it had only a fiercely isolationist ideology to preach, while Turkey could offer investment and new technology; and, most important of all, the Iranians were characteristically incapable of

planning a proper campaign and carrying it through without politicking
against one another. We were to find, as we crossed into Central
Asia, that Iran's closest neighbours were well aware of the damage
that the revolution and its long aftermath had done; and aside from
Tajikhistan, which was Persian-speaking and strongly influenced by
Persian culture, none of the other countries of Central Asia seemed
interested in following the same path.

As we headed in the direction of Iran's border with Turkmenistan,
and approached the Golden Road to Samarkand, our caravan was not a
great deal more modest than many earlier ones which had set out on the
same journey. There were eight of us, in three cars; Mahmoudi's white
Paykan, a four-wheel-drive truck for the camera equipment, and a shiny
new black Mercedes-Benz provided for us by the Foreign Ministry and
driven by a chauffeur. We had taken the hint provided by Sir Roger
Stevens and insisted on an early start:

> Unless the weather is exceptionally hot it is not usual, or necessary,
> to follow the custom of leaving in the evening and travelling by
> night; nor yet the more normal Iranian practice of setting out
> in the afternoon of the first day and travelling only a short
> stage – so that the servants can go back and fetch what has
> been inadvertently left behind.

Accordingly, we set out from the Laleh Hotel at five o'clock one
clear, cool morning in early autumn, with the first light of the new
day beginning to appear over the hills and plains to the east of the
city – the direction in which we were heading. Tira and I were in
the official Mercedes – the protocol car – which led our procession.
Ali, our young and genial Foreign Ministry 'minder', sat in the front
passenger seat next to the driver. For the previous five years we had
always avoided the company of 'minders', but Ali had been quietly and
efficiently helpful during the past two weeks of filming in Tehran,
and had once had to extricate us from the grip of the Komiteh when
we were filming in the bazaar. He was looking forward to the trip; he
had never been to the area we were travelling to.

Mahmoudi drove the director, a relaxed and witty man who had to
bear all the pressures from an independent production company which
was distinctly unenthusiastic about spending the kind of money required
for an elaborate documentary like this. He and the cameraman and
sound-recordist switched cars occasionally, so that there would always
be someone with the man driving the Jeep, which was carrying the
camera gear. The driver was a particular friend of ours.

The road north-east out of Tehran followed the line of the Albourz
Mountains flanking Damavand. The mountains rose on our left, while
to our right lay the arid plain stretching from Tehran to Mashhad,

described by Thomas Herbert as a 'howling desert'. As we drove backwards and forwards up the twisting mountain roads we could see the sites where caravanserais had once sheltered travellers in the days when twenty miles constituted a day's journey. Now there were frequent *chai-khanehs* for the drivers of the trucks which carried their loads to and from the Caspian and the Turkoman steppe. As we followed the road which clung to the mountain range and descended towards the Caspian, we left behind the reds and umbers of the dry earth. The scenery became greener and rich patches of agriculture could be seen below us. In the small villages jars of honey and ripe watermelons were set out for sale on wooden boards by the roadside.

We came to Gurgan, the start of the Turkoman country, in the late afternoon, just as the sun was beginning to dip below the jagged edges of the mountain range above. This was the city of which Iskandar, the author of *A Mirror for Princes*, had been the ruler but there was no difference between the architecture of Gurgan and that of every other town and city we had passed through on the way: dull brick, dusty grey in colour, trailing electricity and telephone cables and looking unfinished and gloomy. Yet we could tell simply by looking at the faces in the street that we had crossed an invisible frontier. Persian features – the dark Aryan features and the thick straight black hair – were much less common than they had been in Persia proper; instead there were the flatter, Asiatic faces and the stocky figures of the Far East.

Unexpectedly, Ali announced that we had to drive on to the town of Gonbad to pay a courtesy call on the governor of the province. No one had suggested this before, and it was bound to affect the unrealistically tight schedule which the production company back in London had set for our filming. To keep to this, we had to reach a particular Turkoman village that evening, and film there first thing the following morning. Instead we found ourselves hanging around in the unappealing town hall of Gonbad, waiting for someone to find out where the governor was and tell him we had arrived.

It was two hours before we received a message from him: he was waiting at Golestan National Park, an hour's drive away, where dinner was being prepared for us. It was all very Persian: the sudden announcement of the trip to see the governor, the vagueness of the arrangement with him, the hospitality that would brook no refusal, the complete lack of any thought that we might have plans of our own which might be disrupted by this unnecessary delay. I looked at my watch: it was after 9 p.m., and we were all hungry and in a thoroughly bad temper. Two more cars joined our convoy and we were escorted into the darkness.

At 10 p.m. I was awoken from a doze by the sound of tyres on gravel; we were in the middle of Golestan Park at the Shah's old hunting lodge. The guard outside the door had also been asleep when we arrived, but he jumped up obligingly and went inside to alert the governor's officials.

The governor turned out to be a small, tough character with the kind of eyes that moved around the room swiftly, searching out the most advantageous person to talk to, and watching for the arrival of someone even better. His jokes were raucous and sometimes rather personal: there were comments about my grey hair and the director's fuller figure. He seemed, all the same, precisely the kind of man you would hope to find opposite you at the negotiating table: sharp-witted and keen on gaining his own advantage, to be sure, but certainly not a fundamentalist ideologue. He looked like a Rafsanjani man, through and through.

It was not a particularly lively evening; we made small talk through interpreters across the table, the visitors sitting opposite the home team, and did not finish eating our large, meat-heavy dinner until one in the morning, by which time all of us were nearly asleep. On the wall were mounted trophy heads of the ibex which had once roamed this area. In between the stuffed heads was a photograph of Ayatollah Khomeini.

'Dead heads,' Tira muttered irritably, looking at them. This had once been the hunting lodge of the Shah; now it was reserved for the enjoyment of government officials. Once again the parallels with imperial and revolutionary Russia came to mind. The Communist Party had behaved exactly like this.

The governor, still laughing and making loud personal comments, insisted on driving us home at the end of the feast. It was the middle of the night when we turned off a tiny paved road into a badly-pitted dust track; we had arrived at the outskirts of a Turkoman village. We found the open sleeping platform where the crew decided they would spend what was left of the night: the air was sharp but not really cold, and they were happy to lie in their sleeping bags under the wheeling stars of the steppe. Tira and I decided to sleep inside the small house. We lay on the floor in front of the embers of the dying fire, with dogs around us and the occasional sound of mice running across the terracotta tiles of the floor.

I woke at six. The front door was open, and I wandered out past the sleeping platform and looked across the steppe. I knew what I was looking for: Alexander's Wall, so called, which was built by the Sassanian monarchs in the second century AD to keep out the Asiatic nomads advancing across the Turkoman steppe. I could see it in the distance: not a wall at all, but a barrier of earth six, eight or sometimes ten feet high, cutting its way across the flat landscape. I walked the mile or so towards it in the early-morning light, the dew splashing up under my feet, shivering a little in the keen air.

This was one of the great frontiers of history, where the Indo-Europeans of Iran, settled, agricultural, ordered people, confronted the wild horsemen of the endless plain who drove their herds from pasture to pasture, moving constantly and acknowledging no overlord except their own immediate headman. For well over a thousand years this was one of the dividing lines between the Sunni Muslims of the steppes and Shi'ia Iran. Then, after the Bolshevik Revolution in Russia in 1917, it became a frontier once more, between the Soviet-controlled People's Republics of Central Asia and the capitalist empire of Iran. In due course this faded, too, and it now divided the post-socialist regimes from the world's largest and most aggressive Islamic republic.

The sun started to rise, red and fierce, and tombs and burial mounds from ancient times abutted on to the skyline. The Turkomans, being simple people and good Sunnis after their fashion, regarded it as wrong to break into the tombs to find the Scythian gold they contained, so most remained intact. Farther off I could see two entire buried cities, vast mounds completely untouched, whose very names no one here now knew.

I came across a group of Turkomans: hardy, jolly men in baggy breeches and boots, with large, slightly conical caps of lambswool on their heads and the women in brilliantly coloured scarves and costumes; *hejab* meant a great deal less here than it did in the central parts of Iran. Most of the men were heading for their farms on the steppe, where they grew cotton, watermelons, wheat, sunflowers, soya beans. In the villages the women make *namads*, felt carpets, not by weaving but by laying down strips of felt and melding them into a tightly-packed design. At a meeting of the Imperial Geographical Society in St Petersburg in 1872 the Russian explorer and adventurer Colonel Stebnitzky, who played a significant part here in the 'Great Game', described the Turkomans admiringly:

> They are Sunnis and good Muhammadans although not fanatical and they will divide their food and live on friendly terms with people of other religions. They admit a plurality of wives and often marry their Persian and Kurd captives. Almost all the domestic work is performed by women and slaves; they watch the flocks, prepare the food, make felts and weave carpets; while the men spend most of their time in pleasure sometimes sallying forth on an '*alaman*' or raid into Persia to obtain plunder and carry people off to sell as slaves. Their horses are of Arab race, very enduring, swift, of a good height and handsome in appearance. The Tekke horses are particularly famous; the high quality of the Turkoman horses and their perfect subjection to their riders enable them to make distant plundering forays into Persia.

Later that day as we filmed the women kneeling side by side in a row of seven or eight, rolling out the *namads* and fixing the strips of felt as tightly as if they were hand-knotted like a carpet, we heard the voice of an old woman singing a song louder and higher than the rest. She was dressed mostly in yellow, and her face was turned up to the sky, the eyes sightless. She had been blinded by her brother fifty years before for committing some supposed indiscretion: accepting the compliments of a man, perhaps. The Turkomans are settled now, and live in houses of brick and stone; but they have never quite forgotten the more savage ways of their nomadic past.

It was here that we said goodbye, with a good deal of sadness, to Mahmoudi. His work for us was now over, and he would head back for Tehran while we crossed the border into the newly independent state of Turkmenistan. Somehow in the past, whenever I had left him, I had always been certain I would see him again reasonably soon. This time I had a premonition that it would be a great deal longer; that I might never even work with him again. It was only a passing feeling, but it made me grip his hand a little tighter and a little longer than usual. Perhaps he felt something of the same thing: he pulled me towards him in a bear hug and kissed me on both cheeks. His own cheeks were bristly from being on the road so long. I had become very fond indeed of Mahmoudi, and had come to rely greatly on his steadfastness and loyalty. Not all the other drivers at the Laleh Hotel, I knew, were quite so enthusiastic about him especially when, after the first edition of this book was published in 1988, foreign visitors sometimes asked for him by name and paid him well above the standard price. Later he left the Laleh Hotel altogether. But if he was inclined to be superior to some of his colleagues, he was never so with us. We had already paid him, but I pressed a folded banknote into his hand and he palmed it with the virtuosity of a professional. Back in Tehran he had given us a farewell gift he guessed we would appreciate: a pre-1917 Russian samovar, imported into Iran and inscribed in Persian as well as cyrillic. He stood by his white Paykan for a long time as we drove off down the road, his arm raised high in the air. His figure grew smaller and smaller, and the dust welled up behind us and almost blocked him from our sight. Then it cleared, and I could see him turn and get into his car, and then even that faded into a small white dot in the far distance, and he was gone.

We drove through the Golestan National Park where we had been entertained at the hunting-lodge the night before. In the early autumn light the leaves were beginning to turn. After half an hour of winding road with thick forest on either side, we came out into the open. Once again we saw the rolling steppe. We finally approached the last town on the paved roads before we were to turn due north towards the border. We stopped in Kuchan to take on new supplies; the cars needed petrol and we needed food and drink. Beyond Kuchan we could see the high mountain peaks of the border.

We drank tea from a *chai-khaneh* next to the petrol station, and bought a variety of ripe fruit from market stalls that stood on the main road that went through Kuchan: a bag of ripe plums, a kilo of apples and two different types of melon.

We jostled and bumped our way along a forty-kilometre dirt road to the border. This was the road that was supposed to be the main trucking link between the new Central Asian republics and the Persian Gulf ports of Iran: the Islamic Republic's chief hope of turning the attention of the Central Asian states away from Turkey and towards itself. So far this was nothing more than a dream. Sometimes with sheer rock on either side, the road was barely wide enough for a lorry. In places the surface was so bad that in good weather with two brand-new four-wheel-drive vehicles, it still demanded careful driving. At first we enjoyed the chance to race each other along the dusty road, but what had looked like a short jaunt on the map now turned into a long haul of several hours. When we finally reached the customs house at Baj Giran we felt relieved rather than triumphant. It was also clear that not much had been achieved here in the century since Curzon crossed the border.

> Russia can afford to leave this portion of her Asiatic frontier absolutely unguarded, aggression from Persia being out of the question, and none but Russians or natives going the other way. This is the Persian Baj Girhan, where there is a Custom-house at which dues are levied on caravans from Ashkabad . . . At present there is nothing better than a mountain track, descending upon the other side to Kuchan and the high road to Meshed; a contrast which is due to the failure of the Persians to fulfil their part of the bargain, Russia having undertaken to construct the first section of the chaussée to the frontier, while the remaining portion of forty miles to Kuchan was to be laid . . . by the government of the Shah.

We were the first Westerners to cross the border at Baj Giran since 1919, when the new revolutionary authorities in Moscow began to close off their entire empire to casual visitors from the West. We had permission from the Foreign Ministry to cross here, and Ali, our official 'minder', was here to help us through the border safely, even though the previous week there had been a ruling that this particular crossing-point, which had recently been opened, was available only for Iranians and citizens of the Commonwealth of Independent States.

We created a considerable stir, then: five people with passports that were neither Iranian nor CIS, thirty zinc boxes of camera equipment, and a senior official from a Tehran ministry to see us on our way. There was only seventy minutes left before the border was due to close for the weekend, and we had no desire to go back to Gonbad until Sunday. Ali went inside to negotiate on our behalf, and we walked around and examined the crateloads of Russian motorcycles imported from across the border, which not only hadn't been unpacked but had fallen over in a heap some time ago and been left there. Colloquially, '*baj giran*' means a bribe-taker; perhaps the bribes had been insufficient here.

We knew progress had been made when we were summoned in to the office of the head of customs and offered tea. He emerged from behind his desk, walked out to the four-wheel-drive truck, and looked at the stack of cases and bags.

'What is in here?'

'Just camera equipment.'

'Okay, you are clear.'

We crossed twenty minutes before the border closed.

Some months later VAVAK, the Ministry of Intelligence and Internal Security, hearing that I had crossed by an unauthorised route, and not bothering to find out (or perhaps not caring) that the Foreign Ministry had sanctioned us, blocked the issuing of another visa for me. I had, it seemed, been listed as an undesirable. It was typical of the confusion and infighting of the Islamic Republic. It was also, as our predecessor through the Baj Giran border post, George Nathaniel Curzon, had found, very Persian:

> I felt certain that my footsteps would be at once dogged by spies, if I was not actually turned back. The Persians are so extravagantly suspicious of foreigners, and particularly of such as sketch, or ask questions, or measure, or pull instruments out of their pockets, that no successful exploration would ever be undertaken if they were to be forewarned of the traveller's intention.

We passed across a short area of no-man's-land and headed towards an unremarkable metal gate across the road. Three soldiers in old Soviet uniforms stood there watching us speculatively. Tira, having left the Islamic Republic behind her, started to pull off her *hejab*. One of the soldiers grinned at her.

'You don't need that here,' he said in Russian.

For her, it was a huge relief to be liberated from the headscarf and long clinging cloak, and she stood there in the pale afternoon sunshine enjoying the sense of freedom. I looked around at the mountains on either side of us, and the great Central Asian plain opening out below, and once again felt that faint premonition that I might not see Iran again for a long time. Neither Edward Granville Browne nor Curzon ever returned to Persia, though they maintained a deep interest in its affairs. But that was their choice. In my case, it would not be. I thought, as I often had in the past, of a sentence from Harold Nicolson's biography of Curzon:

> He was for ever haunted by those plains of amber, those peaks of amethyst, the dignity of that crumbled magnificence, that silence of two thousand years.

Afterword

Properly regarded, no man lays claim to wisdom, virtue and truth unjustifiably, for there is no person existing devoid of these three qualities. Yet the bluntness of men's understanding and the obscuring of their original path keep the door of these qualities closed against the majority of mankind.

A Mirror For Princes

In the months and years that followed the revolution in Iran there was endless self-searching and bitterness about the failure of embassies, intelligence services, scholars and politicians to foresee the downfall of the Shah. The fact is, it all happened so quickly that someone writing a book about Iran in, say, the spring of 1978 – only nine months before the triumph of the Islamic Republic – would have been perfectly justified under the circumstances as they then were in assuming that whatever difficulties the Shah might endure, he would survive them. That he did not was partly his own fault, and partly the effect of the natural volatility of the Iranian people.

The Islamic Republic has been subjected to precisely the opposite process: everyone has been forecasting its downfall since the moment of its birth. In 1982 Massoud Rajavi, the head of Mojaheddin-e-Khalq (now the commander-in-chief of the National Liberation Army, based in Iraq), assured a group of British journalists with great intensity that the Khomeini regime would collapse by the end of that year. The Iran desk at the State Department in Washington believed it to be a near-impossibility that the regime would survive the death of Khomeini himself. The one question everybody asks a traveller from Iran is, how long can the system last?

Part of the problem lies with the leaders of the regime themselves. Iran has not yet decided whether it is a revolutionary society, still pushing back the frontiers of the old system and promoting revolution abroad, or a post-revolutionary society which can afford to consolidate the gains it has made and come to terms with its former enemies. As a result, the defining issue in Iranian politics is the country's relationship with the West. The radicals believe that any accommodation with the forces of Satan will do further damage to the revolutionary creed that brought Ayatollah Khomeini to power; the moderates are worried that the economic decline which has resulted from Iran's isolation is a greater threat to the Islamic Republic than anything else.

Most Iranians now seem to believe that corruption is worse under the Islamic Republic than it was under the Shah; and while this is probably not literally true – the sums of money available are far smaller than they were in the days of the enormous foreign contracts of the Shah's last years – it is the impression that counts, not the precise figures. Since the government has to keep expenditure down, it has embarked on a new policy which encourages corruption at the level of ordinary people. Each government department has been told that it must generate its own revenue. As a result, civil servants are paid lower salaries and are told to make up their money as best they can: in other words, through bribes. Local authority workers will knock down a fence round a garden and invite the owners to buy it back. Contractors working for the government will be told that entire phases of their work will not be paid for. Even the Revolutionary Guards – especially the Revolutionary Guards – demand instant 'fines' from anyone they choose to stop in the streets. Under a system like Iran's, it is always possible to find some infringement of the rules. This has lessened the moral force behind many of the Islamic prohibitions; women no longer think 'Do I dare wear lipstick?' but 'Can I afford to pay the fine if I wear lipstick?'

As a result of the growing corruption and the economic decline, the natural constituency of the regime is being progressively eroded. Discontent is probably higher in Iran at the time of writing than at any other time since the revolution. The dispossessed, in whose name the revolution was carried out, are no better off than they were in the final months of the Shah's reign. Large sections of south Tehran in 1978 lacked water, power, decent housing and sanitation. Most of those areas lack them still, and the huge influx into the city has created new and worse slums which make the old ones look moderately comfortable.

The expansion of urban life has created conditions which the regime finds extremely difficult to control. Tehran is growing faster than almost any city in the world. Karaj, some twenty-five miles to the west of the capital, was a smallish provincial town at the time of the revolution. Now it has a population of three million and is the second-largest city in Iran. A little further west along the motorway is the new industrial city of Hashtgard. Eventually the entire region from Tehran to Qazvin, ninety miles away, will constitute one enormous urban development, containing a fifth of the population of the whole country. The supply of housing and the availability of adequate social services will never catch up. At the United Nations International Conference on Population

and Development held in Cairo in September 1994 a great deal of
press attention was paid to the opposition of Islamic fundamentalists
to notions of birth control, abortion and sex education. Few observers
noticed that the Islamic Republic of Iran ranged itself firmly on the side
of better education about birth control.

The median age of the population in Iran has now dropped to 17.5
years. Younger people, by and large, have less sense of commitment to
the revolution than older ones; for them, the Islamic Republic tends to
represent restriction and old-fashioned values. Nor does it hold any great
terror for them. Anyone arrested for purely 'social' offences – going to a
party, being caught alone with a member of the opposite sex, or playing
loud music – can expect to be held in prison for a couple of days.
According to a police officer in the Tehran anti-vice squad, 80 per cent of
those his men had arrested in the previous two days were under twenty;
that is, they were educated under the Islamic system. Whereas the voting
age was dropped to sixteen, because it was felt that young people, many
of whom were fighting the Iraqis, were the strongest supporters of
the Islamic Republic, the government is now considering raising it to
eighteen or even higher; the youth vote is no longer reliable.

A government facing problems like these should in theory be on its last
legs. Maybe it is; but that is by no means certain. For one thing, there is
no tradition whatever in Iran of governing with popular support. Except
for a couple of years at the start of the Islamic Revolution, governments
have not looked for popularity. The main task of an Iranian government
is to be strong, and to command the obedience of the people; it does not
have to court public support and is unlikely to get it. The problem for the
Islamic Republic is not its unpopularity, but its perceived weakness. If it
can no longer make people afraid, then it will be in serious trouble.

Even so, it still has some unexpected strengths. Whatever Westerners
may think about Iran, it is not nowadays an autocracy like the Shah's
regime or the old Soviet system: pyramids of power, which could be
destroyed merely by lopping off the topmost few layers. Iran under
the Islamic Republic is a highly devolved state with any number of
competing power-centres. Nowadays it can scarcely even be said to
have a single ideological faith, since the various religious authorities
are so divided among themselves. It certainly does not have a command
economy, like the Soviet Union or, say, Iraq. In other words, the sources
of political and economic power are many in number and quite difficult
to capture under the diffuse system which the Islamic Republic has
introduced.

None of which means that a takeover by a modern Reza Khan is
necessarily impossible; though the regime has weeded out the old regular
army time and again to rid it of anyone with the necessary ability to stage
a coup, and the Revolutionary Guards still seem to be rock-solid for the
Islamic Republic, if only because they have no one else to turn to. As for

a widespread popular uprising, there seems little sign of that at present. Qazvin erupted into violence against the regime in August 1994 when tens of thousands of people clashed with the police and Revolutionary Guards. The city was placed under martial law, and during the two days of fighting at least fifty people are thought to have been killed. It was a serious blow to the regime; but the main cause was economic discontent and the demand that Qazvin should be regarded as part of the province of Tehran, which would give it a number of economic and commercial advantages. Although the crowd shouted 'Death to Khamene'i' and 'Death to Rafsanjani' and the government tried to blame it all on the Mojaheddin-e-Khalq opposition, there seems no reason to believe that the trouble was stirred up by any of the exile groups.

The Mojaheddin's umbrella organisation, the National Council of Resistance (NCR), headed by Maryam Rajavi and her husband Massoud and based partly in France and partly in Saddam Hussein's Iraq, has worked hard to bring together as many opposition groups and leaders as possible. It includes supporters of the old nationalist parties, and even some royalists; its main journal is now entitled *The Lion and the Sun*, royalist emblems that are quite remarkable for an organisation which only fifteen years ago was far to the revolutionary left. The NCR is particularly adept at public relations, and knows how to attract support among Western politicians and interest among Western journalists; but it has little discernible support inside Iran. This could change, however, as the memories of the war with Iraq fade and the NCR's policy of throwing in its lot with Saddam Hussein becomes less offensive to ordinary Iranians.

As the Shah found during the course of 1978, governments can lose power very fast in Iran. The dynamic of crowd politics can build up with frightening speed, and the unpopularity and political weakness of the Islamic Republic make it potentially vulnerable. Yet it survived its biggest crisis, the death of Ayatollah Khomeini, without difficulty; and if it is able to break out of its gridlock and develop in a way which will allow the economy to grow, there is no reason to expect that the system will collapse. If it does not break out, it may be a very different story. Yet for the time being – which is all that matters in Iran – the position now is what we felt at the time of our visit in 1986: the system is stable, but it does not feel permanent.

Bibliography

ABRAHAMIAN, ERVAND, *Khomeinism*, I. B. Tauris, London, 1993.

ACHESON, DEAN, *Present at the Creation: My Years in the State Department*, Hamish Hamilton, London, 1970.

AFSHAR, HALEH (ed.), *Iran: A Revolution in Turmoil*, Macmillan, Basingstoke, 1985.

BAKHASH, SHAUL, *The Reign of the Ayatollahs: Iran and the Islamic Revolution*, I. B. Tauris, London, 1985.

BEKHRANDIA, SHAHIN, 'Zoroastriasm in Contemporary Iran', *International Journal of Moral and Social Studies*, Oxford, 1991.

BERNARD, CHERYL AND KHALILZAD, ZALMAY, '*The Government of God': Iran's Islamic Republic*, Columbia University, New York, 1984.

BILL, JAMES A., *The Eagle and the Lion: The Tragedy of American–Iranian Relations*, Yale University Press, New Haven, 1988.

BILL, JAMES A. AND LOUIS, WM. ROGER, *Musaddeq, Iranian Nationalism and Oil*, I. B. Tauris, London, 1988.

BROWNE, EDWARD GRANVILLE, *A Year Amongst the Persians*, A. & C. Black, London, 1893. Republished by Century Publishing, London, 1984.

BYRON, ROBERT, *The Road to Oxiana*, Macmillan, London, 1937.

CARTER, JIMMY, *Keeping Faith: Memoirs of a President*, Bantam Books, New York, 1982.

CHUBIN, SHAHRAM AND TRIPP, CHARLES, *Iran and Iraq at War*, I. B. Tauris, London, 1988.

CLOAKE, MARGARET MORRIS, *A Persian at the Court of King George 1809–10: The Journal of Mirza Abul Hassan Khan*, Barrie & Jenkins, London, 1988.

Constitution of the Islamic Republic of Iran, Ministry of Islamic Guidance, Tehran, 1985.

COOPER, ROGER, *Death Plus Ten Years*, HarperCollins, London, 1993.

CORDESMAN, ANTHONY H., *The Iran–Iraq War and Western Security 1984–87: Strategic Implications and Policy Options*, Jane's Publishing, London, 1987.

CURZON, GEORGE NATHANIEL, *Persia and the Persian Question*, Frank Cass, London, 1892. Republished by Sidgwick & Jackson, London, 1986.

DEHQANI-TAFTI, BISHOP H. B., *The Hard Awakening*, Triangle, London, 1981.

ELM, MOSTAFA, *Oil, Power and Principle, Iran's Oil Nationalization and its Aftermath*, Syracuse University Press, Syracuse, NY, 1992.

FARMAIAN, SATTAREH FARMAN, *Daughter of Persia: A Woman's Journey from Her Father's Harem through the Islamic Republic*, Bantam Press, London, 1992.

FRYE, RICHARD N., *The Heritage of Persia*, Weidenfeld & Nicolson, London, 1962.

FULLER, GRAHAM E., *The 'Center of the Universe'*, Westview Press, Boulder, Col., 1991.

GRABAR, OLEG, *The Great Mosque of Isfahan*, I. B. Tauris, London, 1990.

GRAHAM, ROBERT, *Iran: The Illusion of Power*, St Martin's Press, New York, 1979.

GUPPY, SHUSHA, *The Blindfold Horse, Memories of a Persian Childhood*, William Heinemann, London, 1988.

HALLIDAY, FRED, *Iran: Dictatorship and Development*, Penguin Books, Harmondsworth, 1979.

HEIKAL, MOHAMED, *The Return of the Ayatollah*, André Deutsch, London, 1981.

HIRO, DILIP, *Iran Under the Ayatollahs*, Routledge & Kegan Paul, London, 1985.

—*Islamic Fundamentalism*, Paladin, London, 1988.

—*The Longest War*, Paladin, London, 1990.

—*Between Marx and Muhammad*, HarperCollins, London, 1994.

HOBSON, SARAH, *Through Persia in Disguise*, John Murray, London, 1973.

HOVEYDA, FEREYDOWN, *The Fall of the Shah*, Weidenfeld & Nicolson, London, 1980.

HUNTER, SHIREEN T., *Iran After Khomeini*, Praeger with the Centre for Strategic and International Studies, New York, 1992.

HUYSER, ROBERT E., *Mission to Tehran*, Harper & Row, New York, 1986.

Iran-Contra Affair, Report of the Congressional Committees, Random House, New York, 1988.

ISKANDAR, KAI KA'US IBN, PRINCE OF GURGAN, *A Mirror for Princes*, translated and republished by Reuben Levy, Cresset Press, London, 1951.

ISLAMIC PROPAGATION ORGANISATION, *Fall of a Centre of Deceit*, Tehran.

KAPUSCINSKI, RYSZARD, *Shah of Shahs*, Quartet Books, London, 1985.

KEDDIE, NIKKI R., *Roots of Revolution: An Interpretive History of Modern Iran*, Yale University Press, New Haven, 1981.

KEDDIE, NIKKI R. (ED.), *Religion and Politics in Iran*, Yale University Press, New Haven, 1983.

KEDDIE, NIKKI R. AND ABRAHAMIAN, A., *Iran Between Two Revolutions*, Princeton University Press, NJ, 1982.

KENNEDY, MOORHEAD, *The Ayatollah in the Cathedral: Reflections of a Hostage*, Hill & Wang, New York, 1986.

KHOMEINI, RUHOLLAH MUSAVI, *Imam's Final Discourse*, Ministry of Guidance and Islamic Culture, Tehran, 1989.

KISSINGER, HENRY, *White House Years*, Weidenfeld & Nicolson/Michael Joseph, London, 1979.

LEWIS, BERNARD, *The Assassins*, Weidenfeld & Nicolson, London, 1967.

MIDDLE EAST WATCH, *Guardians of Thought: Limits of Freedom of Expression in Iran*, Human Rights Watch, New York, 1993.

MILANI, FARZANEH, *Veils and Words: The Emerging Voices of Iranian Women Writers*, I. B. Tauris, London, 1992.

MONTAZAM, MIR ALI ASGHAR, *The Life and Times of Ayatollah Khomeini*, Anglo-European Publishing, London, 1994.

MORIER, JAMES, *The Adventures of Hajji Baba of Ispahan*, George G. Harrap, London, 1948.

MOTTAHEDEH, ROY, *The Mantle of the Prophet*, Chatto & Windus, London, 1986.

NARAGHI, EHSAN, *From Palace to Prison*, I. B. Tauris, London, 1994.

PAHLAVI, MOHAMMAD REZA, *Mission for My Country*, Hutchinson, London, 1961.

—*Answer to History*, Stein & Day, New York, 1980.

PARSONS, SIR ANTHONY, *The Pride and The Fall: Iran 1974–1979*, Jonathan Cape, London, 1984.

RADJI, PARVIZ C., *In the Service of the Peacock Throne: The Diaries of the Shah's Last Ambassador to London*, Hamish Hamilton, London, 1983.

RAMAZANI, R. K., *Revolutionary Iran: Challenge and Response in the Middle East*, Johns Hopkins University Press, Baltimore and London, 1986.

ROOHIZADEGAN, OLYA, *Olya's Story: A Survivor's Dramatic Account of the Persecution of Baha'is in Revolutionary Iran*, Oneworld Publications, London, 1993.

ROOSEVELT, KERMIT, *Countercoup: The Struggle for the Control of Iran*, McGraw-Hill, New York, 1979.

ROSS, SIR E. DENISON (ED.), *Sir Anthony Sherley and His Persian Adventure*, George Routledge & Sons, London, 1933.

RUBIN, BARRY, *Paved with Good Intentions: The American Experience in Iran*, Oxford University Press, Oxford, 1980.

RYAN, PAUL B., *The Iranian Rescue Mission: Why It Failed*, Naval Institute Press, Annapolis, Maryland, 1985.

SACKVILLE-WEST, VITA, *Passenger to Teheran*, Hogarth Press, London, 1926. Republished by Arrow, London, 1991.

SAID, EDWARD W., *Covering Islam: How the Media and Experts Determine How We See the Rest of the World*, Routledge & Kegan Paul, London, 1981.

SHAWCROSS, WILLIAM, *The Shah's Last Ride*, Chatto & Windus, London, 1989.

SICK, GARY, *All Fall Down: America's Fateful Encounter with Iran*, I. B. Tauris, London, 1985.

—*October Surprise*, Times Books, New York, 1991.

STARK, FREYA, *The Valley of the Assassins, and Other Persian Travels*, John Murray, London, 1934.

STEVENS, ROGER, *The Land of the Great Sophy*, Methuen, London, 1971.

SULLIVAN, WILLIAM H., *Mission to Iran*, W. W. Norton, New York, 1981.

TAHERI, AMIR, *The Spirit of Allah: Khomeini and the Islamic Revolution*, Hutchinson, London, 1985.

—*Nest of Spies: America's Journey to Disaster in Iran*, Century Hutchinson, London, 1988.

—*The Unknown Life of the Shah*, Hutchinson, London, 1991.

TEAGUE-JONES, CAPTAIN REGINALD, (published under the name of Ronald Sinclair), *Adventures in Persia: To India by the Back Door*, H. F. & G. Witherby, London, 1988.

The Tower Commission Report, Bantam Books, New York, 1987.

WILLS, C. J., *Persia As It Is. Being Sketches of Modern Persian Life and Character*, Sampson, Low & Co., London, 1886.

WRIGHT, SIR DENIS, *The Persians Amongst the English*, I. B. Tauris, London, 1985.

WRIGHT, ROBIN, *Sacred Rage: The Crusade of Modern Islam*, André Deutsch, London, 1986.

—*In the Name of God: The Khomeini Decade*, Simon & Schuster, New York, 1989.

ZAZIH, SEPEHR, *The Iranian Military in Revolution and War*, Routledge & Kegan Paul, London, 1988.

Index